OVERLOOKING DAMAGE

OVERLOOKING DAMAGE

Art, Display, and Loss in Times of Crisis

JONAH SIEGEL

STANFORD UNIVERSITY PRESS
Stanford, California

Printed in the United States of America on acid-free, archival-quality paper

Library of Congress Cataloging-in-Publication Data

Names: Siegel, Jonah, 1963- author.
Title: Overlooking damage : art, display, and loss in times of crisis / Jonah Siegel.
Description: Stanford, California : Stanford University Press, 2022. | Includes bibliographical references and index.
Identifiers: LCCN 2022004394 (print) | LCCN 2022004395 (ebook) | ISBN 9781503630550 (cloth) | ISBN 9781503632158 (paperback) | ISBN 9781503632165 (ebook)
Subjects: LCSH: Ruins, Modern. | Violence in art. | Art—Philosophy. | Aesthetics.
Classification: LCC BH301.R85 S54 2022 (print) | LCC BH301.R85 (ebook) | DDC 111/.85—dc23/eng/20220325
LC record available at https://lccn.loc.gov/2022004394
LC ebook record available at https://lccn.loc.gov/2022004395

Cover art: Joseph Michael Gandy, *Bank of England as a Ruin*, watercolor on paper, 1830,
© Sir John Soane's Museum | Bridgeman Images
Cover design: Rob Ehle
Typeset by Newgen North America in 10/14 Minion Pro

For Aisa, Carmel, Shay, and—of course—Silvia

CONTENTS

PREFACE

Occasions and Feelings

Broken, we say, as though we could imagine a whole. Stolen, we say, as though identifying rightful owners might be a straightforward matter, as though we had ready access to a system for the proper adjudication of contending claims. I see, we say, meaning, I understand. Your point of view, we say, meaning, I see things differently from you because of what we call my position or my angle of sight, as though geography or the simple fact of location determined how we see things and so our disagreements. And, of course, we know they do—though our certainty about the simplicity of that fact might suggest we probably should spend more time thinking about how and why that is the case.

This is a book about how we see damage and loss at moments when seeing and losing are particularly marked events—when the object at risk or injured is so highly valued or the loss is so irrecoverable that the mind is driven to judgments about how it feels about sight and loss. It is about the relationship between thought and feeling that emerges when overlooking damage—and what is entailed in what we are moved to say about this relationship. The polemical aim of this set of interlocking essays is to challenge what I take to be fairly conventional ideas about the relationship between seeing, knowing, and judging by focusing on a small number of highly charged instances that tantalize with the apparent clarity of the judgments for which they call, a lucidity that I demonstrate is bought at the cost of overlooking a great deal.

But that last sentence sounds more judgmental than I mean it to. I should say at the outset that what is interesting about the disappointments I discuss in this book is that they have structural sources. Thinking about damage is bound to be challenging, as the experience of injury is always incommensurate with the emotions it provokes and with the ideas it inspires in response. The immediacy of injury does not lend itself easily to the processes of generalization necessary for conceptualization to take place, even though damage is probably the most urgent motivation for reflection on causes. Why do I suffer? Why does my loved one? That the questions are inevitable does not make the answers come. But then, such questions are hardly requests for information. We might call this the Job effect: the appeal for the meaning of suffering, which is really more of a complaint about that suffering. This nonquestion is answered in the Bible by an ungenerous reminder of how little we in fact know, of the smallness of the perception that finds great interest in one injured party in a world full of harm. Where were you when I laid the pillars of the world, says a voice out of the whirlwind to the suffering man, an answer that has disappointed for millennia.[1] But the painful disproportion manifested in the relationship between human and divine is only a vast expansion of the gap that limits all human sympathy. I may see injury; you feel pain. But it is also quite possible that I may not recognize damage where you do. When I do feel pain, I will not, in any case, reflect on that experience in the same way as someone who merely sees the moment of injury, or hears from me that I am suffering. I am feeling; you are reflecting. Would we say those words describe a difference of point of view?[2]

This is to speak of subjects in a vague present tense. But injury inhabits time. Its importance to individuals and cultures includes retrospection and projection. I fear injury; I have been injured, or I am injured: the unresolvable ambiguity built into the verb in the last formulation is telling. When does damage end? Though the terms are often used interchangeably, injury suggests a harmful event (the bowl is dropped, the fire set, I fall), damage an ongoing condition (the vessel is cracked, the temple fallen, the hip broken). What is the relationship of the memory of injury to the ongoing experience of damage? My engagement with event and condition will have the attenuated and sporadic character of all my other experiences, especially, as suggested already, when it comes to what others suffer. My responsiveness is fated to a greater degree of failure in that case than even that which typically characterizes other events in my moral and emotional life.

A broken thing has been further damaged. The thing that never belonged to me still does not belong to me. Where do I find *myself* in relation to facts and events that do not clearly include me? Speaking for my own relationship to monuments, I have to admit that I want nothing rebuilt that is broken. Any rendering of Rome I have seen that brings it back to the days of its glory fills me with a dread that is at once aesthetic and ethical. I don't want Rome repaired; I need no new temple. The religious and political murders that took place from

Tenochtitlán to the Roman Forum, the privileged priestly castes or aristocracies that accompanied so many ancient structures: I have no nostalgia for those. Structures that would have excluded me as an outsider or an enemy become welcoming when subjected to injury and the mollifying effects of time. Broken, they let us in. Thinking along this vein, disturbing notions might arise: for example, what if what shocks us when we look at the destruction of the Buddhas at Bamiyan or the Temple of the Sun in Palmyra is not the face of barbarism but a kind of destruction modernity embraces in some contexts, deprecates in others?

Every ruin is a record of loss and neglect, and almost always of a kind of violence. Oblivion and recovery are the two fundamental ingredients of the ruin, with the memory of violence either directly present or easily surmisable from the losses we see before us. Even when the damage is the result of natural processes or accident, we know the absence of caretaking is always indicative of a greater loss, as human hands no longer repair roofs or reinforce foundations. The fascination of the ruin is impossible to separate from the evidence of irrecoverable loss it carries on its surface—though the names we give the experience of that loss may identify a kind of compensatory or more than compensatory experience we might have called picturesque at one point, or poetic, or sublime.

Buildings painstakingly assembled from carefully dressed stone, carved statues of gods and people: they were not made to be broken. Hence the pressure they place not just on aesthetic concepts that quickly naturalize their injuries, but also on the moral life, into which they tend to enter or which they leave with disconcerting ease. There was a time a book might have been titled *Pleasure of Ruins*, suggesting what is indeed the case—that interest in the aesthetic experiences they afford shaped the modern fascination with broken old things.[3] Centuries of visual representations and poems since the Renaissance evidence the pleasure antique fragments have provoked, the creativity they have stimulated. Now we are likely to see titles that suggest the moral concerns embedded in encountering broken things, such as *Ravaged*, *Designs of Destruction*, *Catastrophizing*. An excellent recent catalog was titled, like the show itself, *Ruin Lust*, with the suggestion of a passion that overflows the measure. Susan Stewart's *The Ruins Lesson* advertises its concern with something like instruction, an emphasis further underlined in the subtitle of that magisterial work, *Meaning and Material in Western Culture*. Even my own, vaguely judgmental *Overlooking Damage* hardly leads with pleasure or beauty.[4]

It bears saying that "ruin," like some of the other words with which it has been associated, such as "antiquity," "pagan," or "barbarian," "gothic" or "classical," says less about the object being identified than about the system of values sustained by the existence of the term. Still, "ruin" has that extra charge that a material instance provides—even in imagination or reproduction. Like all matter, it pushes the mind beyond concepts through its sheer contingency as experience. Who managed to carry this massive stone all the way here, to pile it up this way and carve it? How could anyone destroy anything that looked like *this*? Who found it? In what sense was it lost? Would I care about this thing the way I do if it were whole? Are those flowers growing between the ancient stones? Looking at this massive structure I have come a long way to visit should be enough to engross the imagination, so why is my eye drawn toward that dark corner closed off to visitors where a further level of experience seems to wait? Why does an obscure shadow in the engraving tantalize me with an absence that feels heavier than the stone shifted by the passage of time or by an angry enemy? What would the foundations of my home look like after two thousand years, and will anyone care as much as I seem to about this place I am visiting in person or in my imagination?

And this final question, which may or may not be given voice but is always present when we encounter a ruin with any degree of attention, reminds us that while we may tell ourselves that on the other side of ruins glimmer visions of lost wholeness and permanence, just past *that* mirage lie all the broken things about which we do not care. As Dario Gamboni points out in his important study of damage and art, the fate of every thing is oblivion: "It is their normal fate," he points out with disarming simplicity, "to disappear."[5] Vulnerability is written into the nature of things we love, as into everything else. The real tragedy of things is how banal injury and loss are as facts. All the most robust systems of value people have lived by until recently factor in that quality ("We are dust and to dust we return" is just one familiar ritual/textual reminder from one tradition). It is an indication of a particularly modern moral crisis to think that the experience of injury and loss is anything other than the experience of the world over time. Given how much we lose and discard, it is evidently the supplement of our feelings that adds to particular artifacts the aura of vulnerability. Still, there is no gainsaying that the pressure of the ruin is also ascribable to its durability. A ruin is something that has outlasted its moment and is very likely to outlast us. The feeling of loss we experience at the encounter is at once a recognition and a mystification. We see ourselves in the ruin when we experience it as loss. But we also see a permanence that is far more than human alongside an entirely and solely human phenomenon, which is projection itself, which is the cultural experience of recovery that makes us pause over this pile of rocks at this waste space, these columns and arches or foundations, and feel they mean something to us. Whether we are feeling pleasure in reflecting on broken things or are troubled by encountering them, in either case what we are experiencing are emotions in which the self is at issue. How do I place *myself* in relation to damage and loss?

Questions apparently more erudite than the ones I have touched on so far will remind us of the cultural sources of our relationship to broken old things. Did Jesus walk here, or Caesar? What might the whole temple have looked like to either one of them, or to Solomon? How would it feel to worship here? Will the building or monument I myself design ever be able to achieve such grandeur? Then again, is all human achievement not ironized by the passage of time that has brought down even these strong walls, left us only a foundation? The First Temple in Jerusalem stood about 410 years before it was destroyed by Nebuchadnezzar. As a point of comparison, one might note that it was in the world of things a little less than the time the Sistine Chapel has existed, roughly the amount of time that Michelangelo's frescoes have been on its walls. The Second Temple lasted for around 420 years before it was burned down by Roman troops. Every year that passes marks for the world how much more enduring than their physical existence the textual life of these lost structures has been. At this point that number tells us that more than double the length of time that both temples put together lasted has elapsed since the last one ceased to be. And the near coincidence of the Christian Era with the fall of the sanctuary of the Jews is a further indication of how much more widely diffused the power of these buildings has been since their loss. Evidently, some things are more lasting than temples built with hands.

Overdetermination is a concept from psychoanalysis that loses most of its interest when it is used merely to describe something that is inevitable owing to a proliferation of causes. In Freud, the word describes the ways in which apparently immediate preoccupations feel as pressing as they do because of the ways in which they follow or cross tracks laid down in our minds years before.[6] The term is designed to capture a fundamental psychoanalytic concern—both therapeutic and conceptual: the relationship between a past that is never fully lost, although never entirely present to our conscious minds, and a present that feels immediately difficult because of specific current concerns, but in relation to which neither feelings nor concerns can be understood without reaching back to a personal history that the mind keeps telling us about and hiding. In dreams, or perhaps in the neuroses we find impossible to escape, the mind confesses a relationship that it does not fully allow itself to remember but will never entirely forget. The ruin is an extraordinarily vivid manifestation of overdetermination, though it requires some reflection to see it this way. While it participates in the modern tendency to valorize immediate experience, everything about the ruin indicates that its meaning is only available to a mind stocked with the memory of ideas and values that make a relic of neglect and injury feel self-evidently meaningful.

The categories I am interested in in this book, beauty and damage, are experienced with a contingent quality that general concepts will tend to camouflage rather than reveal. As I reflect on recent episodes of damage to prized objects, or to objects that have become prized as we see them threatened, or to objects that are prized by some and deprecated by others, inevitably there are moments I find myself wondering if my aspiration to use the resources of scholarship and theory to understand these things is meant to be a contribution to current debates on these topics or an attempt to avoid the fear that the kinds of human behaviors entailed in the creation of damage are precisely those least liable to respond to ideas at all, especially ideas of any sort of complexity or sophistication. The final thought in this melancholy chain of reflection, compounded, on the one hand, of the scholar's hypertrophied sense of the difficulty of adequately reflecting current scholarship and, on the other, of the fear that my attempts at intellectual responsibility will not compensate for the nugatory effect of my intervention in the very areas of life I am writing about, takes me in another direction altogether. It strikes me at that point that it is silly to imagine a world in which ideas, even quite sophisticated ideas, are *not* shaping the violence that shakes the world. As museums are assembled and taken apart, as works of art are elaborately destroyed, it is a kind of self-protective instinct that tells the student of ideas that the realm of thought is distinct from that of action.

What I own, what I care about, the actions I take or fail to take to protect or damage things and people: for all that these are deeply personal phenomena, they are also clearly the result of concepts that are not fully my own, that are always more than individual and practical. Whether they are front of mind at the moment of violence or not, every terrorist is acting on a concept of terror, every soldier on the basis of an idea of nation. And, of course, something similar can be said about every individual response to injury—otherwise, why would a small number of casualties from a rare event engross the imagination when extraordinary numbers of preventable deaths are accepted every day (in my nation from handguns and rifles, everywhere from the global climate crisis)? Every museum is evidently not simply a structure of concrete and glass with stuff in it that is then retrospectively conceptualized, but the result of a number of intersecting and often contradictory ideas, arguments, and desires. Here is one relatively small, if highly relevant, instance that clearly exists in a space between the practical and the conceptual: in the period during which I have been writing this book, the consensus about what ought to be in museums and where those museums should be have both seen extraordinary changes, as have concepts of preservation and feelings about the destruction of monuments. None of these issues is ever truly discussed in a dispassionate way—nor should they be, as there is nothing about them that does not involve the passions. But it would be absurd to understand these ongoing and not yet stabilized changes in the relationships of individuals to objects and display as free of concepts—of nation, of complicity, of historical or personal responsibility. Emotions, even emotions that seem to militate against ideas or reflection, are always hiding in plain sight when such topics are addressed. Along with the apparently self-evident nature of what we see, the primacy of what we feel in response to witness is among the most mystified components in cultural conversations about violence and injury.

Sometimes the occasion of writing is more marked than others, the moment of creation calling out with particular force to the reader and shaping the later reception of a text. The experience of extraordinary crises drives the writings addressed in this book, most clearly the hopes and fears of the French Revolution, the experience of dislocation and dread that became so important in intellectual responses to the Second World War, and the recent violence to antiquities carried out by religious fanatics. Behind these highly localized topics, the reader will inevitably hear in my discussion the pressure of a set of intertwined crises that may feel different, more distinctly pressing and impossible to locate in the past, notably climate change and the international refugee crisis reshaping world politics, the two chief locations for the overlooking of damage in modern culture.

I have written several books devoted to demonstrating the ways in which nineteenth-century authors address issues still current in our day—indeed, how they anticipate and might help us to reflect on concerns the urgency of which is not unrelated to the illusion of their recent emergence. Like every student of writings on art and art institutions, I have always had to keep in mind another set of historical horizons, specifically the pasts that were the source of so much that the nineteenth century thought about when it reflected on art, classical antiquity, the Middle Ages, and the Renaissance, as well as all the things it came to call modern. Lately the topic of periodization has felt less academic, has become newly pressing, as culture confronts the unavoidable sense of looming change created first by the end of the long period of relative political stability in Europe and the United States associated with the Cold War and, more recently and in an accelerating way, by the ongoing and overlapping crises that press upon us in new variations every day, so different yet so clearly related. Winds bring unquenchable fires, smoke that covers the sun, or unwonted rains that flood areas unused to such extremities. Refugees gather at the borders of wealthy nations or die in perilous crossings. Political institutions the world over are distorted beyond recognition by the power of unmatchable wealth. Most recently the response to an epochal medical crisis becomes a reminder of how much more powerful fantasies are than the reserved nostrums of science. And yet, while it is difficult to avoid the feeling that we are living in a period of profound and anxious transition, it is striking that so many changes to circumstances have been met with relatively small revisions in the concepts shaping critical responses, continuing a trend that has been marked for decades.

Dominant ideas about the nature of progress, power, and knowledge, together with the way these things might be said to intersect in culture, still go back to a set of sophisticated claims that are part of a cultural dispensation shaped by the unparalleled conflagration that was the Second World War and the fears and hopes that followed the end of that struggle, a long moment that history will likely judge to have been as extraordinarily anomalous in the intellectual consensus that characterized it as it was limited in the centers of power around which it developed. In the past few decades, the human experience of the workings of all of those categories—whether power, progress, or knowledge—has entirely changed, along with the dominant elites, interests, alliances, and cultural conventions with which they may be associated. It would be as odd for analyses of society and cultural institutions shaped by conditions between the 1930s and 1970s to be clearly applicable today as it would be for assumptions about communication, manufacturing, and even military power to be based on conditions and equipment from that span. The types of politics imaginable, the demographic makeup of nations, the very winds that bring us rain or stoke implacable fires: the last couple of decades have seen profound changes in all of these. And yet our methods of analysis have adapted poorly. The widespread sense of urgency seems unable to result in a new cultural politics that meets the moment rather than a nostalgic one that keeps reaching for old answers and mourning both their failure and the ongoing success of evil.

This book proposes to take seriously the resources culture provides for reflection on damage, whether visual, literary, or a combination of both. Imperfect things, things that find a place in later culture by suggesting through their partial nature their connections to cultures long lost: my working assumption in this book is that texts participate in the qualities we associate with ruins. Loss, oblivion, and potential recovery are the fate of the written word as often as of more apparently substantial things. While some writings become naturalized into later periods and some are found impossible to assimilate, either eventuality says more about the aspirations of the new era than about the text itself. While the injuries associated with the 1940s are crucial in the formation of concepts of responsibility, judgment, and history that still dominate both in the popular arena and in more academic or theoretical realms, the inheritances of earlier moments of violence are sometimes lost sight of in a general sense that past ideas emerged out of a deluded sense of confident clarity aiming to impose its will on an unsettled future.

A number of deeply thoughtful and erudite scholars have illuminated in recent years the complexity of issues involving cultural property, heritage, collecting, display, and even restitution, and I cite much of that work in the pages of this book. I am interested, however, in ways in which current crises might be recognized as indications of ongoing contradictions in culture. The clash of convictions about the nature and meaning of collecting and display is most easily understood as a phenomenon bound to arise when ignorance is confronted and corrected—the ignorance of certain unilluminated agents, of an entire era, of a people. This book is written otherwise. It does not find the contemporary world particularly clear on what it loves and needs to protect, or about the kinds of actions liable to yield protection or manifest love. Given this sense of our own limits, it is difficult for me to think that earlier periods are distinguished from our own mainly by their blindness to what is right or beautiful or valuable.

My hope is that the historical span I engage with by starting with theorists of vandalism and ruin going back to that great new beginning that was the French Revolution, together with the method I employ of listening to the documents of the past for the emotions shaping ideas, will help in the effort to make sense of the ways broken remains articulate with ongoing revisions of what it means to break, to own, to preserve, and to admire. Elements of the rich complex of topics and materials to which I have so far just gestured have typically been encountered in specialized fields—art history, archeology, anthropology, literary studies, philosophy, the law, and of course, more recently, museum and heritage studies—disciplines that will differ markedly in their concerns and methods and so in their conclusions. Studies that have emerged in the social sciences, for example, sometimes focus on the networks of human agents, or even on what has been called the biography of the object itself, as a way to rewrite histories that in the past were often told as stories of the heroic endeavors of highly valorized individuals or that in some way naturalized the fate of particularly admired objects. Such recovery work may overlap methodologically with engaged scholarship aspiring to lay out the complicity with imperial violence of collections or the act of collecting, but it tends to have a distinct character and aim. (Do objects have lives, and so "biographies," once they are removed from the place they were made, or have they died at that point—or worse?) Curators always live with the practical effects of concepts, spoken and unspoken. Today, they are challenged by insights about provenance, about the neglected or hidden histories of collections, as well as by the stringent concepts of complicity and innocence shaping current cultural politics. They find themselves in a difficult situation: on the one hand, a largely indifferent public with less access than ever to any concepts that might give meaning to the museum and its contents; on the other, a motivated and suspicious intellectual elite for whom the current configuration of the institutions of culture is an ongoing injury because it is related to unresolved and unacknowledged forms of damage.[7]

Within my own field of literary studies and among students of culture more generally, the topic of damage has emerged lately as an important element in discussions of the intersection of human beings with the material world.[8] It strikes me that reflection on the theme might also have something to say to the never fully resolved debate about ways of reading that crops up from time to time in the discipline. After all, the two terms around which the topic was first formulated in a seminal essay by Eve Sedgwick—"paranoid" and "reparative" reading—suggest that how we approach a text is shaped by the assumption of an injury to be feared or repaired.[9] "Critique," the apparently bloodless term that Sedgwick put under the signs of injury and fear, has characteristically been wielded to identify a situation in which the dangerous workings of power that underpin some apparently nonpolitical cultural object are *revealed* through careful analysis. In that sense, injury is what the paranoid reading uncovers, though Sedgwick's terms inevitably put a question mark over the discovery. In the instances addressed in *Overlooking Damage*, the marks of injury are not in fact waiting to be discovered; they are everywhere present on the surface of the object. The sense of imminent threat felt when the bullets start to fly, bombs explode, or a work of art is stolen or destroyed is clearly not adequately described as paranoia. It is also unlikely that repair will be possible when the guns fall silent.

Although this book ranges widely, it returns repeatedly to a small set of texts and the occasions of their writing. The former I want to be understood as making representative foundational claims, the latter as the conditions that ought to shape the reception of works that have often been wrenched out of history to their detriment. Walter Benjamin wrote his much-cited final essay on the concept of history in 1940, the fateful year in which German troops occupied Paris and he himself committed suicide at the Spanish border, a hopeless refugee despairing at a frontier. At every turn, Benjamin's claims about long spans of time are shaped by quite local and immediate, indeed urgent, concerns. The concepts of history Benjamin addresses, the angel of history he summons but can never expect to arrive, and the messiah he evokes if only to remind us of the absence of the real presence—these are eternal creatures *and* births of a moment to which I will make repeated reference in *Overlooking Damage*.

Along with Benjamin's essay from 1940, two intellectual projects dating back to the revolutionary 1790s are recurrent points of reference for my argument. Henri Jean-Baptiste Grégoire, known as the Abbé Grégoire, and Constantin François de Chasseboeuf, the revolutionary nobleman who assumed the name Volney in honor of Voltaire, were both members of the National Assembly attempting to define the future for a revolutionary France that not only saw itself as the model for a better future but lived through the experience of attempting to make that future come about. Volney's 1791 *Ruins, or Meditations on the Revolution of Empires* begins with an elaborately staged emotional response to the ruins of the city of Palmyra. The Abbé Grégoire, often credited with establishing the modern meaning of the word "vandalism," wrote a set of studies beginning in 1793—and so, near the height of the Terror—addressing the need to preserve works of art that the Revolution might have seen as self-evidently pernicious. These texts, from a period that is often faulted for the failure to achieve the values it expressed rather than acknowledged for having established the centrality of those values in the first place, vividly demonstrate the complex relations to be discovered among the topics of preservation, judgment, and damage at precisely a point in history when it might have seemed obvious that all the judgments were clear, that preservation was not necessary, and that damage was an entirely desirable goal.

Who is responsible for injury? What does damage mean? What does it mean to look at it and find it meaningful? And how are the processes of looking best understood in relation to harm? Listening to Benjamin, Volney, and Grégoire, we hear voices speaking at epochal turns in history—global conflagration, revolution. Whether the work of John Ruskin, the great Victorian art critic, inhabits an entirely different register depends on how we understand the nature of modern damage. He is typically excluded from the list of significant theorists, not only because his modes of writing have become difficult to assimilate to later intellectual taste, but also because his nation and period are associated in the popular imagination with complacent prosperity and moralizing, on the one hand, and with the violent consolidation of empire, on the other. Texts from his day are often blamed for their indifference to injuries they are typically held either to ignore or to actively support. Ruskin, however, had no doubt that the moral failures of his era were an urgent question and closely linked to the inadequacy of modern perception.

The tendency to think of a complacent and prosperous Victorian Britain as largely insulated from violence is one of those historical fallacies that is apparently too useful to ever be fully put aside. Certainly, the nation avoided the armed insurrections and revolutions of the continent, but a recent reference book calculates that between Waterloo and the outbreak of the First World War, there were a total of six years in which the nation was *not* involved in military operations, none of which fell during the years of Victoria's reign.[10] It is, in any case, inadequate to constrain reflection on the damage characteristic of this period to what we might associate with swords, guns, and bombs. The advance of an inexorable capitalist project in the nineteenth century is only free from violence and injury when we strictly limit our sense of what those terms entail in ways Ruskin never did. As I will indicate in the chapters to follow, to include John Ruskin in the list of significant theorists on damage and culture is not to suggest his impulses were always correct, but it is certainly to open the door to reflection on kinds of injuries and failures of care that are possibly more urgent today than even those associated with the actions of massed armies.

OVERLOOKING DAMAGE

INTRODUCTION

Ruin and Recognition at the Arch of Titus

Overlooking Damage is a book about the intersection of moral and aesthetic judgments at points when clarity about which faculties are (or should be) making judgments is hard to come by. The episodes that concern this work are not presented because I understand them to be instances of unwonted failures by benighted subjects, but rather because they are extraordinary attempts to negotiate a set of relationships the difficulty of which I take to be entirely constitutive of their nature. The story of culture is full of pleasures. It is also a tale of unbearable losses and partial rescues. It is an account of all the things that we cannot fully leave behind and that we make the effort—always only partially successful—to rescue from oblivion. And so, culture is fundamentally and structurally unfair, both in what it tries to preserve and in what it manages to save.

At a recent discussion with scholars of cultural heritage, I heard the complaint that there is a half-spoken but widely understood requirement for their publications to end with a policy recommendation. As a student of literature and culture, that is a pressure I am never likely to feel as a matter of course. Still, I have sensed it impinging on my work for this volume because at every turn I hear voices making direct or implicit recommendations: "Send them all back," they say; "Look elsewhere," they say; "Knock them down"; "Keep them up." This is a book about "back" and "elsewhere" and "look," and about things falling and rising. When we make claims about where things belong, what should be looked at, and what should be looked away from, we are typically drawing on and ratifying current ideas about property and group identity. This study, however, is designed to provide instances of where thought may go when it does not rush to those categories too quickly for answers. I propose to dwell on the challenging nature of possible and necessary relationships to works of art and the institutions that sustain them, given that the tale of their reception is indeed bound up with histories of violence not liable to eventuating in any kind of repair.

If we resist the surprisingly widespread tendency to naturalize cultural phenomena such as property and social identity, it emerges that the key issue in relation to works of art is not in which nation they reside but the feelings they generate, including those directly shaped by the uncertain experience of violence and of national identity. The location of works of art is certainly an interesting question, but it is ultimately a less significant topic than the ways that the histories of objects put the very concepts we use to organize them into question. In a way it is a good thing that, absent a wholesale restructuring of human nature and political institutions, the most ambitious programs of restitution being proposed in recent years are almost certain to fail, not because those who promote them do not have right on their side, given current ideas of nation and property, but because of how sad it would be for those who believe so strongly in the moral imperative of return to live with the practical disappointments attending every long-deferred arrival.[1]

Overlooking Damage emphasizes moments of violence in relation to art and antiquities that are significant in consolidating or attempting to consolidate new ideas of cultural solidarity and resistance that may fail and be forgotten or may succeed and so attain the appearance of inevitability. The historical approach in this work puts into question the certainties that frequently accompany current ideas about seeing, recognizing, and even owning works of art. My goal is to promote a new acknowledgment of the affective drives that cause apparent insights to take the form of our desires. This is not because I aim to foster a debilitating skepticism either about appropriate ownership or about the right response to art objects when we recognize the injuries that shape our relationship to them, so much as in order to encourage a more generative self-reflexive agency in the face of the nexus of emotions, ideas, and perceptions around which responses to art develop.

I will begin with an instance that illustrates almost too well the kind of irresolvable experiences that concern this study and which, for that reason will return various times in this volume, a celebration of victorious violence and

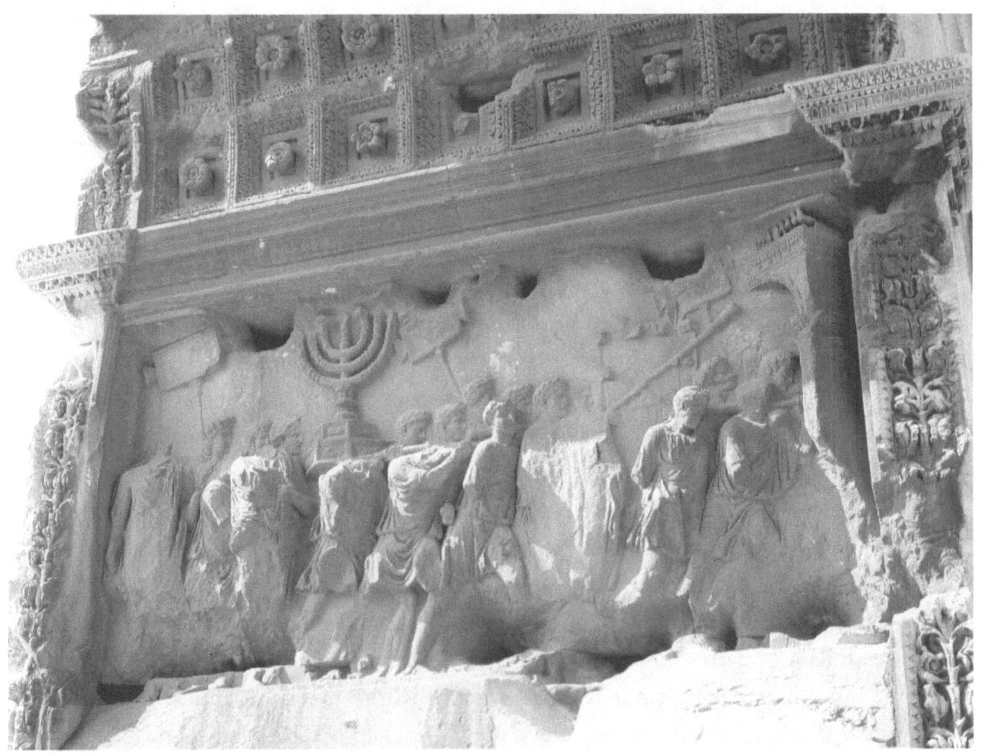

FIGURE 0.1. Relief from the Arch of Titus showing the triumphal procession in Rome after the destruction of Jerusalem in AD 70. Werner Forman Archive / HIP / Art Resource, NY.

humiliating defeat that is both easy to see and hard to fully recognize, though there is no gainsaying its calls on the attention. Indeed, the eye of the traveler will often feel a sense of respite when it falls on the relief decorating the inside of the Arch of Titus at the forum in Rome (fig. 0.1). The simple, unadorned style of the work gives it a modern quality. More than that, a familiar shape comes quickly into focus, a clear point of reference in the midst of that jumble of ancient stone exposed to the glare of the Mediterranean sun by two centuries of excavation, an object that is unusual in the context in which we see it not only owing to its state of preservation—and so, of legibility—but also because it seems so strikingly out of place where we find it. But it is likely we already know what we are seeing, which is why we have sought out this particular carving. In any case the guidebook will quickly explain the brief experience of uncanniness we have sought out or found by chance at this site strewn with so much antique debris less amenable to clear elucidation. The crisp high relief appears to show the menorah and other sacred objects from the Second Temple in Jerusalem being carried off by Roman soldiers following their destruction of the holy site.

In fact, the commemoration on the arch is not quite as direct as it can seem to eyes trained by the immediacy of modern chronicles of violence. What the carving represents is not the event itself (which surely will have looked more confused and chaotic, as violence and injury will tend to do), but rather the elaborate procession, or triumph, that was organized to greet the army on its return to Rome.[2] The men bear the relics with some effort but with commitment. No part of the representation is able to suggest that the seeds of their own destruction have been sown by the act of violence the arch celebrates, an event that was to be of fundamental importance to the emergence of the new religious dispensation that would make every other object in the forum meaningless or worse for nearly two thousand years. The sense of recognition we may feel, whether clearly or at the edge of our consciousness, is one that spans millennia. Writing in the nineteenth century, a time better informed on these topics, the bishop of Durham, an extraordinarily distinguished theologian and student of early Christianity, refers to the fall of Jerusalem as "the most significant national event in the history of the world" precisely because of the way in which it articulated with the rise of Christianity ("national event" becoming world history). He goes on to offer the following account of the Arch of Titus: "It is more than a memorial of a Roman victory. It constrains us to reflect how . . . the conquered, in one sense, trampled on the conquerors; and yet more, how a vigorous remnant of the vanquished still remains, when Rome has perished, and awaits a fulfilment of Divine promises after age-long chastisements."[3]

Today this memory of ruination and of the despoliation of sacred relics is in itself (and not simply in what it represents) a souvenir of yet another moment of now-lost power. The restoration of the arch by Pope Pius VII in 1821 was just one of many post-Napoleonic attempts to shore up state authority with the aid of damaged old rocks. A tellingly understated seventeenth-century painting attributed to Viviano Codazzi shows the structure not simply injured by the depredations of time (columns broken off, vegetation sprouting in the damaged stone at different levels) but firmly embedded in later structures (fig. 0.2). When a new sensibility called for the monument to be separated from the accretions of subsequent ages in order to return it to its ancient dignity, restorers were forced to disassemble the entire structure and rebuild it. A similar commitment to recovery, or at least to differentiating as much as possible the

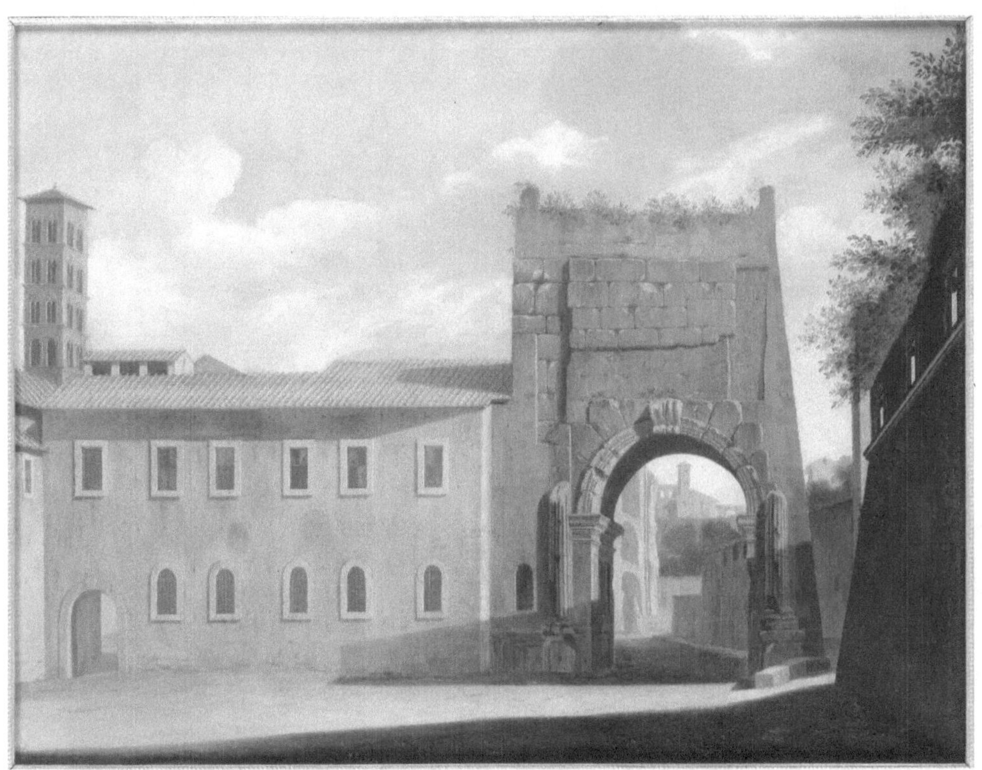

FIGURE 0.2. The Arch of Titus in Rome in the seventeenth century. This painting, attributed to Viviano Codazzi (1603–72), shows the dilapidated structure shored up on one side by masonry introduced for the purpose. On the other side it is attached to one of the many buildings in the area long since removed. RMN-Grand Palais / Art Resource, NY.

periods of history with which material may be associated, is manifested in the ascetic probity of the restoration itself, which is widely recognized to anticipate modern principles: different marble and a distinctly simpler style were deployed for the new sections in order to foreclose the possibility of viewers confusing later additions with original work (fig. 0.3). Everything about the attempt to link modern moment to antique origin requires the careful marking out of periods, not to say the forced forgetting or attempted obliteration of the evidence of vast tracts of time—for example, the long period during what we sometimes call the Middle Ages, when the ceremonial arch served as an actual gate for a fortified structure belonging to the powerful Frangipani family. During their time controlling the imperial city, the French had separated the arch

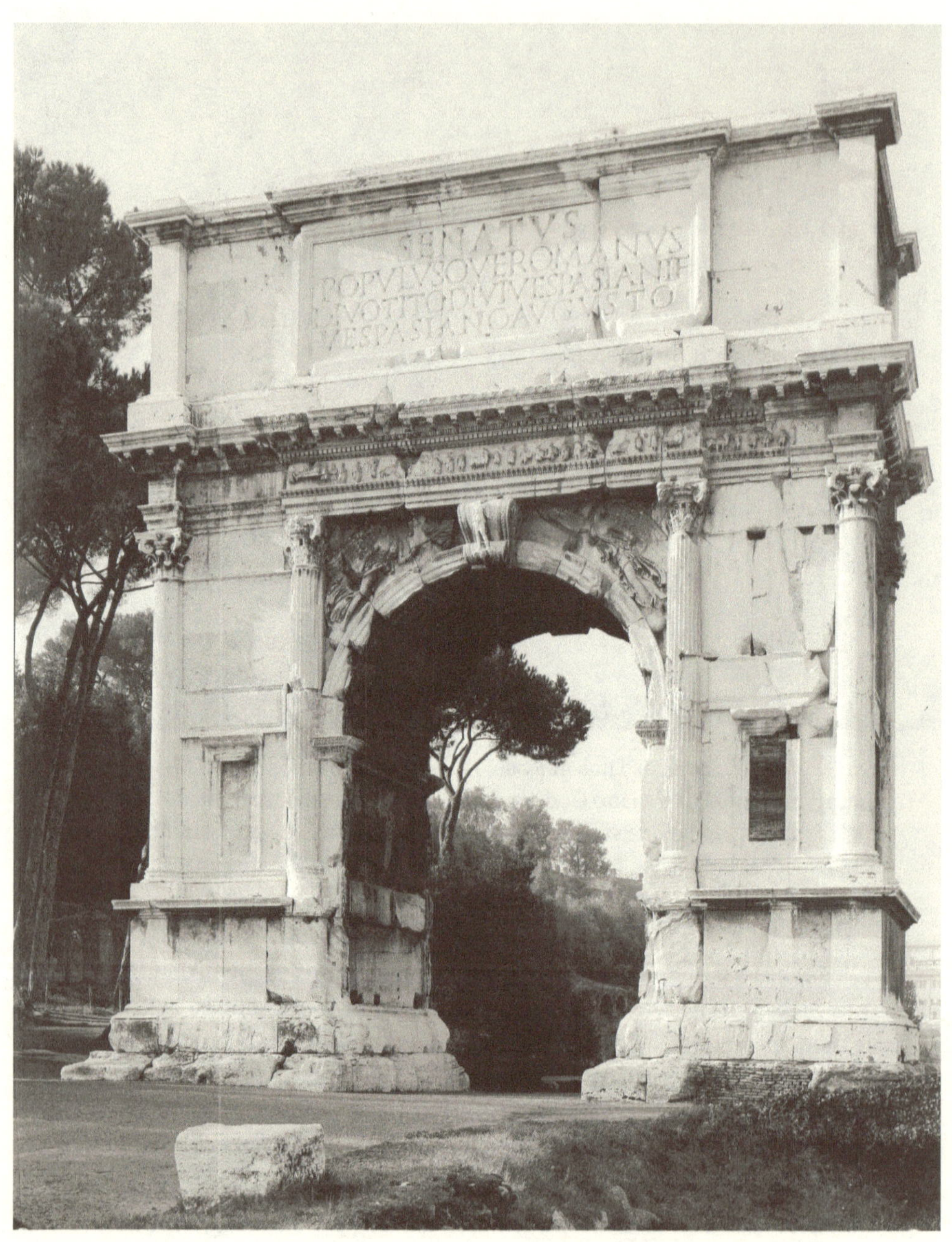

FIGURE 0.3. The Arch of Titus in the twentieth century. Restoration by Giuseppe Valadier, 1821. Erich Lessing / Art Resource, NY.

from surrounding buildings, a freedom from history that left the structure unstable and needing new support, an opportunity for the returned pope to carry out a material restoration, though one that took its object back to a condition unknown to anyone for hundreds of years and in several ways entirely novel.[4]

The inscriptions that dominate on either side of the arch, with more pride of place than the representation of the soldiers and the treasures they carry inside the vault, also mark the change between what the monument was at its outset and what it became at the moment of what we call renovation (when, that is, the history of nearly two millennia was, as much as possible, stripped away). The original dedication is as misleading as it is simple: "The Senate and People of Rome to the Divine Titus Vespasian Augustus, son of the Divine Vespasian." While the graven text identifies the structure as a tribute from the people to their dead ruler, Titus Flavius Vespasianus (emperor AD 79–81), the work was commissioned by Titus's brother, Domitian (emperor AD 81–96).[5] The dedication does not otherwise comment on the reasons for the structure having come into being. And why should it? A commemoration of military prowess carved in hard stone certainly appears to speak for itself. The representations of the triumph and, especially, the apotheosis of the divine emperor, which are the other principal carvings on the arch, though they mean little to the modern tourist, are a further indication of what the original viewers of the work would have understood about the social meanings of the decorative program of the structure, a monument after the death of a ruler, his divinity in the afterlife serving as a warrant for the ongoing merits of his dynasty.

The events the arch celebrates are what its artists have chiseled out; the actions it endorses are the very ones it still does not allow us to forget: conquest, despoliation, victory marked by the acquisition of what others have prized, power manifested by the transformation of sacred relics from another culture into booty, emblems no longer of religious continuity within one community but of individual martial glory in another. A holy object associated with the rituals of one people (and, indeed, with a story not only of continuity but of national recovery—as it was the *Second* Temple that the Romans looted), becomes an exotic decoration at the heart of the metropolis, making the imperial center a location at which knowledge of the periphery is gathered and given new meaning, even if that meaning amounts to little more than an affirmation of the power of the metropolis to ineradicably remake culture at the margins of empire. The symbolic violence of the art program is implicit in the movements between human and divine power it illustrates. Through the force of arms the sacred objects of a people are transformed into emblems of the military prowess of an individual leader, thereby ratifying a political dispensation and a manifestation of divinity unimaginable by those who made those objects or encountered them in their original context.

The nineteenth-century inscription was bound to be longer than the dedication to the emperor because it had to do so much more work than the original in order to justify the presence of a new name, but also because what it commemorates is so much more novel. The renovation of the arch is an opportunity to celebrate the pope in terms distinct from the martial glory the monument originally memorialized. But if the grounds on which he enters the history of the object (not to say its very fabric) are less self-evident than conquest, they are not for that reason less interesting. "Pius the Seventh, Supreme Pontiff," the inscription reads, "ordered that this outstanding monument of religion and art, deteriorating with age, should be stabilized and conserved by new construction imitating the original pattern in the twenty-fourth year of his sacred office."[6] Rather than the *object* being a tribute of gratitude from the people and their representatives to the supreme power, its *restoration* is identified as a boon offered by the pontiff to an unspecified public. The motivation (arresting deterioration) is assumed rather than declared, and the credit taken is not for conquest of the sort Titus and Domitian were concerned to endorse, nor for a new construction like that paid for by the Senate and People, but for stabilization and conservation. (And it is in the nineteenth century that those words of extraordinary political force, "restoration" and "renovation," started to find their meanings in the refurbishment of damaged things.) Ultimately, for all its boldness, the inscription hedges its bets as to the ultimate sources of interest in the arch ("this outstanding monument of religion and art"), leaving as the clearest point the importance of the ruler, who recognizes and makes known the link between past and present—and, indeed, between art and religion. He restores what has been weakened, and his name and title are set off on their own line, inscribed in letters larger than the rest of the text mounted on the entablature.[7]

I have noted that the eye resting on this monument finds some respite from the challenging environment of the forum, which presents such a difficult accumulation of heterogeneous fragments that it is notoriously impossible to take in for any but the most experienced archeologist. But it bears saying that the reason the arch and the menorah are so easy to see, in comparison to many of the other structures and partial structures around the monument, is because we have seen them before. Even before its restoration, the arch was the model for

Napoleon's Arc de Triomphe (commissioned in 1806, and so under construction during the period when the pope was held in France by the emperor, when Rome itself was under French control) and for arches that followed that one. Whether a different source was selected—as is the case with Marble Arch in London (construction begun in 1827), which uses three arches, like the Arch of Constantine and the Arc de Triomphe du Carrousel in Paris (1806)—or followed the model of the Arch of Titus, as with the Wellington Arch (begun 1826) and the Washington Square Arch in New York (1892), the arch form became a recognizable pattern for commemoration that could be evoked even with quite distinct variations, such as the Monument to the Revolution in Mexico City (1910) and Baghdad's notorious Victory Arch (1986).[8] In a process not at all unusual in the history of antiquities, works inspired by an original come to reshape the destiny of the model, which is given new life precisely because of its adoption as archetype. A related anachronistic phenomenon further reinforces the uncanny familiarity of the carving on the arch: the looted menorah has returned to modern eyes as the emblem of the modern State of Israel, which is based on the one the soldiers are carrying, the design having been preserved by the commemoration of the object's capture at the moment of the destruction of its last home.[9]

This book is premised on the idea that if the relationship between beauty and damage has proved so difficult to address, that is at least in part because the topic can seem too self-evident—not just because most antiquities of interest make some claim on our aesthetic categories and because they have all suffered damage in order to become ruins, but because other categories we bring to bear on the topic have seemed themselves almost equally clear-cut, causing reflection to stop prematurely, at an early moment of ethical judgment that is comfortingly clear. It is wrong to break things; vulnerable objects ought to be protected; a culture should always be allowed to maintain ownership of things produced by those it identifies as its ancestors; the experience of an object is always lessened when it is encountered at a distance from the place where it was made to be. These and so many other related and corollary axioms come quickly to the modern mind—with the speed characteristic of judgments one makes about the behaviors of others—so that the project of analysis can seem to involve little more than proposing versions of these nostrums of greater or lesser degrees of sophistication, with more or less colorful detail.

But, is damage more integral to our experience of beauty than such worthy ethical premises may allow us to recognize?[10] The unspoken sense that the objects we admire would as a matter of course be more beautiful if they were not injured, if their original form were intact, is given the lie by every controversial restoration of an Old Master, by every virtual or actual rendering of Greek antiquities in their jarring polychrome glory. Still, while it is an old insight by now that fragments can be beautiful (the culmination of a number of nineteenth-century tendencies rediscovered repeatedly in the twentieth and twenty-first), the role of damage and injury has not typically been celebrated so much as deprecated.

Coming at the question with an interest in the category of things we vaguely call antiquities, it is easy to say that the broken things we learn to admire in museums have typically entered the institution at a point well past the moment of violence that liberated them into the condition of fragments, allowing us to experience damage as something akin to a fact of nature, not as evidence of an injury to be deplored but as a poignant reminder of the inevitable changes that an agentless history will wreak on the things we love or simply live with. With a few telling exceptions (the well-documented revolution or natural catastrophe, for example, or the act of military conquest), the moment of destruction tends to be as much lost to memory as that of the making of the original thing. As various writers on the museum have suggested, one element of the social work of the institution may be understood to be to cast into the light of retrospection violence that is not at all distant from the moment in which an object is put on display. In that sense the concept of primitive art—now entirely and rightly out of favor—is worth remembering for the ways in which it transferred a temporal term used to indicate the absence of civilization from the agent whose brutal actions captured the object to its maker or owner.

The interest of a damaged or isolated object depends on the imaginative relationships it facilitates with an absent whole that may be associated with a past referenced with specificity and detail or, more typically, evoked in a general way for a few characteristic associations. While much of this book will focus on responses to ancient objects, it will be interested in laying out the contemporary pressures shaping their reception, the ever-unsettled temporal disjunctions at the heart of the concept of antiquity making the modernity of the concept at once manifest and impossible to stabilize. "Ancient" and "antique," like "classical," are terms that gesture beyond the horizon of immediate knowledge, toward an uncrossable gap separating objects from the present. But a small number of specialists aside, the same may be said of more concrete regional categories. Ancient Egypt, ancient Greece, ancient Rome, Mesopotamia, Babylon, Assyria,

Nineveh, Carthage, Tyre, Scythia, Palmyra, Angkor Wat, Gandhara, and more: vanished empires or regions or fallen cities are less often understood as specific political and social arrangements from the past than felt as names for the charisma of lost things. And yet the engagement with fragments, and with the fantasies of risk and protection they provoke, is itself inevitably shaped by current losses and fears.

A challenge this book attempts to embrace is putting into relation the distinct historical horizons that might be said to overlap or even to cut across each other at the moment of breaking. The combination of violence and neglect that goes into producing a monument matches up poorly with the ethical and political claims typically at issue when the question of what is to be done about some particular political loss or gain becomes urgent. Relatively straightforward ethical goals such as protecting and preserving irreplaceable objects can be as complicated in practice as adjudicating degrees of complicity on the part of specific agents in order to determine who is at fault for things being broken, lost, or at risk. Even in cases when agency and responsibility are entirely clear, determination of the appropriate moral response of the contemporary subject may be far from self-evident.

Making, breaking, and recovery are the three fundamental acts that form an antiquity, but each one of them will typically take place in a distinct epoch—if, indeed, it does not mark the arrival of the moment of disarticulation or break between periods. The duration of each of these events may vary immensely: some damage takes a matter of seconds, some an extraordinary length of time. Some acts of recovery have become projects of preservation that have lasted millennia; some have come to an end soon after they have begun. Inevitably, then, relics of broken things, admired antiquities, are always reminders of more than two moments in the past, and so of the pressure we put on time to make and support meaning. The urgency of all of these elements—especially breaking, preservation, and the role of time itself—will vary depending on immediate circumstances, as when the museum you have walked by without entering since you were a child becomes pressingly important to you when it is being shelled by enemy forces, or—in a different kind of instance that is nevertheless not unrelated to the first—when the protection or destruction of a statue you had never heard of in a place you have never been comes to feel like an urgent matter.

Overlooking Damage is a study of the ways in which concepts of beauty intersect with periods of epochal violence such as that commemorated in the frieze on the Arch of Titus or that later one that provoked the arch's nineteenth-century restoration. It is also an attempt to resist the separation of broken things from the worlds into which they have come to be embedded. When Walter Benjamin famously proposed in his final essay, the 1940 "On the Concept of History," that every document of culture was also a document of barbarism, he further stipulated that the means of transmission of such documents were tainted with the same quality.[11] The temptation in citing this well-known maxim (itself inescapably a document of worldwide conflagration) has been to identify institutions of culture as unavoidably complicit in the creation of damaging alignments of power and knowledge. It is the role of criticism, this line of argument goes, to reveal the manner in which the drives or motivations of barbarism are woven into each apparent manifestation of civilization, to illustrate the truth of the thesis. *Overlooking Damage* works in another direction altogether, however, not because I find anything to disagree with in the premise of the critic's aphoristic claim, but because I have found room to doubt the narrow range of analytical insights and even ethical options that have typically emerged in response to the process of complicity and resistance Benjamin has sometimes been taken to identify.

I have suggested that the frieze showing soldiers carrying sacred objects from the Second Temple with which the Arch of Titus is decorated offers the modern viewer an experience of immediate comforting clarity in the disorienting Roman Forum. But that is not to say that sustained reflection on the monument is liable to result in either clarity or comfort. An irreconcilable clash of faiths and cultural identities is captured in a work of art that is evidence of what today we would not hesitate to identify as crimes of the worst sort: the destruction of an ancient religious structure, the subjugation and dispersal of a people leading to a period of unfinished exile that culture has naturalized—if that is the right word for embedding a catastrophe in sacred history. Each one of those soldiers stands for legions doing the will of a brutal empire. Behind the men, out of sight, is rubble, devastation. Ahead of them is the glory of their emperor and the validation entailed in any triumph. Further ahead is oblivion, recovery, repurposing.

If vandals damage Rome, what do we call the violence Rome carries out? Fastidious modern sensibilities make injury a perpetual surprise. But earlier periods, which had a more immediate access to—not to say interest in—the classical and religious sources that make the destruction of the temple a turning point in history are explicit on what was entailed in the triumph represented on the arch. The nineteenth-century text I have already cited on the importance of the monument, a publication of the Religious Tract Society endorsed by the bishop of Durham himself, offers a summary of the human cost of the conquest of Jerusalem it celebrates, reminding us simply by its dispassionate tone that recent efforts to contend with the intersection of violence and admiration do not exhaust the range of possibilities:

> The people that survived the fall of the city were variously disposed of at the will of their conqueror. Those that resisted were put at once to the sword; the factious brigands were also executed; the tall and handsome youths were reserved for the triumph; others were condemned to servile works in Egypt; many were sold, and many were distributed for gladiatorial victims throughout the provinces.
>
> According to the generally received estimate, eleven hundred thousand perished during the siege; ninety-seven thousand were made prisoners, exclusive of nearly four hundred thousand who perished in the war in various places.[12]

Four hundred thousand dead "in various places." A people "variously disposed of," in a variety comprised of execution, enslavement, and sadistic abuse. Various places, various dispositions: historical indifference is well captured in one vague adjective that does not judge but simply reports "the will of the conqueror."

In Flavius Josephus, the main classical source on the topic and a witness to much he describes, we find a fuller description of events after the conquest of Jerusalem and an extraordinarily detailed account of the carefully designed triumph that commemorated the arrival of Titus and Vespasian in Rome with their booty, including the massive structures created to showcase the violence carried out in the recent wars. Josephus is himself an equivocal figure, at first a general fighting on the side of the Jews, but then coming over to the Roman side, prophesying the victory of Vespasian and adding the emperor's name to his own: *Flavius* Josephus.[13] The only way to capture the intersection of descriptive richness and brutal celebration of martial violence in the account he left us is to quote in full a passage that begins with aesthetic wonder and ends with military subjection, but which at every point works to weave both elements into an inextricably joint experience:

> The magnificence also of their structure afforded one both pleasure and surprise; for upon many of them were laid carpets of gold. There was also wrought gold and ivory fastened about them all; and many resemblances of the war, and those

> in several ways, and variety of contrivances, affording a most lively portraiture of itself. For there was to be seen a happy country laid waste, and entire squadrons of enemies slain; while some of them ran away, and some were carried into captivity; with walls of great altitude and magnitude overthrown and ruined by machines; with the strongest fortifications taken, and the walls of most populous cities upon the tops of hills seized on, and an army pouring itself within the walls; as also every place full of slaughter, and supplications of the enemies, when they were no longer able to lift up their hands in way of opposition. Fire also sent upon temples was here represented, and houses overthrown, and falling upon their owners: rivers also, after they came out of a large and melancholy desert, ran down, not into a land cultivated, nor as drink for men, or for cattle, but through a land still on fire upon every side; for the Jews related that such a thing they had undergone during this war. Now the workmanship of these representations was so magnificent and lively in the construction of the things, that it exhibited what had been done to such as did not see it, as if they had been there really present. On the top of every one of these pageants was placed the commander of the city that was taken, and the manner wherein he was taken.[14]

A recent scholar is not exactly wrong in describing as "lavish" and "magnificent" this extraordinary ekphrastic memorial of an exuberant celebration of death and ruin that reads like something between the account of the shield of Achilles in the Iliad and the descriptive passages in Keats's "Ode on a Grecian Urn"—if the latter had been undertaken by a cheerful sociopath.[15] The account culminates with the carrying in of the spoils. And "those that were taken in the temple of Jerusalem," Josephus notes, "made the greatest figure of them all" (251).

The massive and carefully planned triumph pauses at the temple of Jupiter Capitolinus to await the completion of a ritual requirement: "It was the Romans' ancient custom to stay till somebody brought the news that the general of the enemy was slain." The Jewish general, Simon bar Giora, had been captured on the grounds of the ruined temple after a long period hiding underground (itself an elaborate and strange episode in Josephus [239]). At this point in the festivities he is removed from among the captives with whom he has marched on the long trek from Jerusalem to Rome. Perhaps he is lowered from a float showing the circumstances of his surrender. Or perhaps he is simply pushed forward from the rear of the column. In any case, a rope is put around his neck and he is tormented as he is led toward the forum, off the Capitoline Hill, where the massive temple to Jupiter stands. The procession waits in silence. The rhythm of Josephus's account appalls the imagination. The large crowd that has been moving through the imperial city in noisy celebration pauses in anticipation of the news of an execution they know to expect as a man is singled out and dragged away. After a gap of some unspecified time, they release an exhilarated cry when they hear he has been killed. "Accordingly," the historian writes, "when it was related that there was an end of him . . . all the people had set up a shout for joy" (251). At this point the Romans can resume the sacrifices and feasting that will take up the balance of their celebration.[16]

In an important study of the modern fascination with ancient monuments that I will be discussing in the third chapter in this volume, Alois Riegl, the great Austrian art historian and theorist, finds one anticipation of the phenomenon in the early years of the Roman Empire. "This," he writes of the mania for antique objects that coincides precisely with the period of the chilling triumph of Titus, "may well be one of the most striking among the many analogies to our own age which that time offers us."[17] And indeed, the antiquities of the Jews are highly valued. They come to be placed in a massive temple Vespasian builds soon after the events Josephus describes, a museum and trophy case for the nation given the Orwellian name "Temple of Peace." The historian seems to understand the collection and display of antiquities as a reasonable project for the capital of the empire, his terms evoking an explanation of looting that would gain currency in the nineteenth century: "In this temple were collected and deposited all such rarities as men aforetime used to wander all over the habitable world to see, when they had a desire to see one of them after another" (Josephus, 249).

The triumph, the temple, and ultimately the Arch of Titus are so many indications of a society in which imperial power needs to stage elaborate performances in order to validate its practices—to share complicity, even—and to ensure the public support on which it depends. I will return later in this book to the fate of the implements taken from the temple in Jerusalem, as well as to the topic of triumphs. What I want to emphasize here is the openness of the violence behind what we see at the Arch of Titus. For generations, traveler after traveler has crossed the spot where Simon was taken from the crowd to be killed. The execution itself quite possibly took place in the prison, or *carcere*, that would gain fame in later years as Peter's place of captivity, a location now occupied by two churches.

It would be a rare visitor to Rome who did not pause after climbing the stairs of the Campidoglio to take a moment in the courtyard designed by

Michelangelo, in the space where once stood the massive temple to Jupiter, where the crowd waited to hear news that Simon had been executed. All this violence is unseeable, of course. And Michelangelo so reoriented the approach to the hill that it would take an extraordinary act of sympathetic imagination for one to try to think oneself back to that moment, even when on location. Still, this place of violence so transformed by millennia of damage and reinvention is not unavailable to reflection, though the injuries on which the mind may pause are without hope of repair. And, indeed, the instances I cite in *Overlooking Damage* provide occasions for reflection, because they are not liable to a cure. To ask what broken things can do is to be resolved on the fact that in the world of culture—like elsewhere—damage does not as a matter of course eventuate in remedy.

In *Civilization and Its Discontents*, Freud famously used Rome as a model for the unconscious because history tells us that so many distinct structures occupied the same locations over the centuries. His point is to draw a contrast between the coexistence of all the eras of our lives in our minds and what is possible in the outside world.[18] The forum recovered would be a sublime nightmare, not just because of the blood that ran on its stones over the long centuries but because only in the unstable condensations of the unconscious is it possible to experience so many overlapping temporalities. To return to the Arch of Titus as I have done is to insist that it is only by looking again—by moving beyond merely seeing—that the meanings of the encounter with the monument are liable to emerge. Sight itself is an inadequate guide to the moral implications of things, and our first emotional response is barely a beginning on the way to addressing the moral nature of our aesthetic experiences.

Sometimes when we talk about Rome, it is a way to not talk about Jerusalem. Sometimes we use "historic" to indicate neutral topics of purely academic interest. But the presence of irrecoverable objects on the Arch of Titus reminds us that the issues at stake when reflecting on antiquity may be more current than the damage caused in the name of Roman peace. It is not just the case that rebuilding the temple in Jerusalem could only be the result and the cause of a vast loss of human life, nor that doing so would entail the impossible project of forgetting nearly two thousand years of Jewish and gentile culture that has been shaped by its loss. It is that its recovery could only ever be a new start, and in that sense not a recovery at all. And to say Rome and Jerusalem is just to pick two of the capitals around which these always asymmetrical topics have revolved in European thought. Related issues might be raised about other contested sites around the world.[19]

It is hardly a new discovery that war damages things irrecoverably, nor that cultures are built on the broken pieces of other cultures, some of which they acquire through violent means. The goal of *Overlooking Damage* is to address the ways in which the forms of attention we give to precious objects from the past may or may not be connected to the forms of attention and neglect we give other challenging parts of our lives, as individuals or as political or ethical agents. It is not that the categories in which we put forms of attention to antiquities (beauty, sublimity, antiquarian learning, culture, and so forth) have ever been kept entirely separate from those by which we judge the ethical crises of our lives (such as responsibility, culpability, and blame). The conceptual challenges in which this book is interested arise from the fact that the relationships of elements in each category are linked by so many lines of connection that it has been tempting to reduce them to one thing.

The question of which episodes of violent conflict or simple damage count as world-historical and which are fated to oblivion is always liable to more revision than our ethical sensibilities would prefer to recognize. The instances I discuss in this book are inevitably shaped by current relationships to violence, from the discomfort that came to be a characteristic—if relatively novel—twentieth-century response to military conflict sometime around the middle years of the First World War, to the more recent articulation of the modern subject with the uneven and apparently unresolvable struggles involving popular opinion and proxy battles that we might associate first with the Cold War and then with the response to terrorism in the United States and Europe. Important recent work on the cultural manifestations of war has highlighted the effects of armed conflict even in places where we might not have thought to find it, an insight itself shaped by the experience of living at once with the dread of violence (the terrorist outrage, the nuclear strike) and of complicity in unjust action (the elaborate military adventure, the sudden bombing of a putative or actual enemy justified as a form of self-defense, the drone strike).

My treatment of the topic of the Arch of Titus has revolved around the question of recognizability, of what we see and what we are liable to miss when we look at that monument. Indeed, I evoked a figure not shown on the arch but important in Josephus's account: Simon, the Jewish general who trudged for miles in captivity, who rode or rowed on shipboard, living every long mile in the intimacy with his captors inevitable in such circumstances. The limited and tendentious record we have leaves a lot out, but the timeline is thought-provoking, as are the small hints we find in Josephus. The conquest of Jerusalem was complete by September of AD 70. The carefully staged triumph of Titus took place the following summer. Between those two points in time there passed almost a year of unchronicled living for the Jewish captives transported from Jerusalem to Antioch to Alexandria and ultimately to Rome, an unimaginable unrecorded hiatus of the sort that has been experienced by the displaced for millennia.

Josephus's account of the aftermath of the sacking of Jerusalem amounts to a grand symbolic imperial progress culminating in the triumph at Rome. It is an elaborate performance of authority by Titus, accompanied by a great deal of displaced rage at the Jews (who are blamed for the violence entailed in quashing their uprising).[20] Indeed, Titus is in the middle of participating in one particularly savage war crime when he hears the news that the last remaining general has been taken:

> But as for Titus, he marched from that Cesarea which lay by the sea-side, and came to that which is named *Cesarea Philippi*, and staid there a considerable time, and exhibited all sorts of shows there. And here a great number of the captives were destroyed, some being thrown to wild beasts, and others in multitudes forced to kill one another, as if they were their enemies. And here it was that Titus was informed of the seizure of Simon. (Josephus, 238)

We see here the source for the cold-blooded tone of William Knight, the Anglican divine I have already cited, writing about acts of extraordinary cruelty some 1,800 years later. Ultimately reaching Alexandria, and with the glory of his triumph in mind, Titus reserves some seven hundred of the prisoners (picking those who are "eminently tall and handsome of body" [243]). Along with Simon, he has this group of select captives sent to Rome via ship.

"Sent to Rome via ship." The passive tone of the phrase feels like the language of complicity. But I find I can do no better. I hesitated on the verb as I wrote it: "embark" suggests agency to my ear, as one enters a vessel for a trip one has chosen to undertake; "they were shipped" indicates acquiescence in the commodification of these individuals who clearly lost the power to determine their own destinies when they became captives but did not become objects at that moment. It is far easier to say what the sovereign ordered to be done than to determine how the actions and feelings of individuals articulate with the effects of sovereign decisions. And then, only speculation can fill in the gaps the narrative leaves as to the actual conditions of travel in an era when the size of transport was small and when long periods of time were part of the experience of traversing significant distances. Though the nature of their relations was established and modified by orders from above, guards and prisoners were bound to be physically very close to each other—eating, sleeping, sweating, shitting, pissing in a relatively narrow space.

Out of all the likely delays and mysterious activities of this group of soldiers and prisoners, possibly the most baffling pause may have been the stop during which the elaborate preparations for the triumph were carried out. We cannot know what Simon understood about what was happening when, among the hundreds of captives, he waited (if that's the word for the experience of a pause in motion for people with no expectations of any kind of arrival) as the army did the hard work of preparing massive floats and organizing the commemoration of his defeat for an imperial capital that had seen its own recent internecine military struggles but was at the moment at peace (as we say about cities that take war elsewhere). Joining a parade may have seemed like more of the forced movement and humiliation to which he had been subjected for months. But surely it would have felt different to be one of many in the crowd advancing through the imperial capital, surrounded by the noise of a jubilant metropolis after the long marches in the Mediterranean countryside that had brought him to that point. And what could he have known about how it would all end for him that day? Given what Josephus tells us about the actions of Titus, it was hardly likely that any degree of cruelty on the part of his captors would have surprised Simon. Still, it is difficult to imagine that the traditions involved in a triumph would have been explained to the captive leader. Whether he knew what to expect or otherwise, what can we imagine him feeling in the sudden silence when he realizes that he has gone from constrained subject or example—from one among many—to the object of every eye as he is pulled from the parade and taken to be slaughtered, removed from the triumph in order for his death to be its culmination, to provide the occasion for a joyful noise he will not be able to hear?

Evidently, as I write I orient my moral compass around the experience of the defeated, and my prose encourages the reader to do the same. It is easy enough to do so. And I suppose my Jewish heritage—is that what we call it these days?—may be understood to give me some particular warrant for doing so. But why does that miserable, hopeless identification seem so self-evidently the moral one to take in relation to the situation I have briefly sketched out? What am I denying in the process of identification I claim? I have no problem distancing myself from the man who put the sword in—if that is how Simon was killed—or with those who threw him to his death or throttled him, or with those who tortured him on his way to whichever kind of death the Roman ritual required. But I do find myself hesitating as I pull myself away from the crowd attending the spectacle.

Reflecting on what the immediacy of my identification with the victim may be protecting me from, I find myself thinking back to a memorable opportunity I once had to visit an institution in the same city as the Arch of Titus, yet a world away. The Museum of Roman Civilization is in a fascinating corner of Rome, though not one typically visited by the tourist. The Esposizione Universale Roma, or EUR, as the district is generally called, was built in the southern periphery of the city in the 1940s, its architecture combining classicizing and modernist gestures into a monumental style we associate with the period and its politics. The area was developed with the goal of creating the locale for an ambitious ("Universal") exhibition celebrating the anniversary of the 1922 March on Rome that led to Fascist control of Italy. History outran the slow development of plans and the work of builders, so that the exhibition for which the area was developed never took place. Indeed, American GIs found themselves quartered at EUR at the end of the war. But the museum designed to celebrate Roman civilization—originally intended to illustrate continuities between antique and modern glories—was ultimately constructed and opened in the 1950s, less than an afterthought now for visitors with so many other calls on their attention in the Eternal City, and so an easy economy when the state is looking for institutions to shutter. The museum was closed to the public when I visited in 2004; it is currently closed again, as it has been since 2017.[21]

I had accompanied some classical art historians and archeologists who had received permission to see one of the few recognized treasures at the museum, though one that was itself more a visitor than a resident. The *Forma Urbis Romae*, a massive marble map of the city displayed on a wall of the Temple of Peace from early in the third century, was largely destroyed in the course of the Middle Ages, made into lime for mortar or simply broken up to be incorporated as building material. But fragments of this extraordinary work, which measured around sixty by forty feet when complete, have been recovered (and, indeed, are still being recovered). In the post-Napoleonic period the work had been prominently displayed at the Vatican Museum, but at the time of our visit its pieces had been consigned to boxes at the Museum of Roman Civilization, an extraordinary resource for knowledge of the ancient city and a challenge to the puzzle-solving talents of archeologists. On our way to see this evocative and humbling sight of broken marble fragments carefully wrapped and stored in cases in a disused room in the melancholy halls of a closed modern museum, we were brought up short when we came up against a quite distinct kind of display, one we could not easily ignore, though it was not what we call original and its elements were composed of a far more modest material. Our steps faltered and paused as we entered a splendidly arranged gallery of casts of Trajan's Column dating back to the nineteenth century but displayed with stark modernist flair (fig. 0.4).[22] Yet another structure commemorating the victories of a Roman emperor, the column was completed in AD 113, so a little less than fifty years after the triumph of Titus. It is decorated with events from the wars in which the

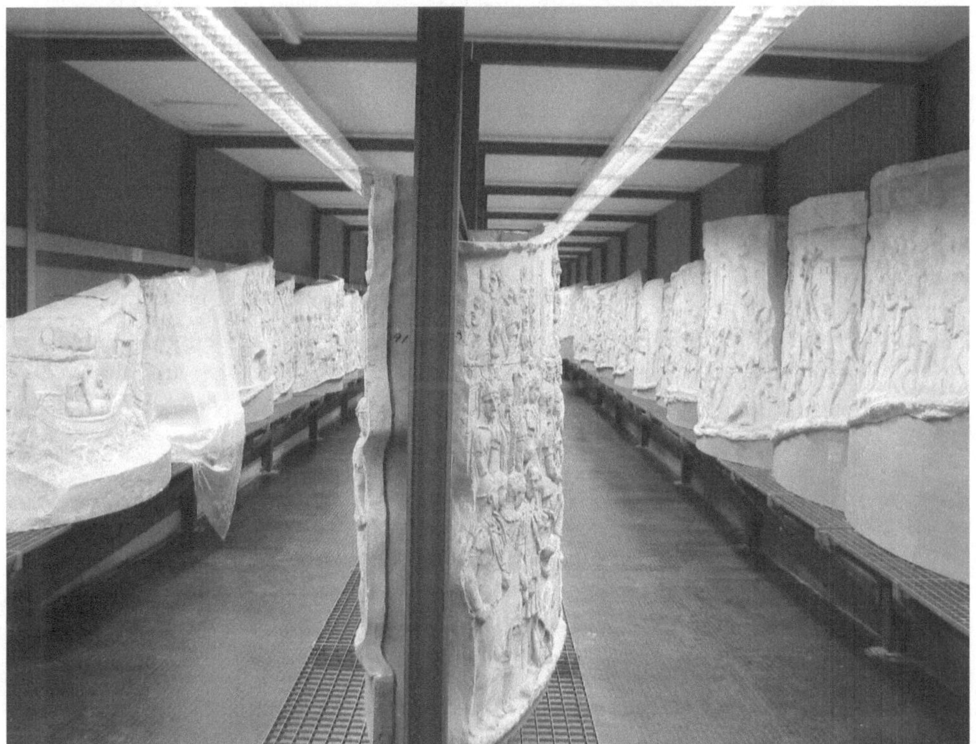

FIGURE 0.4. Display of casts from Trajan's Column. Museo della Civiltà Romana, EUR, Rome, 2004. Photo by the author.

later emperor had prevailed, notably the conflict with the Dacians, the natives of a territory now including Romania and other adjacent areas.

The original still stands at the corner of Trajan's Forum, quite close to the busy traffic of the city, a challenging object to take in as a whole, a difficult one on which to reflect in detail—and, of course, also subject to the damage that results when rain mixes with the exhaust of the many cars around it every day (fig. 0.5). While it must always have been hard to make out the carvings, as they rose up beyond sight into the Roman light, that challenge has become an impossibility as the buildings that afforded views of its higher levels in its own day are long gone. The original object is in many ways less available to examination than the copies that were made before modern technology had contributed to the degradation of the carved marble. As a further aid to perception, the curators at the Museum of Roman Civilization have laid out the reliefs to look as much as possible like a narrative. Other collections tend to pile the casts on top of each other insofar as space allows, in order to emulate the original object—maintaining thereby the experience both of grandeur and of illegibility. (The casts at the Victoria and Albert Museum in London are displayed in two halves, a compromise simply based on architectural limits.)

There is much of interest in this extensive illustrated record that the curators in Rome have made appear more narratively straightforward than in fact it is, much that catches the eye of the walker in the museum headed toward the fragments of something more authentic but harder to understand, the broken marble map of a great capital that both does and doesn't exist. Indeed, the relief that gave me pause as I unexpectedly encountered this antique celebration of military prowess is as shocking as it is clear. It shows a torch-wielding Roman soldier dispassionately setting fire to the thatched roof of a building that gives the appearance of being a home (fig. 0.6). It is the kind of thing we have seen in footage from Vietnam in the 1960s. The disquietingly modern look of the unadorned style of the sculpture, the urgent documentary feeling we have learned to associate with the display of disconnected images edited together on broadcast news—these formal qualities make the scene all the more reminiscent of a film clip showing a methodical GI using his Zippo lighter to burn down the huts that make up a hamlet, as apparently indifferent to the dismay of nearby residents looking on in misery as to what we might be tempted to call the heartbreaking efforts of those residents to rescue their belongings from the burning structures. But perhaps the soldier's indifference should lead us to mistrust our wishful sense that some events are of themselves liable to break

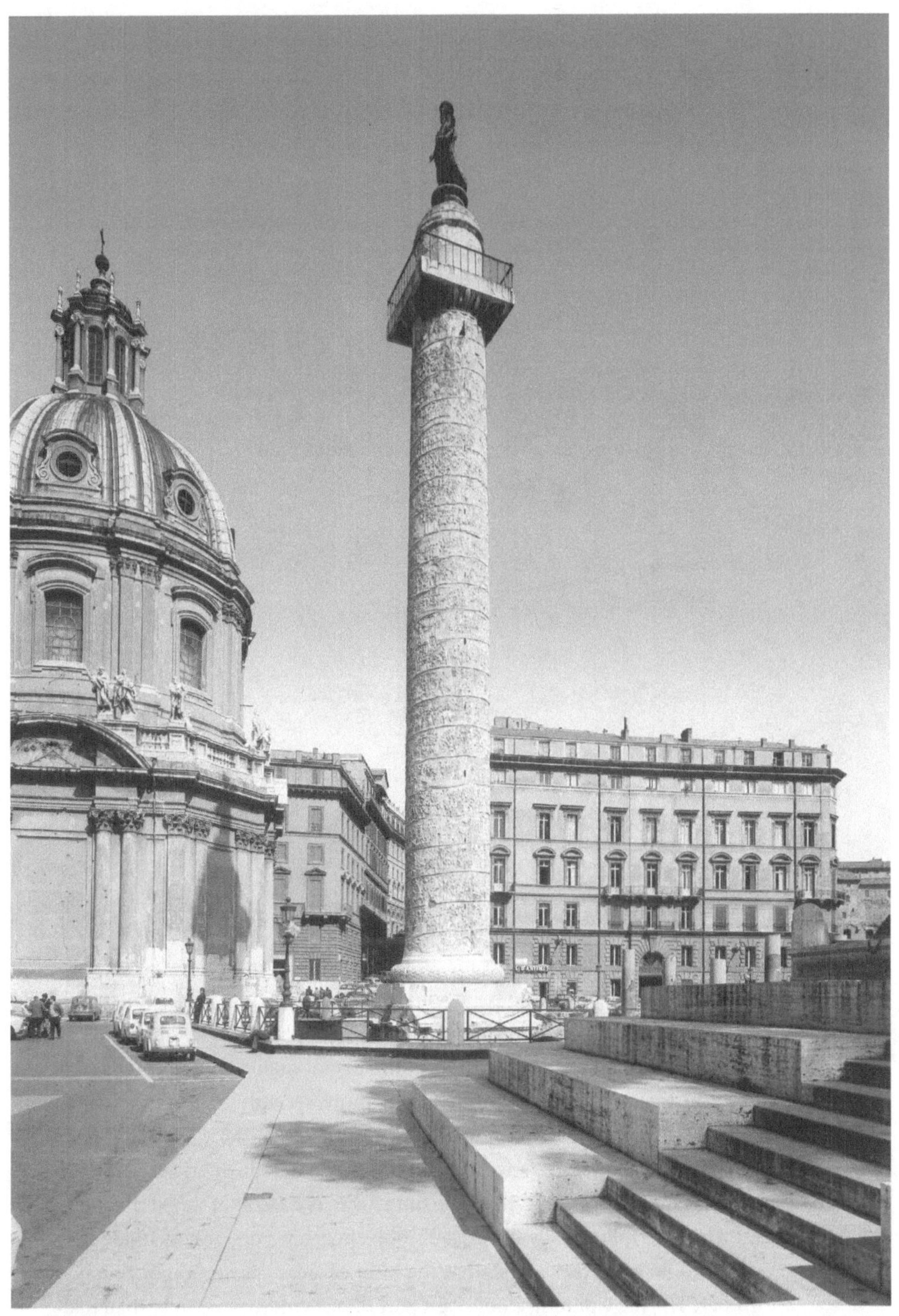

FIGURE 0.5. Trajan's Column (AD 113) in the twentieth century. Scala / Art Resource, NY.

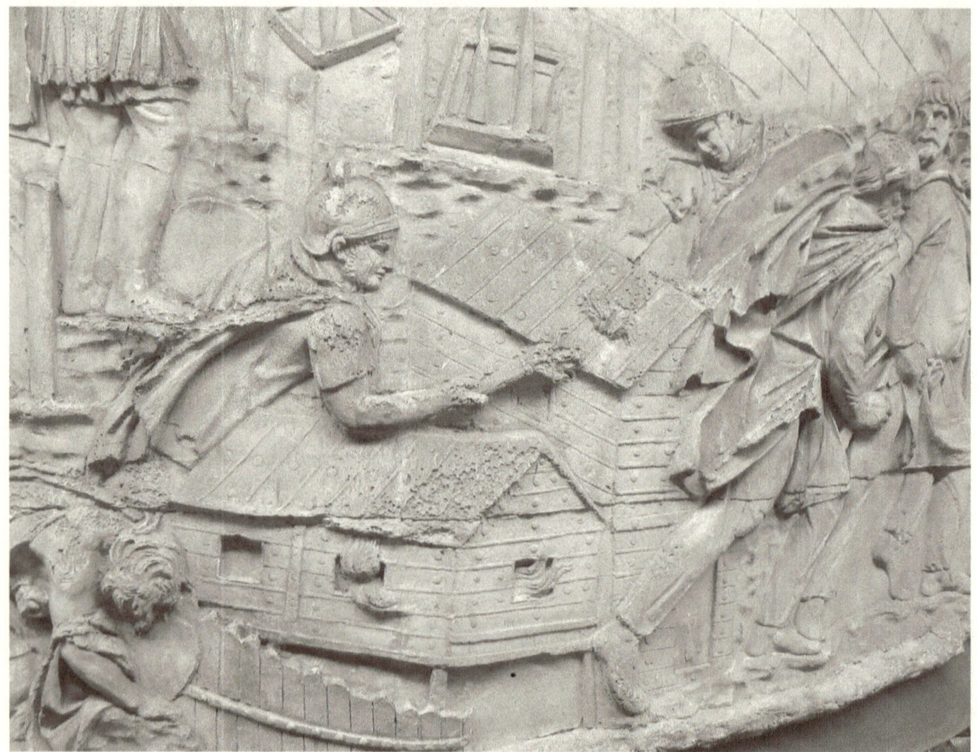

FIGURE 0.6. Roman soldiers setting fire to Dacian buildings. Cast from Trajan's Column. Museo della Civiltà Romana, EUR, Rome, 2004. Photo by the author.

a heart. A contrast stood out to me as I stopped before the cast. Openly acknowledged in the heart of Rome, if somewhat camouflaged by circumstances, we find a carved record of the kind of injurious actions on which the power of the imperial capital depends, a vision of the brutal nature of war comparable to an event that soldiers and commanders more recently had every right to expect would be forgotten, like so many wartime acts of cruelty, had it not been captured by the television cameras and ultimately entered American history as part of the tale of the gradual rejection of the war as a result of the revelation of brutal strategies followed by American troops fighting a difficult insurgency.[23]

It would be perverse to wish that the kind of clear celebration of brutality we find on Trajan's Column should be a part of our culture any more than it already is. And the evidence of the column itself tells us that it would be foolish to think that if it were, we would find the cruel actions of armies brought to a halt. But I do find myself wishing we could feel a relationship to the damage we wreak that was fuller than either denial or regret. It may seem strange and appalling to us that the triumph of Titus does not end before the death of the foreign general and the celebration that attends it. But as we think of the fate of Simon, related events from recent years may spring to memory, such as the complex public feelings and elaborate forms of commemoration that followed the deaths of Saddam Hussein, Muammar Gaddafi, and especially Osama bin Laden.

The nineteenth century is the crucible in which conditions for modern forms of cruelty were formed—not in the sense that the period was more prone to causing pain. On the contrary, the consolidation and diffusion of novel concepts of political subjecthood made cruelty newly challenging to think about even though it is hard to say they reduced the occasions for causing damage. Crises of knowledge, vision, and judgment are our inheritance from this earlier period, along with characteristic and even emblematic figures that reflection on those crises has provoked, some of which will be discussed in this book. We cannot save Simon, and I am not interested in making a hero out of a defeated general with a decidedly mixed profile in the sources. But I can reflect on the crowd in the city that had committed itself to open witness of the injuries it caused and on which the power of its leaders depended. Evidently, every act of state brutality makes witnesses accomplices, and one cannot recapture the conscience of any skeptical participant or of those who may have turned away. But let us say that the brutal act commemorated in fragile plaster in a closed museum and on a decaying marble column seen and ignored by centuries of travelers and residents may stand as a reminder of two facts: the possibility of acknowledging the acts of war subtending our apparent peace and the limits of immediate witness as a prompt for ethical action.

• • •

Writing on beauty and collecting and display has frequently found its conceptual energies in recent years by working through a compelling but fairly constrained set of claims about what it means to see things and to collect them, and even what it means to try to come to know objects (on display or otherwise).[24] The powerful critical machinery that has been brought to bear on these topics notwithstanding, a fairly narrow set of insights has typically resulted, largely ratifying the expectation that the main interest of cultural institutions and the concepts that subtend them is to endorse or otherwise support the structures of social power in place at the moment of analysis. Often, as in the Benjamin essay briefly mentioned above (and addressed at greater length in Chapters 1 and 4 of this study), that moment is understood to be a remarkably long one, so that current rulers are blameworthy heirs of guilty ancestors and those who manage the institutions of culture are perhaps best understood as the viziers of a cruel dynasty, priests of a brutal cult. This book is premised on the sense that a more punctuated idea of continuity and rupture is necessary when addressing the nature of institutions of culture, especially in relation to episodes of violent struggle.

Overlooking Damage resists the desire to identify ongoing hidden dynamics and structures of power linking phenomena over time. The vicissitudes of war and other forms of overt struggle, while clearly not unrelated to the inequities and cruelties of the bloodless rationalizing powers that are the more characteristic targets of critique, nevertheless also pose some fundamental challenges to those by now conventional structural analyses.[25] At the very least, the open face of violence is bound to present problems to methodologies that depend on the gesture of uncovering or revelation. The kind of violence and loss that interests me in this book is no obscure fact needing revelation; it is carried on the surface of my instances, almost as vividly as the Arch of Titus carries its evidence of violent theft or Trajan's column its representation of arson. It is a different kind of mystery when the murderer stands before us, dagger drawn or torch raised, or when he stops for his portrait, accompanied by his loot, than when we have to discover the nature of the crime even as we become ever more certain that the perpetrator is standing beside us. The diverse set of approaches sometimes identified in a general way as critique has in recent years generated a powerful counter-discourse, even a small polemical subgenre in its own right, typically motivated by a concern about the ethical limitations of the broad project embraced by the term.[26] And, indeed, the instances discussed in this book illustrate the tendency of the disposition toward critique to sometimes distort the nature of the objects under consideration or simply to miss key elements.[27]

The crimes discussed in *Overlooking Damage* are generally carried out in broad daylight. If anything has been hiding in plain sight, it has been the troublingly productive nature of the experience of damage in the nineteenth-century culture of art. Certainly the existence of a relationship between imperial expansion and the creation of collections will not be news to anyone reading this book. But discussion of the relationship between empire and culture has too often stopped at its identification or has seemed concerned with trying to use analysis to somehow run history backward in a desperate attempt to undo damage in the cultural sphere that is beyond cure in the world of practical experience.[28] I am interested in highlighting not complicity or ideological blindness in my treatment of these topics, but the sense of passionate engagement, responsibility, and even caretaking provoked by encountering art and antiquities at moments of violent crisis. My point is not that these responses are inevitable—the historical record tells us they are not—but that including these affects in the conversation will enrich reflection on ongoing disappointments of the modern moral life.

This book began as an attempt to think about the conceptual limits that were quickly reached when twenty-first-century subjects tried to formulate the emotions appropriate to episodes of violence against antiquities, notably in the case of the destruction of irreplaceable objects at Bamiyan and Palmyra. I asked myself how those acts might be understood in relation to other notorious instances of politically motivated vandalism, and then how the responses of the period in which the modern concepts of art and the nature of art institutions were established might provide resources for thinking about these topics. I have found that some of the most compelling writing on museums and violence comes from a different direction of late, not from reflection on museums of art and antiquities as they were formed around the beginning of the nineteenth century, when the immediate political crisis was shaped by the French Revolution and its aftermath, on the one hand, and the rise of industrial capitalism, on the other, but from analysis of the emergence of museums of anthropology and the links of those institutions with military violence and the pseudosciences associated with imperial expansion in the late nineteenth and early twentieth centuries. Recent polemics against conventional museum practices have made a powerful case for the need to recognize—and respond concretely to—specific acts of violence with which museums have been associated, the damage that the institution is sometimes said to hide or even to inevitably perpetuate.[29] It is not an accident that the energy of these works comes from their accounts of collections formed at the high-water mark of European imperial aggression, indeed, that the material that came to be known as the Benin Bronzes, stolen in 1897 from the living culture in which it played a vital part in the course of a particularly well-documented episode of brutal imperial violence, is the paradigmatic episode for many of these accounts.

"Looting became something new during the three decades between the Berlin Conference of 1884 and the outbreak of World War in 1914," Dan Hicks proposes in his impassioned recent book on the Benin Bronzes, "through the actions of anthropology museums" (233). The fact that the combination of new or newly ascendant race theories, open institutional participation, and raw economic interest all were component parts in events that caused extraordinary damage to people and social structures in Africa is impossible to gainsay and vital to recognize. Still, one might pause over Hicks's formulation, in which cultural markers associated with epochal violence (the First World War, the scramble for Africa) are leveraged to talk about the moral failure of institutions for display. One can imagine a multitude of ways in which events and attitudes between 1884 and 1914 might be understood to have led to a recalibration of the meaning of looting, and for most of those the actions of museums will not be the chief component. The violent role of the institution is central to Hicks's argument; indeed, his insistence on the harm caused by museums in the period of European imperial expansion is emphasized not to address a historical fact to be deprecated in retrospect—that works in museums were sometimes acquired through brutal means—but as part of an argument that holds that their continued display in those museums is part of an ongoing process of injury in which every viewer is interpellated. "The damage is renewed," Hicks writes, "every day that the museum doors are unlocked and these trophies are displayed to the public" (xiv). Hicks is desperate for his readers to hear the violence of bombs and rifles that echoes in this argument exploding in the museum itself, which is what drives what one hopes are tactical moments of hyperbole such as "The invention of ethnological displays was surely as significant a technology in the history of Victorian colonialism as the Maxim gun" (11).[30] It is otherwise hard to know what Hicks means by "surely as significant." Still, it is difficult for me to find a way to understand the claims of the sentence that strikes me as morally or conceptually sound. Indeed, tendentious comparative constructions are characteristic of the way Hicks leverages claims in order to put in the same register what might seem to be quite distinct phenomena, hence the patchwork of evil linked with "in the same way" in the following sentence: "Displays of loot are an endurance in the same way as apartheid was an endurance, or how the poisoning today of the Niger River by oil companies is an endurance" (227).

Hicks's formulations at once express an impassioned faith in the object lesson of the museum—the sense that material on display will as a matter of course or inevitably teach a certain lesson—and confess how difficult in fact it is to see what is before one and come to a clear determination of meaning and values in relation to things on display. The operating theory of ongoing harm one sees in Hicks and other similar critics is characteristic not only of an ostensibly political position in relation to the museum but also of an effort to mount a powerful ethical challenge to the institution by arguing vigorously for restitution and reparations. In this context, the report commissioned by the French government from Felwine Sarr and Bénédicte Savoy in 2018 after President Emmanuel Macron indicated a new openness to restitution distinguishes itself not simply by the official imprimatur under which it was produced but by the combination of nuance and detail it offers in its treatment of specific regions and objects. These elements, along with the report's engagement with a wide set of stakeholders in Africa, we may understand as putting into practice the bold demand for what the authors call, in the subtitle to their report, "a new relational ethics." "Thinking restitutions," Sarr and Savoy argue, in a simple formulation of notable ethical and conceptual weight, "implies much more than a single exploration of the past: above all, it becomes a question of building bridges for future equitable relations" (2). The report resists the sentimental tendency to believe that certain objects can only belong in their native settings, but it also does not look away from the violence that has at this point become formative to what certain objects have become:

> These objects which for a large part have been ripped away from their cultures of origin by way of colonial violence, but which were welcomed and cared for by generations of curators in their new places of residence, from now on bear within them an irremediable piece of Europe and Africa. Having incorporated several regimes of meaning, they become sites of the *creolization* of cultures and as a result they are equipped to serve as mediators of a new relationality. (87)

To see the museum as the site of an ongoing violence comparable to that waged with bombs and machine guns or by means of environmental degradation, a violence shaped and determined by the keepers of museums whose current descendants share their guilt as they keep opening the doors and reenacting the injury that led to the acquisition of the objects on display—this is a very different vision from that of the welcoming and caring curators suggested in the Sarr-Savoy report. While "welcome and care" are evidently simplifications that might be felt to soft-pedal the actions of agents at institutions that care for things ripped by violence from where they originally belonged, it bears pausing before we assume that emphasizing an unbroken line of evil actions and results is a more accurate version of the facts. Indeed, the affective lives of curators—precisely because they will be as inadequate and self-deluded as all our most serious passions inevitably are—might be a more promising phenomenon alongside which to think about culture than the juridical desire to identify and pass judgment on an original crime and to determine forms of expiation. As they emphasize the urgent need to repatriate a heritage easily available in Western capitals but all too rare in the areas in which that heritage arose, Sarr and Savoy point out that at the time of writing, 60 percent of the population of sub-Saharan Africa were below the age of twenty (5). The subjects they have in mind are these young people. Oriented toward the future as they are, as well as toward recognizing not one fallen condition but a complex set of relationships that exist and must be addressed (something suggested in their use of the term "creolization"), Sarr and Savoy's conceptions of restitution are not premised on nightmare visions of the violent repetition of old conflicts so much as in understanding culture as available for new beginnings. The confusion of moralizing absolutes with ethical clarity runs the risk of promoting the kinds of errors associated with the worst instances of decolonization of the past at precisely a time when a more expansive sense of global responsibility and interconnection seems urgently necessary.

My discussion in this book of well-established aesthetic categories, especially the sublime, will revolve largely around the ways the forms of attention these categories describe relate to apparently more mundane topics such as gathering, organizing, and protecting works of art. I am especially interested in the intersection of ethical claims about objects with the emotional responses those same objects provoke. My sense is not only that concerns we typically associate with the vicissitudes of the emotional life of the individual are consistently useful when thinking about beautiful things at risk or injured, but, perhaps more surprisingly, that paying close attention to the nexus of affect and concept manifested at crisis points when subjects are forced to reflect on the unstable situation of works of art is a fruitful way to orient oneself around questions of historic significance and urgent political import, such as the ongoing crises provoked by the rise of the modern nation-state and the emergence of mass public opinion as a political force. Guilt, responsibility, failure, love: all of these are liable to be at stake when we talk about the monuments of culture at risk, and each of these emotional states may be thought of variously as causes or as symptoms of the political events with which they are associated.

• • •

The word "war" is used in popular discourse as though its meaning were not only clear but among the clearest meanings available. Indeed, it is one of those terms that typically stand at the edges of discourse, marking a limit because of their apparently self-evident nature. Hence its application to evoke a natural state of hostility tending toward open violence (as in Thomas Hobbes's famous war of all against all) or a full national commitment to active resistance against a foe that will not be defeated with partial measures (as in war on crime, war on drugs, war on poverty, and so on). It has also been used to describe a condition of foundational disharmony not lost once a presocial state of nature is left behind but disguised by convention or by a kind of linguistic legerdemain that denies a condition by refusing to name it. The idea that a state of war exists whenever a sense of inequality between groups of people is allowed to prevail would be an example of this usage.[31] And yet, precisely because "war" is a term that can suggest collective action or fragmentation, organized violence, or chaos, it should be evident that far from standing against discourse or figuration, it is among the most conceptual of terms—albeit one that is used to mobilize our feelings about apparently very concrete things such as group identity, the status of property (including but not limited to territory), and damage itself. This book is premised on the idea that there is little that is self-evident about war, that we need a great many words about feelings and ideas to understand this phenomenon that can seem so distant from both.[32] Overdetermined relationships to loss and recovery of the sort that concern this book were a foundational part of what institutions constructed to preserve and display art offered the nineteenth century, and military conflict is one place to look for the most forcefully concrete recalibration of the meaning of things: treasures are broken or change possession owing to the force of arms, and new social dispensations that will organize these objects come to the fore when nations rise or are reshaped, when the boundaries of empire are altered, and when new forms of faith come to predominate, often through military conflict. While war is often, and with reason, treated as fundamental, a material determinant defining later conditions, this book focuses on a far more dynamic view of the cultural effects of military struggle: the effects of dread, the role of memory, and the experience of the limited successes attending victory.

Overlooking Damage develops its arguments in a set of interlocking essays tracing the relationships among witness, knowledge, and feeling at points of crisis where the intersection of damage and the fine arts comes to be particularly marked in culture. Part 1, "Views of Damage," will, ideally, be read in sequence, as it develops a sustained account of the ways in which the centrality of damage is registered and avoided in a period running from the time of the French Revolution to today. Chapter 1, "Rising above the Ruins," addresses the elaborately intertwined representation of sublimity and ruins in a deeply influential if surprisingly understudied text, *Ruins, or Meditations on the Revolutions of Empires*, published by Constantin François de Chassebœuf, comte de Volney, in 1791. This chapter marks the beginning of my discussion of a characteristic figure that will be important throughout the book: the viewing self rising in the air in response to the conceptual and ethical challenge of damage, an indication of a crisis in perception and the emotional life. The chapter also begins my discussion of the ruins of Palmyra, the location around which Volney's text is oriented. Both rising and Palmyra return in Chapter 2, "Height and Damage / Virtual Reality," which addresses the ancient city in what is now Syria as one of the sites of the much-discussed violence against objects of cultural heritage carried out by ISIS and related groups. To think about the cultural nature of violence is to reflect on the terms by with which its effects are typically categorized. This chapter brings to the twenty-first century the topic of rising begun in the previous one, but it links the crisis I see in those moments of rising to the history of the two concepts around which discussion of cultural damage has typically been organized: vandalism and iconoclasm. Chapter 3, "Terror and Judgment / Dating the Ruins (Ruskin with Volney, Grégoire with Riegl)," addresses the foundational attempt by the Abbé Grégoire to describe, account for, and limit the meaning of modern vandalism around the time of the French Revolution, a project that I put into conversation with the sophisticated account of the modern cult of ruins laid out by the great Austrian art historian Alois Riegl at the beginning of the twentieth century. Reflections on damage in both authors become important occasions for recognizing a modernity in which injury and preservation are two sides of a tantalizing and troubling relationship between the self and the material world. As my goal throughout this sequence of essays is highlighting the place of ethical claims in accounts of admired antique objects at risk, it is inevitable that John Ruskin should emerge as an important voice in this chapter. For Ruskin, an impassioned critic of far more nuance than is generally realized by those who do not read him, as for Volney before him, artworks at risk become occasions to think about human agency and the limits of human perception, not to lose reason in a sublime impasse. Attentive reading of the art historian's bold historicizing claims reveals a searing challenge to modern forms of social violence underpinning his fascination with ruined things and his challenging account of perception itself.

The book closes with a section focusing on the intersection of strongly marked yet unstable identities with the experience of irreparable loss. Chapter 4, "Owning Art after Napoleon: Destiny or Destination at the Birth of the Museum," addresses an important and deeply productive crisis in the very early years of the modern museum, that extraordinary nineteenth-century invention for the preservation and display of art. By highlighting responses to the dissolution of the Musée Napoléon, at once the greatest art museum ever assembled, and also an open manifestation of the power of arms, this chapter creates an occasion to reflect not only on the intersection of violence, looking, and collection but also on the complex nature of restitution as a practical act. Having, giving, and losing emerge not as contradictory but as mutually dependent elements in this foundational moment in the history of the public display of art.

Old ruined monuments that glimmer on the edge of our understanding in forms their makers would not recognize, feelings about loss we cannot quite describe, works of art partially preserved or fully lost, and the constant pressure of violence: call these figures for the experience of culture, or call them culture itself. Arguments about art can seem trivial in the face of ongoing crises or historical injustices, or of what appear to be self-evident cycles of repeated violence. *Overlooking Damage* is intended to illustrate the ways in which the visual evidence of injury that tantalizes with its apparent clarity may well call for deeper care and attention. In this view, the acknowledgment of limited sight may become the basis of a moral claim. Chapter 5, "Revelation and Uncertainty, or What You See in the Water," works its way toward the only kind of conclusion available to this project by bringing the arguments of the book back to a number of fundamental nineteenth-century formulations while proposing their relevance for understanding a set of topics of pressing contemporary significance. The chapter frames a discussion of recent creative and critical responses to Joseph Mallord William Turner's 1840 *Slave Ship* and to Ruskin's account of the work with a brief summary of the power and limitations of seeing things in the water as laid out in major texts going back to the nineteenth century. To end with this set of topics—slavery, the danger of rising waters, the challenge of responding to the representation of injury—is to propose recognition of the moral force of partial sight. The topics seem particularly germane today, as we continue to fail to rise to the level required to deal with two crises shaping human existence today at every turn and yet consistently unavailable to a social consensus, the ongoing crisis of climate change and the constant pressure of racism as a historic and current fact.

As I close this introduction, I'd like to highlight a few elements about my treatment of sources that I do not want to come as a surprise my readers. As I have indicated, this book returns repeatedly to writers from the late eighteenth and nineteenth centuries. All of these authors were moralists, careful thinkers, and splendid writers. I understand each one of them to have been both deeply responsive to the culture of their day and profoundly original and useful for later readers. I know they are often wrong about important things. Still, I do not take what I or others might understand to be their moral or conceptual errors to remove them from the list of people I read and encourage others to read. Neither do I do my own reader the disservice of explaining at every turn that my writers were not always right. I trust that the widespread nature of human fallibility is as evident to others as it is to me. Ultimately, this book is written with a sense that the failings of my own day are more of a concern to me than those of earlier times. It is also written with an all too vivid sense that shortcomings, whether moral or perceptual or in right execution, are the fate of all human projects. This being the case, the recognition of a particular flaw need not mark the end of reflection on a topic so much as a promising beginning for analysis.

Part 1

Views of Damage

RISING ABOVE THE RUINS

Rising

Prepositions used to describe perception easily become tendentious; the physical relationships between viewer and object they suggest can seem all too ready to take an emblematic turn. To look over indicates a kind of attention denied when we overlook. To look down on a thing is so very different from looking down upon it. We may try to gain some perspective or be charged with losing perspective, depending on whether we look over or overlook or look down on or look down upon a sight. To look up to someone or something is, of course, itself more than a matter of sight lines. As we swap prepositions and discover new feelings in the same root verb, we may take the labile character of the language as an indication of a cultural uncertainty about the meaning of the kinds of experiences they suggest (*looking* can be so many things!) or an indication that disparities in the location of the point of view carry an unavoidable affective charge that the English language effectively captures in the variations available through its phrasal verbs.

My general point can be refined: prepositions used to describe perception from a height are especially prone to becoming tendentious. That this quality is baked into the language (and not English alone) is an indication that the phenomenon that underpins it is not only the product of recent years—of, say, the symbolic egalitarianism that has been so important to our dominant ethical orientation of late, a disposition whereby the only difference that is not celebrated is one that looks like a difference of level (of power, of ability, of rank).

Though recognition of differences of perspective has come to seem of crucial important in a surprisingly wide set of intellectual and even political orientations, the claim to see from a different vantage point than that of the object under consideration has become, in some circles, a troubling proposition. The recent importance of a kind of morphological ethics can make it difficult to track the nuanced nature of the condition of eminence. While to look down from a height can appear to be a position of power, can it also be a manifestation of panic or confusion, or pain? I will develop this question with a great deal of concrete specificity below, so I will only note abstractly here that it is possible to understand just about any visual representation of the achievement of a higher vantage point in two distinct ways: we can tell ourselves we are seeing a condition of essential difference or even emancipation, or we can reflect that much as the image itself cannot avoid showing us what lies below, there is no full escape from what is being left behind.

Inevitably, a figure caught in midair quickly acquires a freight of symbolic meanings. As it looks out of a work of art, it interpellates us at once as objects and as subjects in the course of an unresolved transition that we may understand as a rising or falling depending on the assumptions we bring to bear—and what we call context. We may see ourselves in the figure caught in motion or we may understand ourselves to be earthbound, in contrast to the entity hovering above the horizon. Still, we have reasons to find both kinds of identification uncomfortable. Falling is problematic for obvious reasons. But, as I have begun to suggest, rising may well strike us as not without its own challenges, especially if we come to understand it as the only way to make sense of conditions from which humanity doesn't as a rule manage to separate itself. Take, for instance, Raphael's *Transfiguration* (fig. 1.1), which shows in an upper register Jesus manifesting his glory on Mount Tabor, while in a lower section the disciples, helpless without him, fail to cure a boy subject to fits. It is not just the exalted condition of Jesus that matters in this complex image, any more than its truth is the hideous suffering boy (prone to *falling*, the text tells us, into fires, into water) and the baffled excited crowd that surrounds him and that stands for so much mundane suffering, for the world that Jesus leaves behind at his moment of transfiguration. As critics have realized since the work first went on display, it is the combination that is of interest: the divinity rising out of the world of the disciples is shown alongside the helpless condition the disciples inhabit as he rises. Indeed, even Peter, James, and John, those privileged enough to accompany Jesus on to Mount Tabor, throw themselves down and hide their

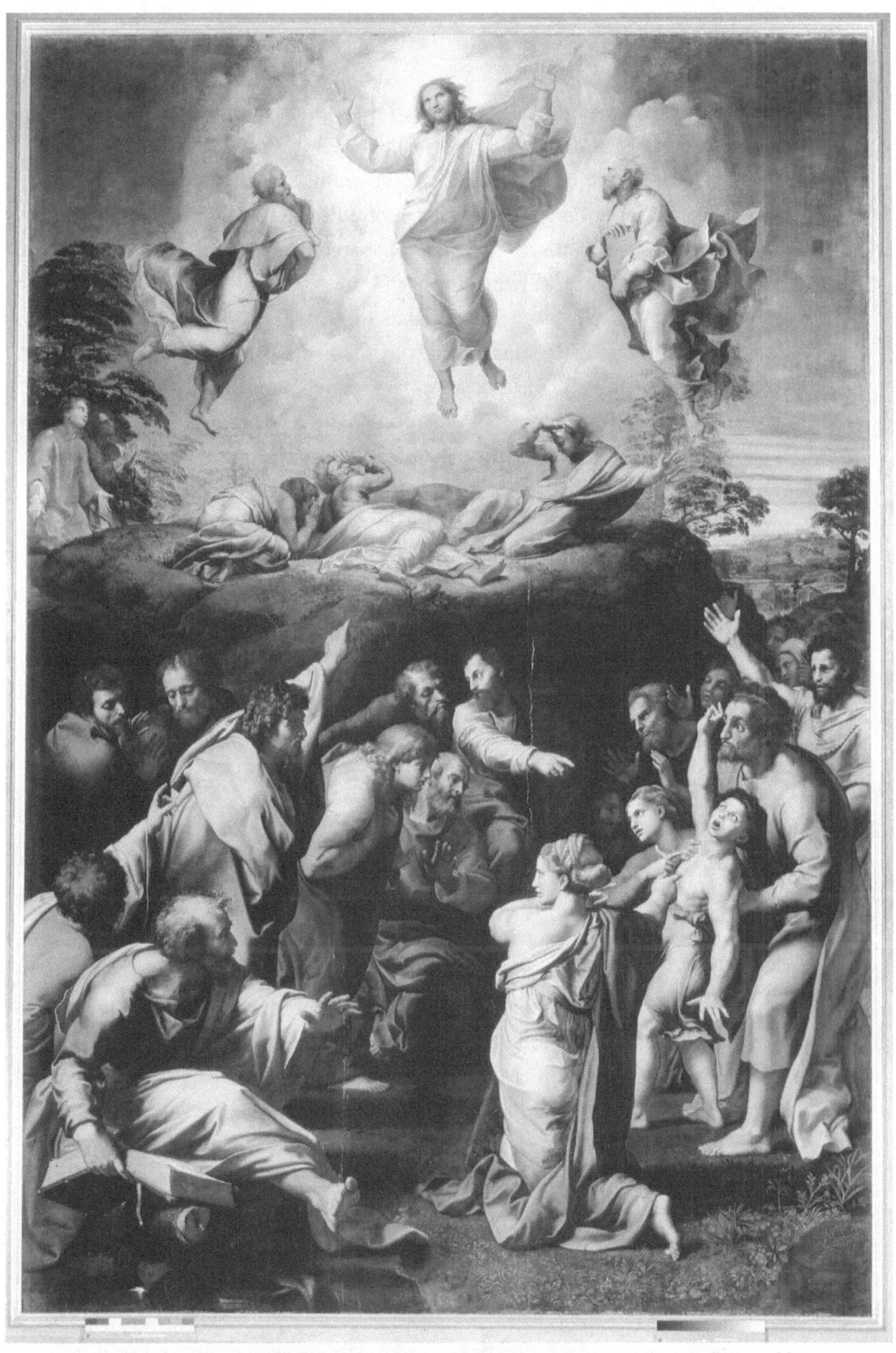

FIGURE 1.1. Raphael (Raffaello Sanzio), *Transfiguration* (1520). Oil on wood, 410 x 279 cm. Scala / Art Resource, NY.

eyes when he is transfigured. Nietzsche draws our attention to the unresolved relationship between divine and mortal captured in this work, which, I have argued elsewhere, we may identify as representing the characteristic form of material inspiration.[1] From "the eternal contradiction, the father of all things," the philosopher writes, there "rises like some ambrosian perfume, a vision-like new world of semblance, of which those who are trapped in the first semblance see nothing." What Nietzsche identified as the Apollonian world of beauty—which he associates with Jesus—comes to us in the painting along with the ground on which it rests, which leads us to grasping, intuitively, "the reciprocal necessity of these two things."[2]

Raphael's uncomfortable painting, taken all in all, represents the ways that a longing to experience or at least witness transcendence arises from discomfort with the actually existing relationship (say, unbroachable distance) between matter and something beyond its limits. Neither longing nor discomfort is escaped by means of the widespread certainty in our own day not only that it is in fact impossible to rise beyond the material conditions we inhabit but that the wish to do so is liable to amount to no more than a bad faith attempt to avoid an ineluctable human situation of which injury and uncertainty are both constituent parts. Like the boy at risk and his family, we are faced with an ongoing threat amounting to a certainty that we will experience damage. In response we may be driven to seek aid in a world that cannot satisfy our desire for safety. Or, like the disciples, we may try to help. But in the final accounting we will fail. And for all of us—vulnerable, caring, failing as we are—the imagination of true safety can only take the form of an absolute separation from the very condition that makes the need for escape feel so pressing.

To address the relationship of the aesthetic and damage, it will be necessary to talk about the association between broken things and the sublime, the category in which the experience of damaged objects is often placed. But I propose in this book to address the sublime not in the sense in which it is frequently understood, as the limit of thought, as an experience of the faculties overwhelmed before a thing about which they cannot adequately reflect. To include damage in the analysis allows one to identify the sublime as a phenomenon that can seem quite similar but is in fact the opposite condition to thought overwhelmed, something we might describe as the experience of the pressures to reflect avoided. To clarify my argument I have to be more than a little literal about a term into which height is written at every point. "Sublime," that is to say, indicates not only a difference of merit or achievement but of position; it marks a distinction understood typically through figures of height. As a quick reminder of what I mean, here is the etymology given in the *Oxford English Dictionary*, in which merit and height always come together:

> Middle French, French *sublime* (adjective) excellent, admirable, perfect (*c*1470 with reference to a thing, probably 1549 with reference to a person), (of a person) occupying a high rank or office (1540), (of a person or thing) rising up high, attaining a great height (1552), (of a thing) set or raised aloft (first attested later than in English: 1572), (of a muscle) superficial (1745 or earlier), (noun) the brain (1659; now obsolete), the grand and elevated style in discourse or writing (first attested later than in English: 1669), that quality in nature or art which inspires awe, reverence, or other high emotion (1690), and its etymon (ii) classical Latin *sublīmis* (also *sublīmus*) high up, elevated, high, (of breath) shallow, panting, tall, lofty, aspiring, grand, elevated in style, majestic, exalted, noble, eminent, illustrious.[3]

High, tall, lofty, elevated, majestic, exalted, noble, eminent, and so on (even panting enters the mix, suggesting breath that does not go deep): rising is written into the word typically used to describe the aesthetic experience when an individual encounters an object that suggests to the mind a vastness before which it feels overwhelmed. In modern accounts of the phenomenon, an original moment of distress is typically just the first phase of a sequence wherein the power of the mind is in fact affirmed through a process of recovery that ultimately recognizes how much the faculties are able to encompass—including those very things that at first dismay us by their extraordinary size or other overwhelming characteristic. And so, the subject rises.

When the object of perception provoking the sublime experience is a relic of human violence, we may experience the sublime as something more disturbing than the faculties of the mind unbalanced and restored in the way Immanuel Kant describes them to be by the vastness of space or the immensity of a cataract, or the boundlessness of numbers.[4] As Gerard Passannante has recently put it, the sense of recovery and self-affirmation written into the Kantian sublime (Passannante calls it a "triumph") is "often an unpersuasive ending to the mind's metaphysical horror story."[5] I will be suggesting in what follows that we identify in manifestations of what we will be tempted to call the sublime not the play of faculties of *perception* so much as—on the side of the subject—the failure of the faculties we might devote to moral judgment and—on the side of the object—the evidence of something awful on which we are refusing to reflect. In her magisterial recent study, *The Ruins Lesson*, Susan Stewart reminds the reader of the roots of the word "ruin" in the Latin for fall or collapse: "What should be vertical and enduring," she notes, "has become horizontal and broken."[6] To take seriously the conceptual play between verticality and horizontality when it comes to broken things means to reflect on the act of rising in reaction to ruins, which will be a recurrent concern in this text, the body projected into space in response to earthbound collapse.

The ethical challenge written into the experience of what we call sublime is manifested in situations in which (we feel that) all that is available to us in the face of damage is an affective response that leaves careful reflection to the side and certainly obviates the possibility of a clear judgment that will eventuate in action.[7] The roots of the word tell us that sublimity always involves an act of rising. But a change of levels leaves many questions unanswered, including pressing ones, such as what is the effect of rising on the subject, and what does that effect in turn tell us about the cause or meaning of the original moment of elevation?[8] Although this book looks back to texts written in the very early days of the modern sublime in order to identify how the political import of the category is registered at the site of its first emergence, my goal is not ultimately historical. My discussion of difficult moments in the past is intended to make possible a fuller reflection on the urgencies shaping more recent responses to the attempt to find a view of the whole that may or may not be sublime, or in which we discover a concept of sublimity that may well be understood to indicate the limit of our thoughts and feelings when confronted with challenging topics or conditions.

Raphael shows us a rising and a separation, along with the thing from which a being has risen and become separated. The presence of the divine in an exalted realm is not what the elaborate machinery of the painting is designed to illustrate—hence the awkwardness of a work the religious force of which is marked precisely by its commitment to capturing transitional moments best indicated by the inclusion of human inadequacy (and outright failure). In heaven, after all, there will be no transfiguration. Transfiguration is evidence of the *need* for the divine on earth. The sick and vulnerable boy in the lower register, together with the disciples unable to cure him, are indications of what the experience of the world is like when we feel it at its most painful. It is that common experience that may make us long for a transcendent realm that, while it cannot solve our problems, may be said to give them meaning. Later periods learned to mistrust a condition that an earlier era understood to entail salvation on one side and irreparable loss on the other, hence the recurrent need to explain the underlying harmony of a work so clearly composed in two distinct registers.

I want to compare a well-known visual representation of the suspended figure from the twentieth century, Paul Klee's *Angelus Novus* (1920), to Raphael's divided final masterpiece. But in order to make clear the stakes of such a comparison, it will be helpful to pause at an important polemical moment in the writings of Jacques Rancière addressing the sense of impasse at which the category of the sublime has arrived in modern thought. The philosopher's discussion of Jean-François Lyotard's influential account of the sublime reaches back to the early nineteenth century in order to describe a disappointment. According to Rancière, the aesthetic and the ethical come into close connection in the turbulent period following the French Revolution, inaugurating an era characterized by the emergence of what he calls "modernatist thought" (*la pensée modernitaire*), his term for the widespread conviction that the emergence of aesthetic autonomy will of necessity map onto desirable developments in politics. From the work of Friedrich Schiller forward, Rancière argues, this line of thought has been marked by the certainty that a greater formal freedom in the arts will anticipate or participate in the emergence of a freer humanity.[9] The postmodern sublime described by Lyotard—which is the topic Rancière has in his sights—arises as a response to the double failure of this project, the emergence of a better political situation having been thrown into question by the grim facts of modern history and the centrality of autonomous art having been challenged by any number of creative movements moving beyond the formalist conventions of high modernism.

Rancière's response to Lyotard in the polemical foreword to *Distribution of the Sensible* (2000) merits sustained attention in order to bring out the intersection of historical and ethical claims that motivate his animus. If his argument encompasses a surprising amount and comes to a conclusion that can appear to be a little forced and more than a little dark, both the expansive nature of what Rancière includes and the affective crisis he reaches are, as we will see, typical of the tendency he is attempting to address. We may attribute the apparently hyperbolic nature of these elements to Rancière's attempt to make explicit characteristics that are often left unspoken precisely because they have been so fundamental to contemporary thought that they generally go without saying. The philosopher brings to the surface a network of affects (and the complex disappointments from which they arise) that has consistently underpinned the pervasive tendency in critical thought to group together a variety of failures—conceptual, aesthetic, and political. "Modernist faith," as he says, "had latched on to the idea of the 'aesthetic education of man' that Schiller had extracted from the Kantian analytic of the beautiful" (29). The aesthetic is a political question in Schiller's *The Aesthetic Education of Man* because it is in the beautiful that we find the interpenetration of what in the Kantian system are the antithetical elements of reason and nature, a harmonization of contraries that may serve as a model or object lesson for the overcoming in the realm of culture of fissures in the social whole that had been revealed in the violent crisis of the French Revolution. This is the structure Rancière finds put into question by the line of thought he associates with Lyotard. Instead of looking to the fundamental argument of *The Aesthetic Education of Man*, whereby a set of difficult relationships are negotiated through the faculties we associate with the Kantian concept of the beautiful, the postmodern tendency has been to emphasize a different part of Kant's *Critique of Judgment*, the one devoted to the overwhelming experience of the sublime.[10] And this difference is more than a detail in the history of the reception of German philosophy; it is part of a hugely consequential reconfiguration of the possibilities of political agency and despair.

"The postmodern reversal," Rancière argues as he develops the distinction, "had as its theoretical foundation Lyotard's analysis of the Kantian sublime, which was reinterpreted as the scene of a founding distance separating the idea from any sensible presentation." The debate comes down to distinct responses to a fundamental gap. Instead of the space between idea and experience of the world that Schiller recognizes but hopes to heal or ameliorate, Lyotard finds a foundational division that will never be repaired. And so, the project of the postmodern sublime becomes an endless—and endlessly reiterated—process of mourning that is easily transposable from object to miserable object. "From this moment onward," continues the passage from Rancière I have been quoting and paraphrasing, moving aggressively from theory to history and back in an emulation of its subject,

> postmodernism came into harmony with the mourning and repenting of modernatist thought, and the scene of sublime distance came to epitomize all sorts of scenes of original distance or original sin: the Heideggerian flight of the gods, the irreducible aspect of the unsymbolizable object and the death drive as analysed by Freud, the voice of the Absolutely Other declaring a ban on representation, the revolutionary murder of the Father. Postmodernism thus became the grand threnody of the unrepresentable/intractable/irredeemable, denouncing

> the modern madness of the idea of a self-emancipation of mankind's humanity and its inevitable and interminable culmination in the death camps. (29)

Rancière's account of the political claims he identifies with the postmodern sublime, with its wild expansiveness and appalling final instance, is designed to bring out in a florid form the often unspoken causal elements shaping the function of the aesthetic category in culture. The fundamental losses that have in recent decades been associated with what he calls "the scene of sublime distance" turn out to be part of a symmetric turn away (a "reversal") from a faith in the social value of art traceable at least as far back as Schiller's concept of an aesthetic education. The linking of aesthetic autonomy to political emancipation is the foundational element (the original error) in a process the failure of which Rancière proposes as the underlying cause of the emergence of the postmodern sublime. In this telling, the sublime is always available to stand for the gap between the sensible and something beyond it that Schiller and those who followed his lead were working to close but that is now understood to be unbridgeable.

I will return to the ethical charge of this passage below, as part of my discussion of Benjamin's angel of history. But before doing so it will be helpful to lay out the elements in Lyotard motivating Rancière's indignation, the play between event, idea, and fated disappointment that leads to the dirge he hears rising from so many voices in contemporary culture. The philosopher likely has in mind moments such as the close of Lyotard's *The Differend: Phrases in Dispute* (1983), a sequence too long to quote in full, in which the discussion of the sublime culminates in a treatment of historic despair that contrasts "philosophies of history" influential in the nineteenth and twentieth centuries—by which Lyotard (who puts the term in quotation marks) evidently means the formulations of Hegel, Marx, and other rationalizers of the events of the past—to what he calls "the names which are those of '*our* history.'"[11] The book as a whole is shaped by Lyotard's attempt to address the arguments of a French Holocaust denier, and yet, at this concluding moment, we find the particularity of one unspeakable event wielded first to advance a philosophical claim and then in a peculiarly generalized way to create a broad and murky nimbus of disappointment.

"What is rational is actual and what is actual is rational," Hegel famously wrote in an important aphorism in the preface to his *Philosophy of Right*.[12] Not without cause, Lyotard identifies this claim with a characteristically Hegelian vision of history that aims to reconcile events and values, real conditions with the demands of reason. In response he offers not so much a counterargument as a name, one of those names that are those of "our history," understood as the opposite of rational: "This crime at least, which is real," the philosopher writes about Auschwitz, paraphrasing Hegel in order to counter his axiom "is not rational." The challenge presented to any kind of rationalization of history by this name that is real, by the crimes for which the name stands, is forceful. A pile of other names follows, however, names for important disappointments experienced by the French Left from Berlin in 1953 to Paris in May 1968 and including other locations: Budapest, Czechoslovakia, Poland. The crises of faith in the relationship between values and events a French progressive might identify with these names and dates (and so find inimical to faith in progress *tout court*) are then counterbalanced with the disappointment of liberal economic nostrums such as "Everything that is the free play of supply and demand is favorable for the general enrichment, and vice-versa." This claim is given the lie by "the 'crises of 1911 and 1929'" as well as "the 'crisis of 1974–79.'" The dates begin to pile up in the paragraph, and their proliferation, along with that of the quotation marks evidently meant to indicate the irruption of contradictory events that cut across the speculative promise of systems from the left, right, and center, starts to suggest an inflationary pressure that reduces the value of any one item in the heap. The listing of failures on all sides concludes with a full embrace of the condition of sorrow understood as one in which particular events really are, after all, just instances: "The passages promised by the great doctrinal syntheses end in bloody impasse. Whence the sorrow of the spectators in this end of the twentieth century."[13] Sorrow, the last emotion Lyotard proposes, has always been at the heart of this discussion of the sublime. The feeling emerges as a step toward a sublime conclusion to rationalization that is better than the vague hopes of a resentful reform that is unable to recognize the mismatch between "ideas and realities."

It is possible to be more sympathetic to the melancholy drives Rancière discovers in Lyotard's sublime, but there is indeed something ethically distasteful about the grab bag of sources he identifies: the proliferation of dire instances makes human crises with distinct moral implications because they involve such divergent historical circumstances into so many returns to one underlying disappointment. Someone interested in truly preserving the resistant particularity of the name "Auschwitz" for the specific events that have made that site memorable might well resist its placement in this long list of distinct disappointments, like some strongly flavored ingredient intended to lend its flavor to a stew, though too strong to be consumed on its own.[14] The events and ideas cited in Lyotard's argument lose their specific qualities (including causes, agents, victims, and victors) as they enter the category of instance, as they become mere manifestations of the ongoing failure of a hoped-for emancipation (the kind of thing indicated by place names such as Budapest, Czechoslovakia, and Poland, not to say Paris in 1968). To be made an instance of a greater loss is ultimately to become part of a process of minimization that might well give the ethical thinker pause and that Rancière evidently aims to resist. The repetition of miserable events amounting to more of the same establishes the rhythm and keynote of that perpetual song of mourning commemorating the unrepresentable or intractable or irredeemable, the dirge that accompanies the process that inevitably culminates with the death camps of Europe. The relationship between specific crises in the world and fated sublime catastrophe is at the heart of a failure that is at once conceptual and ethical. Instead of a responsive politics, Lyotard, in Rancière's telling, can only offer a kind of neurotic repetition, a Möbius-strip relationship between idea and event in which immediate cause and effect is seldom fully distinguishable and never really germane, a situation in which a vague sense of agency or responsibility may shape an affective crisis but is not available to respond to its cause. Like a passage in a long dirge that we have heard many times before and so know to expect at set intervals, its returns set a mood; they do not amount to a call to action.

As Rancière goes on to explain, the politics entailed in what he sees as a reformulation of the account of the sublime we find in Kant is based on the incapacitation of reflection at the moment of aesthetic experience. The aesthetic opens up to the sublime *because* the sublime is the experience of reflection paralyzed. In that sense the sublime is an indication of an experience of trauma understood as precisely what is not available for thought:

> It is . . . the work of Jean-François Lyotard that best marks the way in which "aesthetics" has become, in the last twenty years, the privileged site where the tradition of critical thinking has metamorphosed into deliberation on mourning. The reinterpretation of the Kantian analysis of the sublime introduced into the field of art a concept that Kant had located beyond it. It did this in order to more effectively make art a witness to an encounter with the unpresentable that cripples all thought, and thereby a witness for the prosecution against the arrogance of the grand aesthetico-political endeavour to have "thought" become

> "world." In this way, reflection on art became the site where a mise-en-scène of the original abyss of thought and the disaster of its misrecognition continued after the proclamation of the end of political utopias. A number of contemporary contributors to thinking the disasters of art or the image convert this fundamental reversal into more mediocre prose.[15]

"Cripples" is the word the translator uses for *désempare*, a term that suggests incapacitation, like a crippled ship, unable to move. And Rancière cannot be said to be overstating the matter. Drawing perhaps as much on the kinds of missed occasions that are so important in the works of influential figures ranging from Martin Heidegger to Jacques Lacan, Lyotard finds in new developments in art a preoccupation with matter that is of interest because of the way it confirms a relationship between mind and world that is sublime in the sense that it overwhelms thought, that it instantiates again and again a repeated moment of unthinking, unthinkable encounter with an unassimilable other. The model of baffled engagement with something imagined as more real or more material than the subject (so much in excess as to be unavailable to the subject) comes to stand for the recognition of the melancholy (because inevitable) fact of political catastrophe:

> The paradox of art "after the sublime" is that it turns towards a thing which does not turn towards the mind, that it wants a thing, or *has it in for* a thing which wants nothing of it. After the sublime, we find ourselves after the will. By matter, I mean the Thing. The Thing is not waiting to be destined, it is not waiting for anything, it does not call on the mind. How can the mind situate itself, get in touch with something that withdraws from every relationship?[16]

Lyotard's sublime is an encounter with the thing that can never take place, that freezes thought before it can happen, or sets it reeling away from the very element (call it object, call it thing) that provoked it. Such a model of inherent sublimity will inevitably lessen the ethical charge of the encounter with damage—and will certainly negate any engagement with topics that require the mind to do more than throw up its hands.

Responsibility and regret, like agency itself, are made impossible concepts before the fact of the sublime. Indeed, Lyotard's complaint about Kant in his more historical account of the topic is that the philosopher "strips Burke's aesthetic of what I consider to be its major stake—to show that the sublime is kindled by the threat of nothing further happening."[17] Though (or because) the thing is there, we experience it as sublime; in this (non-)encounter we can recognize the limits of thought in relation to the world. As we will see below, Lyotard is right that the experience of a non-event is precisely not what happens in the sublime in Kant—an insight that at the very least should remind us that the sublime is not an aesthetic experience we should as a matter of course associate with the end of reflection.

I recently proposed a brief contrast between the figure of Jesus in Raphael's *Transfiguration* and Paul Klee's *Angelus Novus*, the image that has become well known as Benjamin's angel of history since the account the critic gave of it in "On the Concept of History."[18] I will expand on that comparison here because it helps me establish the parameters of the kind of suspended viewing that I want to put in relation with the sublime and with damaged antiquities in this book. The figure suspended in the air is a characteristic one for the imagination of a material crisis that goes quite far back (fig. 1.2).[19] But I want to emphasize the particularly modern quality of the image Benjamin selected—and of the terms by which it has been understood since he wrote about it—because the critic's response to the Paul Klee monoprint is probably the most compelling version of the painful sensibility that becomes the cliché of endless disappointment Rancière finds in Lyotard. My point is not to deprecate the limits of the image or of Benjamin's extraordinary analysis but to underline, on the one hand, the historical sources of Benjamin's legacy and, on the other, the power of its characteristically constrained vision of possibilities. As often as it is cited, the urgencies in this well-known passage are impossible to put in perspective. The difficult sight lines described in staccato sentences and brief clauses of a mysteriously axiomatic nature suggest a vision of the future as a dark mirror of history, while the represented figure that is the all-in-all of the piece is a subject who interpellates the viewer as an object—though one stripped of agency and even of history understood as anything other than catastrophe:

> There is a picture by Klee called *Angelus Novus*. It shows an angel who seems about to move away from something he stares at. His eyes are wide, his mouth is open, his wings are spread. This is how the angel of history must look [*muß so aussehen*]. His face is turned toward the past. Where a chain of events appears before *us*, *he* sees one single catastrophe, which keeps piling wreckage upon wreckage and hurls it at his feet. The angel would like to stay, awaken the dead, and make whole what has been smashed. But a storm is blowing from Paradise and has got caught in his wings; it is so strong that the angel can no longer

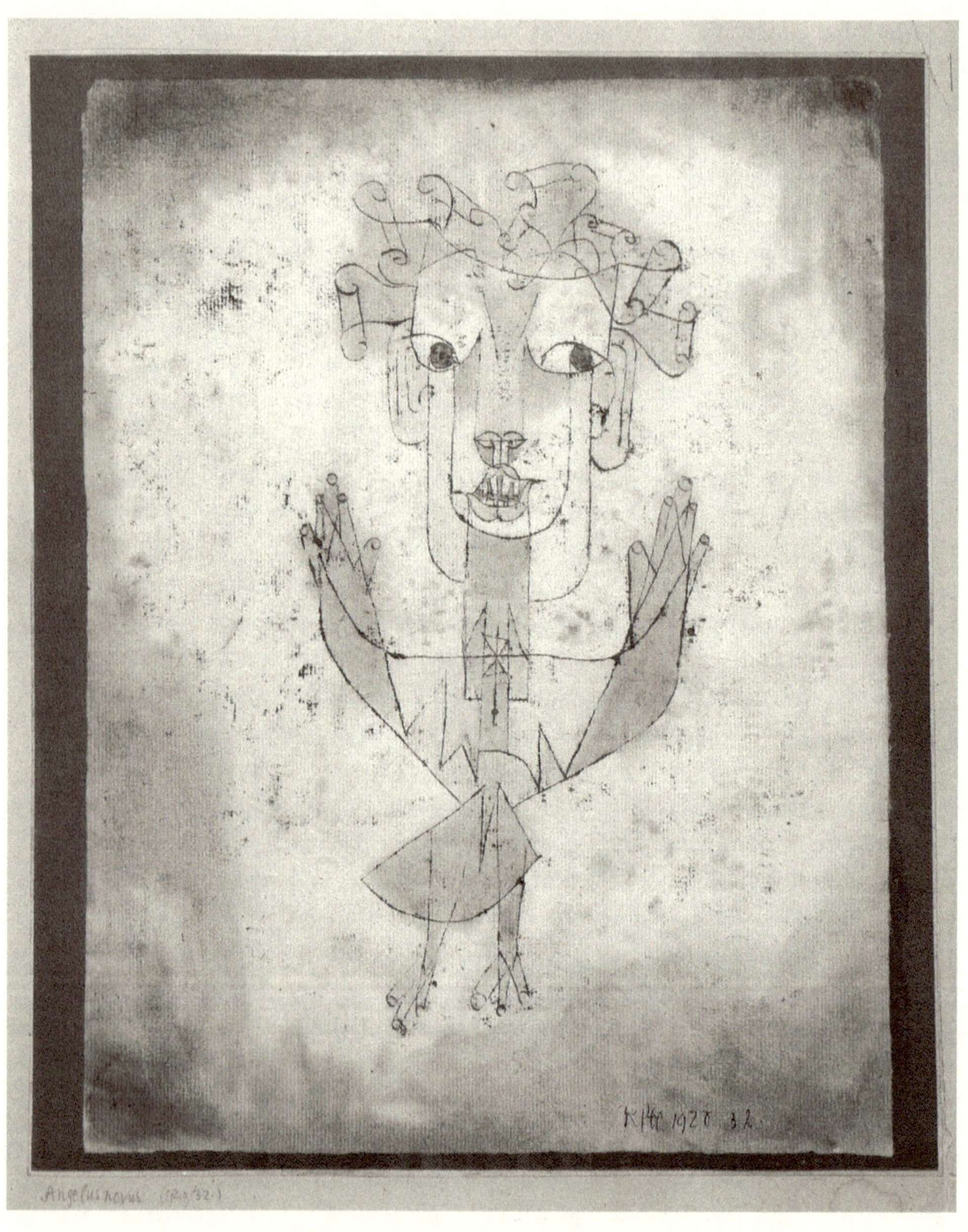

FIGURE 1.2. Paul Klee, *Angelus Novus* (1920). Oil transfer and watercolor on paper, 31.8 x 24.2 cm. ARS, NY. HIP / Art Resource, NY.

> close them. This storm drives him irresistibly into the future to which his back is turned, while the pile of debris before him grows toward the sky. What we call progress is this storm.[20]

In Klee's *Angelus Novus* Benjamin sees a separation from the world understood as a loss that calls for a repair that will never come. In that sense, the representation of this airborne figure is entirely different from the one that rises at the center of the *Transfiguration*, a painting that lays out with vivid emphasis the distinct spheres of experience of its subjects by providing a lower register in which the viewer can identify a recognizable version of human fallibility. Raphael's image represents an unachievable bliss entirely distinct from any human experience. Its promise of salvation depends on the acknowledgment of a gap that has been crossed only once, by an omnipotent divinity become briefly human, a divine entry into the human condition that makes possible the fated moment of redemptive sacrifice. Benjamin's vision of an impossible nostalgia compounded out of guilt and despair describes something quite different, a preposterous condition driven by the hopeless wish that the divine (angel/paradise) be as responsive to history as we are, the way we are, that its losses be our own. After all (before all), no angel is blown out of paradise in the story of the Fall, although a number of them stand in front of its gate ensuring that we can never return. "So he drove out the man," Genesis tells us, "and he placed at the east of the garden of Eden Cherubims, and a flaming sword which turned every way, to keep the way of the tree of life" (Gen. 3:24). Klee's angel, in Benjamin's telling, effects a fantastic reversal whereby the guardian of paradise does not stand as an obstacle before our hopes but instead takes on the burden of witnessing the human misery that is either the cause of those hopes or the result of our failure to live up to the demands of paradise. In this reversal, the viewer stands in the place of a history that cannot be shown in any way except by its violent effects on the angel being driven ever further from paradise—without thereby leaving the way clear for our return.

Political disaster is at the heart of the sublime preoccupations of "On the Concept of History," the essay Benjamin wrote in Paris in 1940, a year of dread that saw the German army occupying the French capital in June and Benjamin dead by his own hand at the Spanish border in September. If the relatively simple image the critic calls to the attention of later generations comes to be charged with the burden of witnessing an extraordinary set of events, including those that would determine his own tragic death, the pattern is set by the original analysis. In the fixed eyes of Klee's angel Benjamin finds the occasion for what appears to be all kinds of observation:

Showing
Staring
Wide eyes
Must look
Face turned
A chain of events appears before us
He sees a single catastrophe

And yet has any representation of looking ever seen so little? Unlike the play of glances that gives meaning to the mundane world in Raphael's *Transfiguration*, Klee's image offers eyes locked and unable to look away, a constrained two-way relationship shaped by the force of an overwhelming world. By the time of Rancière's analysis of Lyotard (call it our own day), a grab bag of accusations of obscure complicity mark not a vision of traumatic exile from Eden including angels as well as a mortals but a recurrent unredeemable sin, the originality of which is merely conventional. "The scene of sublime distance came to epitomize," the philosopher writes disdainfully in a passage from "The Distribution of the Sensible" that I cited above "all sorts of scenes of original distance or original sin" (*toutes sortes de scènes de péché ou d'écart original*). Rancière's tone does much of the work here: the unique quality of every trauma or loss is absorbed into the aggregated category of a generalized blame, much as the undifferentiated excess of blame awkwardly combines formlessness with judgment into an endless dirge the music of which is made up of a flamboyant overlapping set of negations, a "grand threnody of the unrepresentable/intractable/irredeemable" in which the Holocaust itself becomes a facile (non)terminus ("an interminable culmination") in a well-rehearsed argument for hopelessness.[21] With that self-protecting logic with which the disappointed are most familiar, disappointment is symbolically mitigated by the retrospective proleptic magic of insisting that there was never reason for hope. The possibility of moral judgment, like that of political action, is surrendered in exchange for the dark fantasy of inevitable and ongoing failure to represent / to solve / to redeem.

I have made this brief return to Rancière's account of the school of thought or feeling (or thoughts about feeling) represented by Lyotard in order to suggest why Benjamin's angelic vision has been so powerful in the period after he wrote it. And the relationship is more than accidental. The need to reflect on a history that, rather than match up with our hopes, is a constant demonstration of their failures motivates Benjamin as it does Lyotard. And the choices Benjamin offers, though intellectually galvanizing, are nevertheless in some measure incapacitating. Benjamin's powerful project, composed in a period of ongoing and profound political despair, begins and ends with feelings. The emotional investments entailed in various kinds of historiography become, in his analysis, a way of tracking political commitments. *Einfühlung* is the root term that Benjamin's translators give variously as "sympathy" or "empathy," and the *Einfühlung* provoked or demonstrated by distinct historical sensibilities is at the heart of Benjamin's diagnostic project. The question at the heart of the section of the essay devoted to identifying the barbarism unavoidably present in all documents of civilization is "With whom does historicism actually sympathize?" And Benjamin's answer is a network of forceful declarations, passionate, tendentious syllogisms driving a relationship with the past into the present: "The answer is inevitable: with the victor. And all rulers are the heirs of prior conquerors. Hence, empathizing with the victor invariably benefits the current rulers." The tendency of the argument is not to propose an alternative method of doing history but to declare a knowing relationship to the ethical failure of a historicism that pretends to neutrality by locating its emotional investments in the past, when it is in fact complicit with an ongoing present-day moral failure:

> The historical materialist knows what this means. Whoever has emerged victorious participates to this day in the triumphal procession in which current rulers step over those who are lying prostrate. According to traditional practice, the spoils are carried in the procession. They are called "cultural treasures," and a historical materialist views them with cautious detachment. For in every case these treasures have a lineage which he cannot contemplate without horror. They owe their existence not only to the efforts of the great geniuses who created them, but also to the anonymous toil of others who lived in the same period. There is no document of culture which is not at the same time a document of barbarism. And just as such a document is never free of barbarism, so barbarism taints the manner in which it was transmitted from one hand to another. The historical materialist therefore dissociates himself from this process of transmission as far as possible. He regards it as his task to brush history against the grain. ("On the Concept of History," 391–92)

The options in the passage are stark but quite limited: empathize with the victors and join the crowd of onlookers giving assent to brutality by attending the triumphant celebration of violence, or run one's brush against the grain of history. And yet these alternatives are not choices at all so much as claims about identity (tyrant or civilizing barbarian on one side, historical materialist on the other; between them the perhaps unwitting but nevertheless complicit participant in the triumphs of victors). Whether we call it identity or allegiance, both terms bring us back to feelings, to that empathy with the victors Benjamin deprecates or to a melancholy identification with the losers of history that will shift the direction in which the historical materialist orients his brush. This latter option amounts to an evocative but ultimately thin metaphor that pulls us away from the one in operation up to that point. And it doesn't seem adequate in the face of what precedes it: suddenly we are not talking about history as a triumphal march but as something one does with fingers. Feeling the texture of history as a rough thing when moving the hand in one direction or as a smooth thing when running it in the other: these are actions in the world only in a very limited or a very heady sense (amounting as they do to figures for ways of thinking about something or for feelings about thoughts about something). And they would certainly be odd actions to take in response to recognizing that one has inadvertently found oneself participating in a brutal parade. For all the vividness of Benjamin's language—the barbarians, the triumphal procession marching heedlessly over its victims, the hands that feel—the scope for responses in the text is strictly constrained. Even the range of feelings is extraordinarily narrow: feel against the grain or feel with the grain, feel with the victors or feel with the vanquished. The considerable power of this model resides in its utopian vision of sympathy, its invitation to identify with the vanquished or to at least stop swelling the parade of the tyrant victors, to abandon the barbarians to celebrate alone.

"On the Concept of History" is about feelings, so perhaps it makes sense that it should generate emotional responses. Still, it has at its heart a disappointment I cannot claim to feel, because it depends on contending visions of historical development neither one of which I feel myself to share. More than this, in spite of its commitment to the claims of history as a process, its apparent desire to escape the indifference Benjamin identifies with a purely synchronic historicism, the surprising tendency of this wartime document is toward passivity or passive forms of action (if they can be called actions in more than a metaphorical or grammatical way). And so, the most important operating metaphor is the one that feels most substantial, the one for which we have an illustration, that of the angel, rising up before a world that it cannot touch but the violence of whose winds keeps reaching it and constraining all actions beyond seeing and feeling. Original sin without the hope of expiation is just the kind of horrifying vision we may imagine Klee's angel is looking at when he gazes with unblinking eyes at something we might call history but that we are also bound to recognize as ourselves (looked at, overlooked, looked over). And after all, the perpetual renewal of evil is the consequence of original sin right until the moment a messianic new sacrifice makes another compensatory or supplemental structure possible. I will return to the figure of the angel of history in the third chapter of this book, in the course of my discussion of terror and judgment. Suffice it to say at this point that Rancière's description of the sublime in influential critical formulations serves as a reminder of all that is lost when catastrophic thought becomes conventional and unreflective. The balance of this chapter will propose that at the moment of self-reflexive separation we may be able to imagine an alternative to an unproductive political despair in which both responsibility and agency are subsumed in a generalized melancholy gazing.

Ruins

In 1791 Constantin François Chasseboeuf, the comte de Volney, delegate to the National Assembly and bold traveler, published a book set in a place he had never been. *Ruins, or Meditations on the Revolutions of Empires* is an Enlightenment text still surprisingly understudied though often cited as a resource for Romanticism. It arrived in England with impeccable radical credentials, having been translated in 1792 for the publisher Joseph Johnson by James Marshall, William Godwin's dear friend. *Ruins* is a frequent footnote for students of *Frankenstein*, as it is the text with which Felix teaches French to Safie and so the work from which a creature newly formed from reanimated dead fragments and hidden in a closet learns language (and also history—and generally what a mixed bag humankind is). The work is also sometimes mentioned because of its association with Thomas Jefferson, who knew Volney personally and apparently was the author of much of a new translation that appeared in 1802.[22] My own discussion of this work that evidently mediates between an era that we might identify as the revolutionary Enlightenment and later periods will be quite limited, revolving around Volney's elaborately staged opening, the point at which the themes and location of the work are most closely connected.

The adventure of the text begins with an unnamed traveler surveying Palmyra, the great ruined city in the Syrian desert, in 1784, an event anticipated for the reader on the frontispiece (fig. 1.3). The specificity of the date, we will

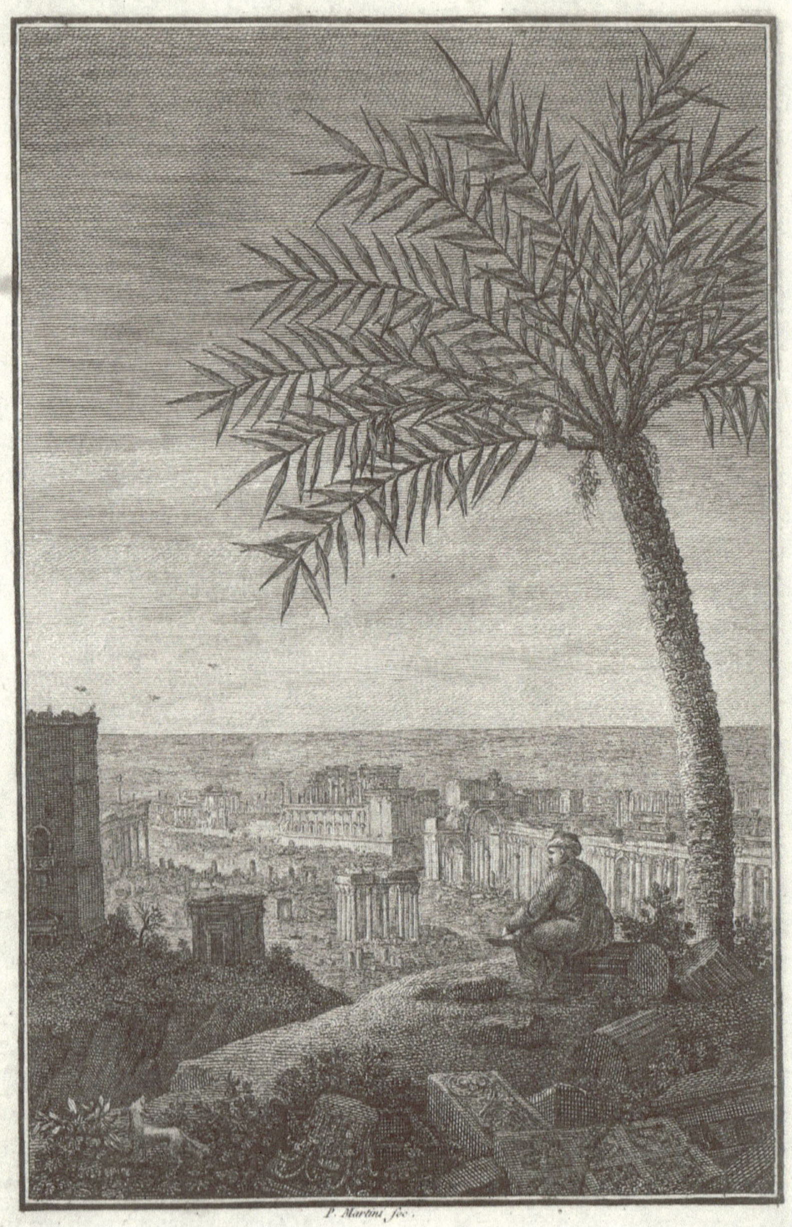

FIGURE 1.3. Frontispiece of Volney, *Les ruines, ou Méditation sur les révolutions des empires* (Paris, 1791).

see, intersects in important ways with the feeling of timelessness that a ruin is conventionally understood to provoke. But this play between extension and specificity will only become clear as the perspective of the text broadens well beyond the long, melancholy survey of contemporary human life inspired by experiences earlier in the traveler's journey:

> I visited cities, and studied the manners of their inhabitants; entered palaces, and observed the conduct of those who govern; wandered over the fields, and examined the condition of those who cultivated them; finding in every place nothing but plunder and devastation, tyranny and wretchedness, my heart sunk with sadness and indignation.
>
> I saw, daily on my road, fields abandoned, villages deserted, and cities in ruin. Often I met with ancient monuments, wrecks of temples, palaces and fortresses, columns, aqueducts, and tombs. This spectacle led me to meditate on times past, and filled my mind with contemplations the most serious and profound.[23]

These important anticipations notwithstanding, the intertwined project of social reflection and the contemplation of ruins reaches its high point in Palmyra, and the process of arriving at that extraordinary apex is carefully detailed in order to emphasize its sublime character:

> After three days journeying through arid deserts [*solitudes arides*], having traversed the Valley of Caves and Sepulchres, on issuing into the plain, I was suddenly struck with a scene of the most stupendous ruins; a countless multitude of superb columns, stretching in avenues beyond the reach of sight. (3)

A sense of what the traveler would have seen is available to us in the views of the site produced by Giovanni Battista Borra for Robert Wood and James Dawkins's important 1753 folio, *The Ruins of Palmyra*, a work on which much in Volney is based, as he never actually reached the city himself and certainly his illustrator did not (fig. 1.4).[24] Indeed, at first Volney's text seems bound toward a picturesque narrative of antiquarian travel following the written descriptions and images in Wood and Dawkins:

> After three quarters of an hour's walk along these ruins, I entered the enclosure of a vast edifice, formerly a temple dedicated to the Sun; and accepting the hospitality of some poor Arabian peasants, who had built their hovels on the area of the temple, I determined to devote some days to the contemplation of these beauties in detail. (4)

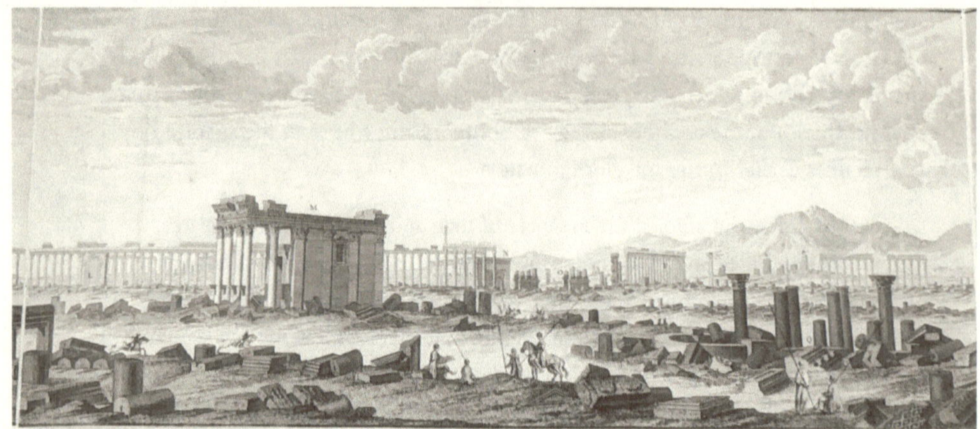

FIGURE 1.4. Giovanni Battista Borra, "View of Palmyra Taken from the North East." James Wood and Robert Dawkins, *The Ruins of Palmyra* (London, 1753), plate 1, detail.

Detailed contemplation is not what the traveler will ultimately experience, but already the text has suggested why that might be his goal; the manifold sublimities of this location present a clear challenge to perception, as vast and solitary desert tracts give way to that "scene of the most stupendous ruins," a vision of countless columns going beyond the reach of the eye. In an improbable domestication of that sublime divinity, the traveler takes up residence at a hovel built within the temple of Bel (fig. 1.5), the Mesopotamian sun god and chief deity of Palmyra—an important structure that gets pride of place in Wood and Dawkins (figs. 1.6 and 1.7).

I have pointed out in another context the overdetermined sublimity of the city to which Volney brings his traveler.[25] It is not only its setting in a vast desert or the overwhelming antiquity of its ruins, or even their unusual extent and preservation, that brings this aesthetic phenomenon to mind. Wood and Dawkins, erudite adventurers that they were (and they traveled with an extensive classical library), remind the reader that, as the home of Longinus, Palmyra has a long-standing association with the concept:

> As to the state of Literature among them, we have great reason to judge favourably of it: nor could they have left a more lucky specimen of their abilities in that way, than the only performance of their's [*sic*], which has escaped, viz. Longinus his Treatise on the Sublime.[26]

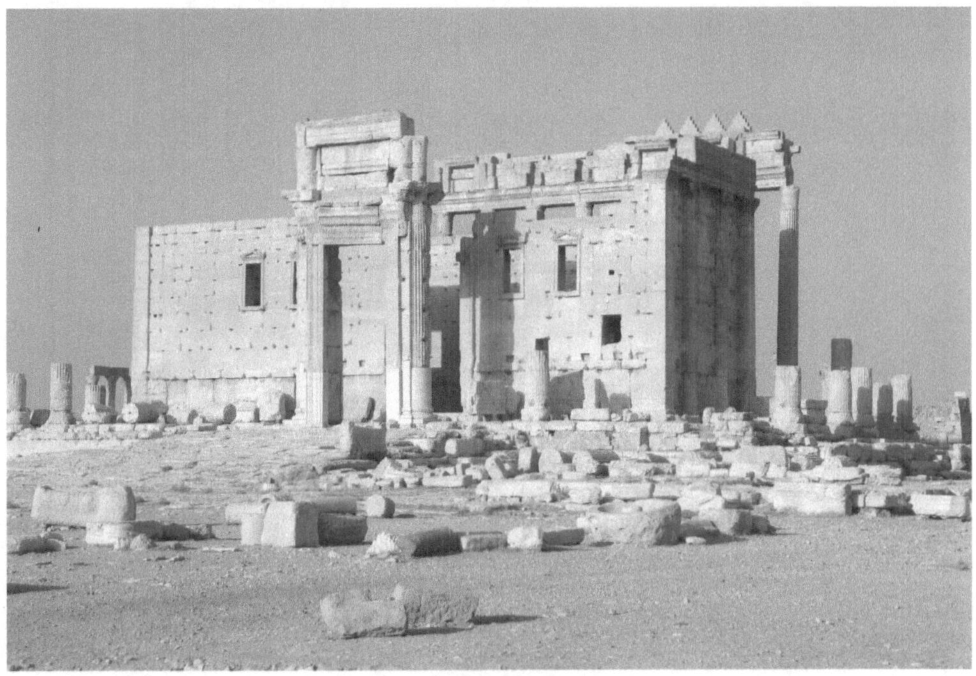

FIGURE 1.5. Temple of Bel, Palmyra. Manuel Cohen / Art Resource, NY.

As Longinus was minister to Zenobia, the famous queen whose vast expansion of the Palmyrene Empire ultimately provoked the destruction of the city by Roman forces in the third century, the association between ruin and sublimity is both historical and phenomenological; it is a sublime location at which the topic finds a noted exponent. Volney has this nexus in mind when his sensitive traveler steps out one evening for a walk that brings him to a panoramic vantage point on the scene, the important moment captured in the frontispiece (see fig. 1.3):

> Absorbed in reflection, I had advanced to the Valley of Sepulchres. I ascended the heights which surround it, from whence the eye commands the whole group of ruins and the immensity of the desert. The sun was set; a red border of light, on the distant horizon of the mountains of Syria, still marked its tract: the full-orbed moon was rising in the east, on a blue ground, over the plains of the Euphrates; the sky was clear, the air calm and serene; the dying lamp of day still softened the horrors of approaching darkness. . . . The eye perceived no motion on the dusky and uniform plain; profound silence rested on the desert;

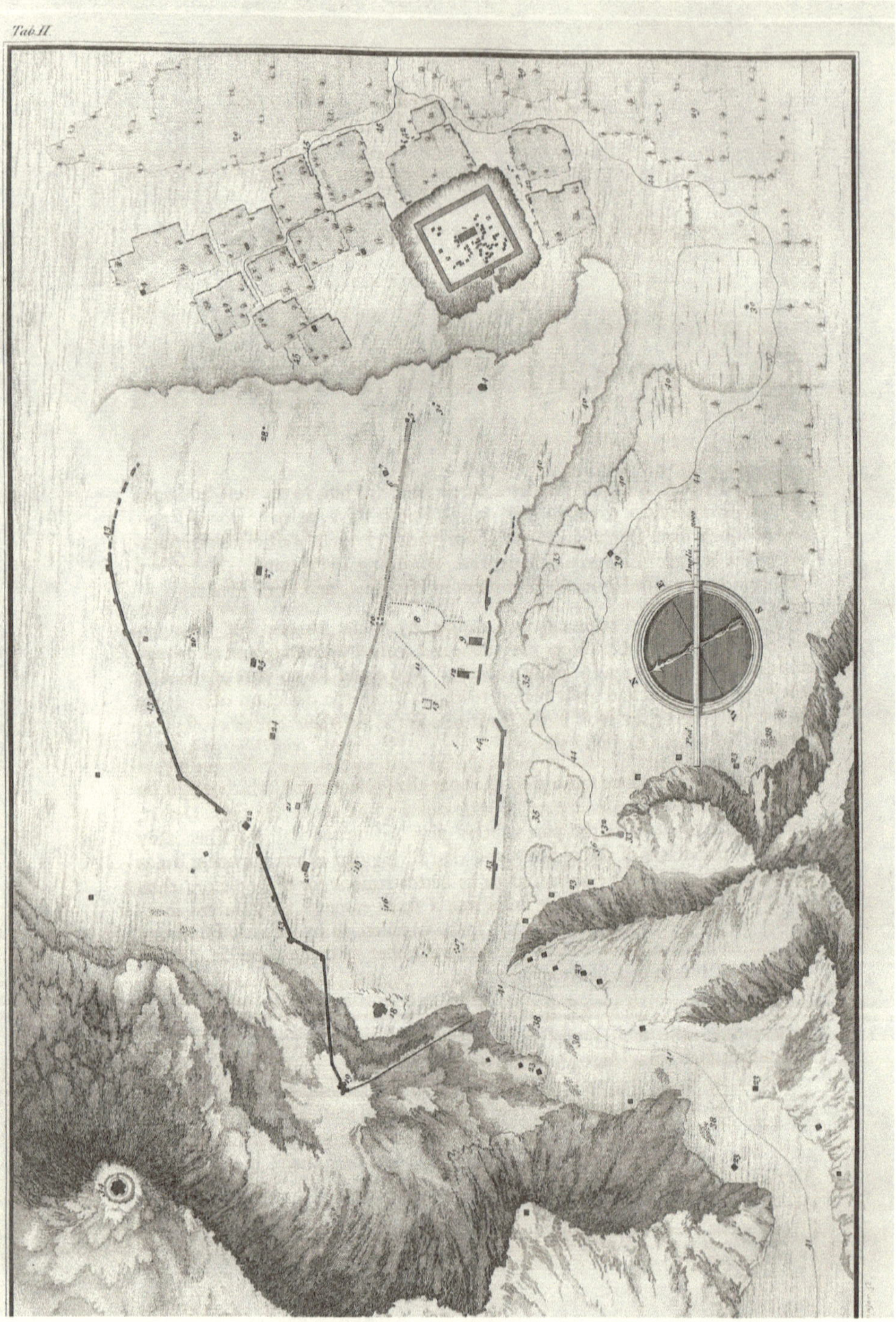

FIGURE 1.6. Giovanni Battista Borra, "A Geometrical View of the Ruined City of Palmyra." Wood and Dawkins, *The Ruins of Palmyra*, plate 2. The square shape at the top of the plate indicates the compound housing the Temple of Bel.

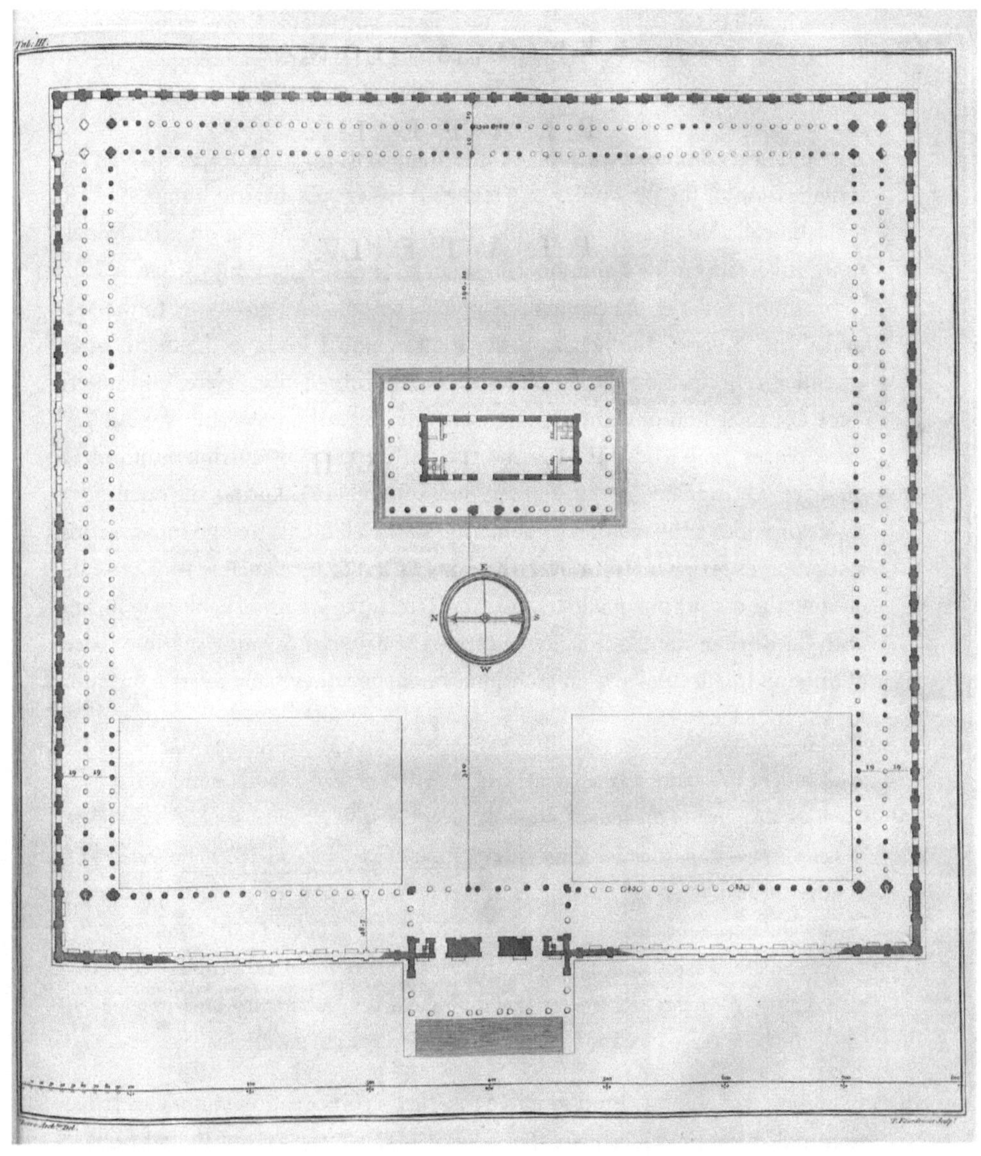

FIGURE 1.7. Giovanni Battista Borra, "The Plan of the Temple of the Sun and Its Court." Wood and Dawkins, *The Ruins of Palmyra*, plate 3.

> the howlings only of the jackal, and the solemn notes of the bird of night, were heard at distant intervals. Darkness now thickened; and already, through the dusk, could only be discerned the pale phantasms of columns and walls. (4–5)

His isolation combines with the circumstances of the scene to provoke an internalization of the play of levels Volney's traveler sees around him: moved to what he calls "high contemplations" (*hautes pensées*), he sits on a fallen column, his head on his hand, his elbow on his knee, falling into what he calls "a profound reverie." As the first chapter, "The Journey," gives way to the second, "The Reverie," the height of the contemplation leads to the depth of an extended reflection on the moral lesson of the ruined city: "Here, said I; here once flourished an opulent city; here was the seat of a powerful empire. Yes! these places, now wild and desert, were once animated by a living multitude; a busy crowd circulated in these streets now solitary" (6). And so, the opening of *Ruins* provides a thorough representation of the elements that go into creating a sublime experience, from overwhelming space to incalculable time, and including the disturbing qualities students of the topic are more liable to associate with Burke than Kant: obscurity and fear. The experience of the sublime space, at once an intellectual and an emotional challenge, inevitably raises a question for the traveler:

> I sought the ancient inhabitants; and their works; and I found nothing but a trace, like that of the foot of a traveller over the sand [*la trace, semblable à celle que le pied du passant laisse sur la poussière*]. The temples are fallen, the palaces overthrown, the ports filled up, the cities destroyed; and the earth, stripped of inhabitants, is become a place of sepulchres. . . . . . Great God! whence proceed these fatal revolutions? From what causes are changed the fortunes of these countries? Wherefore so many cities destroyed? Why has not this ancient population been reproduced and perpetuated? (10; ellipsis in the original)

Experience, idea, and emotion move together as observation stimulates reflection; reflection provokes tears that do not indicate the end of thought but its beginning—the long ellipsis serving as a transition point between emotion-laden observation and passionate speculations. The impressive ancient city the traveler is visiting is itself identified as a kind of transient mark in the sand, like his own footsteps, which he has seen come and go in his long passage through the desert, putting his own actions into the same condition of impermanence that is the immediate cause of his effusion.

It is worth emphasizing the relationship between thought and the sublime at this juncture because doing so may allow us to nuance and even historicize recent claims about the political work of the aesthetic. I have already cited Jacques Rancière's argument that the revival of interest in the sublime he traces back to the late 1970s in French critical thought—and which has had a long and fruitful influence on writers in the years since—has shaped it into "the privileged site where the tradition of critical thinking has metamorphosed into deliberation on mourning." While it might at first blush make sense to align Volney's traveler with the melancholy sensibility Rancière describes, a gap opens up in the comparison when it becomes clear that it is precisely not a *deliberation* in any true meaning of the word that the critic is describing, or at least not as it is for our traveler, for whom the desolation he sees around him opens up real and pressing questions.

I laid out a debate about the sublime from the close of the twentieth century earlier in this chapter because it seems to me useful to emphasize that the structure of aesthetic-political paralysis at its heart is precisely *not* what we see in Palmyra in 1784. Our historical sense would be at fault were we to project the reaction to the political disappointments of a later era back to a period that had yet to learn our own characteristic versions of hope, regret, and intellectual self-soothing. Clearing out as much as possible the inevitable accretion of the intellectual predispositions of a later time may allow the reader to discover in the traveler's sad meditations a model of melancholy, reflection, and politics that is not always already at once utopian and disenchanted. And, after all, Volney is evidently not at all interested in the nonspace we call *utopia* but in some very concrete locations—hence his painstaking orientation of his traveler at various degrees of height at a meticulously rendered site. Published two years after the storming of the Bastille, though set seven years earlier, evidently the "revolutions" in the subtitle are no more solely a matter of a *lost* historical past than are the empires available for the traveler to contemplate. Sitting on the eminence overlooking the Valley of the Sepulchres in Palmyra, the traveler's thoughts turn to France, and an initially comforting contrast with his modern, dynamic nation is followed immediately by the anxious fear that Europe as a whole might be fated to the same destiny as Asia:

> I was gratified to find in modern Europe the departed splendor of Asia. But soon the charm of my reverie was dissolved by a last term of comparison: reflecting that such had once been the activity of the places I was then contemplating, who knows, said I, but such may one day be the abandonment of our countries? (13)

The reflection leads to an image that will have a long life in literature and the arts, the projection of the traveler's experience onto some future voyager coming to a European capital and finding a similar desolation:

> Who knows if on the banks of the Seine, the Thames, or the Zuyder-zee, where now, in the vortex of so many enjoyments, the heart and the eye suffice not for the multitude of sensations, who knows if some traveller, like me, shall not one day sit on their silent ruins, and weep in solitude over the ashes of their people, and the memory of their greatness? (13)

The sensitive traveler weeps for the people whose losses he can imagine as he considers the damaged city below him and for those whose future desolation he can anticipate, and he proposes to himself two possible reasons for the degenerative tendencies of human affairs. In a Hardyesque vein, he identifies either chance or the workings of an inscrutable, and perhaps malevolently judgmental, deity as the source of all this disappointed civilization, which briefly leads him to hide his eyes, as though not seeing were a solution to the problems sight had brought to his attention:

> My eyes filled with tears; and covering my head with the fold of my mantle, I sunk into gloomy meditations on all human things. Ah! hapless man! said I in my grief; a blind fatality sports with thy destinies! A fatal necessity rules with the hand of chance the lot of mortals. But no: it is the justice of heaven fulfilling its decrees! a God of mystery exercising his incomprehensible judgments! Doubtless he has pronounced a secret anathema against this land; blasting with maledictions the present, for the sins of the past generations. Oh! who shall dare to fathom the depths of God? I remained motionless, and sunk in profound melancholy. (13–14)

The traveler will not remain immobile for long, or sunk: this carefully developed crisis of sight, feeling, and thought is what will provoke the next—and most remarkable—phase in his ascent. It is just when the traveler has traced the melancholy outcome of human efforts to a divine malediction that "the pale phantasms of columns and walls" he had described earlier precipitate a more substantial anthropomorphic form.[27] A genie appears. Moved at first to indignation by the traveler's self-indulgent misunderstanding, this spirit of the place will ultimately become a guide, an interpreter, and the means by which the traveler's rise reaches its apogee:

> A sound struck my ear, like that of the agitation of a flowing robe, and of slow footsteps on dry and rustling grass. Startled, I opened my mantle, and looking about with fear and trembling, suddenly, on my left, by the glimmering light of the moon, through the columns and ruins of a neighbouring temple, I thought I saw an apparition, pale, clothed in large and flowing robes, such as spectres are painted rising from their tombs. (15)

The vision, associated with the place by his dress and his emergence from the tombs, has evidently been motivated to appear by his irritation at the shortsighted reflections of the traveler, whom he immediately addresses and to whom he offers a third option beyond blind fatality and a cruel God. "How long," the genie exclaims, "will man importune heaven with unjust complaint? how long, with vain clamors, accuse fate of his sufferings? Will he for ever shut his eyes to the light, and his heart to the insinuations of truth and reason? . . . If, for a moment, you can suspend the delusion which fascinates your senses, if your heart is capable of comprehending the language of reason, interrogate these ruins! read the lessons which they offer." The genie calls on the "evidences of twenty centuries" to testify against the false piety he hears in the melancholy ruminations of the traveler, which cite divinity only to have someone to blame. The genie's lesson in responsibility ("it is falsely that you accuse fate and heaven! it is with wrong that you refer to God the cause of your evils!") is worth quoting at length, given its force and the terms it entertains and rejects as it develops a vivid and consequential imagination of a desolation in which agency and cause are not truly difficult to identify:

> Say, perverse and hypocritical race, if these places are desolate, if these powerful cities are reduced to solitude, is it God who has caused their ruin? is it his hand which has overthrown these walls, ruined these temples, mutilated these columns, or is it the hand of man? is it the arm of God which has carried the sword into your cities, and fire into your fields, which has slaughtered the people, burnt the harvests, rooted up trees, and destroyed cultivation, or is it the arm of man? And when, after the destruction of crops, famine has ensued, is it the vengeance of God which has produced it, or the mad fury of man? When, sinking under famine, the people have fed on impure aliments, if pestilence ensues, is it the wrath of God which sends it, or the folly of man? When war, famine, and pestilence have mown down the inhabitants, if the earth remains a desert, is it God that has dispeopled it? Is it his rapacity which robs the husbandman, ravages the

> fruitful fields, and wastes the earth? or is it the rapacity of those who govern? Is it his pride which excites murderous wars, or the pride of kings and their ministers? is it the corruption of his decisions which reverses the fortunes of families, or the corruption of the organs of the law? are they his passions which, under a thousand forms, torment individuals and people, or are they the passions of man? if, in the anguish of their miseries, they see not the remedies, is it the ignorance of God which is to blame, or their ignorance? Cease then, mortals, to accuse the decrees of fate, or the judgments of God! (18–19)

The peroration brings home the question of agency the traveler had deflected onto providence or a malign divinity: "The germ of his calamities is not planted in the heavens on high; it is beside him on the earth; it is not hidden in the bosom of God; it dwells within himself, he bears it in his own heart" (19).

Finding the traveler responsive to his instruction, the genie transports him far above even the eminence he has already reached, giving him a new perspective on the world beyond the one he had achieved on the rise overlooking the ruined city at which his profound reflections began:

> Rise, mortal, said he, and extricate thy senses from the dust in which thou movest. Suddenly a celestial flame seemed to dissolve the bands which hold us to the earth; and like a light vapour, borne up on the wings of the Genius, I felt myself wafted to the regions above. Thence, from the aerial heights, looking down on the earth, I perceived a scene altogether new. Under my feet, floating in the void, a globe like that of the moon, but less large and less luminous, presented to me one of its phases; and that phase had the aspect of a disk dappled with large spots, some white and nebulous, others brown, green, or grey; and while I strained my sight to distinguish what were these spots—Man, said the Genius, who seekest truth, knowest thou that object? O Genius, answered I, if I did not see the moon in another quarter of the heavens, I should have supposed that to be her globe; it has the appearance of that planet, seen through the telescope during the obscuration of an eclipse: I should take the different spots for seas and continents.
>
> They are seas and continents, said he, and those of the very hemisphere which you inhabit.
>
> What! said I, is that the earth, the habitation of man? (26–27)

At this point we have arrived at the culmination of an elaborately staged process of achieving what Amanda Anderson has described as "cultivated distance." It would be reasonable to see here simply an anticipation of "the wide and long view" she reminds us that an author such as George Eliot aspires to present in its natural home, the late Enlightenment.[28] But it bears emphasizing that some of the modern ambivalence about reaching that view that concerns Anderson's project is written into the process in this text—not just in the long setup required to get there or in the fantastic nature of arrival but in the failure of distance alone to give insight. Thus it is that the lessons of the genie will only be complete with one more magical act, itself indicative of the challenge of linking knowledge and perspective:

> O! Genius, said I, interrupting him, the sight of a mortal reaches not to objects at such a distance. He touched my eyes; and immediately they became piercing as those of an eagle; nevertheless the rivers still appeared like waving lines, the mountains winding furrows, and the cities little compartments, like the chequers of a chess-board. (29–30)

The importance of this moment is indicated by the text's second image (out of the two or at most three that typically accompany the text in its early editions), a "View of the Globe" that relays to the reader in a more concrete—not to say prosaic—register the limited insight accessible from the impossible vantage point occupied by the traveler (fig. 1.8). A note inserted in the text at the point when the traveler queries the genie undermines his improbable confusion about the identity of an orb from which he has just risen by drawing the attention of the reader to the plate "representing half the terrestrial globe." But it is difficult to say if that textual guidance is intended to indicate how little one can make out of the details of the world from a height, or to emphasize how closely connected everything is when viewed from a sufficient distance. The image is, in any case, largely keyed to the exposition of the genie. It identifies a diverse set of important locations of antiquities or of religious centers: the pyramids in Egypt and Mount Sinai but also Nineveh and Constantinople, even Lhasa and—most striking because most urgent and because not typically associated with the history of religion in the way these other places are—Crimea.

The presence of locations associated with world religions on a globe that shows so much and can therefore highlight so little is not fortuitous. The lesson of the genie amounts to a history of the destructive drives of religion, and if the traveler is a willing pupil, it is in part because that history is urgently present to his view. As he gazes down he sees not just the effects of past religious struggles but their current role in shaping the world: what at first looks to him like

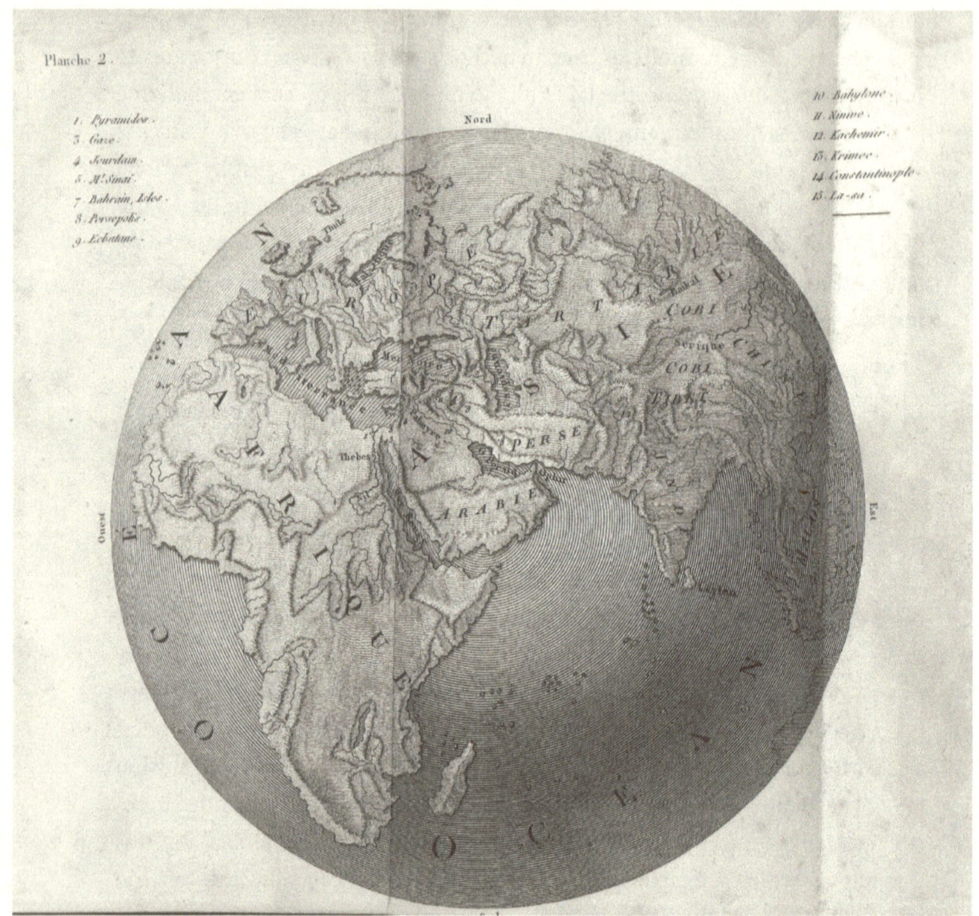

FIGURE 1.8. "View of the Globe." Volney, *Les ruines*, plate 2.

agitated insects turns out to be the armies of Catherine the Great in the midst of annexing Crimea (as they in fact did in 1784), an important development in the long-lasting power struggle with the failing Ottoman Empire that the text sympathetically envisions as an affront to the Muslim world as a whole. That this act of conquest is a vital historic point of inflection for Volney is indicated by the fact that the book opens with reference to this very event, a strikingly specific temporal marker given the otherwise vast timescales of the work. The modern reader may well pause over this opening, commemorating an event that has largely been lost to memory, though it has achieved new topicality in our own day:

> In the eleventh year of the reign of Abd-ul-Hamid, son of Ahmid, emperor of the Turks; when the Nogais-Tartars were driven from the Crimea, and when a mussulman prince, of the blood of Gengis-Kahn, became the vassal and guard of a christian woman and queen, I was travelling in the Ottoman dominions, and through those provinces which were anciently the kingdoms of Egypt and Syria. (1–2)

Whether we think of its setting in 1784 or its publication date in 1791, the text was produced in the early years of what would be a long contest between Russia and the Ottoman Empire, a struggle that would involve other nations over the years, notably the British and the French during the Crimean War. Still, Volney does not bring this attention to global politics down to the level of the nation. The focus he goes to such pains to widen out at the opening of *Ruins* is bigger even than massive empires: it is ultimately the religious struggles shaping and shaped by military conquest that will be of pressing interest.[29]

Mary Favret points out that warfare in the Romantic period is represented "not necessarily as history but as current event, or as some complex combination of the two."[30] In *Ruins* that complex combination of the past and present eventuates in an extraordinarily perceptive reflection on the future. I will be touching on the difficult topic of the displacement of people repeatedly in the course of this study (and indeed, it has already entered this book and been left largely unaddressed in my treatment of the destruction of the Second Temple in the Introduction, where it is displaced onto a story of stolen ritual objects and murdered generals). But it is striking that Volney himself highlights not only the armed struggle and the cultural clash but the dislocation of populations he has in fact already mentioned early in the text: "When the Nogais-Tartars were driven from the Crimea" is one of the several ways he had located the events at the start of his narrative; "In the eleventh year of the reign of Abd-ul-Hamid" is another. Indeed, the opening of the first chapter of *Ruins* draws attention to the very question of whether periodization is to be understood as a matter of sovereigns or of the movement of populations. His concern is such that he returns to the topic in a largely redundant note on the same page on which we find the oddly elaborate characterization of the period with which he opens, "*In the eleventh year of Abd-ul-Hamid*, that is 1784 of the Christian era, and 1198 of the Hegira. The emigration of the Tartars took place in March, immediately on the manifesto of the empress, declaring the Crimea to be incorporated with Russia" (1n; emphasis in the original). Evidently the responsibility for devastation we might learn about in the ruins of Palmyra will include not just the destruction of structures but the memory of people displaced. The distant view afforded by the genie also makes it impossible to miss the interconnections of Europe and Asia of which we may understand the Russian and Ottoman Empires to be most material political manifestations. Indeed, from the book's point of view, these key political entities so often taken to mark the distances between East and West make evident a set of relationships we limit when we reduce them to extreme polarities.

I have emphasized the great efforts to which Volney goes in order to make the fantasy of witness from a height part of a complex affective-intellectual project of moral engagement, a combination of attention and position that marks the beginning of reflection. Recent work on culture and violence has productively noted the suspension that characterizes the modern relationship to military conflict. Paul Saint-Amour describes the period of likely but constantly deferred nuclear annihilation that followed the Second World War (a period in which we still find ourselves) as a kind of perpetual "between the wars." Mary Favret has noted the importance of suspension in representations of war in the Romantic period. She writes beautifully about the unresolved quality we call "suspense, a sort of hanging in time and space" as she addresses the feeling of uncertainty—at once of knowledge and agency—characteristic of modern ethical subjects who know their nation is involved in a conflict but for whom the material experience of the violence of war cannot be fully present (Favret, 191).[31] Favret emphasizes the emotions provoked by partial knowledge, such as those felt by individuals in the early nineteenth century who received the news of military actions carried out by their national armies abroad after substantial delay. Volney's traveler, on the other hand, hangs in time and space as part of a fantasy of clarity, though, of course, it is in the nature of fantasies to compensate for conditions that are anything but clear. Volney begins with the affects inspired by the experience of damage, but these lead his traveler to unanswerable ethical questions, which directly result in the encounter that makes possible the act of rising, which is at once a relief (he had been weeping and covering his eyes) and a challenge to reason (his ocular witness is useless without further elucidation).

Although the guilt and complicity of the safe spectator reflecting on the pain of others—or on injuries for which any given viewer is unlikely to be directly responsible—is a characteristic modern topic, the history of literature indicates that the pain of others is not of necessity the main issue when reflecting on warfare, no more than the proper moral disposition of the noncombatant to the struggle need be a significant ethical issue in relation to military conflict. The sense that the injuries of others are a key question when it comes to war is relatively novel, if not quite as recent as the hypertrophied but always insufficient sense of personal responsibility that characterized response to war in the twentieth century and to which it is closely related. It is this change that causes us to understand anew texts ranging from Felicia Hemans's "Casabianca," in which the child's loyalty to the father eventuates in his own gory death, to Alfred Tennyson's "Charge of the Light Brigade," in which the blunder of leadership stands out to us rather than the fact that not a man is dismayed even though the entire brigade knows someone has blundered.[32] While in these texts the act of self-sacrifice is available to the modern reader for recasting as an ironic failure, the same cannot be said for works going back to classical antiquity, in which gory mayhem is the vocation of heroes. Family members might bemoan particular losses, but a general sense that the fact of death at war is to be deprecated evidently has no place in the epic. The rage of Achilles of which the muse will sing is provoked by a disagreement about the disposition of women taken as war booty. Not the sadness of Briseis, torn from her family, nor even of Andromache, fated to witness the death of her son, flung from the ramparts of Troy, to be widowed by the war, destined to marriage with her captor—none of this is at the epic heart of the Iliad. The devastation of Dido at her abandonment by Aeneas is an elaborate melancholy vision of loss that displaces all of the barely mentioned or utterly ignored human misery attendant on the death of each hero whose end Virgil describes with such relish, as though the hopes and losses of a transient love affair were evidently of more power than those attending the sudden passing of a father or husband or son.[33] The nineteenth century was the period in which the transition to a new vision of the horrors of war took place, a development that would require a number of such thoroughgoing and effective changes in concepts of political subjects, ethics, psychology, and even in media technologies that it can be difficult to remember an earlier era. Still, we may recall here that in 1815 the field of Waterloo became almost immediately a tourist destination whose fascination the evident signs of carnage and ongoing human misery were insufficient to dim.[34]

In *Regarding the Pain of Others*, among the most nuanced and challenging accounts of the complex tradition of sympathy and cynicism involved in the representation of war, Susan Sontag describes Goya's *Disasters of War* as "a turning point in the history of moral feelings and of sorrow," a hyperbolic claim of no little merit about the epochal change for which that series of prints may indeed be taken as evidence. Goya produced this astonishing body of work between 1810 and 1820, in response to the struggles of the Napoleonic era and the violent reaction that followed the defeat of the emperor. But the plates were only published in 1863, after the crisis of the Crimean War and in the middle of the American Civil War, conflagrations each of which has frequently been identified as marking a new departure in the cultural response to military conflict.[35] Goya's relentless dark vision of war as a brutal, pointless, and often grotesque set of episodes characterized by damage and confusion anticipates the world into which it was diffused, in which new concepts of the public and the state and new technological developments in mediation would keep giving the lie to *dulce et decorum.*

We find elements of the modern sensibility running through the nineteenth century, though not yet consolidated into the form it would take in a later era. As Favret notes, "the very contrast between . . . modes of picturing available to the public at the turn of the nineteenth century offers broad hints of how much contemporary culture has inherited—and lost—from romantic views of war" (193). The play with distant perspective and the close-up view that is experienced by Volney's traveler with the magical aid of the genie is an indication, I want to suggest, of a relationship between knowledge and affect that must be counted among the losses separating us from this earlier time (Volney, 193–96). Surely, if we had the genie's gift at our disposal (even just as authors), we'd use it to see (or show our readers) the pain of others. To show the distress of individuals is at the core of the ethical project of representation today: to witness, to testify—or, I suppose, to take testimony, like a magistrate or member of a jury who already knows the verdict, or perhaps like a judge listening to the statement of a victim prior to passing sentence.

The idea of witness is extraordinarily powerful in contemporary culture, though the paradoxical callousness or failure of the imagination at its heart has still not received sufficient critical attention. What are we to make of a system of values or concept of knowledge and sympathy that can only arrive at judgments when it is presented direct evidence of pain? Worse, we learn every day that the moral effects of immediate experience are always overstated. After all, it is hardly the case that we are currently bereft of access to ocular proof of the suffering of others, not when it can be summoned on our computer screens with a few keystrokes—proof, it turns out, of whatever we want to believe. It may well be the case that we call for witnesses less because we lack the knowledge to act than in order to tell ourselves that history may be understood to have the form of a trial, or even that all violence is usefully understood as a crime that will ultimately be brought to the bar of justice.

"There's nothing wrong," Sontag writes, "with standing back and thinking" (118). It is a claim with a long pedigree, in which we might certainly locate the values of Volney's *Ruins*. Standing back *and* thinking are not two distinct actions in Sontag's formulation; one is the precondition for the other. The proliferation of images characteristic of the modern experience of violence can sometimes appear likely to drown our moral senses in experience and first-order affective response. As Favret says about this part of Sontag's argument, with a deceptively simple turn of phrase, "the ethical value of distance demands reconsideration" (196). Aaron Tugendhaft's recent claim about inherited images offers a similar proposition: "We can take a step back," he says in his study of contemporary idolatry, "to ask whether those images suit our needs" (98). Immediacy importunes the feelings, but the response for which it appears to call may be the most inadequate, and it is not unlikely to be distorted by a misleading urgency—not because crises are not urgent but because their urgency may be symptomatic and in no way a path toward a solution. To add one more voice to the set I have already cited, I will just mention the title of a book by Elaine Scarry, *Thinking in an Emergency*, which I will discuss in Chapter 3. While the preparation to act without reflection that characterized strategic thinking in the Cold War, and which Scarry attempts to put into question in that volume, is a typical impulse of the reactionary Right (providing as it does an important basis of support for the concept of the "unitary executive" in the United States), it is possible that on the other side of that coin we may find something that can seem like neutral common sense, or even a progressive value: the claim for immediate experience as the only source for judgment of an ethically significant event. Rational reflection and even imagination become suspect categories when only immediacy matters, as when the appropriate response to injury is understood to be a melancholy unspeakable sublime.

2

HEIGHT AND DAMAGE / VIRTUAL REALITY

The elements on which the elaborate opening to Volney's *Ruins* is structured are clear enough and in many ways not surprising. The visual experience of sublime space becomes readily analogous to the boundless expanse of time because it is more available to perception: vast regions we can almost see come to stand in for millennia we cannot. As a relic from an otherwise unreachable antiquity the ruin plays a unique double role, teaching a lesson at once about the accidental durability of things and the actual vulnerability of the systems in which those things come into being. Still, there is more to say about what Volney has taken so much trouble to stage: the *rising up* to generalization, to perception—the movement first onto the hill and then into the heavens, which the reader in some ways emulates. And that is the topic of this chapter, the relationship between rising and the recognition of injury.

We don't have far to search in order to find the political work of the ruin in subsequent periods, most famously perhaps in Shelley's "Ozymandias"—a text the sources of which in Volney are hard to miss but which acquires its power by vastly simplifying the formal and thematic material in that source: "Look on my Works, ye Mighty, and despair!" the statue famously enjoins Shelley's traveler. But when the view pulls away, it leaves the traveler and reader who is also the speaker all in the same desolate situation:

> Nothing beside remains. Round the decay
> Of that colossal Wreck, boundless and bare
> The lone and level sands stretch far away. (lines 10–14)[1]

Shelley's is a very flat poem, topographically speaking. A towering statue is brought low: its trunk is gone; its topmost parts are "half sunk." But the reader rises to take in the wide view. The poignancy of the close, what makes it more than the ironization of the claims of power (which, of course, it also fundamentally is), is the sleight of hand that makes "lone" appear to be a reasonable adjective for "sands" and somehow parallel to "level." The statue, evidently, cannot feel alone or anything else. The subject who gets to feel that is the composite figure interpellated by the statue—namely, the traveler, the speaker who is quoting him, and ultimately the reader, each one alone remembering an encounter with a traveler, a statue, a poem—and all reduced in the long view.

The movements provoked by broken antiquity characteristic of Volney's spatialization of time are closer to those of the reflecting mind in Keats's "On Seeing the Elgin Marbles." The manifold incoherences of that short poem mark the wonder it contains by making the stones into mountains ("pinnacles and steeps") to be climbed, by gesturing toward an empyrean range in which the speaker cannot stay, as he rises toward a height that the mind can faintly descry but at which it cannot in fact arrive:

> . . . each imagined pinnacle and steep
> Of godlike hardship tells me I must die
> Like a sick eagle looking at the sky.
> Yet 'tis a gentle luxury to weep
> That I have not the cloudy winds to keep
> Fresh for the opening of the morning's eye.
> Such dim-conceived glories of the brain
> Bring round the heart an undescribable feud;
> So do these wonders a most dizzy pain,
> That mingles Grecian grandeur with the rude
> Wasting of old time—with a billowy main—
> A sun—a shadow of a magnitude. (lines 3–14)[2]

The unstable fantastic projection of rising and falling is captured in the pinnacles and steeps but above all in that peculiar simile whereby the speaker imagines himself as an eagle, though one too sick to fly. The force of Volney's sublime, like that captured in Keats's poem, involves not merely perception but reflection as well—or rather, an unreconciled combination of both. While the sonnet has no interest in pushing beyond the commemoration of an amazed moment, it does open up to thought, manifesting a crisis that involves brain as well as heart—the former quite dim in its conceptions, however, and the latter subject to the struggles that the vague glories of reflection have provoked ("dim-conceived glories of the brain").

In the lineage of the sensibility going back to Volney, with its spatialization of the poetics of ruins and its particular attention to the location of the emotional viewer, we might place not only Keats overwhelmed at the shed displaying the ruined Parthenon Marbles in London and the fantastic vision of tyrannical overreach imagined by Shelley, but also a figure from the graphic arts that has become something of a convention, the well-known image of the New Zealander visiting a ruined London in Blanchard Jerrold and Gustave Doré's *London* of 1872, itself drawn from various moments in the work of the historian Thomas Babington Macaulay with sources in Volney (fig. 2.1).[3] The image of a traveler from a distant land sketching the remains of a ruined London, which was so quickly taken up in British culture, emerges in the course of an extended reflection on the vigor of the political infrastructure of the Catholic Church in a review of Leopold von Ranke's *The Ecclesiastical and Political History of the Popes during the Sixteenth and Seventeenth Century*. Macaulay begins with a sense of the sublime timescale of the institution of the papacy, the way it forms a still-vital link between antiquity and today. In contrast to other great cultures of long standing now lost, and—surprisingly enough—to Protestantism itself, which, Macaulay argues with more hyperbole than accuracy, has conquered no new lands since the Reformation, "the Papacy remains, not in decay, not a mere antique, but full of life and useful vigour." After citing various instances of that vitality, Macaulay concludes with an odd but extremely influential fantasy, which serves to bring the point of comparison home even as it contradicts the claim that Protestants have acquired no new territories: "And she may still exist in undiminished vigour when some traveller from New Zealand shall, in the midst of a vast solitude, take his stand on a broken arch of London Bridge to sketch the ruins of St. Paul's."[4] Macaulay is fascinated by the contrast between what he takes to be the ever-renewed power of the Catholic Church and the static or even stagnating character of Protestant institutions, hence his bold contrast: the heart of Anglicanism in ruins while the papacy continues its run.

Given that almost everything human ingenuity can fabricate has a good chance of outlasting its maker and that failure attends most human activities, it is little wonder that images such as Macaulay's—or Doré's visualization—slide so quickly into cliché. Can the contemplation of broken things go beyond ironizing human ambition or paralyzing thought and feeling in a sublime

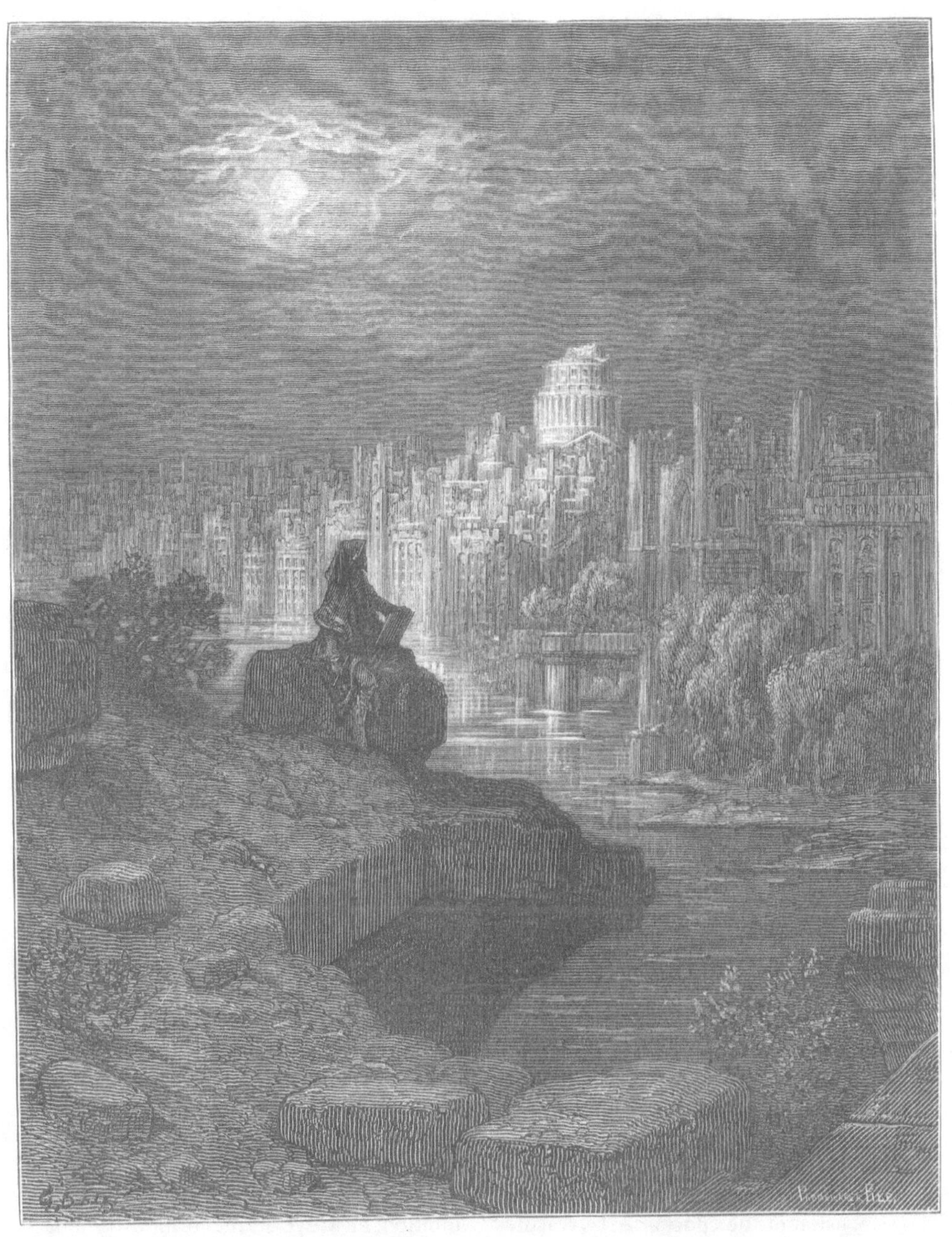

FIGURE 2.1. Gustave Doré, "The New Zealander." Blanchard Jerrold and Gustave Doré, *London: A Pilgrimage* (London: Grant & Co., 1872).

moment? What would it mean not to stop at the point of melancholy encounter but to take seriously the question of responsibility raised by the outburst that provokes Volney's genie as well as the elaborate aftermath of the experience of sublime melancholy that is the burden of *Ruins*? Historians tend to cite Macaulay's review simply to identify a source for the wistful New Zealander, but it bears noting that the text in which he appears is motivated by a complex and textured relationship to historic loss, involving not only the decline of classical antiquity at the time of the emergence of Christianity but subsequent challenges to the totalizing aspirations of the religion, whether the rise of Protestantism or developments during the Counter-Reformation. Macaulay briefly and judiciously lays out the histories of these epochal developments, but he offers no reflection on the pain felt and devastation wreaked at the points of transition as one powerful life-defining religion is superseded by another in the course of events typically accompanied by violent upheaval.

The unavoidable nature of loss can seem to push against the very affective categories that make ruins significant, to ironize even the feelings they provoke. The lone and desert sands put into question not just the sneer of command of the tyrant but the bare life of the traveler contemplating the trackless spaces all around him. It is ultimately this feeling that leaves Keats shaken, that Shelley negotiates by creating a speaker to bear witness to his traveler and to distance the reader from his crisis. To acknowledge the inevitability of decay is to recognize the transience of all we hold dear, including ourselves. On the other hand, to imagine a traveler sitting down and sketching what remains of what we value is to task the imagination with forecasting an existence beyond the unavoidable catastrophe. It is to end one's reading of *Ruins* at the frontispiece, to allow melancholy perception to stand in the place of recognition, to refuse to admit the lesson of responsibility and effortful perception of the genie.

An extraordinary passage in John Ruskin's seminal 1857 lecture "The Political Economy of Art" would have gratified the apparition precipitated by the ruins of Palmyra with its indignant insistence on human agency. The art critic, at the height of his fame as the author of *Modern Painters* (1843–60) and *Stones of Venice* (1851–53) had been invited by the leaders of taste of Manchester, that great center of nineteenth-century commerce, to speak to them on the occasion of the epochal Art Treasures Exhibition, at which so much industry and wealth was to be gilded by the presence of major works of art held in private collections across Britain, gathered and displayed in a purpose-built glass palace. Ruskin did not gratify his hosts by celebrating them or the works they had gathered at such effort and cost. Instead he spoke with urgency about art in danger elsewhere, about the ethical failure of subjecting admired objects to the risk of transportation from one place to the other merely to overwhelm viewers with an experience of unassimilable, ostentatious excess. In the lecture, he invites his viewers to imagine a situation of care, one in which the resources spent on the exhibition had gone to protecting buildings and works of art threatened by war and neglect on the continent. If Keats and Shelley speak to us of the challenges that the relics of time present to the individual ego, Ruskin turns the issue around. His topic is the threat that human actions present to treasured objects:

> Fancy what Europe would have been now, if the delicate statues and temples of the Greeks—if the broad roads and massy walls of the Romans—if the noble and pathetic architecture of the Middle Ages, had not been ground to dust by mere human rage. You talk of the scythe of Time, and the tooth of Time: I tell you, Time is scytheless and toothless; it is we who gnaw like the worm—we who smite like the scythe. It is ourselves who abolish—ourselves who consume: we are the mildew, and the flame; and the soul of man is to its own work as the moth that frets when it cannot fly, and as the hidden flame that blasts where it cannot illuminate. All these lost treasures of human intellect have been wholly destroyed by human industry of destruction; the marble would have stood its two thousand years as well in the polished statue as in the Parian cliff; but we men have ground it to powder, and mixed it with our own ashes. The walls and the ways would have stood—it is we who have left not one stone upon another, and restored its pathlessness to the desert; the great cathedrals of old religion would have stood—it is we who have dashed down the carved work with axes and hammers, and bid the mountain-grass bloom upon the pavement, and the sea-winds chant in the galleries.[5]

I will return to Ruskin in later chapters, but I place his voice here now as a reminder of how much needs to be forgotten in order to make any ruin an agentless product of time. "Human industry of destruction" is the extraordinarily rich formulation Ruskin arrives at to capture the hard work it takes to create ruin. "Fancy" he had begun, as though he were going to invite us to dream with him. But it is a nightmare reversal he brings to the listening industrialists—and perhaps not only to them—in a figurative overload that is meant to make us understand the metaphors we create for agentless unwanted damage as so many ways of not talking about our own responsibilities. We are worms and flames and scythes because we are the hammer-bearing and axe-wielding destroyers who consistently reduce objects endowed with far greater staying power than human beings to the transient condition we know to expect for ourselves. Call it a counter-poetics of ruins we hear in the words of the genie at Palmyra, of Ruskin in Manchester. Moving forcefully past the long-standing convention of the melancholy ironization of human hopes by the experience of broken old things, Volney and Ruskin both identify in the emotions provoked by damage a forceful demand for the recognition of agency.

Toward the end of August 2015, about eight months before I first started drafting the material in this chapter, the group known as Islamic State of Iraq and Syria, or ISIS, blew up the temple of Bel at Palmyra, where Volney's traveler stayed, along with other irreplaceable ruins (fig. 2.2). Insofar as contemporary culture is familiar with the city of Zenobia and Longinus, it is largely because images of the event and its aftermath were widely distributed at the time, including extraordinary views documenting the damage from a height (fig. 2.3). Originally I had thought it would be useful to address this event in relation to similar episodes of recent iconoclastic destruction, such as—most

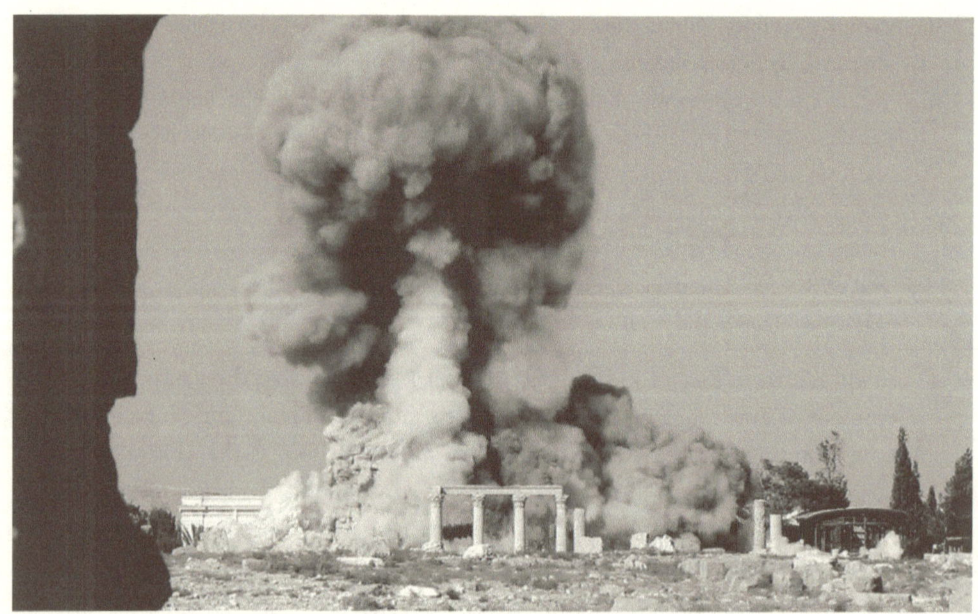

FIGURE 2.2. Destruction of the Temple of Bel, Palmyra, August 2015. History/Bridgeman.

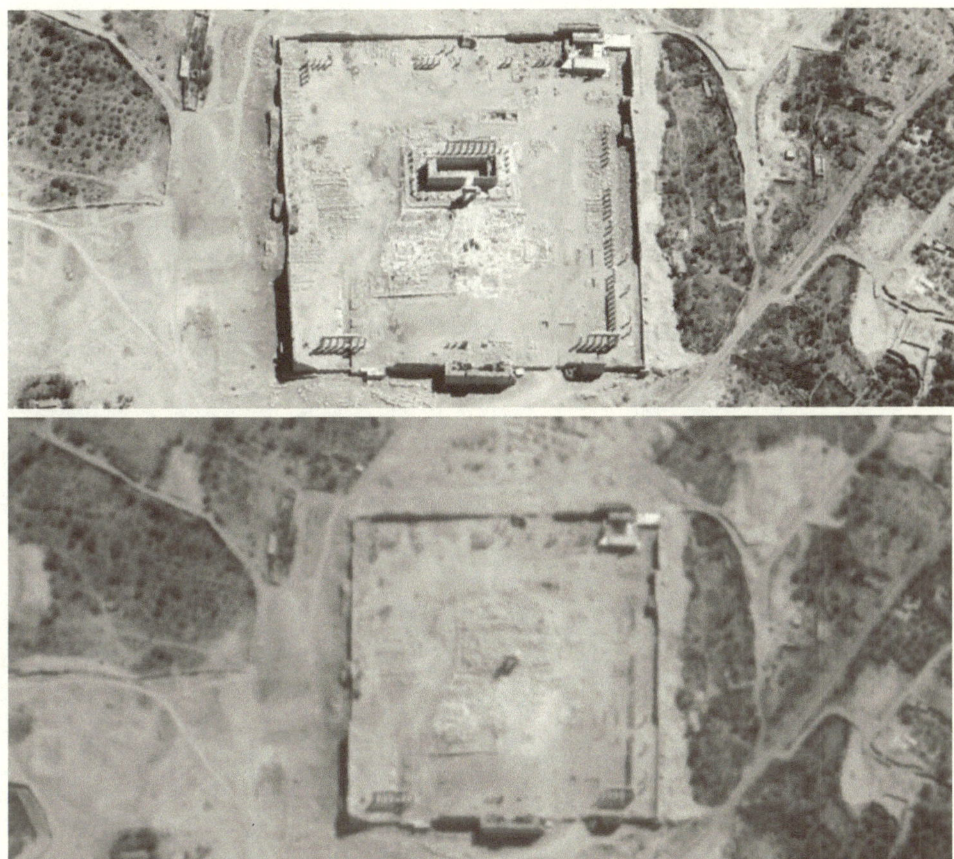

FIGURE 2.3. Satellite images of the site of the Temple of Bel before (*top*) and after (*bottom*) its destruction in Palmyra, Syria, August 27, 2015, and August 31, 2015. History/Bridgeman.

dramatically—the Taliban's 2001 dynamiting of the Buddhas that had stood at Bamiyan for only half a millennium or so less than the walls of the Temple of Bel had risen above the plain of Palmyra (fig. 2.4). Perhaps I might have focused on the easy but nevertheless important paradox that a new admiration for a broken past tends to follow closely on acts of vandalism and pointed out to my readers that the term "vandalism" is closely associated with the emergence of a museal sensibility responding to the depredations of the French Revolution. Indeed, historians have dated the emergence of the concept precisely to January 11, 1794 (otherwise, 22 Nivôse, Year 2 of the Revolution), when it appears

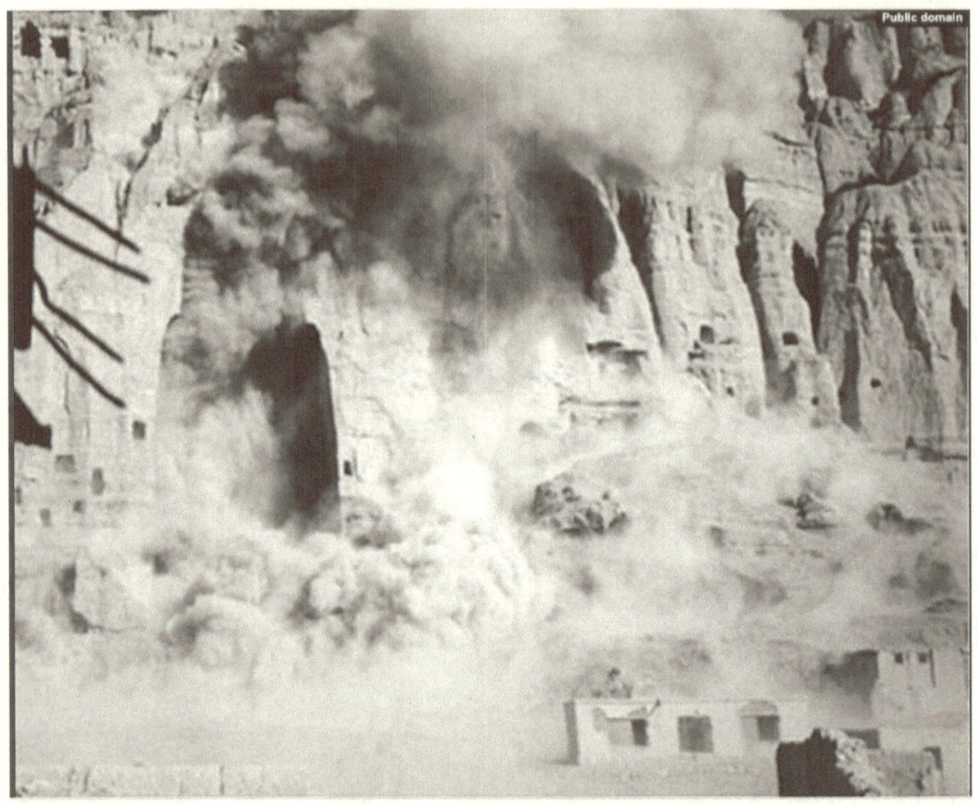

FIGURE 2.4. Destruction of the Buddhas at Bamiyan, March 2001. History/Bridgeman.

in the course of the first of three important reports on the topic presented by the Abbé Grégoire to the National Convention.[6] For practical reasons, too, the actions carried out in the course of most manifestations of popular vandalism have a morphological similarity across time. The winds will carry echoes through an empty niche in a similar way, whether the work it once protected was destroyed in living memory or centuries earlier (see figs. 2.5 and 2.6). A statue being pulled down in Paris in the eighteenth century (fig. 2.7) will look like one being pulled down in 1989 or in 2003—or any year since). Surely, one feels, the relationship between events that look so similar and result in such similar effects is bound to be more than simply formal.

Miguel Tamen's equivocal description of "the writer on Vandalism," which I read around this time, gave me pause: "typically a person who, when given to theoretical pronouncements, regrets general ignorance and, when given to empirical descriptions, denounces shocking instances of the effects of ignorance."[7] Reflecting on the long-standing and ongoing connection between museums and vandalism, and in particular on the fact that the first museum of medieval art was founded to house the very objects that had been eagerly broken by the *sans-culottes* a few years before—emblems of ecclesiastical power and royal prerogative that became sources of nostalgia or formalist appreciation—I came to feel a pressure to do more than regret and denounce ignorance.[8]

It was only in the late 1970s that the statues of the kings of Judah that had been torn from the church of Notre-Dame in Paris nearly two hundred years earlier by revolutionaries were found and put on display at the museum established in 1843—we might say, with very little hyperbole, for this very purpose. One sometimes reads that violent men mistook the works for representations of ancient rulers of France and so destroyed them. What is certain is that with

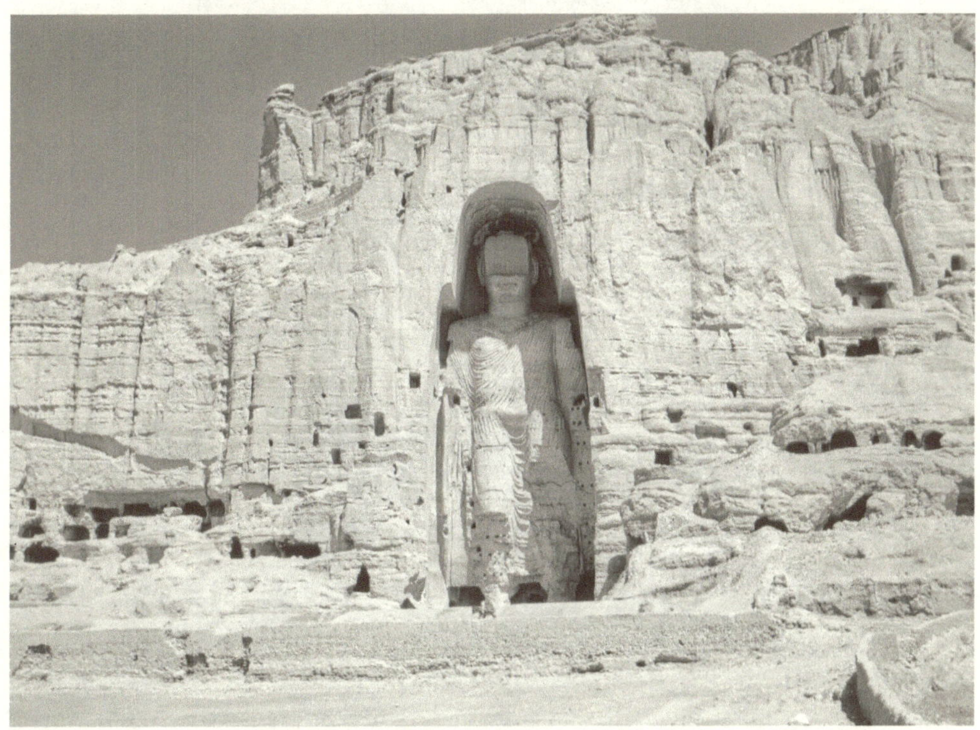

FIGURE 2.5. Taller Buddha at Bamiyan before its destruction. Ann & Bury Peerless Archive / Bridgeman Images.

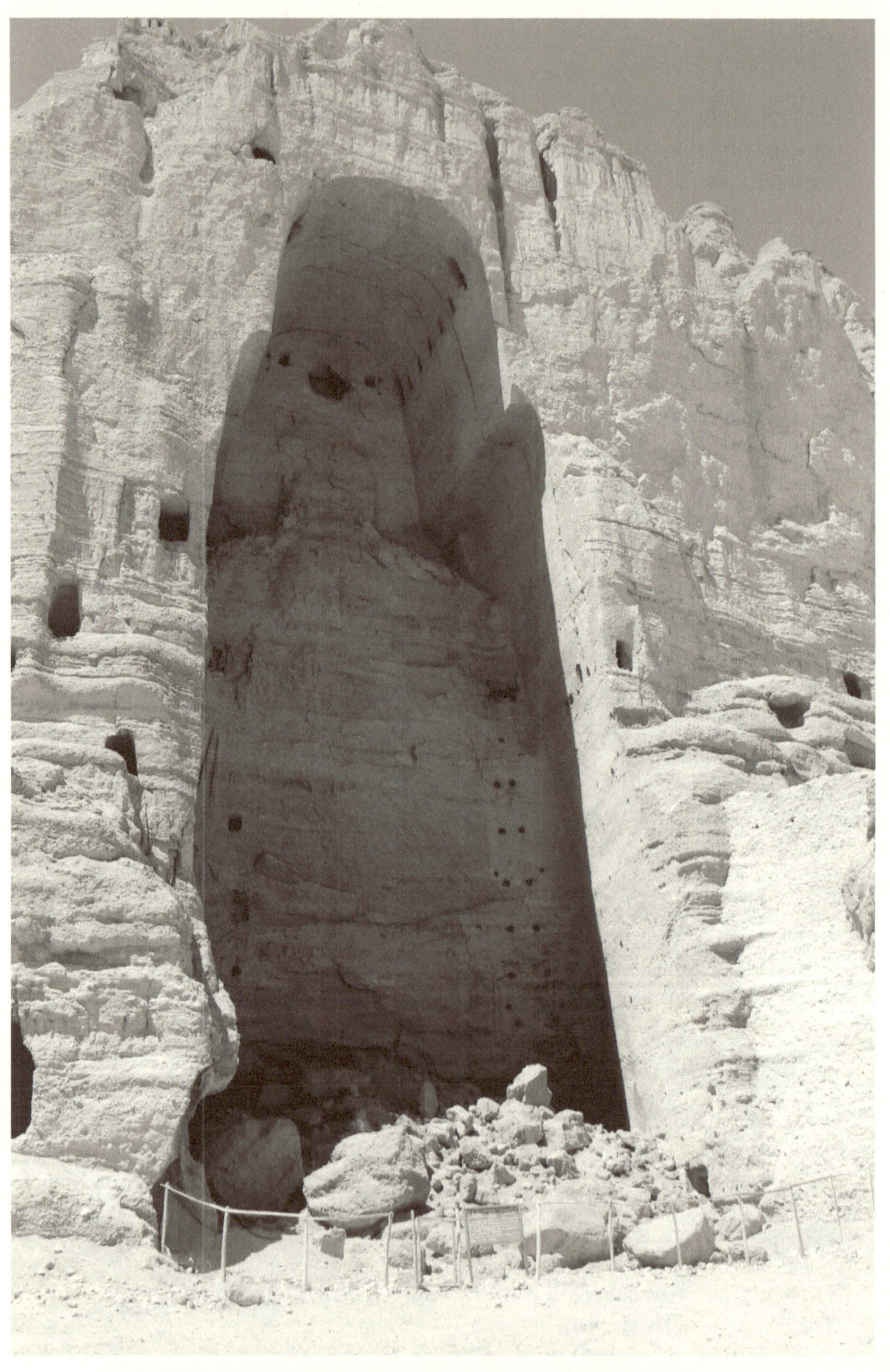

FIGURE 2.6. Niche of taller Buddha at Bamiyan, after destruction. Private Collection©. World Religions Photo Library / Bridgeman Images.

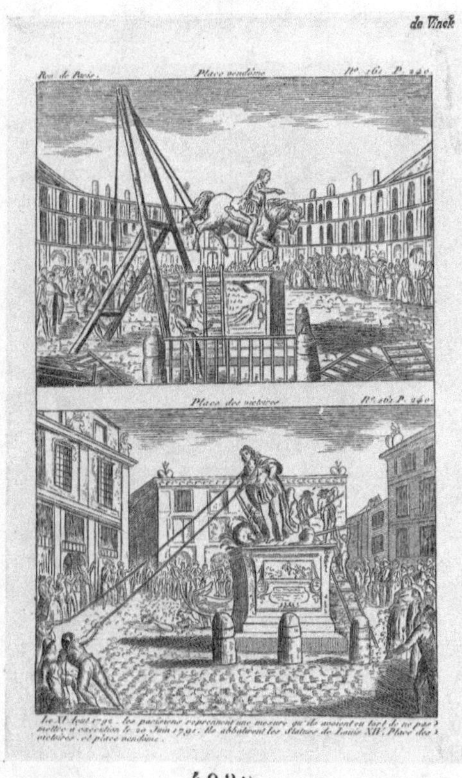

FIGURE 2.7. Destruction of statues of Louis XIV at Place Vendôme and Place des Victoires (1792). Part of a set of six engravings celebrating the toppling of statues around Paris. Bibliothèque nationale, Paris / Bridgeman Images.

no little effort these heavy objects were lowered to the ground and systematically decapitated (fig. 2.8). Practical matters aside, mistaking old Jewish kings for more recent French ones might appear to be a perfect instance of what Tamen describes as the shocking effects of ignorance typically associated with the efforts of vandals. But such an eminently reasonable thought depends on ignoring the committedly anticlerical ideas that played an important part in revolutionary iconoclasm, themselves evidently something more than an ignorant response to what we may understand to be the links between commemorating distant biblical monarchs and enforcing the rule of kings.

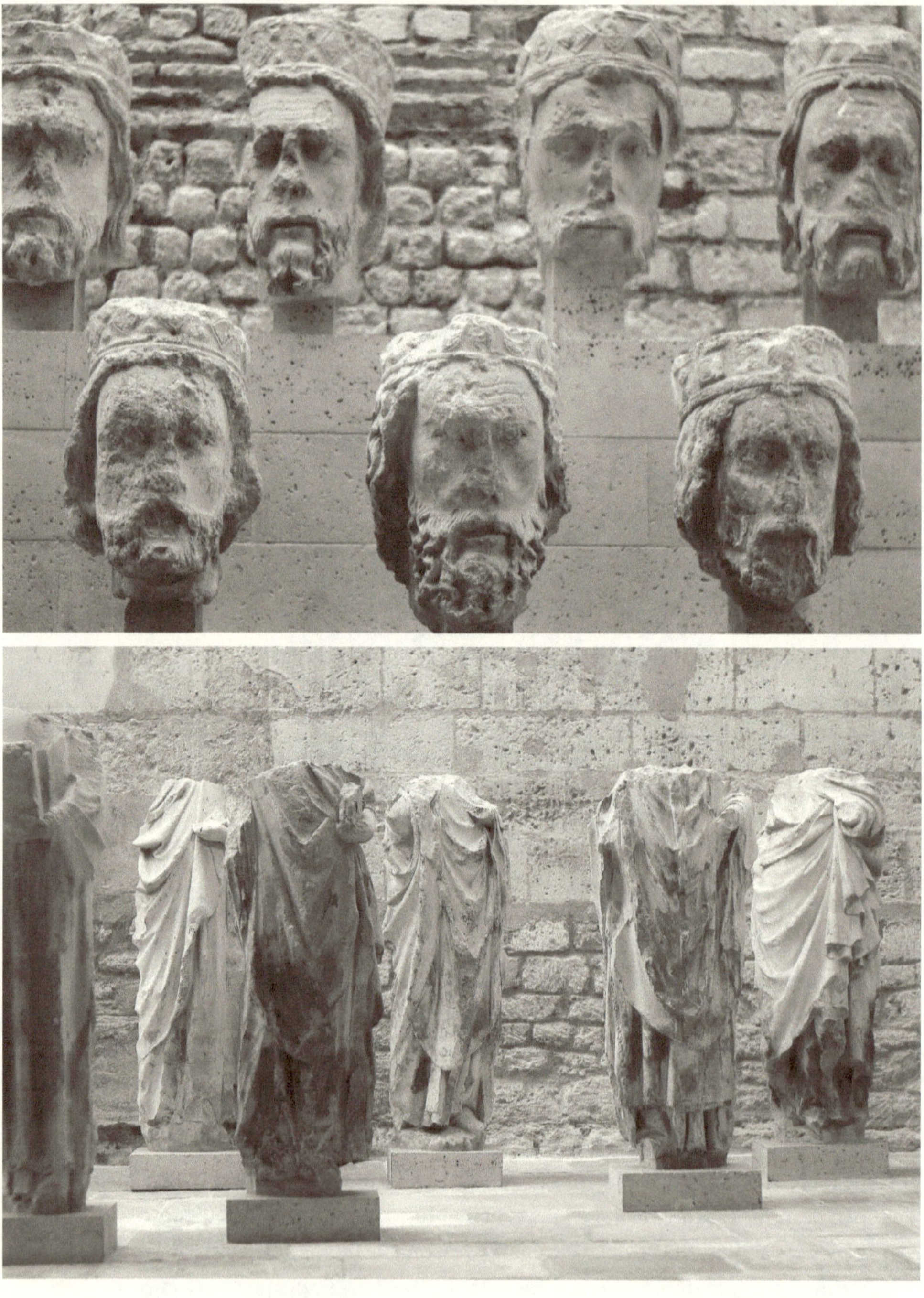

FIGURE 2.8. Heads and bodies of the kings of Judah from the façade of Notre-Dame (ca. 1200–1240), beheaded and buried during the Revolution, rediscovered in 1977. Cluny Museum of Medieval Art, Paris. Top photo: Tom Hilton, CC BY 2.0 https://creativecommons.org/licenses/by/2.0, via Wikimedia Commons. Bottom photo: Adrian Scottow, CC BY-SA 2.0 https://creativecommons.org/licenses/by-sa/2.0, via Wikimedia Commons.

It took scaffolds and tools to remove the statues decorating the west façade of Notre-Dame Cathedral. To tell oneself that it was the confused frenzy of an enraged crowd that caused the damage would be an act of willed ignorance. There is something awful about the thoughtful, informed embrace of violence, which can make it more comforting to think of episodes of injury as matters of immediate unreflecting rage. But such an account of the matter would certainly be inadequate when it comes to understanding the historical actions in question or attempting to establish what we might recognize as we gaze at broken objects at the museum. Given the general obliviousness in most quarters when it came to the very existence of the Temple of Bel at Palmyra or of the great Buddhas at Bamiyan before their destruction, it would be foolish to predicate an argument about these events in relation to knowledge and ignorance—or at least we need to move beyond any simple account of how knowledge and ignorance do and don't map onto violence. In that sense, I may be following an insight of Tamen's appended in a footnote to the description of writers on vandalism I have cited above: "*theories* on Vandalism tend to be disappointing, whereas reports on certain actions thought to be deplorable tend to be useful" (160n13; emphasis in the original). It should be difficult to claim that the men who placed the dynamite around the statues in Afghanistan knew them less well than those individuals who, on seeing the pictures of their destruction, felt a spasm of rage and then went about their business. As has been pointed out by a number of thoughtful writers on the topic, the acts of violence against antiquities at ancient sites or modern museums were highly staged media spectacles, designed to generate the videos that were then diffused around the world (fig. 2.9). Aaron Tugendhaft perceptively notes about those who undertook the destruction in the Mosul Museum that "the hammer wielders are attentive videographers." Clearly the care of the individuals who produced the videos of the destruction of the Temple of Bel and the Buddhas at Bamiyan, as of other acts of violence at museums and elsewhere, demonstrates the centrality of the project of documentation and promulgation that determined the action of the destroyers.[9] The proof is in the video: compelling angles had to be identified, and the cameras needed to be rolling at a precise moment to capture the sudden violence of a planned explosion or the iconoclast shoving the statue.

Immediate reactions to the destruction of irreplaceable objects will tend to illustrate the difficulty we have in clearly identifying the bases for our response to their loss: in the dust and smoke we may trace the outline of our own powerful ignorance, not just of the history of particular object but of the sources

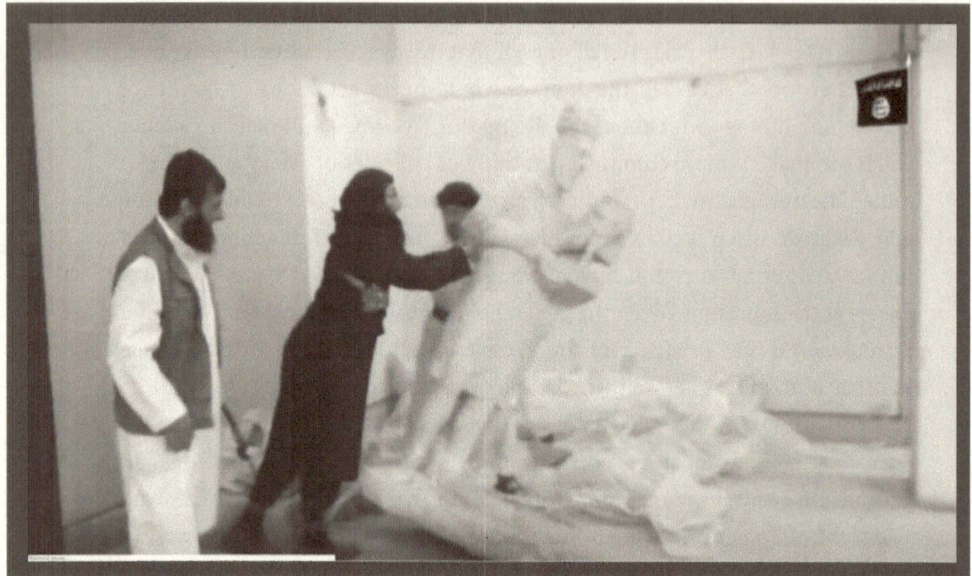

FIGURE 2.9. An ISIS militant toppling a statue inside the Mosul Museum. ISIS video.

of our desires. "Don't destroy those idols from the past," we want to tell the religious fanatic; "they don't matter to us (or not in the way you think they do)." "Don't destroy these idols from the past," we want to say; "they matter so much to us, though in ways we can't explain to you, or that you will never understand."[10] As the militant pushes the statue to the ground the words we can't quite formulate and he will never hear may come back to us in an empty echo to suggest that he also has something to say to us, or that perhaps he understands our desires in ways that we do not. In the eventful years since the explosions at Palmyra and Bamiyan, writing on damage to works of art has become substantially more sophisticated than the initial dismayed formulations these events initially provoked. But Tamen does capture a feeling that has proved hard to resist, that urge to simplify that in itself we may want to recognize as a characteristic response to a sense of panic about emotions and ideas we need to think of as self-evident but that we are suddenly forced to recognize as deeply contingent.

The distinction between iconoclasm and vandalism is a topic that has seen renewed interest in recent years. Iconoclasm traditionally has been shaped around controversies over worship or admiration; vandalism can suggest indifference as well as rage. Damage from either motivation has released objects to be what Ruskin described as "treasures of human intellect," works calling out for recognition and preservation for reasons other than those for which they were originally created.[11] Given that there is no real religious competition either from Buddhists in Bamiyan or from worshippers of Bel at Palmyra, no controversy about orthodox practice, we need to be clear on the fact that it is the recognition, the preservation, the treasuring that the leaders of ISIS had in mind as they ordered these monuments destroyed. In that sense, as recent analyses have made clear, ISIS and the Taliban are not motivated to act by what we might be tempted to call a misunderstanding of the modern role of the objects they destroy with such effort.[12]

It is we who smite, Ruskin declared to his listeners in Manchester, ourselves who abolish and consume. We are moths to our own works. And the actions of ISIS demonstrate the responsibility he describes even as they rebuff the implicit solidarity that is the basis for Ruskin's moral charge. Indeed, their actions are declarations evidently intended to proclaim their refusal to be included in the "we" of cultural heritage that makes us claim to mourn things we had never heard about before they were damaged. The refusal to see monuments as objects of universal human interest is part of the denial of a concept of international community that has responsibility written into it, if seldom fully embraced. A great deal of embarrassment and bad faith rises up to greet us out of the smoke and ashes, along with a challenge: if we hold that humanity owns a share of all great human achievements, how much does it own a share in the violence that determines how that inheritance comes to us?

Injury to objects whose meanings are deprecated, once a new dispensation, comes to predominate: that is a common event in the history of religion, one likely to be justified on principled grounds. Damage to admired objects the value of which is itself the result of quite secular drives will, however, be of a different order. When Ruskin spoke to his audience in Manchester in 1857 of "lost treasures of human intellect," he was wielding the kind of periphrasis that would become characteristic of generalizations about heritage. But it is worth highlighting the relative novelty of the idea in his day and the remarkable nature of its particular source.[13] After all, the sect in which Ruskin was raised as a fervent devotee did not worship in those "great cathedrals" he identifies with "old religion," any more than they prayed in the temples of the Greeks.[14] Indeed, he is quite right in associating the former structures with the violent work of axe and hammer—as any visitor to the remains of St. Andrews Cathedral in Scotland or any number of derelict religious structures around Britain might confirm. One can hazard a guess that at least some of Ruskin's ancestors would have celebrated the destruction of the great cathedrals that have become "lost treasures" for their descendant. But then again, it was not "human intellect" that was on the minds of those who threw down the monuments of the old religion.

ISIS and its collaborators have destroyed Islamic shrines they understand to mislead the religious or pervert the faith. But that is not typically the issue that has exercised Western sensibilities (any more than the recent destruction of a historic mosque in India by nationalist Buddhists has). It is the injury to the Temple of Bel (a shrine for no god now worshipped) and to the Buddhas at Bamiyan (objects of religious veneration for nobody around them) that have scandalized the modern sensibility—as these actions were intended to do. In what is certainly the most ambitious attempt to address the modern topic of the destruction of art across the widest possible span, Dario Gamboni proposes that the lack of sustained attention to the topic in the twentieth century—as opposed to the recurrent interest that has been shown in related actions in earlier eras—comes down to the emergence of artistic autonomy:

> In the context of a purely aesthetic conception of art, aggression must appear as irrational, meaningless, irrelevant, and of course threatening. Nothing can be learnt from it, and it must be condemned, or better still ignored. The Byzantine and Protestant attacks can be explained by the religious functions that images then fulfilled, just as revolutionary "vandalism" can find its source—if not its justification—in politics. But with the advent and spread of the modern conception of the work of art as an end in itself—art freed from every extrinsic goal or purpose—aggression can only be understood as an expression of ignorance and incomprehension, a barbaric regression.[15]

While Ruskin would never accept the idea of an art freed from every extrinsic goal or purpose, it is certainly the case that putting cathedrals and Greek temples, as well as statues of the Buddha and a ruined antique city at an ancient crossroad of trade, in a related category will inevitably indicate that the value of objects is very distant from their original social function, that the common concepts behind the most ambitious drives for preservation will advance the claims of autonomy. The intellectual crisis provoked by the actions of ISIS involves a violent rebuttal of a half-understood commitment to autonomy and an insistence that that commitment might itself feel, at least outside the realms in which it was developed, like what it is: an entirely heteronomous project associated with the very things (call them secularization or call them foreign interference) that those who ordered the destruction have been moved to resist.

• • •

In the intervening years since the period of acute ISIS violence against antiquities, I have found myself thinking not so much about the objects that are gone as about something that may seem an evasion of the horror of the act of their destruction, though I hope it is instead a way of responding to the experience of that difficult feeling. I have found myself reflecting, that is, on the way in which the troubling encounter with damage calls for a casting of the self into space, for a movement up and away: a kind of sublime escape into rationalization that is at once like that of Keats's viewer gazing at the Elgin Marbles and becoming something like a sick eagle and like Volney's traveler raised above mere human contemplation, but not for that reason immediately granted insight about what lies below. What intrigues me about the movement is that it can be understood as both evidence of an unavoidable condition (of being overwhelmed, of feeling and thought clashing with no outlet for the emotion generated in their clash) and as a manifestation of a kind of psychic resistance (thought motivated by feeling seeking out a point of view that will allow the opportunity for engaged reflection).[16]

At a presentation I attended some years ago on the topic of cultural artifacts at risk in zones of conflict, the audience was shown an aerial view of an area in southern Iraq that had been subjected to very aggressive plundering. It took a moment for the eye to adjust, because what it initially recognized as a lunar landscape proved to be something quite different. What we were seeing was a field riddled with the kind of pits looters dig at archeological sites in order to reach antiquities they may trade on the black market (fig. 2.10). The speakers described an ethical problem of extraordinary complexity in relation to these objects. Reputable museums are expected to shun antiquities acquired by means of such violent prospecting, which at once steals from the nations we like to say have a property in the objects—even as the conditions in which the ostensible theft takes place puts the nations themselves into question both practically and conceptually—and funds further military activities on the part of the looters. If institutions do not acquire the pieces pulled out of the ground in these contested territories, their likely destiny is to enter private hands and

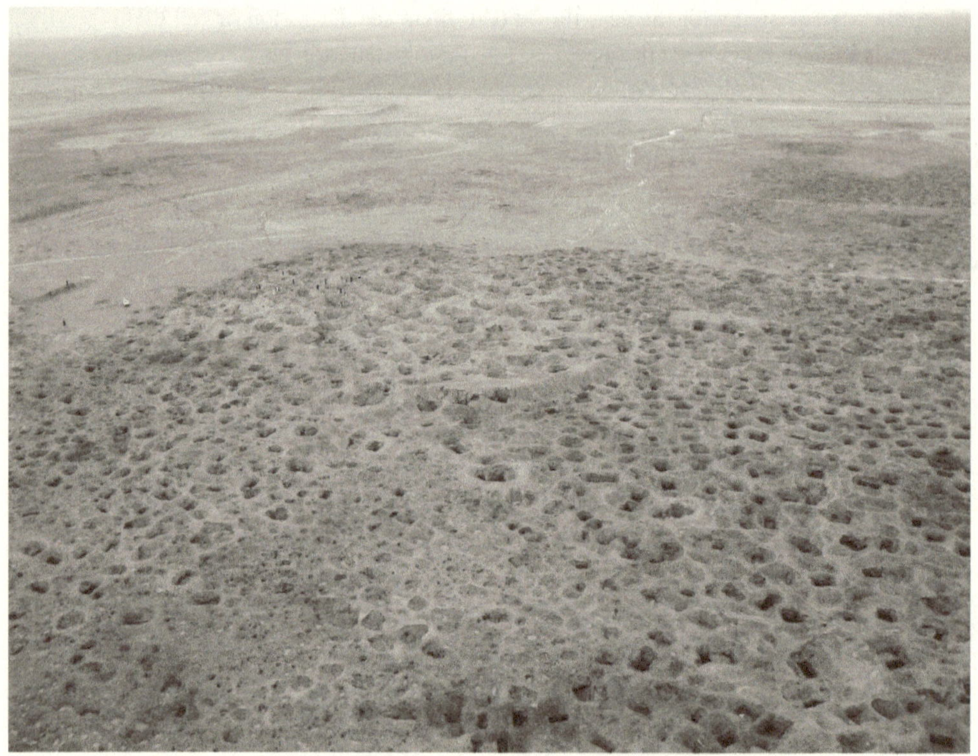

FIGURE 2.10. Looters' pits, Isin, Iraq. Photo by John Russell.

never be seen again by the general public or by scholars. If they do purchase, the museums promote more looting—which destroys the archeological evidence of a site, again reminding us of the unstable nature of the value of the archeological object itself.

To address this topic fully would require us to take seriously the political claims written into the name ISIS, which not only posited a state at once old and new—an Islamic state—but did so while acknowledging and displacing more recent forms of political organization, the nations of Iraq (founded 1921) and Syria (founded 1945). Tamen has pointed out the "link between valuing something for its exemplary properties and not being able to justify the desirability of its preservation without referring to notions such as that of the state" (73). In that sense the looters' pits are not just marks of a challenge to professional protocols of archeology; they are evidence of an attempt to reimagine the relationship between object and state premised on throwing the nature of the modern state into question, along with the secularizing (or at least ecumenical) relationship to religion of modern culture. Fundamentalist iconoclasm challenges the value of the art object that helps to consolidate the modern idea of the state (as an entity that has a history it must treasure and protect, and by which it knows itself and is known to others), because its aim is to move beyond that model. The unresolvable ethical crisis of the museum that may or may not buy objects of dubious provenance is a subset of a broader set of issues, which run in two directions: the validation of the modern state through concepts of culture its members may or may not recognize and the value of antiquities when the state is in question.

The image up on the screen in the course of the discussion of this urgent and yet intractable situation rang a bell even after I realized it was not the moon. It reminded me of the widely distributed double photograph showing the Temple of Bel in Palmyra before and after its destruction (see fig. 2.3). The similarity was more than formal, having to do with the role of distance in trying to provide the evidence of violence or in just organizing its effects for thought. As I was myself reflecting on the relationship between height and damage, between evidence and reflection, and even between the things we call news and those we understand as history, it happened that technology provided a new opportunity to think about this complex of issues.

In November of 2015 the *New York Times* distributed a virtual reality viewer to its subscribers. The disarming cardboard contraption combined the look of an old-school stereograph with a humble and recyclable construction material to create, improbably enough, a new receptacle for one's smartphone, not to say a new mode of intimate cyborg contact with that device—making it experientially what it often seems to be figuratively: one's whole world (fig. 2.11). Of course, the most significant innovation entailed in virtual reality is not its mode of distribution but its being a kind of filmmaking that takes in every conceivable direction—with the result that if you look up while watching a movie, or down, you will see not what is above or below you in fact but in the reality of the film. In short, virtual reality is a form of representation of almost infinite variety because of the range of depth it allows the viewer—not just the planar three-dimensionality that has become common at the movies, which still leaves room to step outside of its illusion by merely turning one's head to see the theatre around one, other members of the audience lit by the glow from the screen. It is a full visual experience that immerses one, like reality itself—if reality were experienced alone.

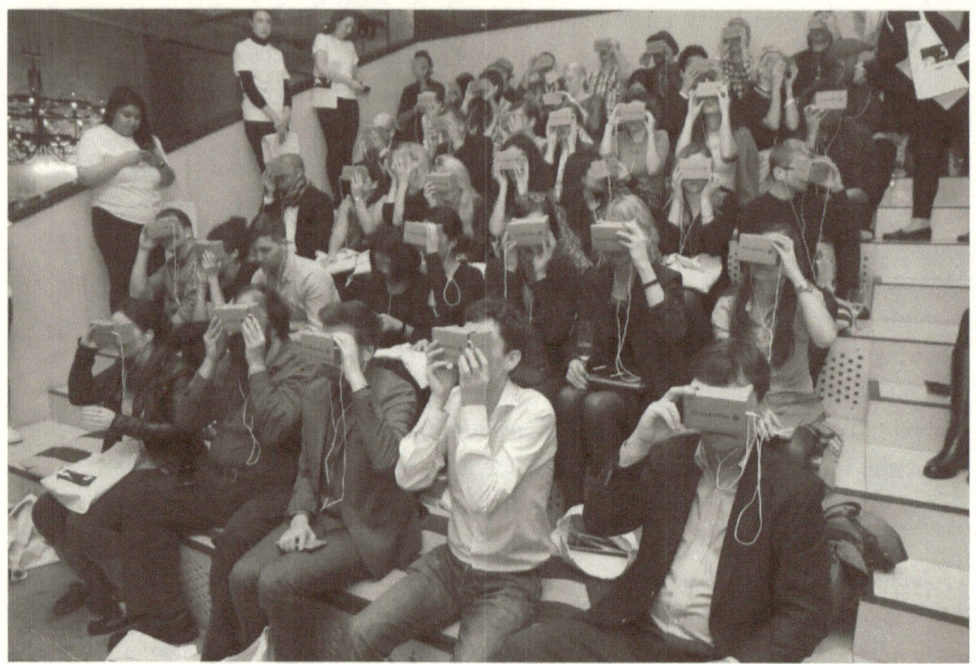

FIGURE 2.11. Photo of *The Displaced* premiere on November 5, 2015. Neilson Barnard / Getty Images for *New York Times*. Madeline Welsh, "The *New York Times* Hopes Its First Virtual Reality Film, 'The Displaced,' Kicks Off Mass Adoption of VR." NiemanLab, https://www.niemanlab.org/2015/11/the-new-york-times-hopes-its-first-virtual-reality-film-the-displaced-kicks-off-mass-adoption-of-vr/.

The distribution of this newly augmented experience through the phone is bound to affect its nature in ways predictable and otherwise, especially when the event replaces the kind of acquisition of knowledge and calibration of social emotion that had until relatively recently come from opening a newspaper or even from sitting down to watch a publicly delivered, regularly scheduled broadcast news program. It is sufficient for my purpose to point out that while we have grown familiar with the observation that there is something isolating and limiting in getting, as it were, one's own news, as one does these days over the internet, picking and choosing sites one consults for information—or letting various algorithms choose, based on one's prior choices—there is a kind of urgency of address built into the telephone even today. Instead of being a punctuated social event to be taken in with others, or at least at the same time others do, as the news used to be, or available when we check in for it, as it is now at various websites, this information (if that is what the news is) is liable to be importuning. The device on which the new medium is delivered makes it similar to a call or message that we may try to ignore but cannot deny receiving, as if the news one chooses to view on the phone might be at once an escape from the world immediately around one and a bell tolling for each of us.

The launch by the *Times* targeted potential audiences with two distinct offerings, both of which to my mind worked together. The first, titled *The Displaced*, was a brief and moving film introducing viewers to the lives of three children living in the aftermath of violent conflict in Ukraine, South Sudan, and Syria (fig. 2.12).[17] The power of the medium to show a world in the round is evoked by the astonishing distances covered by this terribly melancholy film that introduces us to three lovely children whose lives have been placed beyond the hope of repair. Its sad theme notwithstanding, the film is beautiful and full

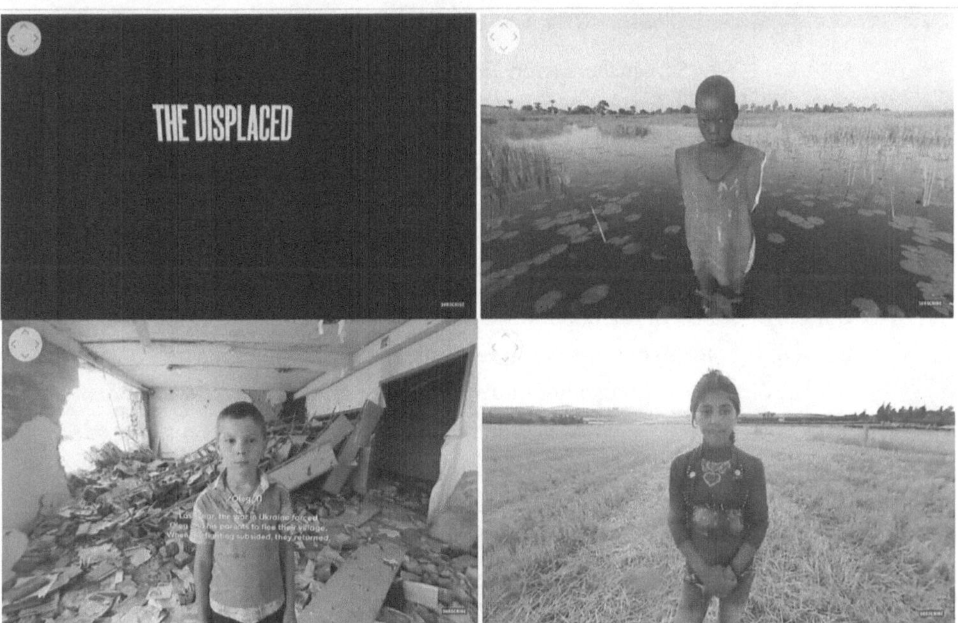

FIGURE 2.12. Screenshots of the children from *The Displaced* (360 VR video). dir. Imraan Ismail and Ben C. Solomon, creative dirs. Chris Milk and Jake Silverstein (Hollywood, CA: Vrse.works, 2015), *New York Times*, November 6, 2015, https://with.in/watch/the-displaced/.

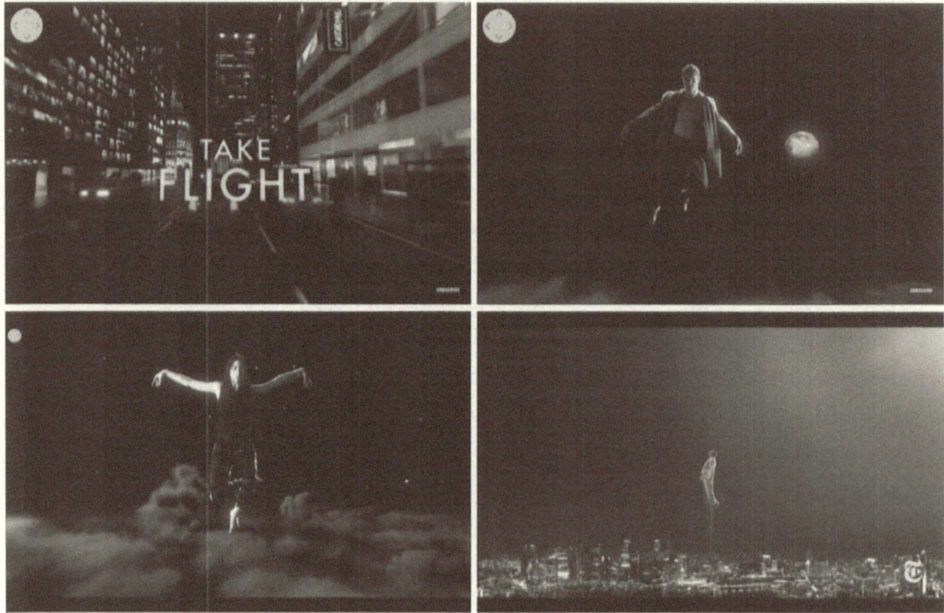

FIGURE 2.13. Screenshots from *Take Flight* (360 VR video). *New York Times*, dir. Daniel Askill, written by Lorin Askill, Daniel Fletcher, and Gregory Stern (New York: The New York Times Magazine and Radical Media, 2015), November 6, 2015, https://www.nytimes.com/video/magazine/100000004084936/take-flight.html.

not only because of the hope we cannot help projecting onto children but because of the wealth of sensory impressions that the medium makes available.

The other film is altogether more trivial, though in its way more ponderous. *Take Flight* features a number of famous actors floating in the air above New York City (fig. 2.13).[18] Abandoning entirely the detailed realism that characterizes *The Displaced*, *Take Flight* finds glamor and magic in the technology. The opportunity to play with depth is highlighted as the film stars rise above the nighttime metropolis in an apotheosis of the category that may also be understood as effecting an unintentional satire of its circularity. Why do they rise, these lovely men, women, and children? Because they are lovely and we want them above us, the film seems to suggest, because they are stars. Why do we follow their ascent within our Virtual Reality Viewer, on our phone, wherever we are? Because they have risen above us, weightless objects of admiration defying gravity. By contrast, the only place where any kind of height is evoked in *Displaced* is in a heartbreaking sequence showing food being dropped from a plane and gathered at a refugee camp in Sudan (fig. 2.14).

"Google Cardboard's *New York Times* Experiment Just Hooked a Generation on VR," *Wired* magazine explained to its online readers, with an enthusiasm that doesn't just seem misplaced half a decade later but had the quality of forced excitement even at the time that occasionally allows us to perceive

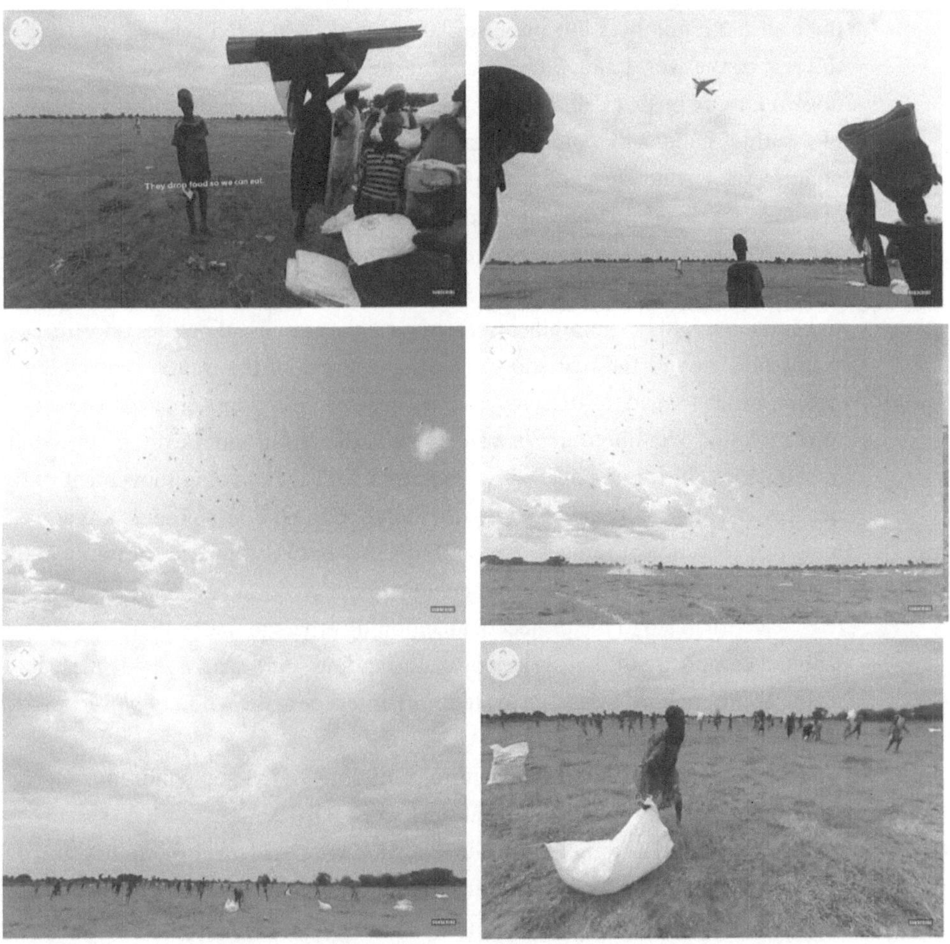

FIGURE 2.14. "They Drop Food, So We Can Eat." Screenshots from *The Displaced* (360 VR video). *New York Times*, November 6, 2015, https://with.in/watch/the-displaced/.

the hard work that goes into agitating our popular culture.[19] Still, this cultural relic has stayed with me as a manifestation of a phenomenon worth more substantial reflection. It led me, at least, to keep thinking about how *The Displaced* carries out the work in its title. According to annual figures from the United Nations High Commissioner for Refugees, in 2014 there were almost 60 million refugees and internally displaced people (IDPs) around the globe: 1 in every 122 people on the planet (today the ratio is closer to 1 in 97). Not since the Second World War had there been so many refugees or IDPs. And it must be said that these were displacements of particular note not because of their absolute numbers but because the individuals affected refused to leave the rest of the world alone, to suffer and die in place. The refugees flooding toward Europe made a call on the capacity for conceptualization and sympathy of wealthier nations that proved impossible to answer. The pressure of the tide of humanity—which reached over a million in 2015—overturned all possibility of simple response and overwhelmed prior existing mechanisms and the values and conventions that subtended them.[20] Europe reimposed internal borders, and experienced politicians found themselves unable to understand what the right action might be—morally or pragmatically—as internal politics reformed themselves around the real and imagined pressures of the influx. Inevitably, chance events shaped the discourse: a baby drowned and doors opened; women were molested over the course of a New Year's celebration and the doors started to shut; enough terrorist acts were associated with the ongoing movement of peoples and the call came to throw the bolt across all doors. The actual and imagined presence of refugees has subsequently reshaped politics not only in Europe but in the United States, where one major political party has committed itself with gusto to the project of abandoning others to their suffering—our national complicity in their crises notwithstanding—and where the displaced on our southern border emerge to attention or recede at the whim of politicians and their allies in the media.

Displaced, with its focus on beautiful, suffering, individual children is evidently motivated by a fairly conventional, even old-fashioned vision of sympathy: the aspiration to help those insulated from a crisis feel the injury and pain of others even at a remove. Still, and paradoxically, the space opened up by virtual reality gives us an illusion of *not* being there, of being at a distance, just looking around, uninvolved, lacking a point of view because every point is available and nobody is around us.[21] Neither political responsibility for the crisis nor strong political action is called for, just feelings. My point is not to judge what the filmmakers failed to do, nor to deploy a well-worn critique of the limits of this kind of sentimental philanthropy. We are better off for having the film and for its being seen. It is no small thing to simply humanize the damaged people who can be so overwhelming in the aggregate by focusing on some lovely individuals. Still, there is no way this kind of representation is adequate in the face of the human catastrophe that is precisely not best understood as a matter of *distance*, not when it is clear that no accurate account of the principal political crises shaping the West in the past decade can ignore the movements of displaced people at their core.

I left Volney's traveler and his genie hanging in space in the previous chapter—and, indeed, that is where they remain forever. Like Tom Stoppard's Rosencrantz and Guildenstern never arriving at their date with destiny, they also never touch down. The raised perspective is the only way to take in the totality of what they are trying to see, though that is not to say that taking it in is easy. The rising is the easy part, and it does not in any way clarify things. It takes further magic and careful exposition to see the actual damage taking place and to think of it in as full a way as is necessary. It will be interesting to stop on the way back to these fantasies from the eighteenth century at a few twentieth-century moments that illuminate the suspended engaged viewing of Volney's traveler.

We say "sublime" and we mean almost too much by the term. As I suggested in the previous chapter, what is particularly powerful about Volney's project is that the sublime marks not an impasse at the limit of thought but an opportunity in the first instance to feel and then to reflect. Perhaps it is not even the sublime at all, in the contemporary understanding of the term, that Volney wields as the genie of the ruins raises his traveler up in the air but then helps him make out and understand the human life below him, to look over without overlooking—to gain, while in some ways losing, perspective. When I was a boy, there was a movement to convince NASA to publish the first photograph of the earth as a whole ever taken from space (fig. 2.15). The image was an incidental offshoot of the race for space, which in itself was driven by the Cold War between the Soviet Union and the United States, part of a competition that was at once symbolic and all too concrete; the propaganda struggle over the technical or scientific ascendancy ascribable to two systems of social organization was the surface manifestation of a deeper practical project aimed at perfecting the rockets able to put military satellites in space and land nuclear weapons on enemy territory. Nevertheless, the hope was that when the view

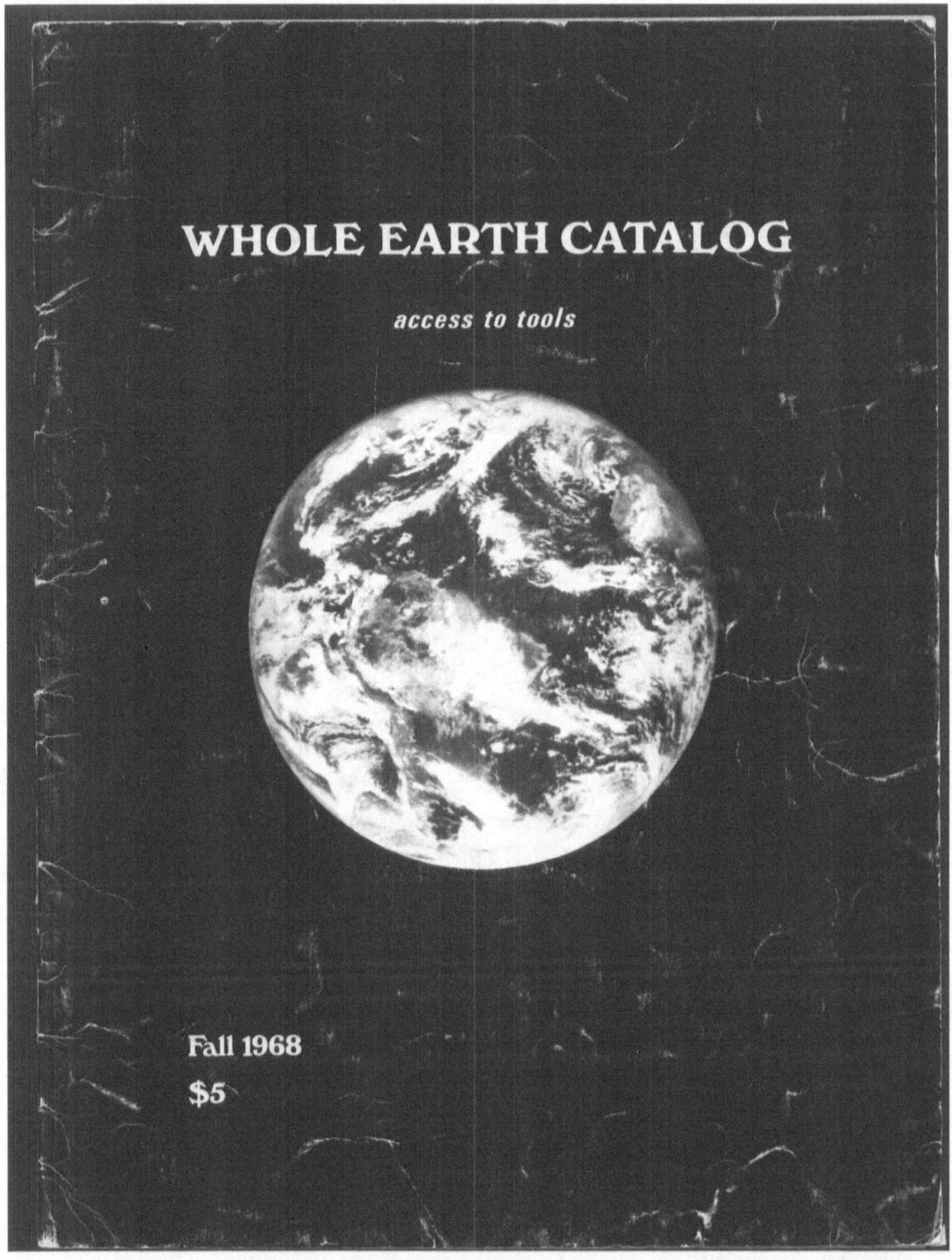

FIGURE 2.15. Cover, *Whole Earth Catalog*, Portola Institute (1968). Courtesy of the Department of Special Collections, Stanford University Libraries, RBC TS199 W5 1968 ff BB: 1968 Fall Whole Earth Catalog.

of the earth as a whole moved from being a state secret to a public experience, it would lead to greater kindness and care for each part of the whole, that the vulnerability of the planet and those upon it would be recognized and result in new kinds of caretaking—of the environment, or of the less fortunate, disenfranchised inhabitants of a world bound to feel more accessible to thought as it became more available to view. The place one saw the image most often was on the cover of the *Whole Earth Catalog*, a countercultural compendium of equipment and tools with the paradoxical aim of making emergent alternative communities self-sufficient by putting them in touch with others. And, in fact, the creation of the catalog was closely related to the movement to see the earth whole.[22] Stewart Brand was the founder of the movement and the creator of the catalog, and it is striking that both of his accounts of the key moment of creative inspiration—and there are two distinct ones, so the commonality is significant—describe an upward trajectory almost as elaborately staged and fanciful as the one Volney designs for his traveler. The elevated position from which he "sort of look[s] and think[s]" described in an interview in which he tells one of the stories is at once physical and metaphorical, as he had taken LSD just prior to the moment of epiphany:

> I went up onto the roof and sat shivering in a blanket sort of looking and thinking. . . . And so, I'm watching the buildings, looking out at San Francisco, thinking of Buckminster Fuller's notion that people think of the earth's resources as unlimited because they think of the earth as flat. I'm looking at San Francisco from 300 feet and 200 micrograms up and thinking that I can see from here that the earth is curved. I had the idea that the higher you go the more you can see earth as round.
>
> There were no public photographs of the whole earth at that time, despite the fact that we were in the space program for about ten years. I started scheming within the trip. How can I can I make this photograph happen? Because I have now persuaded myself that it will change everything if we have this photograph looking at the earth from space.[23]

Every element of Brand's account works to bring perception and thought together; rising up to see leads to his "scheming within the trip," and this scheme is all about taking that long and distanced view to its logical conclusion, toward changing everything by seeing everything. The other widely reported inception story for the project also emphasizes the process of rising as the source of inspiration. It has Brand flying over Nebraska after his father's funeral while reading Barbara Ward's *Spaceship Earth*.[24]

In *From Counterculture to Cyberculture: Stewart Brand, the Whole Earth Network, and the Rise of Digital Utopianism*, Fred Turner has laid out in fascinating detail the historical and conceptual connections linking the utopian hopes that Brand identifies with the view of the whole earth to the networked computing projects that eventuated in the World Wide Web and virtual reality. Andrew G. Kirk's *Counterculture Green: The "Whole Earth Catalog" and American Environmentalism* emphasizes the place of the project in developing significant lines of American environmentalism. There is evidently no denying the force of Brand's insight and the power of the greater interconnection he anticipated and hoped for from disseminating the image of the globe suspended in space that he worked so hard to make public. Still, the failure of the view of the whole to lead inevitably to the achievement of greater global harmony may be inscribed in the extensive list of innovations that did not live up to the hopes of their most utopian promoters, another in the long train of instances of technology—even of knowledge itself—failing to make things better for us as a matter of course. Today, with footage from drones and other military equipment giving us recurrent access to higher vantage points right before they destroy the objects they reveal, not to mention the vulgarization of the view of the whole promised by Google Earth (with its slogan "Gain a New Perspective"), it can seem difficult to recuperate the utopian hopes associated with perspective (fig. 2.16).

As I write, Jeff Bezos, the wealthiest man in the world (his money coming from his creation of what is the closest thing we've ever had to a whole earth catalog), has just returned from a privately funded rocket ride into space, the culmination of a project that will make such jaunts accessible to anyone able to pay but that has also fascinated the general public. Commentators could not help pointing out that as he blasted off he was rising from a planet in which record-high temperatures were causing unparalleled damage and portending worse: multiyear droughts, towns and vast forests on fire, the moon itself taking on a new color on account of the particles thrown into the wind by flames a continent away, animal life dying in unwonted heat, material that had not been liquid for millennia melting and releasing gases bound in place millions of years before any structure had been formed by any human being. What made the venture of this billionaire appear more symptomatic than ironic is the fact that two other individuals were simultaneously working toward a similar goal,

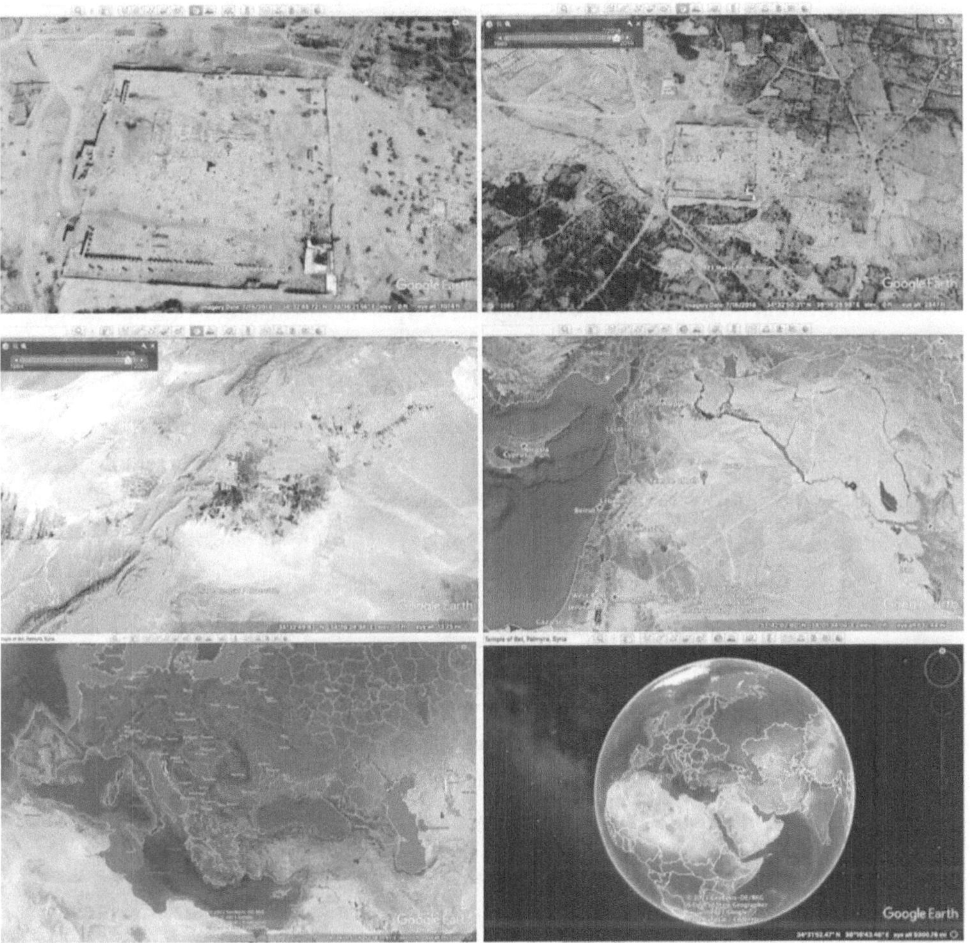

FIGURE 2.16. Screenshots from Google Earth, beginning at the Temple of Bel, Palmyra. Google Earth, https://www.google.com/earth.

as though a season of brief escapes and momentary suspensions had been announced for the wealthy and those who follow their activities.

Down to Earth: Politics in the New Climatic Regime, the English title to a brief polemical 2017 book by Bruno Latour, sounds more declarative than the original, *Où atterir? Comment s'orienter en politique*, which might be translated more literally with a question, if not two: *Where to Land? How to Orient Oneself in Politics*. The original title, suggesting something between a query and an instruction manual, captures very well the spirit of a work at every point shaped by the sense of global uncertainty Latour associates with the abandonment of the common good by the powerful in the face of the ongoing climate crisis. Latour describes a situation, felt as a sensation of intolerable suspense, in which what he calls "the obscurantist elites" who supported the decision by Donald Trump to abandon the Paris Climate Accords "*had to stop pretending, even in their dreams, to share the earth with the rest of the world*."[25] It is almost too easy to say that this abandonment of our shared earth receives its most flamboyant illustration in the little symbolic hops away from the gravitational pull that keeps the rest of us down that have come to preoccupy the wealthy of late. Latour proposes that the escape from a shared ground should be understood as an attempt to make into a giddy fantasy a feeling that is in fact widely shared, a dispossession not at all unrelated to those felt by every victim of the great imperial projects of the nineteenth century but now affecting all of us, including those belonging to nations that had once advanced their interests by displacing others:

> What is striking in the current situation is the degree to which people experiencing deprivation feel disoriented and lost, for want of such a representation of themselves and their interests, and the degree to which they all behave in the same way—those that move and those that stay put, those that emigrate and those that remain behind, those who call themselves "natives" and those who feel like foreigners, as if they have not lasting inhabitable ground under their feet and have to find refuge somewhere. (98)

Latour distinguishes between the "Global" and the "Terrestrial." It is his desire to emphasize the latter, far more concrete category that determines the French title of his book, with its query about where we might *land* (*Où atterir?*). The feeling of vertigo, of suspension, we live with is evoked but by no means solved by the attempt to rise above and get a view of the whole, which Latour associates with the Global and which is more symptomatic of the problem than anything else. "One cannot pass from the Local to the Global," Latour notes, "by moving through a series of interlocking scales, as in the illusory impression of zooming that we can get from Google Earth" (93). As Latour agitates for a recognition of the widespread sense of a need for grounding (for ground), the attempt to rise emerges as a characteristic manifestation of the moral separation from the world and its needs that is at this point quite evidently shaping the very crises that make the question of where to land far more urgent than the desire to briefly rise.

I have mentioned that my train of thought about the place of height in our attempts to rationalize damage was originally provoked by viewing a slide of the work of looters taken from a plane or satellite in the course of a presentation on the challenge that thefts from sites of antiquities present to modern museums. I should note that I have learned in subsequent years that the use of landscapes viewed from high above as a way to trace the actions of looters is at once a deeply impressive and highly limited way to find evidence. A pit might have been dug but nothing found. Pits might be old or new. Looters might return to work in old pits. Errors of visual analysis are easy to make: bushes and marks in the soil can be confused with pits, or old pits can come to look like natural features as they are eroded by environmental conditions. Recent work evaluating the effectiveness of space-based methods points out that aerial views always need validation through "ground truthing," that is, assessing conditions from on-the-ground observation.[26] GlobalXplorer, a site designed to crowdsource review of satellite imagery, is one manifestation of the challenge of extracting useful knowledge out of the information available from a height. The project breaks up the view from space into small "tiles" each of which is reviewed by many individuals who attempt to ascertain whether looting is taking place. While we might say that in its use of imagery from a height and its call to the reiterative work of a potentially vast public this initiative illustrates the promise and the limits of the technology, it bears pointing out that in this process, too, ground truthing is the ultimate requisite step.[27]

The most interesting attempts to understand looting need to carry out their own kinds of ground truthing, to recognize the local conditions, and even traditions, that may motivate those digging in the pits—that may make excavations and other forms of what we call looting recognizable as more than a challenge to fairly recent concepts of nation, of artistic autonomy, and of national culture.[28] Down to earth. Where to land? In proposing the "terrestrial" as a more material and more deeply local concept of shared habitation than the "global," Latour works to promote recognition of a condition in which suspension at a height is at once symptom and cause of a condition of real material danger that may be lost sight of without a great deal of ground truthing.

• • •

Wood and Dawkins give an evocative account of the destruction of the Temple of the Sun by Roman forces in the year 273, the act of retribution preceding by nearly two millennia the cloud of dust that rose across screens around the world in the summer of 2015, that frozen moment of violence that evidently must have been carefully planned by the perpetrators themselves in order to commemorate their action. As we will see, it is tempting to think poignantly of the original damage as retaliation for an act of resistance to empire, but to do so would be to project modern nationalist fantasies and imperial antipathies onto a different cultural moment. History suggests that it is more accurate to see the destruction as the result of a struggle *between* empires, though one was vastly more powerful than the smaller upstart it quickly crushed.

The Roman sources (which are the only ones we have on this topic) are no shyer about the brutal actions they record than the media specialists of ISIS. We may pick up the story of Zenobia's ambitions for expansion and independence, and of her subsequent clash with the Romans, after the emperor Aurelian has defeated and captured the upstart queen and left a contingent of archers in charge of the city. His progress back to Rome is interrupted by a moment of resistance on the part of the citizens of Palmyra that would have dire consequences. The following passage from Wood and Dawkins's retelling describes three turns, only two of which make sense: the revolt of the Palmyrenes in the first instance, the return of the emperor in response, and then the implausible story of repairs to the temple:

> So quick a transition from long enjoyed liberty to a state of slavery, is apt to suggest desperate measures. The inhabitants cut off the Roman garrison. Aurelian informed of this in his road to Rome, returned with uncommon expedition, took and destroyed the town, putting to death most of the inhabitants, without regard to age or sex. For the particulars of this cruelty, we have the emperor's own authority in his letter to Bassus, whom he ordered to repair the temple of the sun, damaged by the soldiers, and appropriated to that use 300 pounds weight of gold, found in Zenobia's coffers; with 1800 pounds weight of silver, from the goods of the people, besides the jewels of the crown.[29]

Was Titus a vandal when he sacked Jerusalem and placed its treasures in the Temple of Peace? Was Aurelian, who destroyed a town and murdered most of its inhabitants but used their own confiscated wealth to carry out repairs to the Temple of the Sun? For whose use would the temple have been rehabilitated in any case, one might ask. Who is left to worship when most of the inhabitants of a town have been killed? Indeed, as it is said that he took the statues of Bel back to Rome to place in a new temple there, the claim is entirely improbable.[30] One can surmise that the repairs were ultimately part of the process that transformed the temple into a fort, as Palmyra shifted in its historical role from a major hub of trade to a military outpost. It is indeed clear to Wood and Dawkins that the physical remains of the temple reveal work from various periods (21). But it is implausible that all that gold and silver and the jewels of the crown went to refurbishing a temple stripped of idols and bereft of worshippers.

Vandals, we say—and we mean both less and more than we like to admit. Given the popular imagination of heedless destructive violence associated with the term, there is room to doubt that many member of the tribes that descended on a weakened Rome in 410 to participate in the sack, from which is often dated the collapse of an empire, paused to look up and reflect on the representation of a crowd of men carrying a menorah from a temple. And yet, quite early traditions suggest that a scene much like the one memorialized on the Arch of Titus took place at the time.[31] The menorah, along with other treasures, was said to have been captured by the Visigoths when the ironically named Temple of Peace was looted. It came to be believed among Christians that the items ended up in a church in Jerusalem—thereby in a sense returning to where they belonged (the church being understood to be a place that merited lodging them more than their now-vanished original home). A much later tradition—as implausible and tendentious as all the others—proposes that the objects are still in Rome, hidden in the Vatican, perhaps.[32]

Jewish losses and Roman triumphs are given new meaning by the emergence of the Christian dispensation, a new cultural development that stands in a complex adversarial relationship to both prior traditions. Given the networks of dependence and rejection involved in the emergence of Christianity, the proliferation of legends in which the losses of others are restored by being placed in locations with which they had never been associated is perhaps not surprising. The Temple of Peace, that museum stocked with sacred booty, makes a peculiar cameo in an important place in *The Golden Legend*, the deeply influential medieval compendium of the lives of the saints generally dated to the thirteenth century, in the section devoted to Christ's life. The temple, it is said, had an inscription on it indicating that it would fall if a virgin ever gave birth. The collapse of the structure thereby becomes evidence of Jesus's virgin birth, and so its damage works at once as a paradoxical manifestation of intactness and a reminder of the Christian victory over paganism. The virginity is preserved, the temple is destroyed, and the paradoxical blend of human and divine in Jesus is evidenced in the material world. The confusions and conflations of the medieval text capture much that is important about the relationships it is concerned to lay out:

> During the twelve years when Rome enjoyed peace, the Romans built a Temple of Peace and placed a statue of Romulus in it. Apollo was asked how long the temple would stand, and the answer was that it would be until a virgin bore a child. Hearing this, the people said that the temple was eternal, for they thought it impossible that such a thing could happen; and an inscription, TEMPLUM PACIS AETERNUM, was carved over the doors. But in the very night when Mary bore Christ the temple crumbled to the ground, and on its site the church of Santa Maria Nuova stands today.
>
> The birth of the Lord was not less miraculous as regards the Child himself. As Bernard says, in one person the eternal, the ancient, and the new wondrously came together.[33]

Vandals, we say, or barbarians, and we mean those who brought violent conquest to the heart of an empire that had been used to doling it out, not taking it. And among the garbled elements in this medieval patchwork of memories of antique culture, it is striking that the author of the legend cannot imagine that a Temple of Peace might be the product of a warlike people, designed to commemorate not a peaceable state but bellicose victories. Benjamin's well-known claim that every record of civilization is a record of barbarism runs very much in two directions. "Barbarism" is only ever going to be a category of something that likes to call itself "civilization." Like "vandalism," it is a pejorative invented to exalt the civilized by contrast. But both terms also bear within them a theory of willful damage that is most improbable because it requires that most unlikely thing: a violent actor driven to great efforts of destruction by a hostility born of ignorance. The existence of such an actor is a recurrent fantasy in disagreements, not to say a defensive projection. *You are angry at me because you don't understand me* is certainly a common feeling in argument. And, more broadly, the claim that people who do not understand us because they are so different from us are a danger to us is a common political gambit because it is at once alarming and flattering. The main affect of ignorance, however, is indifference; its principal action vis-à-vis antiquities is neglect. Acts of iconoclasm, like most of the damaging actions that take place during significant periods of vandalism, can hardly be said to be driven by ignorance. Indeed, the vandals who sacked Rome in 410 were Goths (and Christian), and ancient sources indicate that, while—unlike Aurelian—they did not devote themselves to a project of restoration of what they had destroyed, they also did not massacre the population they had defeated.[34] This sack was something of a military anticlimax, though it loomed large in retrospect, as the first of the several subsequent attacks on the storied capital of the failing empire, including the one carried out by the Vandals themselves in 455, which *also* was not as devastating as Aurelian's retaliation against Palmyra.

Volney dates his *Ruins* from a moment of East-West crisis, the Russian conquest of the Crimea in the late eighteenth century. But he takes his point of view from a ruined city in a Syrian desert combining elements of Roman culture with a number of other local traditions and with Roman violence. He stages the fantasy of his traveler rising to contemplate a totality that is both the world as a whole and a specific episode of violence of the sort that ensures the ongoing creation of ruin by acts of human will. I have suggested that the carefully delineated process of rising allows the reader an opportunity to think anew about the moral force of looking things over. This is not Lyotard's sudden sublime that leaves nothing to say, discussed in Chapter 1. It is more akin to what Kant described the year before the publication of Volney's *Ruins*, an experience characterized by a temporal dilation and by affective changes that are not always credited in the literature. It is

> a pleasure that arises only indirectly, being generated, namely, by the feeling of a momentary inhibition of the vital powers and the immediately following and all the more powerful outpouring of them; hence as an emotion it seems to be not play but something serious in the activity of the imagination. Hence it is also incompatible with charms, and, since the mind is not merely attracted by the object, but is also always reciprocally repelled by it, the satisfaction in the sublime does not so much contain a positive pleasure as it does admiration or respect, i.e., it deserves to be called negative pleasure.[35]

Negative pleasure: like that felt by a sick eagle looking at the sky, perhaps. What the traveler is shown once his eyes are adjusted so that they can deal with the challenge of distance is the entire world and its religious conflicts. Indeed, the balance of the book is a long and learned account of the variety of irreconcilable beliefs driving the religions of the world, as well as a subtle anthropological account of the rise of religion itself—followed by a fantasy of an enlightened new harmonization of all the faiths by a divinely appointed, absolutely rational legislator. But, as I have tried to suggest, the account of the difficulties entailed in the simple act of rising for a view is among the most interesting elements in this extraordinarily interesting text.

It has become a well-established convention to identify the failings of the kinds of aspirations embodied in the genie—aspirations for the long view, for perspective, even for rational reflection arriving at a resolution through the establishment of common aims or values.[36] And yet, as I have been trying to suggest, Volney's approach makes the relationship between the process of destruction, reconstruction, and new ruins available for a kind of reflection that may yield new insights. This is in part because the text is quite clear, not to say hyperbolic, in its embrace of the distinctions to be drawn between flawed human activities and the higher project of rationalization that the text identifies with a quality that is their opposite, the divine:

> Sovereign and invisible Power of the Universe! mysterious mover of nature! universal soul of beings! thou who art unknown, yet revered by mortals under so many names; being incomprehensible and infinite; God, who in the immensity of the heavens directest the movement of worlds, and peoplest the abyss of space with millions of suns.

This invocation by the traveler is designed to draw a contrast between the sublime knowledge and control that appertains to the divine, and the abject human condition:

> Say, what do these human insects, which my sight hath already lost on the earth, appear in thy eye? To thee who art guiding stars in their orbits, what are those wormlings writhing themselves in the dust? Of what import to thy immensity, their distinctions of parties and sects? And, of what concern the subtleties with which their folly torments itself? (105)

The viewpoint of the deity as imagined by the human speaker is liable to put in perspective—in the sense of minimizing—human action (to confound people with wormlings writhing in the dust and insects). But this is, of course, the flawed human perspective on perspective. If the deity were indifferent, the traveler would have been left wallowing in his confused misery on the hill overlooking the city.

The actual representation of military crisis within the text is designed to bring out the impossibility of arriving at a single scale that combines knowledge of the whole and of the detail.[37] Its play of distance and intimacy emphasizes not human actions taking on the disgusting undifferentiated quality of the writhing of worms but the inevitable limitations of human perception. I will quote the passage at length in order to illustrate the necessity of constant motion—and attendant changes in focus—of the perceiving eye at this moment of current conflict that so preoccupies Volney. The traveler has just had a lecture on the cycles of development and social decay that lead to the rise and fall of states in general (63–92) when a specific instance catches his eye—and every ellipsis in the following passage is in the original, indications of pauses to think or to take another view:

> I kept my eyes fixed on Asia, suddenly in the north, on the shores of the Black Sea, and in the fields of the Crimea, clouds of smoke and flame attracted my attention: they appeared to rise at the same time from all parts of the peninsula, and passing by the Isthmus into the continent, they ran, as if driven by a westerly wind, along the oozy lake of Arof, and were spent in the grassy plains of Cuban: and following more attentively the course of these clouds, I observed that they were preceded or followed by swarms of moving creatures, which, like ants or grasshoppers, disturbed by the foot of a passenger, agitated themselves with vivacity. Sometimes these swarms appeared to drive in collision against each other; and numbers, after the concussion, remained motionless. . . . While disquieted at this spectacle I strained my sight to distinguish the objects:—Do you see, said the Genius, those flames which spread over the earth, and do you comprehend their causes and effects?—O Genius! I answered, I see those columns of flame and smoke, and something like insects which accompany them: but when scarcely I can distinguish the great masses of cities and monuments, how should I discover such little creatures? I can just discover that these insects mimic battles; for they advance, retreat, rush together, pursue:—This, said the Genius, is no mimicry, these are real battles.—And what, said I, are those mad animalcula which destroy one another? beings of a day! will they not perish soon enough? . . . . Then the Genius, again touching my sight and hearing, Look, said he, and listen!—Immediately directing my sight toward the same objects: Ah! wretches, cried I, pierced with grief, these columns of flame; these insects; oh! Genius, they are men! these are the ravages of war. . . . These torrents of flame rise from towns and villages! I see the squadrons who kindle them, and spread with drawn swords over the fields!—Before them move the crowds of old men, women, and children, fugitive and desolate. I perceive other horsemen, who, with shouldered lances, accompany and guide them. I even recognise them to be Tartars, by their

> led horses, their kalpacks, and tufts of hair. And, doubtless those who pursue, in triangular hats and green uniform, are Muscovites. . . . Ah! I now comprehend; a war is kindled between the empire of the Czars, and that of the Sultans. Not yet, replied the Genius; this is only a preliminary. These Tartars have been, and yet would be, troublesome neighbours. The Muscovites are driving them off, finding their country would be a convenient extension of their own limits; and as a prelude to another revolution the throne of the Guerais is destroyed.
>
> In fact, I saw the Russian standards floating over the Crimea, and soon after waving on the Euxine. . . . But the empire of the Musulmen was moved at the cry of the flying Tartars. They are driving off our brethren, cried the children of Mahomet: they are outraging the people of the prophet! infidels occupy a consecrated land, and profane the temples of Islamism. Let us arm; let us rush to combat, to avenge the glory of God and our own cause. And a general movement of war took place in both empires; in every part they assembled armed men; provisions, stores, and all the murderous apparatus of battle was displayed; and the temples of both nations, besieged by an immense people, presented a spectacle which fixed my attention. (95–97; ellipses in the original)

The fantasy of a full view that the text offers is premised on a mobile optic that can get close enough to recognize breeds of horses and styles of hair but can pull back to show the movements of troops and displaced people. The hesitations and recalibrations that punctuate the passage, as I have suggested, need to be read as indicating the attempt to look again, to distinguish through a more considered view. The promise of a full insight to be gained from achieving a specific point of view is not what the passage illustrates, anymore than it represents an instance of sublime paralysis. On the contrary, Volney's elaborate set piece demonstrates the need for a shifting optic the movements of which are directed by reason and sympathy.

The articulation of the individual with history will consistently tend toward the sublime, both when that phenomenon is provoked by an overwhelming quantity (of time, of individuals, of broken things) that challenges the faculties of the mind through its sheer amount and when it is provoked by a sense of brutality, cruelty, or indifference that challenges the ethical faculties as much as those of perception. The pressure of history, brought to mind by reflection on the ruins of the past, interpellates the self as agent and object: as potential destroyer and as likely to be currently living in what past example suggests will one day be a ruin. The Enlightenment divinity that Volney imagines as distanced witness to the carnage of human history stands in contrast to the human experience of knowledge, which is always partial in several senses: unable to see fully but also liable to find itself everywhere in what it witnesses; to identify, in ways the divine cannot, as agent of destruction, as victim, as mere witness, or—most likely—as an unstable combination of the three.

It is humbling to reflect that Wood and Dawkins, with their small library of classical texts and biblical sources, like Volney, recognize in Palmyra not a lost provincial capital of interest solely as it articulates with the history of Rome but a thriving center of trade between China, India, and the West directly relevant to their own day.[38] If my aim in this chapter had been to advance a new analysis of particular acts of violence when viewed from a height, I might have highlighted the ways in which the distant view would allow us to see Palmyra and Bamiyan as related sites, not simply because they have both recently been damaged by religious extremists but as important stops on the transit network we call the Silk Road, which for millennia linked East and West. Like the Mediterranean, which some in Europe see as a barrier to the free flow of migrants to its shores but which refugees and migrants identify as the route from a dire present to a new future, the Silk Road marks inescapable connection as a historical fact and an ongoing possibility.[39]

• • •

While I have emphasized the limited ethical value of the sublime, the way we may want to read the rising up involved in that phenomenon as insufficient, as more symptomatic than analytic, as presenting a provocation to begin thought rather than an arrival at any insight, the moral life of the concept of the threat to antiquity itself calls out for further reflection. For millennia objects were destroyed—as they continue to be destroyed today—with not a tremor felt in the organs regulating the ethical sensibilities. The cause of damage might be practical or ideological, but the result was the same. Ancient statues have regularly been burned for lime in order to make mortar. From Rome to Tenochtitlán, when new temples were built on foundations established for earlier faiths, the remains of the superseded religion were discarded with little ceremony, or fragments from what the victors destroyed were adapted to a new use. While reuse itself and the attitudes attending it might in some cases be ways of signaling the hegemony of a new cultural dispensation, the lines linking power and remains are not always clear or straight. In England, for instance, ancient abbeys that had dominated the social and cultural lives of entire regions for centuries were often allowed to molder, the power they once housed forgotten, their arches eventually providing a limited shelter for destitute communities. But sometimes these properties found new life as the seats of agents of secular power, distinguished possessors whose families might demolish or embellish the earlier structure over the centuries following the vagaries of taste, whether for novelty or nostalgia.

It is the oblivion that is the common fate of most things that makes it so moving to discover old columns or capitals incorporated in the temples of new religions, or the head of a sacred figure once discarded in an old latrine, a Mithraeum awaiting worshippers who will never return under the cellar of an ancient church. Given all the indifference that creates the conditions for our nostalgia, it behooves the student of culture to put some pressure on the history of responsiveness to broken old things, including on the emergence of a sense of responsibility for care and of blame for damage. As I hope to demonstrate in the next chapter, the topic will bring us back to twentieth- and twenty-first-century reflections on judgment and fear, but inevitably the fundamental formulations will be found to have their sources in the very period in which Volney was writing. How other people's broken things may come to matter for us is a question with a relatively short history, one that takes the form we know it to have between the earliest modern accounts of the concept of vandalism and the most prescient attempts to understand the modern cult of ruins.

3

TERROR AND JUDGMENT / DATING THE RUINS

(Ruskin with Volney, Grégoire with Riegl)

Terror and Judgment

Benjamin's evocation of the angel of history is a reminder that while religion has provided important figures by which culture has structured history, the cultural power of divinity involves a two-way traffic. If belief in a deity requires faith in a higher power's ability to intervene in the world, to make history or end it, it is also the case that the human experience of damage keeps calling out for a perspective that will organize the significance of so much pain or disappointment. Visions of a final judgment are evidently motivated by a desire to stop history in order to give it a just shape, one tolerable for human sensibilities that so seldom encounter fully satisfactory outcomes in the world. Hence the poignancy of Benjamin's reconfiguration of an angel as powerless witness in "On the Concept of History." Volney's *Ruins*, by comparison, demonstrates how secularizing the tradition utterly changes its meaning: the revelation without apocalypse at the heart of that text amounts to a clear-eyed insistence that the end of civilizations is not, in fact, the end of the world.

Secularization inevitably peels apart the various elements of the apocalypse.[1] What one is experiencing at a given moment may or may not be understood as a judgment, but it's not likely to be the last one. Benjamin's angel hovers between the suggestion of faith in an ultimate redemption and the despair Benjamin reads into a gaze combining the perception of all that needs to be redeemed along with a dismayed/dismaying sense of inadequacy for the task (especially given those winds blowing the angel into an uncertain future).

Judging, knowing, and even ending are amalgamated in this figure that binds each of its constituent elements in frustration, the desire for divine resolution exacerbated by the memory of endless disappointments. The angel of history is in this sense the manifestation of a particularly modern sensation compounding judgment with fear, a blend that is probably bound to make itself felt at the juncture where the recognition of a dreadful past becomes the apprehension of a dangerous future (see fig. 1.2).

I have discussed in Chapter 1 Ruskin's insistence on the inescapable fact of human responsibility for the creation of ruins. The great moralist is always alive to the meaning of broken things, hence his brilliant analysis of the print Joseph Mallord William Turner produced as the frontispiece for the *Liber Studiorum*, the collection of prints the artist brought out between 1807 and 1819. And analysis is called for, as that work makes a puzzling introduction to a set of engraved landscapes (see fig. 3.1). Nothing like nature, British or otherwise, the plate illustrates an impossible location with, improbably enough, a painted classical landscape hanging at its center, as though someone had taken the trouble to decorate a ruin or as though a long process of damage and decay had nevertheless left intact an oil painting on the wall of a ruined building. The scene in which the painting hangs is itself flamboyantly incoherent, bringing together too many things at once: what seems to be a Gothic wall decorated with blind arches and accompanied by the debris of fractured classical elements is enlivened by the presence of various animals and fish and some bits of vegetation. The light that falls in the foreground suggests an opening to the outside behind the viewer and to the side, perhaps the breach in the structure that affords us this sight of the canvas. In fact, the location, with its flora and fauna (probably meant to evoke various genres of painting, including still life) gives the impression of being inside and outside at the same time—as ruins often do. But the fictive space of the print and its blocked-off view are formally rationalized and given an opening—and even another source of light—by the painting. In a brightly lit classical landscape at the center of all that historical detritus from later eras than the one represented (though all prior to the emergence of oil painting), the informed viewer can just make out the ruins of Tyre on a hill. In the foreground Europa is carried off by Zeus in the form of a bull while her alarmed companions marvel on the strand (fig. 3.2).

Reflections on agency, responsibility, and judgment may well come together at the contemplation of ruins, along with the question of how we see ourselves articulating with history. Writing in the final volume of *Modern Painters* in

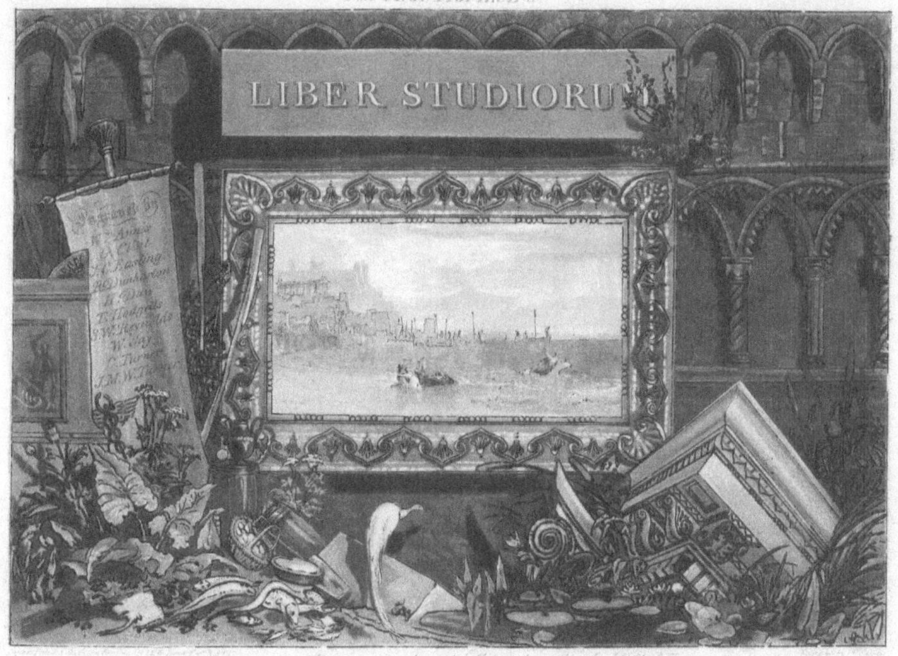

FIGURE 3.1. Frontispiece of Joseph Mallord William Turner, *Liber Studiorum* (1812). Metropolitan Museum, New York, Harris Brisbane Dick Fund, 1928.

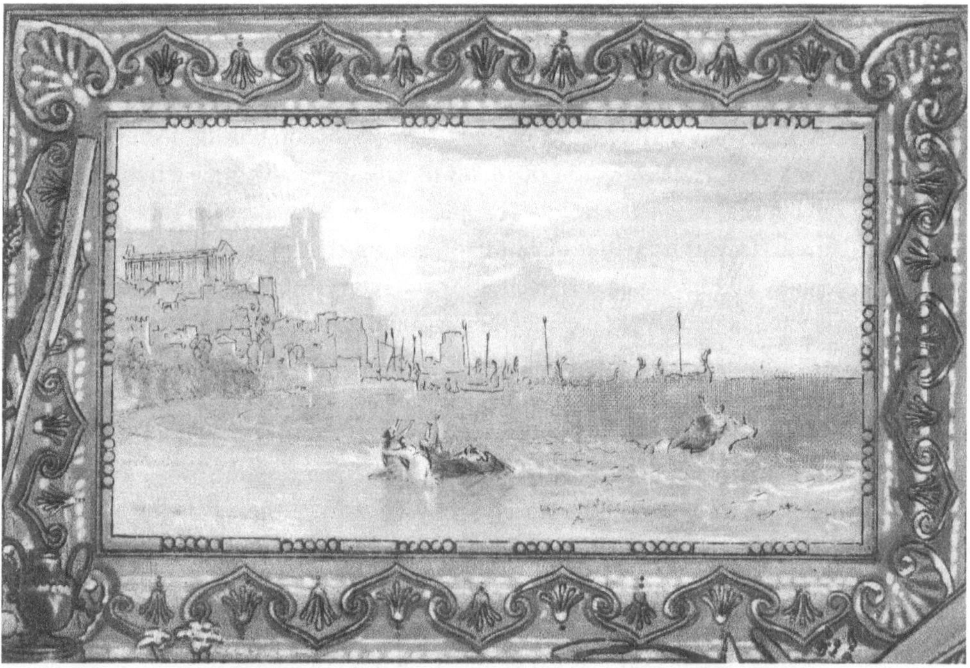

FIGURE 3.2. Frontispiece of Joseph Mallord William Turner, *The Rape of Europa*, *Liber Studiorum*, detail. Metropolitan Museum, New York, Harris Brisbane Dick Fund, 1928.

1860, Ruskin addresses the obvious question: Why would Turner place this classical scene at the center of his frontispiece to a collection of engravings of largely British landscapes, and why set the image in a ruined environment? The critic's answer is characteristically emphatic: "The meaning of the entire book," he writes, "was symbolized in the frontispiece, which he engraved with his own hand: Tyre at sunset, with the Rape of Europa, indicating the symbolism of the decay of Europe by that of Tyre, its beauty passing away into terror and judgment."[2] Ruskin's apparent hyperbole is given support by the evocative incongruities of the piece: what else can the frontispiece be but a symbol, as it certainly is not an indication of the subjects to follow in the portfolio of prints?[3]

Tyre is an ancient city in what is now Lebanon; like Palmyra, from which it is not distant—fifty leagues away, Wood and Dawkins tell us—it is part of that Mediterranean region which, while never quite Europe, is constantly impinging on Europe's identity. And it had a presence in nineteenth-century culture that it lacks today as one of those proud cities that is violently destroyed in the Old Testament. Terror and judgment are overdetermined in Ruskin's reading, being both historical facts and conditions to be anticipated in the future. It is an indication of the density of his treatment of these themes that they open out in two directions. From the snarl of mythic time captured in the image, Ruskin reaches backward into the past of the city of Tyre and its conquest by Nebuchadnezzar and again by Alexander the Great, historic events understood to point further back in time as realizations of Old Testament prophecy, which Ruskin sees here (as he does in *Stones of Venice*) as continuing its mission by offering a salutary warning to Britain, the nineteenth century's great trading nation. But the complex network of temporality represented by the ruins of Tyre (current damage indicative of past injuries manifesting the accuracy of earlier prophesy and its ongoing relevance for the future) is relatively simple when compared to the way the narrative of the painting projects at once forward into the future as well as further back in time, to the consummation about to take place between a god in the shape of a bull and a Phoenician princess.

"Since the first dominion of men was asserted over the ocean," Ruskin had written in ringing tones, and quoting Ezekiel, at the opening of the first volume of *Stones of Venice* (1853) nearly ten years earlier, "three thrones, of mark beyond all others, have been set upon its sands: the thrones of Tyre, Venice, and England." Venice and Tyre are constant warnings for England, though only fragments from the great days of the former remain, and the lesson of the latter is not heeded, precisely because of the extent of its ruination:

> The exaltation, the sin, and the punishment of Tyre have been recorded for us, in perhaps the most touching words ever uttered by the Prophets of Israel against the cities of the stranger. But we read them as a lovely song; and close our ears to the sternness of their warning: for the very depth of the Fall of Tyre has blinded us to its reality, and we forget, as we watch the bleaching of the rocks between the sunshine and the sea, that they were once "as in Eden, the garden of God."

If Tyre is the forgotten ruin in whose oblivion we might discover a meaning close to the one learned from the loss of Eden, Venice—the city that is the subject of the work as a whole—has a more dynamic shape, being a spectral beauty vulnerably flickering on the beach, like Europa before the bull, perhaps, or like some strange Aphrodite rising from the foam, a memory of beauty and violence:

> Her successor, like her in perfection of beauty, though less in endurance of dominion, is still left for our beholding in the final period of her decline: a ghost upon the sands of the sea, so weak—so quiet,—so bereft of all but her loveliness, that we might well doubt, as we watched her faint reflection in the mirage of the lagoon, which was the City, and which the Shadow. (9:17)[4]

Beauty passing away into terror *and* judgment. It can seem that we know the source of fear likely to be felt by a young woman captured by an incontinent deity who has adopted the form of a bull, but Ruskin evidently has in mind something more than personal, something suggested in the ruins overlooking the landscape in which Europa and the bull are only small figures. Every legend of the loves of the gods is a story about the articulation of the human with the divine—of the limited and the contingent with its opposite. The lusts of the gods are in that sense projections of human desires, as are the offspring of these impossible unions who maintain one foot in the vulnerable realm inhabited by humankind and another outside its vicissitudes. The children produced by the union of Europa and Zeus were Minos and Rhadamanthus, Ruskin remembers, judges of the dead in classical antiquity.

Judgment is the name for a fate deserved or earned in the human sphere. Deities are seldom subject to its rigors, and certainly Zeus is not. And so, the terror at issue is that implicit in the *human* memory of violence preserved within the ruin, the injuries that resulted in a destruction that is at once a memory and a prefiguration ("indicating the symbolism of the decay of Europe by that of Tyre"). And it bears saying that Ezekiel's prophesy is astonishingly concrete in its imagination of the violent destruction to be wreaked on Tyre by Nebuchadnezzar, the conqueror of Jerusalem:

> He shall enter into thy gates, as men enter into a city wherein is made a breach. With the hoofs of his horses shall he tread down all thy streets: he shall slay thy people by the sword, and thy strong garrisons shall go down to the ground. And they shall make a spoil of thy riches, and make a prey of thy merchandise: and they shall break down thy walls, and destroy thy pleasant houses: and they shall lay thy stones and thy timber and thy dust in the midst of the water.[5]

Thy stones and thy timber and thy dust in the midst of the water. The image of Europa bound toward Crete and so approaching the moment of conception with the bestial divinity represents a fatal destiny combining in itself and its outcome beauty no less than terror. Judgment is written into the representation, but so is an articulation between East and West that is more immediate than the kind of easy analogy Volney's traveler makes when he reflects on the chance that France might share in the fate of Palmyra, or even the one that Ruskin himself proposes when he suggests that Britain might fail as Tyre did. The point here is not simply that London may come to be like the magnificent city that once stood at the heart of another storied trading empire but that the geographical movements of the myth captured in the print make visible continuities between West and East that are the open secret of the Mediterranean. It is the same secret written in the wake of informal flotillas of refugee ships floating through the same waters as I write. "Now shall the isles tremble in the day of thy fall," Ezekiel predicts, about the lesson of the fall of Tyre, "yea, the isles that *are* in the sea shall be troubled at thy departure" (26:18). At every turn the biblical text finds a lesson in terror and judgment that is not limited to the location in which it takes place.

Volney's traveler and his genie remain suspended in midair as the conflagration between Russians and Tartars in the Crimea develops below them, an event the author wisely understands as a religious struggle not liable to quick resolution even though its damage is immediate, and one that he associates with the ruination of Palmyra that first provoked his emotions. The play between ancient ruin and current judgment emerges with new force in Ruskin's text; the memory of decay is a goad for reflection and creative response rather than an encouragement for passive regret, for sublime paralysis. To emphasize largely *classical* remains, however, is to participate in a convention that of necessity adds an important set of displacements to the topic. After all, ruins are not only to be found on classical soil. They are everywhere in England, the concrete remains of a fundamental religious struggle the force of which Ruskin always recognized (hence the "old religion" of the cathedrals of which he speaks in 1857—see the previous chapter), and which colors at every turn the intellectual structures shaping later understandings of vestiges from the past.

The evidence of violence and subsequent decay encountered in the United Kingdom is often glossed over as so many instances of the picturesque or the Gothic. "Picturesque" is an interesting enough term for what it leaves out: looking like a picture, and so distanced from nature understood as an unstructured given condition and from history as an unresolved phenomenon. But I don't think we pause often enough on how odd the use of "Gothic" is in the British context. By the eighteenth century the understanding that this is a term meant to describe the aesthetically uncouth, along with the distinction from classical work on which that association is based, have all been well established. But the Black Sea is a long way from the British Isles, and wherever these mysterious tribes that bore the name "Gothic" wandered, they were never present in Britain.[6] The descriptor is, in that sense, merely figurative. But, though by the nineteenth century it has largely lost the opprobrium with which it was originally used to describe medieval architecture by those who found it contemptibly primitive, it inevitably suggests that classical antiquity might be a source for British culture in a way that makes more sense than nearly a thousand years of Catholicism. On its surface the implicit argument is about aesthetic values rather than history, the understood premise being that absent classical structures are a more worthy inspiration than models far more frequently encountered in the British Isles.

I am not trying to relitigate an argument between classical and medieval architecture that was current in the nineteenth century so much as to suggest that a few specialized scholars and interested parties aside, it would be no overstatement to say that the naturalization of the term "Gothic" in Britain is part of a thoroughgoing displacement of the memory of an extraordinary national trauma that we may date for convenience to the Act of Supremacy of 1534 that made Henry VIII the head of a church and led to the suppression of a Catholic people by their own political leadership, and ultimately to the destruction or forced abandonment of religious communities all over the island.[7] There are many good reasons to think of classical forms when we think of ruins. But on the British Isles those reasons themselves are evidences of an important historical denial that it is no part of Ruskin's project to support.

In *Material Inspirations*, I addressed the ways in which Ruskin's Turner, a city boy raised at the confluence of two epochal struggles, discovers a new kind of damage when he heads to the country for the first time. While Britain is in the midst of an apparently endless war with France, London is the site of a brutal, irresistible, conscienceless capitalism remaking early nineteenth-century Britain at an ongoing cost to the poor and vulnerable. Uncertain but clearly injurious social structures at home and new types of global military struggle abroad are twinned phenomena in Ruskin's telling. His attempt to explain in *Modern Painters* how a city-bred child grew up to be the nation's greatest painter of nature develops into a diagnosis of the cultural effects of injury. It is precisely what he learns in the city that allows Turner to create a movingly engaged form of landscape art that, as far as Ruskin is concerned, we do not understand when we do not recognize the losses that shape its lines. It is the painter's response to the various kinds of death with which he had grown up that gives the power to his work. Sketches Turner made on his epochal first trip to the north of England in 1797 return as finished drawings and then prints in the *Liber Studiorum*, bearing with them traces of the formation that shaped them. "Grave" means "serious," but it also always means "death" in Ruskin, as in his description of a ruined rectory in Yorkshire Turner encountered on the excursion to the country that was to determine his future work in landscape:[8]

> Beauty, and freedom, and peace; and yet another teacher, graver than these. Sound preaching at last here, in Kirkstall crypt, concerning fate and life. Here, where the dark pool reflects the chancel pillars, and the cattle lie in unhindered rest, the soft sunshine on their dappled bodies, instead of priests' vestments; their white furry hair ruffled a little, fitfully, by the evening wind, deep-scented from the meadow thyme. (*Modern Painters* V [7:384])

For Ruskin, this thyme-scented Gothic ruin is a particularly modern memory of death—of the modern death that gives Turner's art its meaning. The picturesque animal life the modern traveler discovers is no compensation for the losses entailed in making this religious structure a ruin, in banishing the priests and the religious community around them, in letting in the evening wind and the rain that pools darkly around the chancel pillars. Terror and judgment shine out of the ruined space of the frontispiece of the *Liber Studiorum* because, as far as Ruskin is concerned, those are the elements shaping the lines of the etchings in the collection as a whole.

Walking Backward: Agency and the Sublime Politics of History

I began my discussion of Palmyra in Chapter 1 by reflecting on the ways that language can make one feel that an argument, even a political claim, has been advanced whenever the relative positions of self and object of perception are established. I also suggested that the question of the way in which a figure in space interpellates the viewer is a complicated one, given our earthbound existence. A body in the air is either rising or falling, and its gaze may or may not link it to the space in which it is moving in the way our view does (Jesus evidently does not see the world we do at the moment of his transfiguration, to take one easy example). Volney's account of the ascents of his traveler presents the opportunity to imagine a forceful revision of the sublime—one that recognizes the current force of historic damage along with its sources in the past and therefore finds in the urgent crisis an opportunity to reflect that does not despair of judgment. Unlike Volney's garrulous genie and traveler, Benjamin's angel does not speak. He is all the more powerful in his mute symbolic role. And his movements are hardly revelatory (or they reveal only one big thing), caught in midair as he is, blown back by the pressure on his wings, which are driven like sails before the wind of history understood not as a chain of events available to reflection but as an overwhelming catastrophe. Benjamin describes a movement not of transcendence but of the barest survival, something like being thrown clear of the wreckage. Given that both of these figures are fantasies of fuller knowledge, of informed witness, Volney's genie may serve as a reminder that it is possible to imagine options other than wide-eyed, overwhelmed paralysis, or at least that the relationship between angel and wreckage could be more intimate than that suggested by the violent, irresistible wind that catches the angel's pinions and drags him into a futurity he cannot grasp except by witnessing the succeeding piles of debris left in the wake of history.

Always retrospective, always bereft of agency and of any responsibility beyond melancholy witnessing, Benjamin's angel of history is an excellent figure for the project of imagining the response of an informed but powerless victim. It is hardly what one would come up with if trying to visualize agency. It bears saying that the events that made the angel such an evocative figure postdate Benjamin's analysis.[9] The most important sources for modern reflections on despair come back to two historical phenomena directly associated with the close of the Second World War: the betrayals and disappointments that shaped the Holocaust, which came into clear focus at the end of the war and were processed in culture in subsequent years, and the inescapable dread of nuclear conflagration that accompanied the Cold War. The political despair of the period is an overdetermined emotion, shaped as it is by memories that at this point do not quite belong to many of us but that have been readily absorbed into the general culture, and by a fear that has haunted the world for decades, the inexorable logic of mutually assured destruction. The vision of wide-eyed victimhood of the Klee as read by Benjamin has the quality of a proleptic anticipation of disaster that is not free of fatalism. It is a structure Benjamin borrowed more than once from the Freud of *Beyond the Pleasure Principle* (1920), who first described the tendency, when damage cannot be forestalled, for its psychic pain to be mitigated by (the fantasy of) anticipation.[10] In spite of the name he gave it, it is the *prescience* of the shock registered by Benjamin's angel that is at the heart of the long-lasting power of a figure that is at once historical—in the sense of being part of a text written by someone in the course of experiencing the very political damage that shaped the vision—and felt to be prophetic.[11]

"Is the angel an avatar of the historian, of the historian's divine other, or of history itself?" Paul Saint-Amour asks in his compelling study of the complex kinds of proleptic dread shaping culture in relation to the threat of war, in the lead-up to his discussion of the uses of the figure in recent critical writings. "In witnessing a catastrophe it cannot stay to redeem, does the angel figure a fruitlessly passive relationship to historical loss—or a vigilant refusal to let loss be chalked up to the cost of progress? Is the angel's helplessness in the storm of progress epitomized by its backwardness or alleviated by it?" Ultimately Saint-Amour recovers the political value of the figure of the angel with the suggestion that it is not the historian alone but all of us who are being blown into a dreadful future—a future shaped by the dread the angel casts ahead of itself (316). This is a bold solution, both original and of a piece with a contemporary political ethics in which acknowledgment of participation in a condition has come to be recognized as a kind of moral stance. As in Heather Love's work, which Saint-Amour cites and whose identification of the experience of temporal dislocation and out-of-placedness with queer desire may allow us to discover a beginning of politics, not its end, this is a recovery that follows from seeing oneself as the troubled figure of the witnessing angel fated to always gaze at what came before, unable to turn and face that toward which it moves or to change the trajectory on which the past has launched it.

As I suggested in my discussion of recent uses of the sublime in Chapter 2, however, it is entirely possible to read the figure as one of hopeless, passive fatalism, as Wendy Brown does in an important piece to which both Love and Saint-Amour are responding. Brown's subject is a progressive politics stripped of the hope of progress and so limited to actions that amount to little more than anguished retrospection:

> A Left that has become more attached to its impossibility than to its potential fruitfulness, a Left that is most at home dwelling not in hopefulness but in its own marginality and failure, a Left that is thus caught in a structure of melancholic attachment to a certain strain of its own dead past, whose spirit is ghostly, whose structure of desire is backward looking and punishing.[12]

Love's response to the angel is part of her nuanced attempt to recover the power of feeling backward as more than an overwhelming evocation of despair. "Benjamin suggests," Love writes, "that taking the past seriously means being hurt by it. He is damaged both by the horrible spectacle of the past and by the outrage of leaving it behind." This doubled injury, which in both cases is, paradoxically, not at all about experiences we can imagine happening to the angel but about his role as witness to the experiences of others, makes the angel a challenging emblematic figure for those committed to seeking change:

> The angel of history has become a key figure in recent work on loss and the politics of memory, trauma, and history. In contemporary criticism, Benjamin's sacrificial witness functions as something like an ethical ideal for the historian and the critic. Yet this figure poses difficulties for anyone thinking about how to effect political change. What are we to do with this tattered, passive figure, so clearly unfit for the rigors of the protest march, not to mention the battlefield? The question is how to imagine this melancholic figure as the agent of any recognizable form of activism. At the heart of the ambivalence about the angel of history is a key paradox of political life. Although historical losses instill in us a desire for change, they also can unfit us for the activity of making change.[13]

Love's paradoxical project is to acknowledge the despair written into the figure of the angel of history but to move on to action—or at least activism. The key issues at stake are, on the one hand, the relationship of inevitability, progress, and revolution, and, on the other, the place of imagination, belief, and dreams in relation to that apparently more political trio: "Brown asks a series of questions about how to imagine the future after the breakdown of historical master narratives," notes Love, in the course of an argument that recognizes the translation of Benjamin's angel into a contemporary avatar of limitless despair that it could not have been for the essayist (who, after all—as the rest of the piece makes clear—is still working within a narrative that is intended to conclude with socialist change). "She considers our feelings about the future when we no longer believe in the inevitability of historical progress and when our dreams for a global revolution have died" (149). Love's evocative account of Brown demonstrates how fully the angel of history has itself become a relic from a lost past, repurposed in a new dispensation. Both critics agree so far in their use of Benjamin. It is in the acknowledgment of the place of affect in relation to revolutionary actions that the force of Love's political argument lies. Can disappointment and melancholy be the beginning of political action rather than the mark of its end? Love's adjectives are important: *historical* progress, *global* revolution. The loss that shapes the disappointment is the disappearance of a clear articulation between history and progress understood as both global and inevitable. It is the shock waves set off at the collapse of this relationship that power the angel of history.

"Given the scenes of destruction at our backs," Love writes, "queers feel compelled to keep moving on toward a brighter future. At the same time, the history of queer experience has made this resolute orientation toward the future difficult to sustain" (162). The compulsion to keep moving toward a brighter future is, of course, not reserved for one group; it has been the operating assumption of several important strands in culture since the Enlightenment that such a movement is not just possible but inevitable (hence the metaphor of growing illumination written into the term). It is this feeling disguised as a principle that makes the angel of history our particular nightmare. What if the future to which we are heading is not brighter? What if our desire to get there is itself destructive? We feel compelled to keep leaving scenes of destruction behind us in two ways: we move past them, and we abandon them to their fate. The resolute orientation toward the future is an absolute necessity for modernity at the level of the individual and of the culture, and so when we look back we are paralyzed by the shocked experience that we cannot help but recognize but that we cannot pause to acknowledge while continuing the forward progress that keeps driving us.

What does Ruskin say? "You talk of the scythe of Time, and the tooth of Time: I tell you, Time is scytheless and toothless; it is we who gnaw like the worm—we who smite like the scythe. It is ourselves who abolish—ourselves who consume: we are the mildew, and the flame." Or, as Volney's genie puts it, speaking in the third person about all of us: "The germ of his calamities is not planted in the heavens on high; it is beside him on the earth; it is not hidden in the bosom of God; it dwells within himself, he bears it in his own heart."[14] Looking back at the record of human destruction, at the open violence of the flash of the scythe, at the quiet damage of verminous toothless mouthings that consume the things we leave behind, we regret our inability to repair the past even as we fear that our onward flight will entail more injuries to witness—because we will be causing them.

For Saint-Amour, Benjamin raises the question of "how one faces in time." "Conventional historicists," he notes about Benjamin's argument, "may immerse themselves all they like in the past but always face that past's future—either their own present or the future that it self-flatteringly projects—and ratify its triumphalist view of history. The historical materialist . . . refus[es] to countenance a future imagined by the rulers as consummating their aims, vindicating their acts, ratifying their laws" (21). While this is indeed an accurate summary of Benjamin's argument in 1940, it does not account fully for the power of Benjamin's formulation today—at a time when any conventional historicists that were around in 1940 certainly are no longer conventional now—or around. Saint-Amour finds reasons for the ongoing influence of Benjamin's analysis by reference to the conditions that Benjamin anticipated, most notably the multiple kinds of dread that proliferated after the end of the Second World War. It would be hard to do better than Saint-Amour's treatment of the temporal shifts and anticipations entailed in modern anxiety. Still, it will be useful to put a bit of pressure on his formulations. How do we feel when our problem is not our rulers but our hopes? What do we do when it is not "conventional historicists" that trouble us but the history that hurts us and which we cannot escape? The postwar apotheosis of the angel of history takes on a different character when put into relation with superannuated notions of authority, progress, and history that exist in our current political and intellectual lives more as troublesome ghosts (the phenomenon Love illuminates so vibrantly at the affective level) than as fully embodied and effective elements in culture. The failures that paralyze the angel at this point in time are only related to those that motivated

Benjamin insofar as they intersect with more recent preoccupations, notably agency, responsibility, blame, and above all that painful term, complicity.

On June 14, 1940, the Germans entered Paris, and from that point until 1944 the French state largely collaborated with the Nazis, with varying degrees of enthusiasm. It was in September of the year German troops took the capital of the nineteenth century that Walter Benjamin committed suicide at the border with Spain. The defeat, the complicity of nations, and the suicidal despair of the refugee: surely the angel of history is not so much prescient as accurate about the world in which it came into being. But the future has transformed its awful immediacy into prophecy.

Saint-Amour's reference to rulers is striking, as at the heart of the question of historical damage we keep finding the vexed problem of modern sovereignty. Who *are* the rulers we imagine ourselves resisting as angels of history (or at least gazing at in stunned horror), and how does our compromised resistance relate to their dominance? The Holocaust is, of course, the most immediately compelling historical source for the power of the image Benjamin created in the midst of catastrophe, especially as it has been conventional to mean by that term a disaster as unparalleled as it is (or should be?) unrepeatable. "Never again!" people say, as though it had never happened before and is only likely to happen again if it happens the exact same way. "Never again," they say, as though emphasizing the unique nature of a crime will make it not happen again, as if the same crime *were* ever repeated. But the power of Benjamin's image was augmented by the two nuclear devices exploded over cities in Japan, in themselves causing a level of injury requiring a response ("Never again") and also opening up the fearful prospect—lived as a dreadful near-certainty—that there would indeed and inevitably be repeat occasions for that level of damage. The nuclear standoff that emerged at the end of the war became the unthinkable future toward which the angel was being hurled. Its shocked eyes appeared to take in one catastrophe that was only possible because of the development of science beyond Promethean limits and another that was understood to indicate the moral limits of civilization more generally. Dread and a fear that reason was either not enough or in itself complicit with cruel violence became unavoidable in progressive postwar thought.[15]

As the Cold War wound down, we found ourselves in the midst of the inchoate new military project unleashed following the violence of September 11, 2001, itself another lingering blow to the hopes of modernity, as sophisticated technological structures that had been identified with the promise of a new liberation of individual aspirations were used by a movement self-consciously rejecting those aspirations. The smooth international flow of travelers and of money through ever more seamless networks, the internet itself—still at that point possessed of a certain utopian glamor: so many systems that had promised so much could also deliver, it turned out, a great deal that was to be feared. The burden of nuclear dread that had begun to recede—in spite of the continued existence and modernization of vast nuclear arsenals—found a new life, transmuted into the far more uneven preoccupation with the sudden violent acts interrupting civilian life that we call acts of terror or even terror*ism* (the imagination of a concept sharpening our dread). Clearly the prospect of an apocalyptic nuclear conflagration followed by a nuclear winter matched very poorly with the likely damage attendant on even the most extraordinary act of terror. For this reason, perhaps, culture and politics both had to make the effort to bring these sources of alarm together, so that the prospect of a dirty bomb that would release radioactivity on large population centers entered the popular culture with remarkable speed, along with a proliferation of film and television plots in which terrorist acts lost their typically local and limited character and became apocalyptic threats. Nuclear bombs about to be set off, massive releases of toxins into water or air: heroes were faced with all kinds of novel threats that had the same emotional shape, and much of the same fictional signature as the nuclear anxiety of an earlier period. But it was not in culture alone that the continuity was marked. Military commitments and expenditures at risk as the Cold War vanished were newly bolstered in response to the threat of terrorism, which also was seen to require old solutions to ostensibly new problems—so that the terrorist acts of 9/11 resulted in such roundabout responses as the occupation of Iraq and the war in Afghanistan, as well as the growing militarization of local police forces in the United States.

But incoherent and failed military adventures were not the most striking manifestation of the ways in which the war on terror came to support structures in jeopardy when the Soviet Union vanished as a rival. The political and legal system that had ostensibly been set up in response to the fears of nuclear Armageddon was also saved by terrorism. Proponents of the idea that the best way to deal with likely emergencies was to be prepared to act without undue deliberation were given new arguments by the war on terror. No time for trials, no time for due process, no time for the Bill of Rights; it's an emergency! In this context, it may not be going too far to suggest that to acquiesce in the belief that being overwhelmed by history eventuates in a sublime experience bound to paralyze thought is not to resist but to be in agreement with a fundamental tenet of Cold War ideology, the insistence that there is no time to think in a dangerous situation.

The anticipation of panic as a way to proleptically disarm reflection is a characteristic of the period after 9/11. The phenomenon was widespread, but we might cite just one astonishingly clear manifestation of the relationship between fictional dread and military urgency distorting legal thinking: the evocation of the television show *24* by the noted American jurist Antonin Scalia. The conceit of *24* was written into the show's title, as it was a fiction in which the entire adventure was understood to take place in the course of a single day. "The longest day of my life," declared the protagonist at the outset of each episode, making length an emotional experience, not a measure of time; making it a personal matter, not a shared one—though, of course that is what each episode became for enthralled viewers (especially as the political plot was immediately overlaid with a personal motivation when the protagonist's daughter was kidnapped). As each episode notionally took the same amount of time in the life of viewers as in the life of the characters, their stresses were more likely to become the viewers' own, their split-second judgments everyone's.

Produced by Fox, the network that assumed such a central role in managing and guiding the political rage and fear that came to the fore in the years after 9/11, *24* was clearly designed as a site at which the culture could process its own relationship to threat and brutality. Living through the fictional urgency it relayed so effectively produced the sense that accepting injury to others was not only a need but something close to a principle. This is the context in which Antonin Scalia could imagine it made sense to cite a television show in order to illustrate both the need for immediate action and the inevitability of the social rejection of the rule of law (understood as promoting intolerable hesitations in the face of fear). Given the justice's role on the Supreme Court of the United States, we have to understand his words as not only addressing but instantiating, or at least endorsing, the situation they describe. Here is the much-reported moment in the discussion in which the justice participated, which is only one of the times Scalia felt moved to cite the program:

> The conservative jurist stuck up for Agent Bauer, arguing that fictional or not, federal agents require latitude in times of great crisis. "Jack Bauer saved Los Angeles. . . . He saved hundreds of thousands of lives," Judge Scalia said. Then,

> recalling Season 2, where the agent's rough interrogation tactics saved California from a terrorist nuke, the Supreme Court judge etched a line in the sand.
>
> "Are you going to convict Jack Bauer?" Judge Scalia challenged his fellow judges. "Say that criminal law is against him? 'You have the right to a jury trial?' Is any jury going to convict Jack Bauer? I don't think so.
>
> "So the question is really whether we believe in these absolutes. And ought we believe in these absolutes."[16]

Of course, the realism of the fiction the justice celebrated was its greatest illusion. Real injury was what it never represented, any more than the actual consequences of complex moral decisions. And the elaborate facticity of a television show serves to illustrate an important part of Elaine Scarry's thesis, that we have plenty of time to think about what to do in an emergency. That is, in fact, what Antonin Scalia himself was doing. It is just that he was planning on not thinking, and encouraging others to do the same. When the "you" in his instance shifts unstably between the criminal defendant (someone who has a right to a trial) and the member of the jury who will not convict because he agrees about how one needs to act in a state of emergency, Justice Scalia is endorsing the generalized sense of dread along with the complicity that that feeling is designed to create. Perhaps it would be more accurate to say that Justice Scalia creates the supplement the fiction calls for—both the sense of lived urgency and the attendant claim for moral abdication disguised as realism.

In response to the ways in which a society may not just abdicate its political power and ethical responsibilities but abjure its very knowledge of the real-world dangers presented by such abdications, Elaine Scarry proposes a preposterous thought experiment or counterfactual: an alternative reality wherein everyone in a nation that had acquired the technological wherewithal to destroy millions of people by unleashing the power of nuclear weapons would suddenly find themselves only able to walk backward. "The sustained discomfort of walking backwards would surely trouble them on their own behalf," she proposes, before turning to the element in the figure that makes it more than fanciful or even metaphoric. "It would almost as surely prompt them to worry about the enormity of the far heavier price that some unseen population might eventually pay for the mysterious change."[17] This population moving blindly into the future they are creating at every step troubles conventional ideas of progress in a far more bathetic mode than Benjamin's angel of history does, though both angel and public are bound toward a future they cannot face, for all that they may appear to be desperately alert. The difference in Scarry's figure is that it is intended to express a hope that the impaired vision of so many political subjects might mitigate another blindness—might bring to the mind's eye "the unseen population" that pays the cost for things we allow to happen. Scarry is committed to the idea that it is in fact possible to think in an emergency, which in her account makes our abdication of the processes of deliberation something less than—and worse than—a practical necessity.

I find Scarry's arguments on this head deeply compelling, but the main interest to me here resides in the fundamental assumption of her project, that the identification of urgency can lead to an abdication of the processes of thought. The awkward, contradictory, unsatisfactory, compromised, compromising, committed, confused attempt to put oneself in relation to a world toward which one has responsibility and in which one has the agency—what we call thinking—stands on the other side of the permanently alarmed but fundamentally quiescent response to modern conditions Scarry has brought to our attention in relation to the militarization of our decision-making processes during the Cold War. Scarry writes of "the seduction to stop thinking," and certainly when thought itself brings no relief, when it is felt to perhaps even be part of the problem, it makes sense to find the alternatives seductive.

Terror *and* judgment are what Ruskin saw in the image of Tyre destroyed, in the prospect of Europa just prior to conception. While we might well have reason to fear the judgment of a deity as vengeful as the one who rampages through the Old Testament, scattering misery and destruction with an abandon we are not allowed to call reckless because it is a judgment we call divine, the intersection of panic and rational evaluation in the human sphere is a more pressing concern. On the one hand, terror may make us incapable of judgment, paralyzing the very faculties we depend on to make sense of the world, to act as we should. On the other, we may fear that judgment itself may be allied to terror. The political project of terrorism is yet another content that the overriding fear that characterizes modern culture accommodates with dismaying ease. In provoking real fear of events that are almost certain not to happen, terrorism participates in that particularly modern complex linking knowledge and dread in the heart of the fearful citizen.

From the perspective of the perpetrator, terror brings attention to the spaces in which the nation is being active, demanding a response from a metropolis that lives in willful ignorance, avoiding acknowledgment, a sense of agency, responsibility. The helpless fear that may be generated by the actions of the terrorist is not as novel an experience as all that: it is a violent return of the chosen helplessness and ignorance of the citizen in the imperial center. The claim of the terrorist, as of the bomber of civilians, is that the people as a whole are at war, that there is no place that can make the plea for safety based on innocence or ignorance. The temptation, to which we may or may not give in, to stop thinking about the worst things that might happen, is the other side of the coin of the temptation we gave in to a long time ago to not think about all the things we are in fact doing. Well might the emblem of our day be the paralyzed face of a figure we call an angel of history, our exegeses amounting to little more than identifying (with) his horrified, helpless movement though time.

It can seem that what we fear from the proliferation of nuclear weapons, as from terrorism, is sudden, unpredictable violence outside our control. But the deepest despair in relation to both injury and knowledge is traceable, on the one hand, to the sense that we may have more control over our destiny than we are admitting to ourselves—and so more blame—and, on the other, to the dread that greater knowledge is not in itself liable to mitigate our risk. It can seem that the fear in the case of both nuclear annihilation and terrorism is of indiscriminate destruction introduced into a realm in which it does not belong—not the legitimate carnage entailed in the clash of armies but the illegitimate targeting of civilian life and structures. Still, as is also the case with all the major political decisions of our day, the most painful part of the moral experience of these fears is the haunted, anxious sense that while each incident of suffering is painfully arbitrary, in the aggregate, as a community, we are not fully free from complicity in determining the fate we fear (or are almost certain) awaits us.

I mentioned that the question of modern sovereignty is one that will keep coming up in reflections on modern damage. It is a topic I will return to in the next section of this chapter, where it is addressed as a historical phenomenon. I believe, however, that it has been present by implication throughout this discussion of terror and judgment. The question of identification with despotic rulers is one Benjamin challenges in his essay on history. But what if the rulers we most have to fear are not those future ones who will benefit from the documents of civilization being preserved for them or the current ones who are running the triumph but the very ones who are swelling the march of the triumph by their attendance. The paralyzed horror of the angel of history may well be the face of the modern subject recognizing itself in the damage of history—not just as object and victim but as perpetrator.

I have been suggesting that Klee's *Angelus Novus* has been a uniquely rich figure for modern despair because of the ways in which the combination of historical insight, compulsion, and dismay Benjamin discovered in the image aligns it with a range of fears that have been particularly generative for postwar thought owing to their relationship with the hopes they so quickly replace. In the Introduction to this book I touched on an influential tradition of skepticism about the rational faculties shaped by responses to the profound crises of the Second World War and its aftermath. It will be news to nobody interested in such matters that that sensibility was given new energy by the disappointment of political aspirations in French thought associated with the year 1968—though not limited to that date alone. That major cultural movements develop in response to the failure of political aspirations is a convention in the study of European culture that goes back at least as far as that foundational manifestation of political hope and disappointment, the French Revolution. But perhaps we can also recognize the power of a fearful success in Benjamin's image. Its gaze fixed on a past characterized by proliferating violence, the self is blown inexorably toward a future it cannot make out: the figure for history Benjamin found in Klee's print might easily be borrowed as an emblem for the sensibility we see emerging once revolution becomes not just a hope but a practical reality. This chapter will conclude with a discussion of Alois Riegl's sophisticated account of the passionate response to broken old things understood not as a troubling surprise but as characteristic of modernity. But that analysis needs to be preceded by discussion of the most thought-provoking attempt to address the topic—call it vandalism for the moment—in the midst of revolutionary change.

Dating the Ruins: Vandalism and Unintentional Monuments after the Year 2

"Vandalism" is a modern term for what modernity likes to think of as a primitive problem or as a particularly modern form of atavism. Indeed, it is at the very beginning of modern time, in the Year 2 of the Revolutionary calendar, that the Abbé Henri Grégoire produced the series of reports on the destruction of works of art and literature and of scientific instruments for the National Convention, in which he is said to have first used the word in its modern sense.[18] He needs a term under which to categorize his list of recent instances of injury or loss attributable to revolutionary excesses and to help him begin to lay out the case for preserving materials associated with the very elements that the Revolution is in the process of attempting to leave behind, notably the feudal nobility and the Catholic Church, the principal patrons of the arts up to that point in European history. The arguments the abbé develops are driven by immediate and urgent concerns—"I created the word," he would famously write a friend, "to kill the thing."[19] But, of course, the longevity of the term and its ongoing relevance indicate the failure of the Grégoire's project understood this way. Certainly, it would be impossible to argue that vandalism has died.

In fact, the arguments advanced by the revolutionary intellectual at this early point in the new world the revolution aimed to create would prove to be perennially topical, early and powerful manifestations of the never-finished project of justifying support of the arts and sciences in a modern democratic nation. Indeed, that many of the abbé's claims will be distressingly familiar to anyone interested in the arts and sciences *today* indicates that they may best be understood as manifestations of ultimately unresolvable conflicts inherent in the Revolution, whether we trace those back to the political project of destroying the old in order to found something new or to the more heady desire to ground reason in history, history in reason.

Grégoire's account of vandalism first emerges in the course of a remarkable report on inscriptions on public monuments, a topic that has at its heart the crisis of self-validating, self-originating meaning bound to face any truly revolutionary project.[20] And it bears emphasizing that the abbé is quite comfortable with the impulse to destroy in order to remake. That is, after all, the project of the Revolution. The Revolution is certain it owns the future; it is the past that it has doubts about. How can the historical record be remade into something that satisfies the present's aspirations for a new kind of posterity, especially given that the easiest thing to do is to simply obliterate what has come before? It is in the context of the aspiration to make the newest possible historical departure that the abbé needs to find language for preservation. While his immediate topic in the report on inscriptions is quite concrete, it is far from merely practical: What should be the language that is incised on stone memorials? Is it time for the usefulness of Latin to be put into question? Should the nation turn to French in order to make the kind of public address that is aimed at posterity? These are questions that move in two directions: into the past—what to make of the long-standing convention of using Latin as the international and transhistorical language of record; and toward the future—whether French will become a (or even *the*) language of the coming age because the Revolution has changed so much.

The political charge of the topic of inscriptions comes down to the claims for the rationality and permanence of a new vision of popular authority that depends on both qualities to validate its success (rationality and permanence). The question of what kinds of permanent memorials the revolutionary period—imagined at once as a new start and a permanent shift of authority to the people—can envision leaving to its own future is directly related to the challenge of identifying the monuments of a past that a new start needs to understand as now empty of meaning.[21] Does a revolution need memorials—and if so, what kind? "France is truly a new world," Grégoire will argue, as he attempts to lay out the cultural implications of that novelty in his first report on vandalism. "Its new social organization presents a phenomenon unique in the span of ages; and perhaps it has not yet been observed that, beyond the material of human knowledge, owing to the revolution it possesses exclusively a host of elements, new combinations, taken from nature, and inexhaustible means to profit from its political resurrection."[22] The fundamental novelty Grégoire has in mind is an unparalleled change in the sources of sovereignty. "Under despotic rule," he explains, "the people counted for nothing; now they are that which they should be, that is: everything. Public monuments should therefore remind them of their courage, their triumphs, their rights, their dignity. They should speak a language intelligible by all, that is the vehicle of patriotism and virtue, by which the citizen should be penetrated by every sense.[23] The abbé's position is bound to leave open the question he addresses in his later reports: what to make of public monuments that do not self-evidently do the work of celebrating republican virtue?

Remarkably, Grégoire's Rousseauvian insistence on the constantly recursive nature of the representation of the people to themselves does not lead to the obvious solution, the destruction of all prior works of art that remind the people of the long era of despotism in relation to which the Revolution is a new start. Not everyone was so open-minded; Joseph Sax cites a decree of May 12, 1792, that gives voice to the impulse to "eliminate the marks of feudalism and the memories of despotism" made in the following stark terms:

> Whereas the sacred principles of liberty and equality will not permit the existence of monuments raised to ostentation, prejudice and tyranny to continue to offend the eyes of the French people; whereas the bronze in these monuments can be converted into cannon for the defense of the homeland, it is decreed . . . [that all] monuments containing traces of feudalism, of whatever nature, that

still remain in churches, or other public places, and even those outside private homes shall, without the slightest delay, be destroyed by the communes.[24]

The challenge the Abbé Grégoire sets for himself is how to arrive at a situation in which revolutionary subjects will be able to see not offense but themselves reflected in monuments dating back to a period before their full enfranchisement. The aspiration has Enlightenment sources similar to those shaping the cosmopolitan account of religion that Volney, his fellow member of the National Assembly, had produced just three years earlier in *Ruins*. Still, it is deeply moving to discover this sensibility at the height of the Terror.

"Without question," the abbé declares a month after the execution of Robespierre and just eight months after the report on inscriptions, "everything must speak the Republican language to the eye."[25] As he addresses the question of *how* the past is going to be made to speak that language, the abbé runs through a list of types of material, identifying the merit even of objects from outside highly valorized classical categories, including Etruscan work (by which he likely means the Greek vases that at this point were still associated with the people in whose graves they were typically found) and objects dating back to the Middle Ages. The interest in the former he connects to developments in ceramics in England ("Etruria Works" was the name Josiah Wedgwood had given his storied factory in 1769), and so by implication to the support of French industry. The latter are inevitably the most suspect, having been created at the high-water mark of feudal and ecclesiastical control. But Grégoire rescues relics remaining from that period by emptying out their original function as memorials of the privileged and identifying their interest as residing in what they offer the current (presumably republican, now and forever) viewer today, as an illustration of the past: "The monuments of the Middle Ages will form interesting sequences, if not based on the beauty of the work, at least on history and chronology."[26] Novelty, evidently, requires history to know itself. If, as Dario Gamboni has noted, the French Revolution "is generally recognized as a turning point the history of both the destruction and the preservation of art," the works of the Abbé Grégoire are a uniquely sensitive register of the experience of trying to negotiate that paradoxical double pivot. [27]

It has been a long time since the kind of approach to supporting a wide variety of cultural traditions developed in the report has seemed anything more than blandly conventional, so it bears emphasizing just how radical the abbé's approach in fact was. The openness to nonclassical traditions, the scattershot nature of the argument (sometimes pragmatic, about the support for industry; sometimes pedagogic, about the need to illustrate historical continuities), has all the incoherence and overreach of most claims for the social value of the preservation and study of culture proposed in the years since Grégoire advanced his. In his formulations we see Enlightenment values we might associate with the broad engagement with culture of the Encyclopedists, given a new urgency at the Year 2.[28] I will be touching on the work of the great Austrian art historian Alois Riegl below, but it bears emphasizing the particularly modern character of the phenomenon that the abbé participated in bringing about, what Riegl describes as "the past acquir[ing] a present-day value for modern life and work." Evidently Grégoire's project is an important episode in a long process: "Several centuries elapsed," Riegl notes, "before it took on the modern shape we know today . . . an interest inclusive of the smallest deeds and events of even the most remote peoples, who, despite insurmountable difference in character, allow us to recognize ourselves in each and every one of them."[29]

Destruction is at the heart of a revolution aiming to create a new world. And we ought not to mistake the temper of an author who writes with avidity, as the Abbé Grégoire does, about the possibility that major Roman work will be looted and brought to France (as would indeed happen in the years ahead; see Chapter 4).[30] It is because he understands its drives at a fundamental level that the Abbé Grégoire is able to become the great foundational theorist writing against vandalism. The fact that the abbé's writings on the topic have a wider applicability despite the specific political forces and historical events shaping them is the most compelling evidence that at their heart they are part of a condition or complex that will accompany the project of revolution at every turn. Any attempt at a new start will find itself needing to establish its relationship to the past it is leaving behind; this is a conceptual pressure to which the lagging inertial force of culture, and of material objects in particular, will present a constant and not infrequently disturbing check. Sax gets to the heart of the political paradox by reminding his readers how far the values that the Revolution might be said to have helped usher into the world are from the political aspirations of the Revolution itself: "How did protection of cultural values come to be viewed as a proper public concern," he asks, "in a modern world centered on the liberty and autonomy of the individual?"[31] It bears saying that in Sax's formulation "autonomy" takes the place of "fraternity and equality"—a substitution not available in the Year 2 but typical of the ways the drives of the Revolution may be said to have survived into later eras only by being transmuted, sometimes beyond recognition.

As the Revolution did not turn out to be either the end or new beginning of history that some of its more fervent proponents hoped for, the nineteenth century had as its double legacy the aspirations for a violent new start and the fears attendant on that project, as well as the violence and fear that accompanied the reaction provoked by revolution. The question of how to make useful for the future a relic from the very past you are trying to escape or believe you have left behind only grows in complexity when confronted with the uneven success of every human endeavor. Reading through any compendium of the edicts issued in the course of the debates about the destruction and preservation of monuments around the time of the French Revolution, it is impossible to miss the fear of the public, as though the words were coming from a committee of sorcerer's apprentices who are thrilled but dismayed by what they have helped release and now need to manage.

One can hear in the various edicts explicit claims about offensive royal prerogatives and clerical arrogance or implicit ones suggesting the possibility of an autonomous beauty severable from the circumstances of the maker, the expectations of the privileged patron. But motivating these never-resolved debates was a particularly modern fear—that the violence that characterized the first achievements of the Revolution would not be a temporary expedient but a way of life. The concern in such circumstances is both practical and conceptual. The apprehension that the future might need to be secured over and over again for freedom is one manifestation of a fundamental anxiety: that in spite of its desire for a rational system of government, the Revolution will not be able to arrive at a steady state. Above all, and evident at every point in the declarations of the revolutionary authorities, is the fundamental realization that the public may itself be alarming. The source of legitimacy, of power, but also and for that reason a threat, the people—need to be heeded, need to be trained, need to be told what to do with objects the Revolution has taught them to mistrust and that they have the ability to destroy.

I have cited a couple of times already Ruskin's description of the damaging nature of human actions in relation to what might be understood as a vital cultural and aesthetic heritage. His passionate indignation should serve as a reminder that the danger presented to potentially valuable artifacts of culture by human action that had motivated the Abbé Grégoire was to be an ongoing concern in the nineteenth century, though not one that was evenly felt. The agents of the vandalism that concerns Ruskin are everywhere, not just in revolutionary France. And the potential objects of admiration have only proliferated by the time he is speaking in Manchester some sixty years after the abbé promoted the term. In the intervening years, it has become possible for the responsibility for revolutionary damage that in the earlier writer had been a national concern to have become a general condition in relation to the world.[32] Evidently the kind of passionate call for boundless responsibility made by Ruskin was never liable to meet a satisfactory response, and indeed, historians of preservation and cultural heritage can find in the nineteenth century both the emergence of a preservationist sensibility and fabled instances of irrecoverable loss, whether due to armed conflict or—far more often—to a relentless drive for modernization. The sophistication of the response to the question of cultural loss in the period is such that we also see emerge at this time the beginnings of a self-conscious anxiety about restoration itself. This is the era, that is to say, not only of what came to be called the Haussmannization of Paris, which rationalized the city plan while destroying neighborhoods of long standing, creating an almost immediate nostalgia for what had been lost, but also of the bold re-creation of Gothic work that had never previously existed by Eugène Viollet-le-Duc at Notre-Dame and elsewhere, flamboyantly creative restorations that added nineteenth-century monsters and other new elements to medieval buildings, along with an anxious sense that such reinventions might be worse than the genuine damage caused by neglect or rage.[33]

We may bookend this very brief summary of the modern history of responses to damage to antiquities that began with the Abbé Grégoire writing at the threshold of the nineteenth century with Alois Riegl's brilliant 1903 account of the passion for monuments that had emerged in the intervening years, "The Modern Cult of Monuments: Its Character and Its Origin." This later piece lays out a set of useful categories in relation to which the appeal of monuments might be understood, but it is at every point—as its title suggests—concerned with the interplay between historical and conceptual claims (between character and origins). Riegl proposes two principal categories for monuments, *intentional* and *unintentional*, each one allowing him to identify distinct characteristics of the objects of admiration it includes and the relationship to time inherent in the experience of those objects.[34] And yet, in spite of their apparently antithetical nature, the categories are most interesting when it becomes clear how they may overlap in practice (which is to say, in the same object).

An intentional monument, in Riegl's account, is one designed to memorialize something or someone; as such it is a direct address to its moment—say, to a family or community understood to be a current and ongoing phenomenon. A marker, in stone or otherwise, of a memory that someone does not want forgotten, the intentional monument is the concrete manifestation of an attempt to create memories for others protected from the forces of oblivion that its existence acknowledges and resists by means of the durable materials of which it is composed or of its excellence as a work of art. It is working against the losses we know to anticipate from the passage of time. For this reason, the intentional monument is the most familiar and straightforward category. "So long as men can breathe or eyes can see," writes Shakespeare in Sonnet 18, which is both a description and an instance of this type of monumentalization, "So long lives this, and this gives life to thee."[35] The monument aims to last as long as life itself, because its project is to work against the oblivion the reader feels impinging in that repeated "So long," which is intended to mean forever but is given a repeated terminus by the fact that neither the breath of individuals nor their sight is a phenomenon we associate with permanence. It is this shared transience that the poem pushes against in its attempt to memorialize one person—or really two: the lover and the beloved.

An unintentional monument is not the result of human work or desire but the product of time itself. It is brought into existence by the decaying, even entropic, character of existence. And so it is appreciated solely—indeed, it is only recognizable—by those for whom the monument is *not* originally intended. The unintentional monument is the characteristic modern monument because it has an unbridgeable gap at its core. Indeed, it is the loss of intention and even of memory that allows the unintentional monument to come into being. Riegl identifies the admiration—*cult*, he calls it—for monuments as a characteristic development of the nineteenth century and associates it with the veneration for nature that is also typical of the period, as two categories in relation to which care or a sense of responsibility comes to be an indication of newly acquired worth, the recognition of vulnerability serving as an evidence of affection.

Intentional versus unintentional monuments are entirely contrary categories, though the objects they describe may be one and the same. By and large the intention to commemorate a monarch will last no longer than one dynasty. But a later age may find in an object made with a now-lost intention ways of recognizing the passage of time itself or the power of nature, something that requires an acknowledgment that it would not be accurate to entirely distinguish from the project of commemoration. Thus, the intentional monument may be rescued from the oblivion to which it is fated but which it is designed to escape when culture reaches a point at which it can be brought back as an unintentional antiquity. We might hear in this idea a theorization of some of the gestures of recovery made in relation to potentially pernicious pre-revolutionary work by the Abbé Grégoire whereby memorials from a vanished feudal past or superannuated religious dispensation may come to be understood as commemorating human achievement in general or simply national creativity. But these ideas are domestications of the sensibility Riegl is working to describe.

I suggested in the Introduction to this book that a complex network of cross-period interference makes the case of the Arch of Titus particularly interesting. Riegl's terms help us to see why. While the dynasty the structure was meant to commemorate has faded into oblivion, the specific objects represented on its frieze come into new focus. Titus or his supporters were entirely unable to predict that what would mean the most about the arch to later generations was not the apotheosis of the emperor shown at its apex—which my own discussion almost entirely neglected—but the representation of booty from the temple of the defeated Jews. And, of course, neither Jews nor Romans could have anticipated that much of that interest would be traceable to the association of the image with the development of an entirely distinct religion no longer linked to a particular nation. The actions of Pope Pius VII may be understood as an attempt to route the object back into its original function as an intentional monument. But it is evidently not carrying out that role either for the original dedicatee nor for the culture whose objects are remembered on the carving. Ultimately, the antiquity of the arch, and specifically the damage that is its evidence, are as important in making the restored monument feel significant as the emblems or words that inform the viewer what it is intended to mean. Hovering in an indeterminate way between its intentional and unintentional character, the Arch of Titus teases us out of thought almost the way eternity does. And indeed, while Riegl makes the unintentional monument the characteristic one of modernity, for reasons I will address below, the truly powerful instances will tend to be viewed through a scrim of sentiment created by the memory of intention. "I am Ozymandias," the poem tells us, the statue lets us know. We need the intention inherent in his words in order to have something to contrast with the sands spreading all around us.

The categorization of monuments based on the presence or absence of intention that one may identify in them is a relatively simple matter compared to the range of values Riegl associates with monuments, the simple binary matching up poorly with the tripartite system he proposes, as the two kinds of categories of memorials—intentional and unintentional—correspond to more than two kinds of value, each associated with a different relationship to the condition of the object. The first two categories of value are apparently simple enough—*artistic* and *historical.* But they essentially set up the discussion for the category that clearly fascinates Riegl the most: what he calls *age-value.* Still, it bears laying out some of the complexities inherent in these first two categories.

Artistic value, as Riegl understands it, is always linked to a contemporary sense of what counts as art. As it is shaped by the ways in which a monument speaks to taste current at the moment of reception, it is typically interested in the object as it is, in the condition in which it is encountered. Because historical value is characterized by an interest in the origin of the object, its aspiration is to get back, as much as possible, to that earlier point in its condition. The historic sense is driven always to origins, to try to strip away the layers of damage or simple change that time lays on a monument (as the restorers did in 1821 with the structures that had come to accompany the Arch of Titus).

While the concepts of artistic and historical value appear to distinguish historical monuments from monuments that are works of art, Riegl quickly runs these categories together. The art object is always a monument of art *history* in that it belongs to a continuum we need to understand, as the Abbé Grégoire did, as part of a developing whole. It is a historical document because it salvages so much of the past and makes it available for us to know. If each work of art allows us to learn something about the past in which it was created and is historical in that sense, every historical document can be a work of art for at least two reasons. The simplest is that being a made object, it participates in the creative process we identify with that term. More radically, Riegl's system is open to a future that may discover artistic qualities to inhere in kinds of objects that were not, in the past, understood to be available to such characterizations. "The 'art monument,'" Riegl writes in the course of one of his attempts to explain how the sources of value of an object can shift, "is really an 'art-historical monument'; its value from this point of view is not so much artistic as historical. It follows that the differentiation of 'artistic' and 'historical' monuments is inappropriate because the latter at once contains and suspends the former" (22).

Riegl develops not simply a theorical account of relationships to the past that were implicit in the work of the Abbé Grégoire but an analysis of the ways in which the concerns about time and damage that emerged in the revolutionary period led to the emergence of new kinds of value. For example, Riegl's proposal that what the viewer feels in relation to an unintentional monument is evidence of the power of nature itself is ultimately a political claim about where the sources of vaue reside. When he writes that "these monuments are nothing more than indispensable catalysts which trigger in the beholder a sense of the life cycle," Riegl is describing an experience that brings into operation feelings that are always already present in the modern subject. The proposition about age-value being advanced here is ultimately driven by a commitment to the democratization of perception closely related to the Abbé Grégoire's claims about the primacy of the people as sovereign and as perceivers (as sovereign perceivers). And Riegl, like Grégoire before him, is clear on the modern—and therefore not yet fully realized nature of this development:

> This immediate emotional effect depends on neither scholarly knowledge nor historical for its satisfaction, since it is evoked by mere sensory perception. Hence it is not restricted to the educated (to whom the task of caring for monuments necessarily has to be limited) but also touches the masses independent of their education. The general validity, which it shares with religious feelings, gives this new commemorative (monument) value a significance whose ultimate consequences cannot yet be assessed. We will henceforth call this the age-value. (24)

The expansiveness of Riegl's age-value category would be breathtaking if we did not recognize it immediately as the description of a kind of instant nostalgia that would become trite in any number of twentieth-century cultural manifestations, a trivialization of what is an astonishingly open sense of what is liable to matter: "The category of monuments of age-value embraces every artifact without regard to its original significance and purpose, as long as it reveals the passage of a considerable period of time" (24). What Riegl is prescient enough to recognize is an idea that in fact is suggested as early as the writings of the Abbé Grégoire: the collapse of a limited canon of art opens up not only a vast range of possible art to appreciate but a limitless amount of art to protect or mourn. "There are two fundamentally different responses to this question today," Riegl notes about the canon: "an older one which has not entirely disappeared, and a newer one." He proposes that the nineteenth century saw the beginning of the abandonment of an "exclusive claim" for one canon of art, but that the change was limited by the tendency to cling to a not yet fully superseded "objective artistic ideal." It is a sense of the utter inaccessibility of the past that ultimately places the canon associated with objectivity into question, the emergence of "the theory of historical evolution that will declare that all artifacts of the past are irrecoverable and therefore in no way canonically binding." The terms in which Riegl expresses the ecumenical sensibility that makes him an heir of the era of Volney and the Abbé Grégoire have a characteristic spatial organization: "When compared with other values, age-value has one advantage over [*über*] all the other ideal values of the work of art in that it claims to address one and all and to possess universal validity. It rises above [*erhaben zu sein*] differences of religious persuasion and transcends differences in education and in understanding of art" (33). We may note in passing that *erhaben* is often translated as "sublime" or "lofty," as its root is in a verb meaning "to lift."

When Riegl asserts that all historic documents are potentially documents of art and that all art documents are certainly historical ones, he is simply conceptualizing an argument going back to Enlightenment sources—that indeed we heard from Grégoire. But this apparently reassuring mutual support between categories of documents opens up some surprising issues in relation to preservation. In Riegl's account, every drive to admire antique art as an art object is ultimately motivated by contemporary taste, that quality he describes with an important term in his critical vocabulary, *Kunstwollen*. The fascination of art-value is what emerges in response to an object that speaks to current artistic tendencies without having cut itself loose from the past: "It is precisely this apparent correspondence of the modern *Kunstwollen* and certain aspects of historical art which, in its conflicting nature, exerts such power over the modern viewer. An entirely modern work, necessarily lacking this background, will never wield comparable power." Because art-value is modernity seeing itself reflected in the mirror of the past, the traces of time must be present in a limited way for a monument to be treasured for that reason. Age-value, on the other hand, prizes the signs of the passing of time. It needs to see the monument in a state of perpetual decay ("the symptoms of decay . . . are the essence of age-value" [34]).

While monuments admired for their historical value—that is, because they make present some part of the past—are constantly working against the passage of time, whether to show clearly what has happened before or to commemorate something at risk of being forgotten, age-value only exists because the marks of the passage of time are visible on the surface of a monument. And so the restorer and the vandal are both a risk:

> While age-value is based solely on the passage of time, historical value, though it could not exist without recognizing time's passage, nevertheless wishes to suspend time. Intentional commemorative value simply makes a claim to immortality, to an eternal present and an unceasing state of becoming. It thereby battles the natural processes of decay which militate against the fulfillment of its claims. The effects of nature's actions must be countered again and again. A commemorative column with its inscription effaced, for example, would cease to be an intentional monument. The intentional monument fundamentally requires restoration. (38)

It is because the unintentional monument exists in nature, has become a part of nature by entering time, that it must not be interfered with. And so it is that in his account of the age-value of the monument we find Riegl giving a local habitation to that part of the Kantian sublime wherein the power of the subject in relation to nature is lost practically and reestablished conceptually. Modern subjects see themselves in the monument under threat from nature, and nature itself is conceived as an artist and so equated with something like human creative power:

> Every artifact is thereby perceived as a natural entity whose development should not be disturbed, but should be allowed to live itself out with no more interference than necessary to prevent its premature demise. Thus modern man sees a bit of himself in a monument, and he will react to every intervention as he would to one on himself. Nature's reign, even in its destructive aspects—which also brings about the incessant renewal of life—claims equal right with man's creative power. (32)

For the modern reader Riegl's prescriptions may read like the words of a particularly prescient ecological sensibility committed to maintaining the conditions of the world as it finds them. Indeed, in a surprising footnote Riegl himself touches on the relationship: "Another characteristic trait of modern culture," he writes, elaborating on the above passage, "which arises from the same root as the appreciation of age-value, is the protection of animals and of the environment" (50n1). Still, Riegl is far more radical in following out the implications of his thought than the more sentimental versions of the ecological sensibility characteristic of later eras might lead one to expect. Because the place of the monument in time is given special weight by Riegl, the *kind* of destruction entailed in a ruin is important. As decay is fundamental to his vision, physical violence is a problem, given that it threatens the aura that is ascribable to the signs of natural forces at work on the object. However, "preservation should not aim at stasis," he insists, "but ought to permit the monuments to submit to incessant transformation and steady decay, outside of sudden and violent destruction. Only one thing must be avoided: arbitrary interference by man in the way the monument has developed." Because what the monument stands for is the purest possible experience of the intersection of the human and time, the only protection envisioned in this argument is from actions that will compromise the purity of that encounter. Riegl's claims naturalize damage. They participate in the tendency in thinking about ruins to leave out of consideration the human actions that create and promote the existence of unintentional monuments, to only envision the dangers presented by any potential acts of restoration. Indeed, the naturalization of antiquities that plays a role in establishing their need for protection against human action also militates against preserving monuments from the ravages of time:

> There must be no additions or subtractions, no substitutions for what nature has undone, no removal of anything that nature has added to the original discrete form. The pure and redeeming impact of natural decay must not be arbitrarily disturbed by new additions. The cult of age-value condemns not only every willful destruction of monuments as a desecration of all-consuming nature but in principle also every effort at conservation, as restoration is an equally unjustified interference with nature. The cult of age-value, then, stands in ultimate opposition to the preservation of monuments. Without question, nature's unhampered processes will lead to the complete destruction of a monument. It is probably fair to say that ruins appear more picturesque the more advanced their state of decay. (32)

While Riegl appears to suggest a morphology of different kinds of monuments, it is very clear that as far as he is concerned the monuments that truly matter to us are the unintentional ones. We break them or find them broken, and then they mean for us. This insight is the more poignant version of the close relationship between barbarism and civilization suggested by Benjamin, because it is so clearly not an accusation of complicity so much as an acknowledgment of an inevitable relationship. To say that barbarism creates the conditions to which civilization responds, from which it benefits, is not simply to give a name to the acts of open violence that might result in the acquisition of admired objects. It is to make Benjamin's claim a corollary to the axiom that the love of damaged things is characteristic of modernity.

The instances I discuss in *Overlooking Damage* would tend to trouble Riegl's categories, I think, because of their relationship to immediate intentional injury. And yet his formulations help us trace some of the affective power of the ruin, and especially of the ruin at risk. The Arch of Titus demonstrates the kinds of reflections that monuments make possible when we recognize their unstable cultural location, between intention and its opposite. In the restoration of the work, the stripping away of elements from the past, we see the desire to be in contact with origins at the heart of historical value. But as the arch manifests itself in a state as close as the restorers can get it to what they understood to be its original historical moment—shorn of later accretion—it becomes a relic of another era, an intentional monument speaking no longer of the time of Titus but of Pius. And so the arch resonates forever (or for the time being) between too many categories. It is not just an intentional monument repurposed into a monument for another individual and in response to a social and political condition altogether unimaginable by the original makers or viewers. We may think of Abbé Grégoire's arguments for using the vernacular, made some thirty years before the carvers etched the pontiff's claim in the rock, unavoidably in the language of the church, the language of a lost empire, doubling the number of generally unread dedications on the monument. The pope to whom no tourist's mind turns; Titus and Vespasian, lost except to the historian: these are the Ozymandian individuals the monument is meant to memorialize. And yet it is the objects represented on the arch that have had the most powerful life—as lost relics of another vanished monument, as memorials of the violence that ripped a people out of one historical trajectory and threw them into another.

As I have suggested, the arch as it is may also be understood as something quite modern, as an emblem of the pressure on the sovereign in a modernizing world in which, instead of expressing power by creating something they could call a tribute from their subjects to themselves, leaders must act as though their rule provides public benefits that go beyond the practical. The confusion of the religious and the cultural in the pope's inscription speaks to the uncertainty as to the nature of the benefit being conferred by the acts of repair. All that is clear is the bounty of the pontiff. Even though the restoration is a product of a period of reaction, it is all the more (and just for that reason) a post-revolutionary act in its unresolved combination of ancient authority (divine, classical) and modern political anxiety. My instances come together in a modern continuum in which our responses to monuments are fundamentally determined by the vicissitudes of a situation characterized by violence and the rise of a mass public, along with the profound political disappointments that have accompanied both the violence and the emergence of the public. Grégoire, writing in Year 2 of the Revolution, was working against the sentiment that wanted to simply destroy the past. The drive to start time over will always be antithetical to the desire to figure out how the past is related to the new time just come into being. To imagine a concept of development that makes all objects potentially art, potentially history, as Riegl understood culture to be doing at the emergence of the modern cult of the monument, is not to arrive at an ultimate determination of where the value of monuments resides, but to recognize the dynamic nature of what things might mean to a newly enfranchised public. "Everything that has been and is no longer," Riegl notes, "we call historical, in accordance with the modern notion that what has been can never be again, and that everything [*alles*] that has been constitutes an irreplaceable and irremovable link in a chain of development." The losses entailed in recognizing oneself as modern emerge in relation to concepts of development that themselves support the past to which the subject no longer feels connected. "In other words," he goes on,

> each [*jedes*] successive step implies its predecessor and could not have happened as it did without that earlier step. The essence of every [*jeder*] modern perception of history is the idea of development. In these terms, every [*jede*] human activity and every [*jedes*] human event of which we have knowledge or testimony may claim historical value; in principle, every [*jedes*] historical event is irreplaceable. (21–22)

Alles, jedes, jeder, jede: the keywords in this quietly hyperbolic passage are "all," "each" and "every" because what Riegl is outlining is a vast and inexorably growing vision of the past not unrelated to that gazed at by Benjamin's troubled angel. What in Riegl is a chain of development, in Benjamin is a chain of incidents only organized into a sequence by human perception. The absence of an idea of progress fundamentally alters the mental experience of events. From his point of view the angel of history sees no pattern at all, but rather "one single catastrophe, which keeps piling wreckage upon wreckage and hurls it at his feet."[36]

I have argued in Chapter 2 of this book that Kant's sublime was distinct from Lyotard's account of that phenomenon owing to its inclusion of time, which is also the quality we find in the experience of Volney's traveler. The emotional response of the latter to the disjunction between his experience of the world in its broken, inadequate, and precarious condition and his rational aspirations to imagine something more, along with the outburst that accompanies that feeling, provoke the emergence of the genie who will take in charge the traveler's instruction. But the lessons of the genie entail a process of revision that is never comfortable, as it tends to put the self into an awkward position in relation to knowledge *and* the possibility of moral claims. "The disposition of the mind to the feeling of the sublime," Kant insists, "requires its receptivity to ideas." It is a formulation that if attended to as it might be would move sublimity from the realm of visceral immediacy in which it is sometimes placed and allow it to be seen as the clearly reflective category it is. But the claim is a dialectical one. It is because our ideas do not match up with the world to which we bring them that we experience the sublime:

> For it is precisely in the inadequacy of nature to the latter [that is, to ideas], thus only under the presupposition of them, and of the effort of the imagination to treat nature as a schema for them, that what is repellent for the sensibility, but which is at the same time attractive for it, consists, because it is a dominion that reason exercises over sensibility only in order to enlarge it in a way suitable for its own proper domain (the practical) and to allow it to look out upon the infinite, which for sensibility is an abyss. In fact, without the development of moral ideas, that which we, prepared by culture, call sublime will appear merely repellent to the unrefined person. He will see in the proofs of the dominion of nature given by its destructiveness and in the enormous measure of its power, against which his own vanishes away to nothing, only the distress, danger, and need that would surround the person who was banished thereto.[37]

There is nothing more cultured, in short, than the experience of the dominion of nature in the sublime. This is the experience of Volney's traveler in Palmyra and what is registered before Riegl's unintentional monuments. Given what the art historian has argued about the availability of the sensation of age-value to even the uneducated (which is certainly the most sentimental part of an otherwise quite rigorous system), we are left with the clear sense that what is at issue here is a concept of culture that is not about formal instruction so much as what it feels like to be modern.

• • •

Aux armes, citoyens! proposes a double interpellation. The refrain of the bloodthirsty marching song drafted just before Year 1 of the Revolution, the composition that became the French national anthem, indicates with great economy that to be a citizen is to be called to participate in violent military action. War is always awful to its victims. But it is in the nineteenth century that it becomes horrible to culture in ways it had never been before. It would be difficult to argue that the actual experience of military conflict prior to the Revolution was less appalling than it was afterwards, and yet some seventeenth-century precursors notwithstanding, there is simply no document like Goya's *The Disasters of War* (1810–20; published 1863) in an earlier era.[38] There is some merit to the simple explanation for the change, that developments in technology made killing infinitely more effective or more brutal or more knowable. But any student of culture will recognize a transformation in the imagination of war after the turn of the nineteenth century that predates the practical developments that made massacres so much easier to carry out and to present to those who were not there to kill or be killed.

When Hegel tells us, in the course of his discussion in the *Aesthetics* of what kinds of conflicts are epic, that "in war it is precisely the whole nation which is set in motion and which experiences a fresh stimulus and activity in its entire circumstances, because here the whole has an inducement to answer for itself," his aim is to distinguish between the petty squabbles of princes and a concept of war as a struggle in which the project is "the justification claimed by a people at the bar of history."[39] A people justified by war: *Aux armes, citoyens!* It is difficult to avoid the grim thought that along with the concept of citizenship comes the kind of responsibility entailed in modern wartime. If we are not answering the urgent call of Year 1 and taking up arms ourselves and rushing to water our furrows with the blood of our enemies, when can we accurately say that we are at war? Clearly the modern consensus is the one suggested by Hegel: we are at war when our state is in that condition. Mary Favret notes that "the political affiliations of the lexicographer" can be tracked through "changes in the definition of sovereignty."[40] We might argue that the cultural phenomenon of modern war is always to be understood in relation to the crisis attendant on the alarming sense that power is in the hands of a sovereign *people*, hence the ongoing relevance of the question Favret describes as emerging in the aftermath of the Revolution—that is, "how war was understood by those who were, at least as subjects of a sovereign state, often at war, though never actually in battle" (173).[41]

For all their variety, the instances I have touched on in the three chapters I have written on and around Palmyra might usefully be described as participating in a long crisis following the epochal change that was the French Revolution. While the disappointments of Lyotard find a dead end at the Holocaust, that is evidently the terminus for a voyage of hope that began with the enfranchisement of the people during the Revolution. Only three years separate Volney's *Ruins* and the Abbé Grégoire's memoranda on vandalism. Volney's traveler needs to be instructed on the ruinous actions of his fellow men, and he mourns the lives missing in the ruins around him. In the midst of revolutionary violence and hope, the Abbé Grégoire worries not so much about the dead or those likely to die but about antiquities themselves. Is it too much of a stretch to suggest that what has changed between these two works is the lived experience of the Revolution itself? That brief span sees the first use of the guillotine, the storming of the Tuileries, the execution of the king and queen and of Robespierre himself, and so many other deaths. It is also the beginning of the era of unintentional monuments, of works of art newly placed in an irrecoverably unstable condition whereby they must be allowed to decay but must not be either repaired or destroyed by human hands.

Volney sets his *Ruins* in 1784, one of the three years he spent in the Middle East, the eleventh year of the reign of the Turkish sultan Abdülhamid, 1198 years after the Hejira that took the Prophet from Mecca to Medina. Another way of thinking of the matter of dates is that these events take place in a year that will only exist in retrospect: Year –8 of the Revolution. Through this expedient *Ruins* becomes a text of the Revolution set before that extraordinary event has changed the nature of time but shaped by the knowledge that the change is on its way.

Political traumas are typically marked by moments of violence: Grégoire writes at a crisis point in the Terror, Benjamin as the catastrophe of the Third Reich is manifesting itself inexorably as a calamity in his existence and in that of so many others. Lyotard has the death camps in mind as he writes, organizing his vision of the sublime as the paralysis of thought when confronted with human evil. At these undeniable crises of human hope the status of antiquities, whether newly damaged or preserved, can seem at once urgent and trivial. But then, every action of caretaking, whether of human being or material object, always involves a choice of attention. I mentioned in the previous chapter the presentation on cultural artifacts at risk I attended some years ago, at which the impossible response to wartime looting in Iraq and Syria was discussed with sincere and informed passion. Toward the end of the conversation, the event risked going off the rails when a particularly thoughtful curator pointed out that the plight of antiquities in a war zone might draw the eye and provoke a great deal of melancholy hand-wringing, but that in some parts of Asia celebrated economic developments were causing widespread and irreparable damage to a precious heritage with little response from the local or international community. A pair of intolerable questions follow: Is the damage wrought by vandals worse than that licensed by indifference? Is destruction inherent in what it is to be modern? Dario Gamboni writes about an iconoclasm that is "more a matter of daily business than of violent outbreaks," depending on an ideology giving primacy to the economy and "the 'religion' of progress."[42] Clearly the moral orientation of the modern well-meaning individual is to be like the traveler in Ozymandias—taking in the site, understanding its ironies. But is our condition more accurately compared to that of the statue, or worse, to the lone and level(ing) sands? According to Keats, every peak of imagined hardship in the "Elgin Marbles," that great unintentional monument, tells us we must die. Are we perhaps Ozymandias himself in ruins, declaring to all comers that our works *are* the devastation all around us, recommending despair?

While the tendency has been to bemoan the emergence of total war as a particularly modern phenomenon linked to changes in technology, thoughtful writers have nuanced our sense of that term, pointing out that the totality of total war is more conceptual than experiential.[43] Arguably, as a moral phenomenon war has never been total enough. I have touched already on the challenging but inescapable problem of complicity with war of citizens within the modern state. The fantasy of totality may be less morally distressing than the reality that the burden of war always falls unevenly—that its cost is never fairly distributed on any side. "The masterplot of total war," Saint-Amour tells us, "deals badly with instances of restrained warfare in supposedly total theatres and shears off examples of extreme mobilization and civilian-killing in eras it considers too early. Its portrait of a national life completely subordinated to a war effort misses the persistence of the everyday during even the most unrestrained conflicts" (58). Elaine Scarry's imagination of the heads of every citizen in a state becoming permanently turned behind them when their nation becomes a nuclear power is a preposterous attempt to address the simultaneous failure of knowledge and responsibility that is a constant in the modern relationship to armed violence and in that sense more total than any conflict has ever been.

Bloodthirsty though it is, *La Marseillaise* leaves some things out. Though the state is armed, the citizens are not always clear that that means a direct line of responsibility from the battlefield to each individual. Arising, joining, marching, replacing the fallen—these are the actions the song enjoins upon its listeners. The call to arms in the song is motivated by the alarming fact that soldiers doing the will of tyrants are coming to slit the throats of our sons and consorts. Immediately following that call—and as part of the same refrain—we hear not of the deaths of our loved ones and descendants but the ecstatic celebration of impure blood (presumably draining from the bodies of the threatening enemy) watering our furrows. There is no space between threat and bloody relief in the anthem, but neither are the armed citizens represented as the agents of their own sanguinary rescue. Evidently one is meant to fill in the gap with the unspoken understanding that the new state is the agent of the violent relief of the anxiety of its citizens, that function being what justifies their solidarity.

When we think of damage today, especially in the military arena, our reflections have inevitably been shaped by the fear of irreparable injury in the course of a nuclear conflict or perhaps by the knowledge of our own responsibilities for the military adventures and proxy battles that have taken place for the better part of a century under the name "Cold War" or "War on Terror." But the relentless flow of refugees in recent years and the reemergence of religious struggle in so many countries have made the topic of damage, which is always far too easy to naturalize, newly urgent and too unsettling for any broad categories. Conceptual tools developed in a different political and even military situation have come under pressure, given new technologies and also new circumstances. Still, they provide useful tools for reflection, even on the possibility of their revision, as we try to formulate new concepts of responsibility—and perhaps new forms of solidarity.

I noted in Chapter 1 of this book that prepositions related to sight are often moralized, taking on qualities indicative of disparities between self and others in the world that have made us uncomfortable of late. I have emphasized in my analysis alternative models of looking things over, ones in which the identification of a distinction between viewer and object of reflection is not understood as inevitably entailing an unbridgeable conceptual gap with ethical failure as its necessary beginning or end. In the recognition of an experience at once inescapable and damaging with which we cannot help but be in relationship (even complicit) we may begin to identify a new awareness of our place in time—not an analysis that keeps rediscovering the failure of utopia or the destined terminus of our hopes in unspeakable catastrophe. The instances I have addressed demonstrate that the distance between unharmed viewer and the damage that circumstances or interest bring to view constitutes precisely the span or interval into which thought should flow. To have forgotten why buildings have fallen into ruin and populations have been displaced is not—as the genie of Palmyra reminds Volney's sentimental traveler—to be absolved from responsibility. It is rather to participate in the conditions that assure that further damage is inevitable. On the other hand, it would be a poor kind of ethics that finds in the recognition of responsibility the end of reflection rather than the only hope for the beginning of action.

Part 2

Identity and Loss

4

OWNING ART AFTER NAPOLEON

Destiny or Destination at the Birth of the Museum

British soldiers discovered a trove of Old Master paintings hidden in the baggage abandoned by Joseph Bonaparte when he fled the field at the close of the Battle of Vitoria in 1813, the ignominious end of his five years of rule as king of Spain. Years later Wellington offered to return these works looted from various Spanish royal collections to Ferdinand VII, the restored monarch. But Ferdinand—who owed his throne to the duke's victories—declined, leaving in the hands of the victorious commander important canvases by Velázquez, Correggio, and others (fig. 4.1). What in its day would have been called a return to legitimacy, the restoration of the Bourbon line after the defeat of Napoleon, did not in this case result in the restitution of Napoleonic loot.[1] The works remain at Apsley House to this day, the duke's former home in London, on display in the Waterloo Gallery, a usurper's booty transformed by its history into an emblem of military prowess and royal generosity, not to say an emblem of solidarity between two reactionary elites.

The original provenance of its various canvases notwithstanding, this set of paintings is for the foreseeable future inextricably linked to its history by its site of display. Still, it bears saying that the status of the location is no more fixed than that of the art objects it contains. Although the works have remained at the same address where one would have found them if invited to attend a banquet commemorating the victory at Waterloo in the duke's time (fig. 4.2), the traveler visits them no longer in a private home but in the museum established by an act of Parliament in 1947, in the aftermath of another long war.

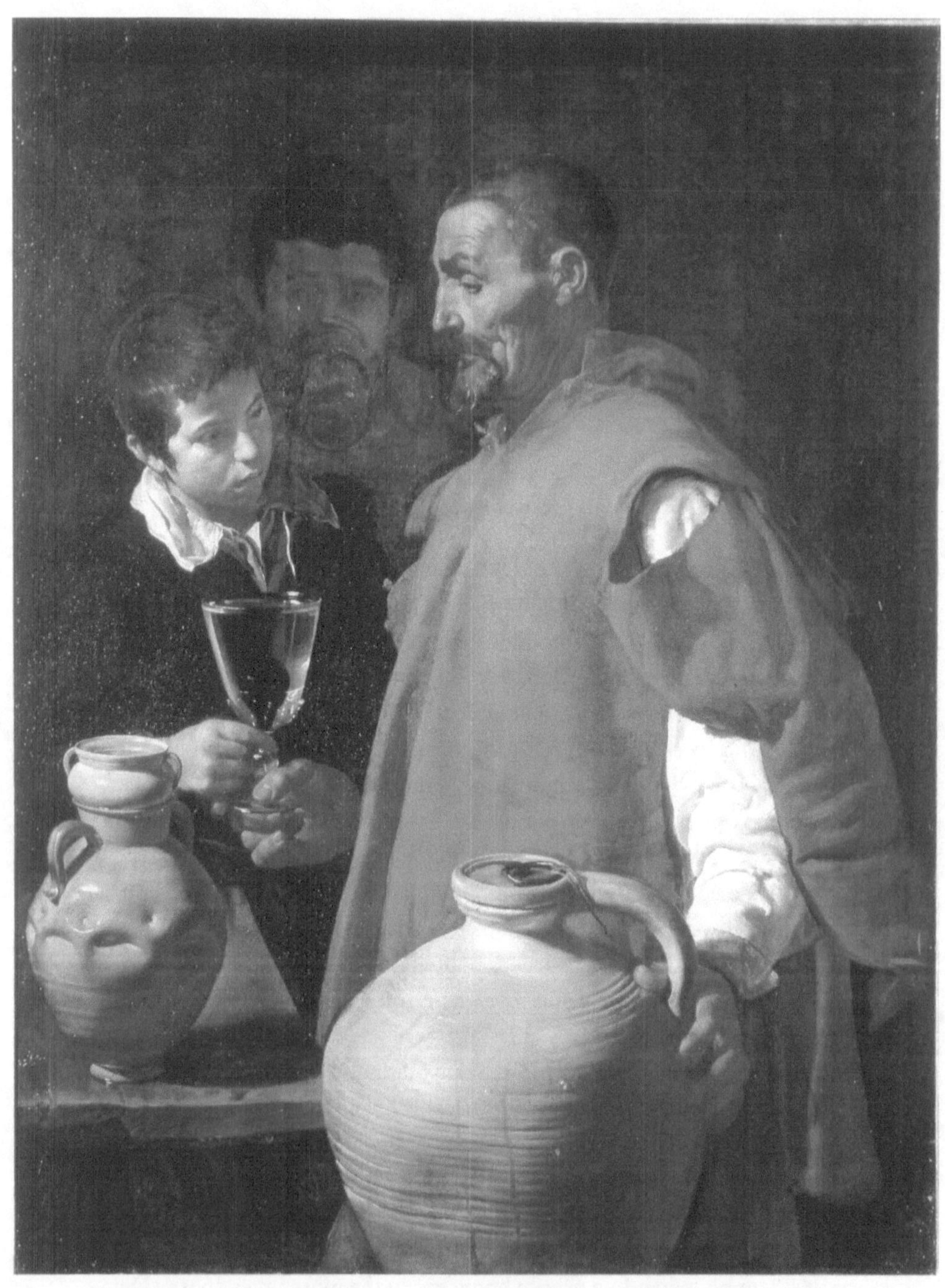

FIGURE 4.1. Diego Velázquez, *The Water Seller of Seville* (1618–22). Oil on canvas, 106.7 x 81 cm. Apsley House / Wellington Museum, London. V&A Images, London / Art Resource, NY.

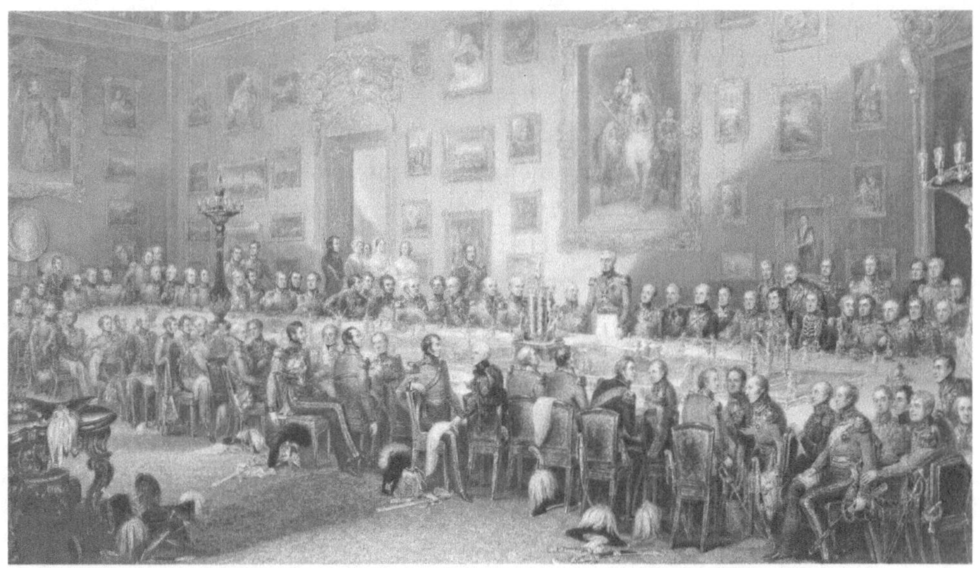

FIGURE 4.2. William Greatbach, line engraving after William Salter, *The Waterloo Banquet at Apsley House, June 18, 1836*. Apsley House, London. The painting was very popular, as was Greatbach's 1846 print, which sold widely. Some of Wellington's collection is visible on the wall, including canvases acquired at Vittoria. (The Velázquez *Water Seller* and the Correggio *Agony in the Garden* are visible to the duke's right.) Courtesy of the Council of the National Army Museum, London.

Does the museum tear objects out of their natural homes, or does it create new kinds of objects? Or does such an apposition presume a distinction that history does not fully ratify? The history of the Wellington House collection might appear almost too good an illustration of Walter Benjamin's axiom in "On the Concept of History" that every document of civilization is also a document of barbarism—and even of his less frequently cited but important development of the claim, that "just as such a document is never free of barbarism, so barbarism taints also the manner in which it was transmitted from one hand to another."[2] Nevertheless, I do not cite the tale of this set of works found on the field of battle in order to belabor moral judgments about rightful owners or barbaric victors, or about the essential brutality of institutions of display, both of which I believe would be limited applications of the critic's terms. It seems to me that an instance such as this one—given the speed and contingency of the changes involved and the distance separating objects from any situation at which we might pretend to descry proper owners—should rather challenge conventional claims about objects than ratify them. Certainly, analyses focusing on original rights and the condemnation of expropriation will prove insufficient. Indeed, even to identify as a "collection," as I have been doing, the group of works gathered by a monarch in flight and refused by another newly installed is to rationalize the existence of an assemblage that has far more to do with violence, greed, and the most expedient personal interest than with the rational practices or the personal taste we might want to associate with that term. But is this flamboyant instance the only one about which we might have such qualms?

The historical force of Benjamin's dialectic is impoverished when we see the two sides of the dyad as separated by a space as wide as the one our ethical aspirations still create between culture (or "civilization," as the earliest translators of the essay had it) and barbarism. It is because Benjamin's hyperbolic formulation fits almost too well in a gap between historical event and moral value that it is pressingly interesting. At the genesis of the collection at Apsley House we find at least two elements that we may be tempted to call barbaric. It is hard to miss in the anecdote with which I opened the role of the unprincipled imposition of power we might identify with the fortunes of war, given that the fate of the collection is determined by military conflict twice over—once when the victories of Napoleon's armies make possible the gathering of the collection and again when Wellington's men defeat those armies and discover the canvases. And then the capricious exercise of royal prerogative is also doubly manifested (along with the contingent and fundamentally arbitrary nature of monarchical rule itself), once in the expropriations of the fleeing King Joseph, the next time in the generosity of the new king, Ferdinand.

We may want to hesitate before the apparently self-evident nature of the alignment of event and principle, even to interrogate our desire to move too quickly beyond the intersection of beauty and damage that shapes Benjamin's insight into a claim about (the failure of) right behavior in a specific instance. A match this close between event and idea, it seems to me, ought to invite new reflection on the practical nature of the theoretical axiom by throwing both theory and practice into sharp relief. A far more general proposition seems to be implied in Benjamin's claim, as in other, more directly antimuseal formulations with which it is sometimes confounded, than anything that might be read into the series of accidents and individual judgments that shape my brief tale of kings and generals.[3] As discussed in the first chapter of this volume, Benjamin's ethical claim in this much-cited part of "On the Concept of History" is premised on the idea that later eras are the political heirs of the barbaric despoilers; the historical sensibility he is arguing for is meant to contest the validation of the triumphs of brutal conquest as a way of resisting current illegitimate forms of power that may be traced back to earlier forms of violence. More recently, we might think that the issue at stake here is something quite distinct, not the ongoing consolidation of oppressive power but the neglect of concepts of cultural property involved in these major works being subjected to the fortunes of war or the whims of tyrants. However, both applications of Benjamin line up awkwardly with this case unless we want to argue for the ongoing legitimacy of political arrangements that may be traced back to the regime of Ferdinand, the "Felon King," returned to the throne by foreign armies, a despot whose regime ended in civil war. Wellington, the legendary general and statesman who would go on to have a long career in British politics, including serving twice as prime minister, but whose resolute opposition could not stop the passage of the Reform Bill of 1832 that placed Britain on the road past oligarchic rule and definitively away from monarchic power, is certainly a reactionary ruler, but the articulation of his actions and the ideas and values that determined them with those of later eras is hardly straightforward.

Evidently, the political continuity suggested in any kind of simple reading of Benjamin's argument would be neither historically nor conceptually useful because of how much it would need to leave out. What about more current application of the claim, to the issue of cultural property, for example? What if the barbarism of transmission is understood as what is manifested in an ongoing process of theft from the weaker by the stronger in the name of a symbolic consolidation of power? In that case the barbarism would be entailed in the use of force to arrive at an apparently civilized or civilizing structure—a collection, say, or museum. This chapter will be arguing for the inadequacy of this particularly influential contemporary version of the Benjamin argument, in part by not shying away from the kinds of reductive claims about actual historical continuities and gaps I have already identified as inadequate. But on my way to that argument it may be worth reviewing what we mean by barbarism.

Arising, as it is said to have done, from a mocking evocation of the incomprehensible sound of languages the Greeks could not understand, the term "barbarism" does not originally identify a stage in human history but a sense of unbridgeable contemporary difference. The word describes a fundamental distinction that, like all borders, is meant to define both sides of the divide it marks. Everyone outside the limits of the city, speaking an unknown language and presenting a likely threat, is a barbarian. (As with "pagan," "gentile," or "native," indifference to distinction masked as the absence of distinction is a feature of the use of these kinds of terms.) Even those later uses that assume that an idea of progress connects the two categories, that hold that a people can or will or should develop from the state of barbarism to that of civilization, typically understand these conditions as the two most distant points between which a society can move. To identify every document of civilization as a document of barbarism, then, is to reveal the darker and more bitter qualities shaping cultural aspirations traditionally associated with what, in an influential nineteenth-century formulation, Matthew Arnold described as sweetness and light, to uncover violence where it is not otherwise clearly present because it should not be there at all.[4] There should be no darkness to hide in the light, and no injurious action making bitter what we aspire to find sweet. To locate barbarism in the documents of civilization is to find either an utterly alien character in that which most identifies us as distinct from that character or a fundamentally atavistic throwback to an earlier time when we were so different from what we are now that it is upsetting to even imagine that earlier state.

All this is just to belabor the obvious qualities that make Benjamin's claim bracing. What is it, however, that makes it compelling, aside from the bold symmetry with which it wrenches together contraries? Where are the edges of Benjamin's assertion? Where do the two sides meet? The long-lasting power of the formulation, I want to say, resides in the way its aphoristic form so effectively covers disappointment in apparent knowledge. I thought I was sad—the formulation allows us to feel—that something I have been identifying as belonging to a higher order because free from base impulses is in fact tainted with those very impulses in their rawest form. Now I realize that what I took to be the disappointing exception is just an instance of a principle at work in the world or, at least, of a regrettable but nevertheless constant condition about which it is just as well that I be informed.

But what happens if we remove the phrase from the vacuum that surrounds any axiom and return it to history? While my questions about Benjamin's claim may seem driven by a literal-mindedness that willfully misses the point, I cannot help but feel that it is worth asking how the categorical propositions about culture and its institutions that the critic proposed in the essay on history he wrote while suffering the immediate effects of global conflagration in 1940 may illuminate other points in history when the form and meaning of ownership and transmission is clearly in question. My interest runs in two directions: Is what we see when institutions of culture are in the course of formation, as they were during the period of epochal military struggle following the French Revolution, and especially at the close of the period of Napoleonic conflict, a vivid illustration of Benjamin's claim? Or is the closeness of the barbarism in the battlefield to the apparently civilized calm of the museum an opportunity to reflect on the limited revelatory quality of Benjamin's aphorism? The events addressed in this chapter, I believe, serve to remind us of the long, violent crisis in Europe that is the very context that makes Benjamin's claim conceptually interesting and historically urgent, because they reveal both how right the critic was and how little surprise should accompany realization of that fact.

The early nineteenth century is not, after all, just another era in the ongoing and inevitable history of institutions, another historical period in relation to which it bears reflecting on the intersection of collecting (understood as a peaceable, civilized activity) with war (associated with barbaric actions and values). The institution of the modern museum developed in the course of a complex, decades-long global military struggle during which the fundamental nature of nations and empires was at stake. It was at precisely this point in history that for the first time the displacement of collections of works of art came to be seen to validate or put into question the meaning of conquest and national identity.

The coming into being of the museum necessarily entails a reimagination of property and the nature of its transmission, developments closely related to those at issue in reconfigurations of political legitimacy. But the process of transmission of valuable things (*Prozeß der Überlieferung* in the original), like that of power, is seldom as smooth or systematic as Benjamin's words would tend to suggest. My discussion of three roughly contemporary instances of acquisition and loss will serve to illustrate the place of accidents of war in the establishment of modern cultural institutions and the development of ideas about their meaning: the magnanimity of a general and a king with which I began, the impact of the Napoleonic model on the acquisition of the Parthenon Marbles by the British Museum, and especially the British response to Napoleon's magnificent Louvre just after his defeat.

The violence out of which the Apsley collection emerges is not hiding. It is at the heart of what matters about its story of origins. French plunder, British victory, Spanish restoration: violence meets us at every turn, along with such primitive social structures as those at work when royalty rewards heroism. (Is *that* civilization or barbarism?) Inherited wealth, martial booty, trophy, gift—in the instance of Wellington and the two kings of Spain the objects remain the same but their meanings shift with vertiginous speed. Given the quite distinct frameworks in which we typically place these categories of ownership—family relations, military struggle, claims of victory, even noble magnanimity or basic social acts of reciprocity—what are the implications of such fundamental changes for our sense of the ethical and aesthetic significance of cultural property?[5] My answer to the question brings me to the most important art museum of the nineteenth century, if not of all centuries, which is a good place to take the measure of what art could mean after Napoleon.

The founding of the Louvre Museum in the early years of the revolutionary period is often identified as marking the origin of the modern institution. And that is certainly a nice story to tell, of royal privilege swept aside by a newly self-enfranchising public. Following on the work of recent historians, however, I want to suggest that we take the creation and incomplete dissolution of the Musée Napoléon as an equally important, if somewhat less edifying and sharply defined, foundational moment.[6] Decades ago André Malraux posited the fecund power inherent in the inevitable failure of all museums; recognition of the gaps inherent in any collection is what drives into being what he memorably called the *musée imaginaire*.[7] This chapter aims to move that point of failure to the very earliest moments in the history of the institution. What is of interest is not only the number of museums that were born or reborn through the imperfect restoration of the Louvre collection but the creation of a nostalgia for a perfect museum that only ever existed through violence, loss, and betrayal.

The development of museums requires not simply the acquisition of material but also the will to make that material available to the public, and even the creation of language for the feelings and actions involved in the acquisition and display of important works of art. A number of political crises contributed to the importance of public display in the nineteenth century, though they did not fully stabilize its meanings. The revolutionary period, and especially the Napoleonic campaigns, not only loosened important pieces from their historic moorings but added new force to traditional ideas of war booty by identifying the possession and public display of important antiquities as a modern symbol of political power.

The trophy, that traditional commemoration of victory going back to the classical period (and to the Romans in particular), which had typically displayed the collected weapons and armor of the defeated armies now emptied of all threat and become emblems of defeat, eventually became so conventional in European culture as to metamorphose into a decorative element that in the main appears to have lost its original military meaning. But at its heart it holds the memory of the ways in which defeat makes the equipment of others useless to them (fig. 4.3). The presence of ritual objects from the Second Temple carried in triumph in Rome in the first century on the Arch of Titus will remind us that the acquisition of the sacred material had served as an indication of cultural predominance in earlier eras, as will the legend of the theft of the remains of Saint Mark, famously taken from Alexandria to Venice in the ninth century.[8] However, it is in the nineteenth century that for the first time we find works of art becoming military trophies *as works of art*, a development that says as much about the forms of power that emerged in the period as about where its vulnerabilities lay but that also must be recognized as a key element in the validation of the modern concept of art.

It makes good sense to think of the acquisition of the Elgin Marbles by the British government in the context of the emerging use of art in politics, as well as in relation to the complex negotiations between the emergent British and declining Ottoman Empires that would be an important subtext in international politics for the century to follow and beyond. But it would be wrong to think of any element in this process as inevitable, particularly the aspiration to mark victory by the transfer of works of art. After all, marble is not an instrument of war as that term is usually understood, one that needs to be taken from the enemy by force in order to assure victory, no more than canvas is—not unless we want to say that new kinds of weapons and even new kinds of warfare are emerging in the post-revolutionary period. The struggle over art objects is evidence of the importance of the battles for legitimacy in which institutions of culture become identifiable not as akin to triumphs in the ancient sense—that is, ritual displays commemorating victory—but as fields of battle for a struggle that is still current. In the unsettled politics of post-Napoleonic Europe we see the will to transmute an ongoing contest into a finished event by the temporal claim entailed in every triumph. The victory parade becomes not a ratification of the successful conclusion to long struggle but a claim that victory has already taken place. The new arrangement of admired objects indicates that the cause was as sound and therefore the struggle as necessary as the outcome is beneficial for the public, that fickle new entity which has become the new measure of legitimacy even for authoritarian regimes. *Noblesse oblige*, is, after all, an early nineteenth-century coinage.[9]

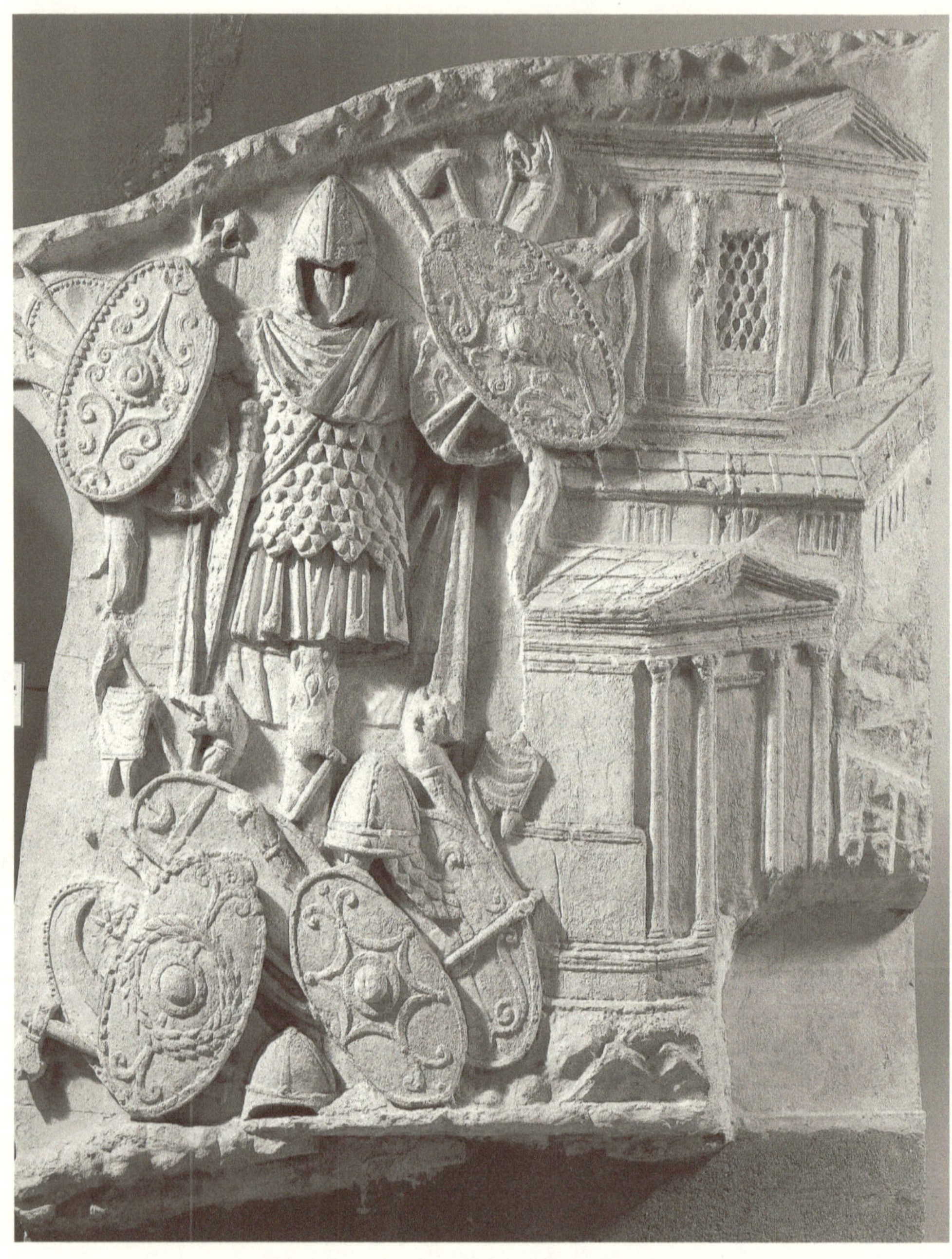

FIGURE 4.3. Trophy of Dacian weapons. Cast from Trajan's Column. Photo: G. Dagli Orti. © DeA Picture Library / Art Resource / NY.

I am focusing on the European part of the story, but the case of the Elgin Marbles is a reminder of the broader imperial processes on which Britain was embarked and which were central factors in power struggles that were global in nature, even though they have largely been remembered for events that took place on battlefields and capitals in Europe. Wellington's military career began in India, where his brother was viceroy, and the financial power that Britain could bring to bear against France had its source in the relative autonomy Britain had developed through its Eastern trade. And so, while, I will follow the lead of my texts and emphasize events in Paris during its time of cultural ascendancy and vulnerability, it bears keeping in mind the far wider scope and effects of local symbolic struggles.[10]

• • •

Between 1803 and 1809 Robillard-Péronville and Pierre Laurent published a sequence of sumptuous engravings with accompanying text designed to be bound into four massive volumes containing most of the known masterpieces of European art since antiquity. However, *Le Musée français* is not the record of an imaginary museum, the sort of thing we recognize as typical of compendia of the eighteenth and nineteenth centuries, in which text and images serve as signs of (and compensations for) the impossibility of seeing all this admirable work together.[11] As its subtitle—*Recueil de gravures d'après les plus beaux tableaux, statues et bas-reliefs qui composent la collection nationale*—indicates, *Le Musée français* is the catalog of the masterpieces making up the *national* collection (their admirable nature was the cause, not the result, of their being assembled in Paris). The frontispiece to all the volumes of the catalog (fig. 4.4) shows Apollo, his lyre at his feet, crowning the muses of painting and sculpture while a similar but uncrowned figure—likely the muse of engraving—looks on and unrolls a scroll (perhaps a print of Raphael's frustratingly unmovable *School of Athens*).[12] The *Apollo Belvedere* is visible to the right of the image, a reminder of the figure on which the representation of the presiding deity has evidently been based and an anticipation of the contents of the volume. Which is to say that the Apollo Belvedere, like the Laocoön, the Medici Venus, and just about all movable masterpieces of painting and sculpture in Europe, had found its way to the assemblage tendentiously named the "National Collection."[13]

"In the course of your victories," reads the 1803 dedication to "Bonaparte, Citizen First Consul" in the first volume, "you have conquered the principal

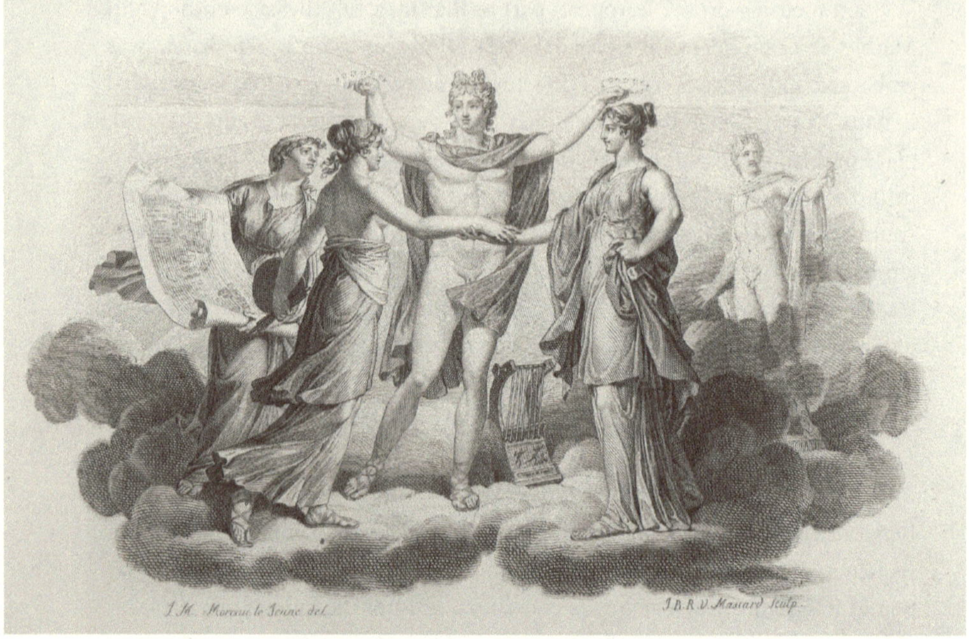

FIGURE 4.4. Frontispiece of *Le Musée français, ou recueil de gravures d'après les plus beaux tableaux, statues et bas-reliefs qui composent la collection nationale*, vol. 1 (Paris: Robillard-Peronville and Laurent, 1803).

masterpieces of the fine arts, and have enriched France with them." For all that it is couched in terms that suggest the publication is motivated by the aim of spreading knowledge, the text, with its splendid type matching its fulsome prose, is unable to hide a desire to publicize French victories and Napoleonic glory. "The collection of engravings that can make them known to the whole of Europe is an homage due to you," the authors write, making the publication a double project, simultaneously diffusing knowledge and projecting something more archaic, the glory of the first consul. "We offer them to you with recognition and respect."[14] Indeed, tributes to power are unmissable throughout the work, as they are in the history of the institution it tracks.

To commemorate the first consul's visit to the Venus de Medici on his birthday in 1803, the director of the museum, Vivant Denon, had had a medal struck with the leader's image on one side and that of the statue on the other, a tribute that the editors of *Le Musée français* reproduce at its actual size and with an accompanying encomium in the 1809 volume devoted to classical statues (fig. 4.5). "This monument, made to last to the most distant posterity, will be the eternal testimony to the munificence of Bonaparte, who donated the Venus de Medici to the French Museum, and will serve to affirm in perpetuity the gratitude of the fine arts towards their illustrious benefactor."[15] "Victory to the Arts" reads the inscription around the medal. But "victory" stands alone on one side for emphasis, and the illustration that displays both sides of the medal at once at the conclusion of the entry on the statue sets up something that looks like a suggestive equation including the idealized visage of the consul and the statue at which he impassively gazes: victory = the arts.

We will see near the close of this chapter that the consolidation of legitimacy through bestowing a Venus on the French nation becomes another of the many practices of the usurper adopted by the returning king, Louis XVIII. But that is still in the future of the tale I aim to tell, which finds its points of reference along the lines of transition separating one dispensation of power from another. Still, it is important to emphasize the wavering and uncertain nature of a division

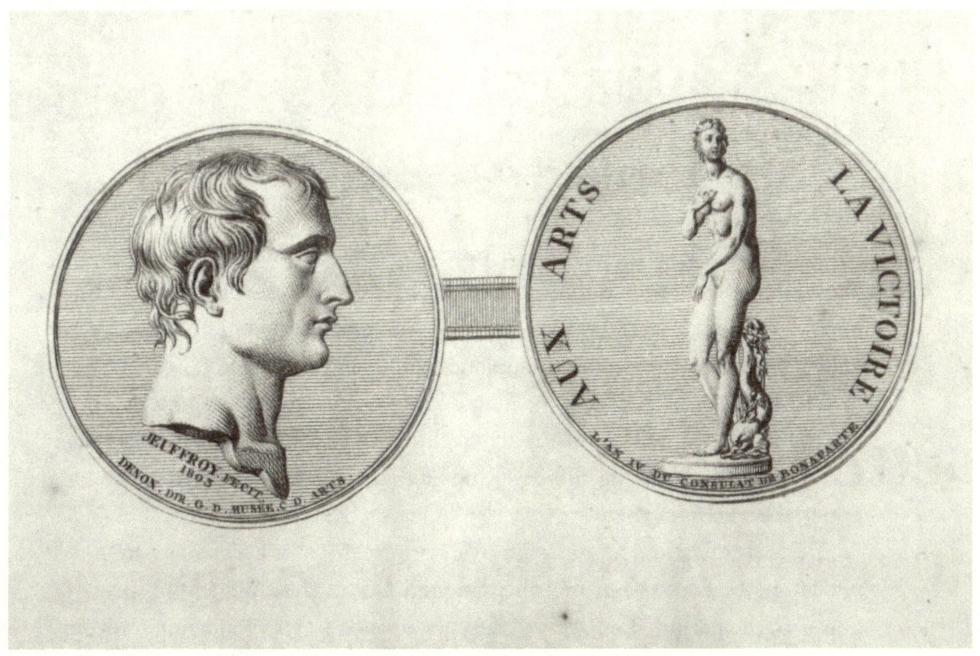

FIGURE 4.5. "Napoleon–Medici Venus Medal." *Le Musée français*, vol. 4 (1809).

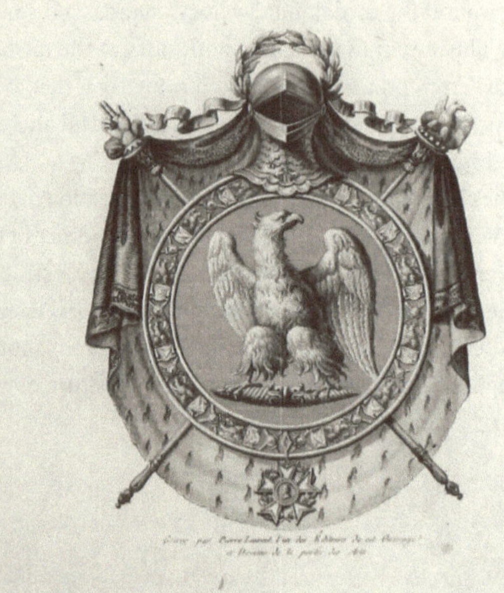

FIGURE 4.6. Dedication. *Le Musée français*, vol. 2 (1805).

that political interests will work to present as absolute, an uncertain margin, like an unsteady natural border, vulnerable to shifts in the geological fault lines it follows, or like a territory contested between neighboring nations, where no matter where the division falls, a relationship is never fully lost. The eventual turn from Emperor Napoleon to King Louis, I am suggesting, is anticipated by the change that is marked in the 1805 volume of *Le Musée français*, dedicated no longer to the first consul but to the emperor, its frontispiece featuring an imperial eagle (fig. 4.6).

The identification of museum with sovereign was a constant in post-revolutionary France, but the phenomenon was as dynamic as the forms of power in the period. The Louvre Museum opened in 1793 following a revolutionary decree of 1791 claiming royal property for the people. While "Musée Napoléon" was first inscribed on the walls of the Louvre in 1803, the ruler's engagement with the institution substantially predates this commemoration of a relationship going back at least as far as the Italian campaign (1796–97), when art objects were systematically expropriated by Napoleon's men and sent with great fanfare to the national collection. It was a process that did not originate with the general but in which he took a personal interest and with which he made an effort to associate himself. It bears emphasizing, given later sensibilities, that contemporary representations indicate no embarrassment at all about the project. In a frequently reproduced ink drawing from the early nineteenth century generally attributed to Charles Meynier, as in other representations of the activities of French agents, neither haste nor furtiveness are suggested so much as a confident claiming of property by right (see fig. 4.7).[16] Under the watchful eyes of their superiors, soldiers carefully lower paintings into crates already labelled with the names of specific items, in this case works in Parma ceded by treaty in 1796. Still, while the canvases themselves are exposed to view and face up, suggesting the openness of the removals, one discordant note is sounded in the image by the presence of a fabric that improbably hangs over

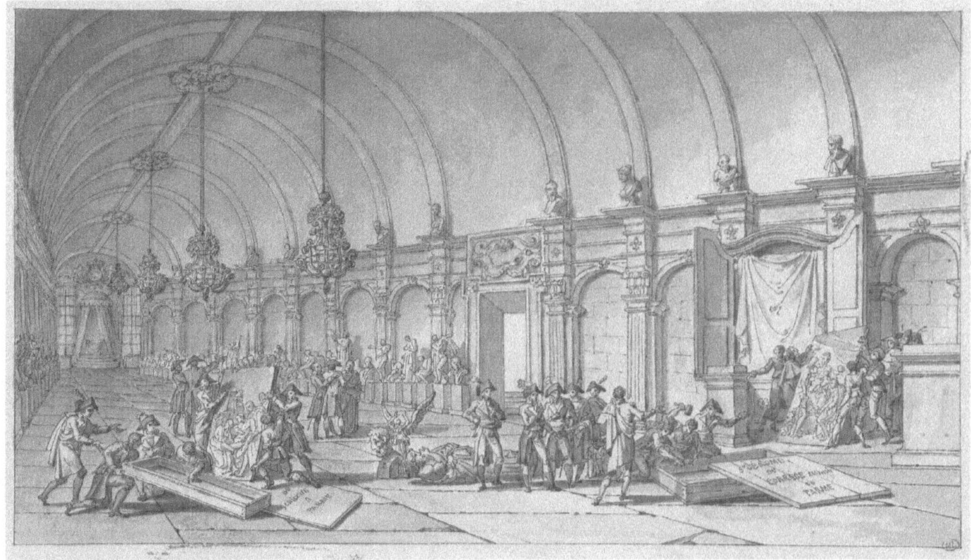

FIGURE 4.7. *The Correggio Madonna Is Taken from the Academy of Parma and Delivered to the French Commissioners (May 1796).* Attributed to Charles Meynier, part of a series of drawings produced between 1802 and 1814 illustrating Napoleon's campaign in Italy. Black ink, 17.8 x 32.4 cm. Louvre Museum, Paris. Photo: Jean-Gilles Berizzi. © RMN-Grand Palais / Art Resource, NY.

the altar from which the soldiers have just removed Correggio's *Madonna of Saint Jerome*, like a screen of modesty protecting an obscene source from view or perhaps a body covered up at death.

The veil Meynier places over the altar draws attention to the blank space that it hides. I will be suggesting below that the imaginative power of the gaps created by the removal and others like it will endure for a longer time than the *Madonna* will be away from Parma. But that period is still in the future of the museum, and loss was neither anticipated nor sympathized with in the rhetoric that accompanied the Napoleonic depredations. Indeed, in a notorious moment in the history of looting, booty from Italy, featuring masterpieces stolen from the Vatican as well as the horses removed from Saint Mark's in Venice, was welcomed to Paris in 1798 with an elaborate four-day celebration culminating in a procession at the Champ de Mars (fig. 4.8). The banner carried at the

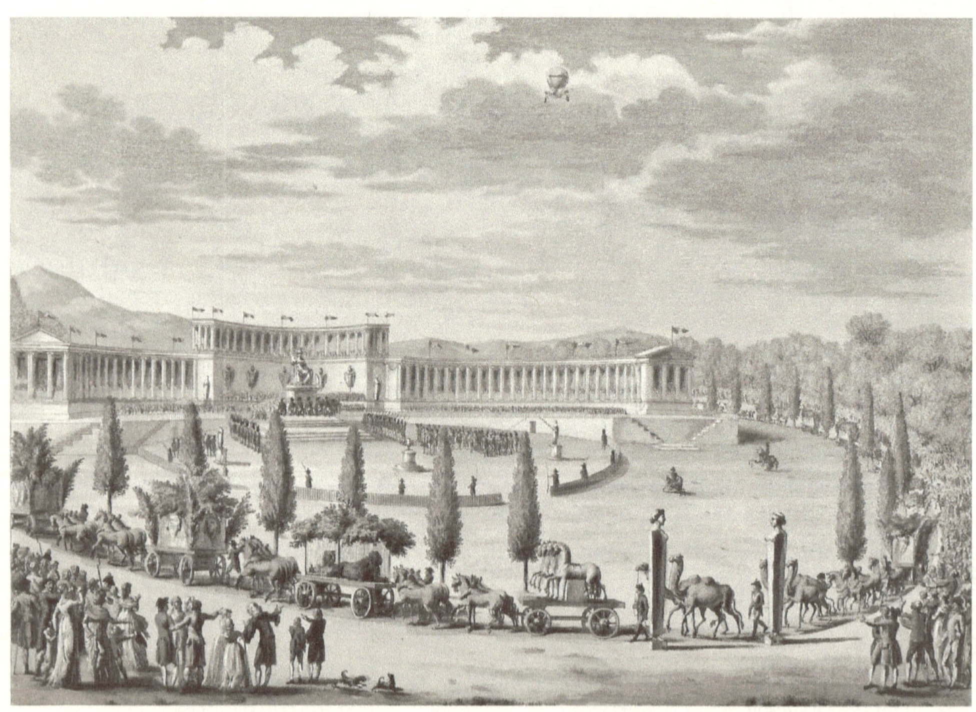

FIGURE 4.8. Pierre Gabriel Berthault, after Abraham Girardet, *Triumphal Entry of the Monuments of Arts and Sciences in France* (1798). (Note the balloon rising over the festivities.) Etching on paper, 20.5 x 29 cm. Smithsonian National Air and Space Museum, Washington, DC.

triumph at once recognized the change that characterizes the history of ownership of works of art and declared an end to that process: "Greece surrendered them; Rome lost them; / Their fate changed twice; it will not change again."[17]

It is hardly surprising that the story of the Musée Napoléon, linked as it was to the fortunes of a political dispensation that was ultimately unsuccessful in securing its continued existence, has largely been forgotten outside of the works of specialists or students of the history of art plunder. But much as it would be wrong to discount the political changes effected in the years of Napoleonic hegemony that were to become a permanent fact for Europe even after his defeat, so it would be an error to neglect the ways in which, in spite of—and in some measure because of—its failure, this museum came to have an epochal effect on the history of art and its institutions. Indeed, scholars have argued for the fundamental importance of the Musée Napoléon to our understanding of the development of the museum in later years. Still, though the fate of material objects in modern concepts of art is a topic of fundamental importance, it can be difficult to keep in view for practical as well as more intangible reasons. It is almost as difficult to credit the power of loss as to talk about the conceptual force of accidents of history based on little more than raw power.[18]

The acquisition of the Parthenon Marbles by Britain, on which I will briefly touch, is in no way separable from the far more elaborate tale of assembly and collapse across the Channel, a relationship reminding us of the complex intersections of theft, restoration, glory, and complicity in the period, and of the challenging nature of the emotions attendant on the experience of damage. Nevertheless, an important element in the story of this chapter is the unevenness in the development of modern art institutions at the international level, so it will be important to be clear on the distinct situations in France and the United Kingdom. Taking our measure from the tale I laid out in my opening anecdote, we find a chasm separating the two nations when it comes to the public display of art. While the paintings assembled by Joseph Bonaparte and captured on his defeat at the Battle of Vitoria arrived in London at the highest point in the life of the museum stocked by his brother's conquests, there was no comparable institution that might have housed the works anywhere in the British Isles during this period. A permanent national museum devoted to the public display of the fine arts would not exist in Britain until the founding of the National Gallery in 1824, ten years after Napoleon himself was first defeated: a modest collection of canvases housed in the home of John Julius Angerstein, the benefactor who had left them to the nation. The heterogeneous nature of the British Museum, which included important holdings in natural history and antiquities from the time of its establishment in 1753, ensured that the role of that institution in relation to the fine arts would remain a question for decades to come. Its admission policies were, in any case, such that only a select few could profit from exposure to its holdings. The Elgin Marbles, the purchase of which would be a milestone in the history of the museum and its relation to the public, were still in temporary quarters at Lord Elgin's Piccadilly home when Joseph Bonaparte was defeated, their purchase for the nation only taking place in 1816.

Little wonder, then, that when the painter Thomas Lawrence finally made his way to Paris in 1814, after the nearly unbroken isolation enforced by decades of revolutionary and Napoleonic conflict, he felt fortunate to arrive before the museum that bore the name of his nation's hated rival had been disassembled (see fig. 4.9). It can be difficult at this distance in time and using the surprisingly simple notions of cultural property current today to fully appreciate the melancholy sense of regret that even Bonaparte's worst enemies felt at the imminent dissolution of this museum built on conquest (perhaps even harder than to fully sympathize with the blend of admiration and disgust provoked in thoughtful Britons such as Lawrence by the emperor himself). And yet traveler after traveler expresses this very sense. Here is Lawrence in May 1814, on his way to paint his important series of portraits of the chief protagonists in the struggles against Napoleon—a commission from the regent himself:

> Had I delayed my journey a day longer, I should have lost the view of some of the finest works of this Gallery, the noblest assemblage of the efforts of human genius that was ever presented to the world. It very much surpassed my expectations, and particularly in its most celebrated pictures. . . . A few days will see the whole taken away; and much as we ought to reprobate the injustice by which the greater part of them was obtained, it is impossible to witness their departure without regret,—at least I know not how to check this feeling. No one can see France and Paris without bowing to the greatness and extent of this man's conceptions. I use a phrase that is forced upon me. I speak of him as present, and every where he is; and it is as impossible that he can ever be separated from the past greatness of his country, as for human efforts to blot out the sun.[19]

The possibility of viewing at a world capital relatively convenient to England objects that had until that point been kept largely in what were essentially

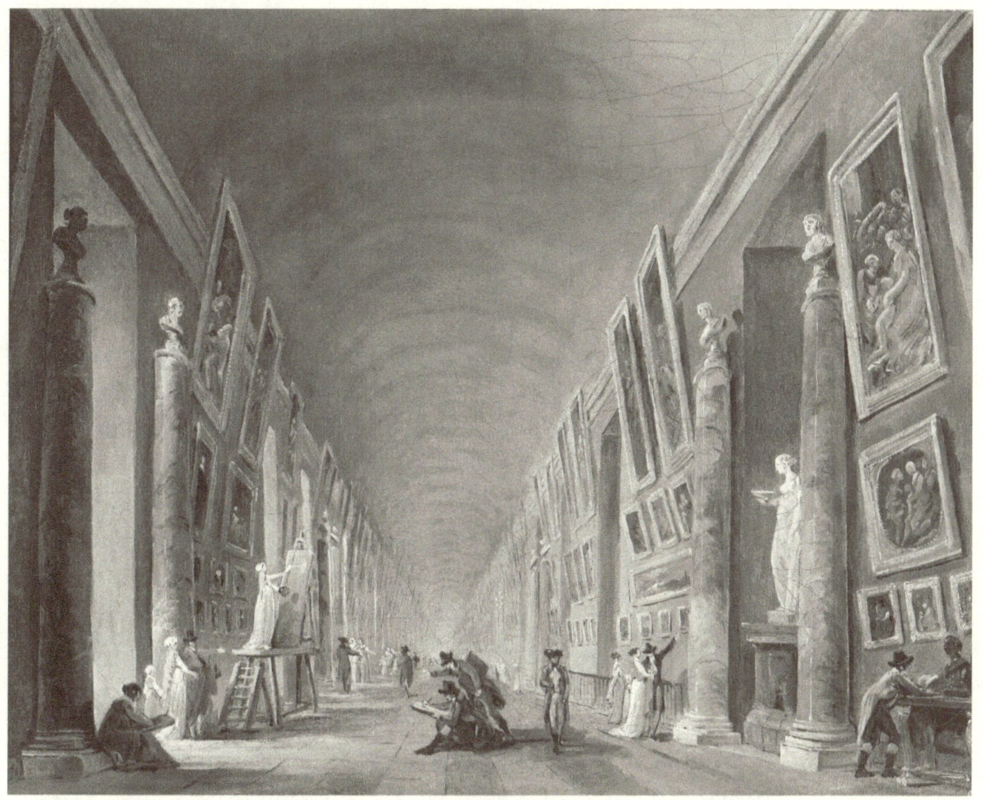

FIGURE 4.9. Hubert Robert, *The Grand Gallery of the Louvre* (1801–5). Oil on canvas, 37 x 46 cm. Louvre Museum, Paris. This work by the early director of the museum and noted painter of ruins offers a view of the museum a decade or more before Thomas Lawrence saw it, around the time William Hazlitt made his first visit. Erich Lessing / Art Resource, NY.

private collections, the chance to see together the principal recognized masterpieces of world art at a time before photography or even rail travel: these boons directly ascribable to the ambitious museum bearing Napoleon's name forced hyperbolic admiration even from his enemies, none of whom had anything approaching the Louvre awaiting them when they returned to their own countries' various capitals.

Here is the voice of another traveler, the scientist Michael Faraday as a young man, writing in his journal six months earlier (October 1813) with a similar blend of moral censure and irresistible admiration:

> I saw the Galerie Napoleon to day but I scarcely know what to say of it. It is both the glory and the disgrace of France. As being itself, and as containing specimens of those things which proclaim the power of man, and which point out the high degree of refinement to which he has risen, it is unsurpassed, unequalled, and must call forth the highest and most unqualified admiration; but when memory brings to mind the manner in which the works came here, and views them only as the gains of violence and rapine, she blushes for the people that even now glory in an act that made them a nation of thieves.[20]

As both these responses make clear, Napoleon's Louvre was recognized as at once something quite new—a site affording the opportunity of astonishing aesthetic edification to a broader public than had ever had access to any collection—and as something all too old, as a concrete manifestation of the raw power of conquering armies. The grandeur of the Louvre under Napoleon participates in the extremely long tradition of military plunder (call it barbarism), while also opening out into a modern world characterized by the drive to public access to culture in which the practice of violent expropriation will typically be seen as not only incongruous but irredeemably unethical (call it civilization). Even in its own day, the relations between reprobated violence and admired achievement manifested by the Musée Napoléon are clear; hence Faraday and Lawrence's quick oscillations between awe and blame.

That the Duke of Wellington was closely involved with the process that stripped the notable Napoleonic accessions from the museum is an indication of the political significance attached to the institution.[21] The project of restitution was complex, controversial, and ultimately incomplete. But its shortcomings made the process of repatriation by despoliation only more resonant. The allies were aware of the cultural force of the museum, and so the removal of the most valuable treasures was almost as well documented as the arrival of that booty, and even more broadly significant. Objects from Italian collections were the most precious, and the British eventually provided important support to their restitution—which in many cases was not to result in anything like a return home so much as a stocking of recently established museums. At the Vatican two new galleries were formed to house material that had been brought together by the French. Works from Rome arrived on January 4, 1816. The Pinacoteca was opened in 1817 for the paintings—and features to this day a large Thomas Lawrence portrait of the prince regent, an incongruous item in a collection of Italian masterpieces but entirely appropriate as a commemoration of the British role in restorations of various sorts. The Galleria Chiaramonti, which had in fact been established by Pope Pius VII a decade earlier in response to Napoleonic depredations, was redesigned to house the antiquities from the Louvre in 1817 in the Braccio Nuovo. The galleries to which the objects were *returned* (to use the conventional verb) did not exist when most of those objects were taken to France. In that sense, even though they ultimately left the museum that bore the emperor's name for about a decade, they came back to a world Napoleon had created.

A lunette showing the recovery of the art objects, which is said to have been commissioned by Canova himself to decorate the Chiaramonte, is notably unresolved about precisely what it is celebrating (fig. 4.10). The famous works of art are not visible, as the artist represents them as having been practically but ingloriously crated for the long trip south. They are transported with all

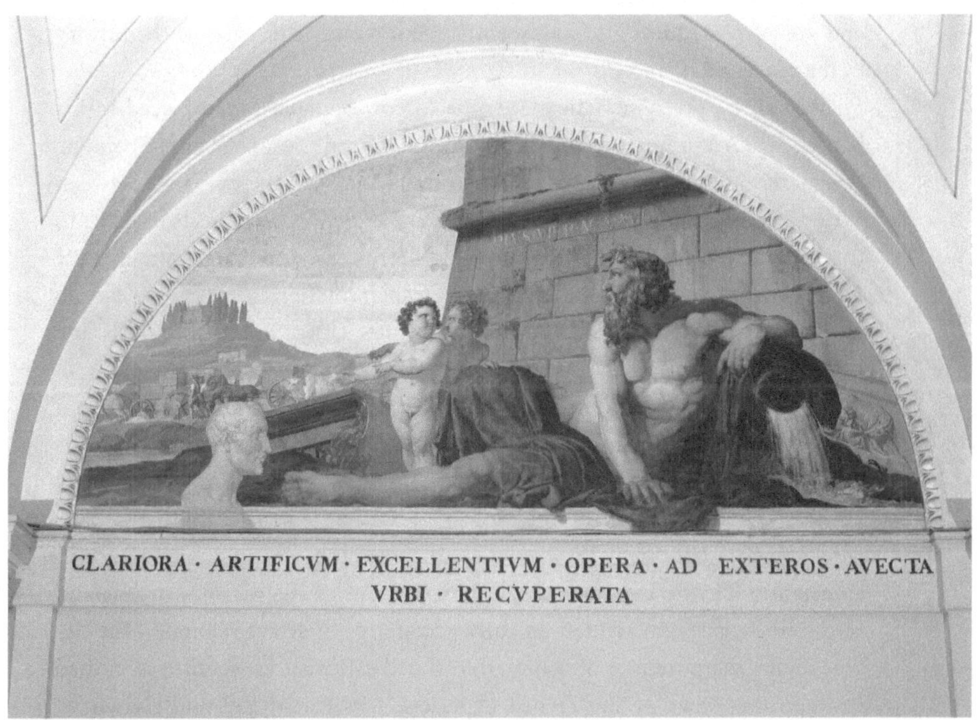

FIGURE 4.10. Francesco Hayez, *Return to Rome of the Works of Art Taken to Paris* (1817). Galleria Chiaramonti, Vatican Museum, Rome. Scala / Art Resource, NY.

the pace and glamour of ox-drawn carts. Meanwhile, a personification of the Tiber, based on a classical model, is vivified into an eagerly expectant Rome turned to gaze in the direction of the procession indicated by two putti (though the actual statue of the Tiber remains at the Louvre to this day). To round out the dislocations illustrated in the work, not to say the surprisingly subdued quality of what might well have been the occasion of a scene of more than a little drama or celebration, in the foreground a modern statue with the air of a Roman portrait bust looks neither toward Rome nor at the works of art being delivered to the city. This representation of William Richard Hamilton, the permanent undersecretary for foreign affairs and an influential antiquarian who played a key role in making the restitutions possible, like the presence of George IV in the Pinacoteca, stands as a reminder of a historical moment and the complicated processes that must be set into motion to undertake any restoration worth the name.[22] But these Englishmen at the Vatican may also be understood to illustrate a more conceptual point: the fact that partial returns and out-of-placedness are not exceptions but constituent parts of the history of the museum.

We can be pretty certain that when Joseph Bonaparte had placed in his baggage train a number of important canvases from royal palaces in Spain, he was merely attempting to secure light, portable loot. It is the exchange between Wellington and the Spanish monarch that transforms these objects lifted from the battlefield into symbols of something more than opportunism and brute force, even into a collection. This kind of transformation is not always easy to effect, however, or to stabilize. A few years after Lawrence's trip to Paris, the painter found himself testifying before a parliamentary committee trying to decide whether the nation should purchase the Elgin Marbles; a letter from Canova himself endorsing the singular merits of the works together with his sense of the privilege of seeing them in London was entered into the record of the committee. It bears noting, just to fill out a little further this list of non-coincidences, that when William Richard Hamilton was Elgin's secretary in Constantinople, he had supervised the shipment of the marbles to England in the first place and written an early account of their acquisition.[23] The debate about the purchase of the marbles for the British Museum was shaped in important ways by the French experience. In Parliament and elsewhere, Napoleon's practice of expropriation was cited as an example to be avoided at all costs. But it is evidently the source of an inescapable, though not always comfortable, model of cultural property (*Hansard*, June 7, 1816). Elgin himself is clear: "Buonaparte has not got such a thing," he notes in a letter in 1802, written as he begins to remove important work from the site, "from all his thefts in Italy."[24] Indeed, the committee asked Lawrence directly to compare the Parthenon sculptures to the masterpieces he had seen at the Louvre, at the time bound back to the Vatican.

George Bankes, chair of the parliamentary committee on the acquisition of the marbles, is not as bold as Lord Elgin in his presentation of the matter. During the course of the debate, he also cites French competition as one reason to make the acquisition, an argument he puts in the context of wartime rivalry. But the official record of the debate shows his eagerness to draw fundamental distinctions, the conventional use of third person in reporting parliamentary speeches adding not a little to the tone of defensiveness that is in any case hard to miss in his words:

> There was nothing like spoliation in the case, and . . . it bore no resemblance to those undue and tyrannical means by which the French had obtained possession of so many treasures of art, which he rejoiced to see again in the possession of their rightful owners. A notion prevailed among some gentlemen, that these treasures also should be restored to their original owners. But how was this to be done? (*Hansard*, June 7, 1816, col. 1028)

Bankes's question may seem disingenuous, but it deserves to be taken seriously. Restitution is sometimes as difficult a project as identifying "original owners." And the matter is more than practical. If there is any interest to Walter Benjamin's declaration that a document of civilization is also inevitably a document of barbarism, it resides in the irresolvable condition it describes. In what sense is it possible to revise the status of a document of barbarism by the simple expedient of a change in ownership?

Art historians have demonstrated the importance of the upheavals that took place during and after the French Revolution in establishing new sources and markets for art, and there is no question that art lovers in the first decades of the nineteenth century knew they were living through an epochal period when it came to the actual possibilities of experiencing admired art objects.[25] William Hazlitt, for one, traced his aesthetic education to the opportunities presented by the era in his extraordinary autobiographical essay "On the Pleasure of Painting" (1820), which memorializes the months the erstwhile painter spent at the Musée Napoléon during the Peace of Amiens of 1802, each canvas he cites having come from a different Italian church:

> A universe of art! I ran the gauntlet of all the schools from the bottom to the top; and in the end got admitted into the inner room, where they had been repairing some of their greatest works. Here the Transfiguration, the St. Peter Martyr, and the St. Jerome of Domenichino stood on the floor, as if they had bent their knees, like camels stooping, to unlade their riches to the spectator. . . . Reader, "if thou hast not seen the Louvre, thou art damned!"—for thou hast not seen the choicest remains of the works of art; or thou hast not seen all these together, with their mutually reflected glories. I say nothing of the statues; for I know but little of sculpture, and never liked any till I saw the Elgin marbles. . . . [ellipsis in the original] Here, for four months together, I strolled and studied . . . and brought away with me some loose draughts and fragments. . . . How often, thou tenantless mansion of godlike magnificence—how often has my heart since gone a pilgrimage to thee![26]

This visit to Napoleon's Louvre would be a constant point of imaginative return for the essayist—giving a political and aesthetic location to his characteristic nostalgia. It is all the more compelling, then, that his argument in defense of the institution in the *Life of Napoleon* (produced nearly a decade after "On the Pleasure of Painting," in 1828–30) is unable to avoid acknowledging the ways in which the nature of the acquisitions in the museum make the institution at once ethically suspect and splendid. Hazlitt's argument turns and turns again uncomfortably, looking for a satisfactory point of view from which to reflect on the nature of a museum created through violent expropriation and the dislocation of objects from their sources of origin. I will mark the sharpest pivots in the passage with italics. Each claim indicates a revision of what is suggested before or is to follow, starting with the first, which is a kind of non sequitur where it occurs, in the middle of a paragraph discussing the uselessness of great art for creating great artists. Dismissing the conventional pedagogical justification for the plunder, which is offered by Napoleon himself when he argues in favor of expropriating Correggio's *Madonna of Saint Jerome* rather than extorting more money from the Duke of Parma ("the possession of such a masterpiece by the city of Paris . . . would produce other *chefs-d'oeuvre* of the same kind"), Hazlitt insists instead on the symbolic, not practical, value of the accumulated works. But his terms are singularly fraught:

> *It was not amiss*, in one point of view, that the triumphs of human genius should be collected together in the Louvre as trophies of human liberty; or to deck out the stern, gaunt form of the Republic which was declared incapable of maintaining the relations of peace and amity with the richest spoils of war: *otherwise*

> these works would make most impression and are most likely to give a noble and enthusiastic impulse to the mind in the places which gave them birth and in connection with the history and circumstances of those who produced them:—torn from these, they lose half their interest and vital principle.

It can be difficult for the modern reader to credit the commitments in the first part of this passage. Still, Hazlitt's experience, as laid out in "On the Pleasure of Painting" and elsewhere, indicates that both the aesthetic thrill and the experience of a radical achievement that could link political ideals with beauty and public edification were crucial to his own development. Nevertheless, at the word "otherwise" the critic turns from justifying the symbolic role of the revolutionary museum to expressing anxiety about the effects of museal deracination on works of art.[27] Still, he cannot leave the matter there. After a brief reflection on the French character, he returns to the project of justifying the museum, answering his forceful recognition of violence and loss with a compensatory celebration of Napoleon's Louvre as a compendium of human genius affording the possibility of new and richer forms of admiration:

> *Still,* justice should be done to the taste and judgment with which the selection was made, which was no less striking than the universality of the sources from whence it was drawn. As a gallery, the Louvre was unrivalled: even the Vatican shrinks before it. Not a first-rate picture is to be met with on the Continent, but it found its way to the Louvre. . . . You walked for a quarter of a mile through works of fine art; the very floors echoed the sounds of immortality. The effect was not broken and frittered by being divided and taken piecemeal, but the whole was collected, heaped, massed together to a gorgeous height, so that the blow stunned you, and could never be forgotten. This was what art could do, and all other pretensions seemed to sink before it. School called unto school; one great name answered to another, swelling the chorus of universal praise. *Instead of* robbery and sacrilege, it was the crowning and consecration of art; there was a dream and a glory, like the coming of the Millennium. These works, *instead of* being taken from their respective countries, were given to the world, and to the mind and heart of man, from whence they sprung. (13:212)

By the end of the passage, the museum itself has become something far more than a repository of deracinated works; the choral effect of the ensemble drowns out the wistful sense of the lost vital home of the original. A resounding paean of universal praise overwhelms any local complaints of robbery or sacrilege.

Behind Hazlitt's hyperbole we may discern the inflated rhetoric provoked by his political disappointment at the collapse of the hope of the Revolution and the subsequent defeat of Napoleon. But, as we will see, conservative responses to the dismantling of the Musée Napoléon have a similar quality as they negotiate the unstable relationship between robbery and sacrilege, on the one hand, and a consecration of art, on the other. Whether sympathetic or unsympathetic to the regimes that made the Musée Napoléon possible, admirers of the institution had to engage a difficult set of issues, some of which may strike the modern reader as entailing distinctions without a difference, while others will seem pressingly current or self-evidently important. When is spoliation a manifestation of martial glory, as opposed to merely theft backed up by military power? What is the relation between the fear that deracinated works of art may be at risk of losing their "interest and vital principle" when removed from the culture in which they emerged, and the admiration those very works of art provoke, precisely because they have been given a new context?

I have cited briefly the ambivalence given voice by Lawrence and Faraday writing in Paris. The conservative triumphalism of Felicia Hemans makes for an interesting contrast. Her *Restoration of the Works of Art to Italy* (1816), written with the forthright clarity and abstraction of an author very distant from events, is an allegory of retribution in which the allied armies appear in the guise of the virtues Justice and Truth:

> Fair Florence! Queen of Arno's lovely vale!
> Justice and Truth indignant heard thy tale,
> And sternly smil'd, in Retribution's hour,
> To wrest thy Treasures from the Spoiler's power.[28]

Helen Maria Williams's nuanced and detailed firsthand account of the process of removal and the response it provoked is far more judicious. Of the angry French she writes, "They were in vain reminded that these precious objects were the spoils of the vanquished, who had now become the conquerors" (342). The cool-eyed symmetry of Williams's claim is part of the subtlety of her analysis of a situation in which concepts of property and supremacy are inextricably entwined. She offers no allegory, simply the unadorned fact of earlier victory and current defeat. And her acknowledgment of the failure to satisfy inflamed feelings of balanced reason or the broad perspective is a reminder of the interests shaping concepts of right ownership when the topic is a proxy for speaking about conquest and defeat.

It is not the losers in a military struggle alone, however, who are liable to be made uncomfortable by finding important cultural determinations ultimately coming down to the fortunes of war. The allies manifest a dominance not practically distinguishable from what Hemans called "the Spoiler's power" when they dismantle the Louvre collection. While Williams recognizes the unmissable fact of retribution, she does not, like Hemans, dress the victor's triumph in the guise of a newly cheerful Justice and Truth. The satisfaction of Napoleon's enemies is as much to be expected as the gloom of his supporters. The matter becomes most interesting when affect does not match up with allegiance. I have noted the ways in which we may hear in Hazlitt's *Life* a rebuke to Napoleonic spoliation that his celebration of the museum would like to ignore. A text written from a different political angle illustrates the power of an ambivalence like that we find in Hazlitt, provoked by the experience of the museum in its last days. James Simpson's small claim to fame as an author was his account of the field of Waterloo soon after the battle. But toward the end of his life this important educator and friend of Walter Scott brought out *Paris after Waterloo: Notes Taken at the Time and Hitherto Unpublished* (1852), a record that includes a vivid account of the inescapable majesty of the Musée Napoléon and the poignancy of its dissolution at a time when both were distant memories.

Simpson's text shows him to have been deeply responsive both to the novelty of a national museum freely open to the public and to the experience of encountering this astonishing institution (he calls it "this wonder of wonders") at its moment of crisis and partial dismantling.[29] His diary entries trace the progress of a significant relationship with a site that is at once overwhelmingly powerful and deeply vulnerable—and not just to critical judgments but to substantial material losses. It will be useful, therefore, to quote from his response to the place over a number of visits, beginning with his first, which establishes all the principal issues—the splendor of the institution, its unwonted accessibility, and the ethical issues raised by its existence:

> Gazing like myself were many spectators, for the doors are open to the whole world; and large parties of English private soldiers, and those of the allies, were wandering through the halls, and in the picture-gallery above. Great numbers of English travellers were there, many with their wives and daughters, and here and there a Frenchman or Frenchwoman. All the sights are without fee in Paris. They belong to the public; and more lately this principle has been pleaded, to endeavour to stop the retributive hands of the Allies, their former owners, in

> the Louvre, that the treasures belong to all Europe, and are merely *collected*, and splendidly accommodated, in Paris, for their admiration. In spite of this view of the question, I was just in time to see the Louvre quite entire. My next visit showed me the work of restoration actually begun. (124; emphasis in the original)

To see "the work of restoration," as Simpson does, is to see particular works of art as transient. Ultimately, it is to *not* see some of them at all. And so, as Simpson himself realizes, what is interesting is less what he gets to set eyes on than what he doesn't. "The great work of restitution is advancing," he notes in his account of a late visit, with his peculiar responsiveness to this process. "Of the many sights I saw and events I witnessed, in a juncture unequalled for wonders, none is more striking to look back upon than to have been present at this" (253). Given that Simpson had witnessed the bloodied field of Waterloo after a struggle during which fifty thousand men had died and had responded passionately to many of the masterpieces of the Louvre collection, his statement that the dissolution was the greatest marvel he had seen is a remarkable declaration. And indeed, throughout his account he is nearly as responsive to the absences around him as to the admired presences: "Pictures belonging to the Prussians were still being removed," he notes at one point, "and a good many blanks were observable" (218).[30]

These "blanks" return in a later passage, transposed back in time and to a different location. As "the work of restoration" continues, they emerge in an oddly nested passage of reference and citation that begins with a discussion of the account of Raphael's *Transfiguration* in the catalog of the collection and ends with an outraged sympathetic evocation of the loss of Domenichino's *Saint Jerome*, a work much prized by visitors to the Louvre, as Hazlitt's reference, cited above, reminds us (fig. 4.11). "It is whimsical enough to note," Simpson writes with forced breeziness, citing the entry on Raphael's masterpiece in *Le Musée français*, "that the 'Transfiguration' was meant for the cathedral of Julius de Medicis, Archbishop of Narbonne; but its destination was changed." It is certainly true that the painting, which was installed in San Pietro in Montorio in Rome upon its posthumous completion, had originally been intended for a chapel in the cathedral of Narbonne, in the south of France. Through a bold telescoping of space and time, the authors of *Le Musée* present the expropriation of the piece as simply the consummation of a destiny that had been delayed for some three hundred years. Simpson, however, becomes ever more exercised

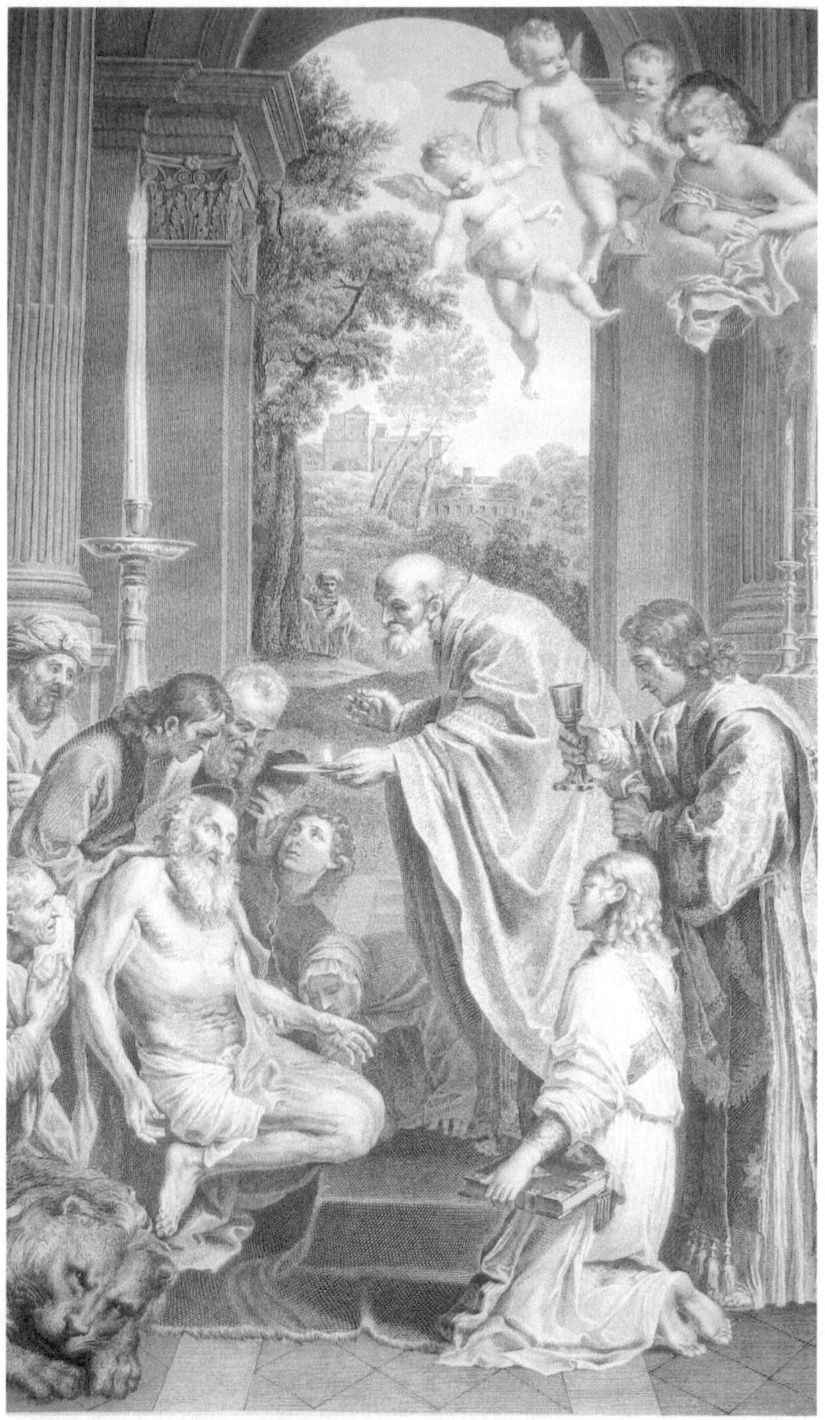

FIGURE 4.11. Henri Laurent, engraving after Domenichino, *Saint Jerome Receiving the Last Sacrament*. *Le Musée royal; ou, Recueil de gravures d'après les plus beaux tableaux, statues et bas-reliefs de la collection royale*, vol. 2 (Paris, 1816–18).

as he reflects on the relation between the destination and the destiny of works of art, a line of speculation provoked in him by a passage in the catalog entry that he quotes in French: "France owes to *victory* this *chef-d'oeuvre qui lui etait destiné*!" (223; emphasis in the original). Although the catalog is accurate on the original plans for Raphael's canvas, its terms inspire Simpson to turn from "whimsical" observation to a more forceful (though oddly interrogative) claim about the destiny of the object:

> Impudent varlets! a few hours more and that destination will be changed again, and the plundered treasure wrested from them! The "St Jerome" of Domenichino attracted my attention even more than the "Transfiguration." . . . This noblest of Domenichino's efforts was plundered from the altar of the Church of St Jerome at Rome, whither it is "destined" to return. What must have been the feelings of the devotees who, with their fathers before them, had associated *its* presence there with the saint's intercessory power, when they first gazed upon the blank left by its removal! What will they be on its return! (223–24; emphasis in the original)

It is difficult not to read in this imagined "blank" above the altar in a faraway church, as in Simpson's retrospective indignation, a proleptic acknowledgment of the loss he works hard to hide in his response to the act of restitution—not to see, that is, the Louvre itself taking on the quality of a despoiled temple where, after all, he has already noted that Prussian action is leaving "a good many blanks." The outburst seems motivated by the uneasy emotional relationship of the individual to two key issues raised by the catalog entry—the debt owed to victory and the destiny of a work of art.[31]

The indignation of the British traveler is part of a strenuous effort to view the despoliation of the Louvre as not simply another manifestation of superior military force but rather a fulfillment of the proper fate of the works of art. (And we might think back to the claim on the banner under which the works were brought to the Louvre, "Their fate changed twice; it will not change again.") In the catalog that exercises Simpson, as for Simpson himself, destiny is another word for a return to origins. Victory, on the other hand, seems to require a displacement to mark its arrival. It bears saying that Simpson is both right and entirely wrong about the fortunes of the works of art he celebrates. Only one of them made it back to the church from which it was removed: Titian's *St. Peter Martyr* was returned to Venice's Santi Giovanni e Paolo (where it met its own unhappy destiny: destruction in a fire in 1867). *The Transfiguration*, removed from the church of San Pietro in Montorio in Rome in 1797, was "returned" to the Vatican, where it remains to this day, along with Domenichino's *St. Jerome*, originally—as Simpson notes—from the church of San Girolamo della Carità in Rome. The phenomenon was widespread, so that—for example—many works from Venice and the Veneto were "returned" to the Accademia, a museum that was itself founded by Napoleonic decree in 1807 (opened in 1817) and whose holdings, like those of so many important museums, were attributable to Napoleonic-era actions (and to the suppression of religious institutions in particular).[32]

The topic of the restoration of art objects becomes all the more complicated when placed in the only context in which it may be properly understood as a historical phenomenon—the political conditions then in effect. But recognition of these is bound to complicate simple notions of *national* recovery. Everywhere one looks, the situation is not as later eras might prefer to understand it. To take one glaring example: at the time of the restorations Venice was part of the Austrian Empire.[33] If it is only at the moment of reunification that we might be able to say that the objects were returned to Italy (an Italy that had never before existed), then we would also have to point out that that same process of unification, which culminated in 1870 with the creation of Rome as capital of the new nation and put a new monarch in the palace that had belonged to the popes, also placed the works at the Vatican into the administrative control of another political entity rather than Italy, or even Rome: the newly forming Vatican State. "What must have been the feelings of the devotees who, with their fathers before them, had associated its presence there with the saint's intercessory power, when they first gazed upon the blank left by its removal! What will they be on its return!" The final question, already identified as rhetorical by its exclamation mark, hangs in space, its bases removed by the history (of the museum, of the nation) that has made it all the more unanswerable.

As Simpson is about to leave Paris, the reader knows there is only one place one is likely to find him (fig. 4.12). And he begins to sound uncannily like Hazlitt in a valedictory passage set in front of the Venus de Medici and within sight of the Laocoön and Apollo Belvedere. The text is worth quoting at length, both for a quality of melancholy regret that seems entirely sincere and well rendered and for the way that it forces itself toward a sublime register that does not ultimately resolve the troubled emotions provoking the evocation of that category. Ultimately Simpson makes recourse to the feelings of angels in his attempt to register the painful experience shaped by the prospect (that is also a memory)

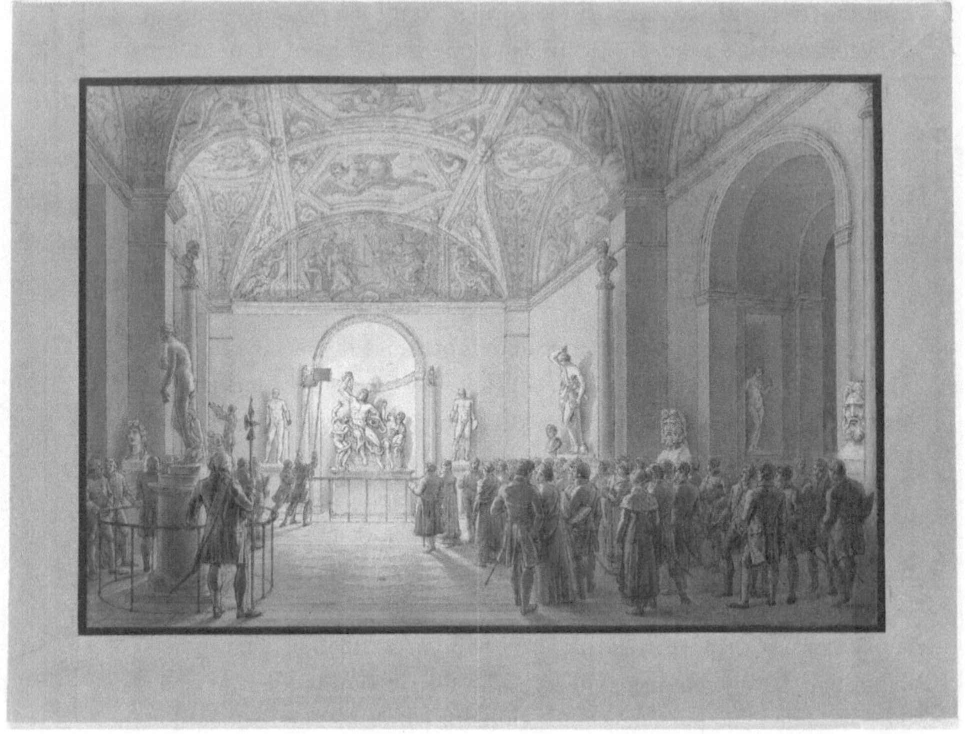

FIGURE 4.12. The Medici Venus (*left*) and Laocoön on display at the Musée Napoléon in 1810. Benjamin Zix, *Emperor Napoleon and the Empress Visiting the Gallery of the Laocoön at Night* (1810). Pen drawing, gray ink, graphite, brown wash, 26 x 29 cm. Louvre Museum, Paris. Photo: Michael Urtado. © RMN-Grand Palais / Art Resource, NY.

of irrecoverable loss. As so often, we may identify in the unsteady evocation of a higher perspective clear manifestations of the unbearable emotions motivating the fantasy of an improbable relief:

> On this my last visit I had gazed myself blind on my favourite pictures, but had new sight when I came down, for the last time, among the statues, whose glories were more and more impressed on me every visit. These latter were now imprinted in my recollection so entirely that, on thinking of them, I see them as distinctly as when present. After a due share of my attention to these towering monuments of art, which refer man to a higher standard, both in the works produced and the genius producing, than he seems now to belong to, I was last in

> the presence of "the statue that enchants the world." Every one had left the halls but the attendants, whose blue-and-silver liveries, cocked hats, and canes, I saw still at a distance. It was within a few minutes of shutting up. In silence like that of awe, I was taking the last gaze for *my* moment of the ages during which that living marble had stood, ever beautiful and young. A glance through the next arch showed me the Apollo, another the Laocoon; around were multitudes in mute excellence, the delight of antiquity, the promised delight of futurity. Every spectator who leaves them seems to go away to die. There is absolutely an involuntary idolatry—a feeling of self-abasement before these enduring stones; till the rapt worshipper, with an effort of reaction, collects himself for a yet higher thought—that the creature of an hour, who gazes on these lifeless monuments, has *that* within him without which these monuments had not been, and for which is destined an immortality which will reduce even their duration to a day in time, and a point in eternity.
>
> One of the attendants interrupted my reverie with "M. L'Anglais, il faut fermer." Perhaps I should not have compared the privilege of seeing the Louvre gallery entire to that of visiting the field of Waterloo so soon as I did, after the battle, and then beholding the whole of Europe in Paris, if it were not for the marvellous thought that the whole has since been swept away as completely as if it had never been.
>
> "So passeth the glory of the world."
>
> Repeating this hackneyed reflection, I walked through the Place Carrousel, where I saw a crowd of amazed Parisians staring up at the operations of several workmen, on a scaffold erected at the triumphal arch under the horses of St Mark, who were actually unfixing the entablatures of marble on which were Napoleon's bas-reliefs, proving that the hour had passed which he had strutted on the earth, vexed the nations, and "made the angels weep." (268–69; emphasis in the original)

Simpson captures beautifully the wistful melancholy of the traveler on his last visit to a treasured site, in this case one that itself is about to be irrecoverably dissolved, a reality clear enough yet difficult to reconcile with the solidity of the objects around him. When he cites what was in his day a well-known tag from James Thomson's *Seasons* describing the universal erotic quality of the Venus de Medici, "the statue that enchants the world," it is part of a sequence of distancing that culminates, as so many uncomfortable moments of transition shaped around the vicissitudes of war do, not with the low and limited human perspective on earthbound events, but with the eyes of angels—benevolent beings who will weep, Shakespeare tells us, where mankind would be prone to laughter.[34]

The play of distances captured so frequently in visual representations of the Louvre galleries in this period and the metaphorical height of achievement instantiated by the statues enter into the very language of the memorialist as Simpson emphasizes the sense of loss of an older man remembering his younger self taking leave of an admired collection to which he knew it would be impossible to return. The passage is also a very full evocation of the kind of sublime rising that I have discussed several times in this book. Surrounded by "towering monuments of art" that abase the mere human individual with their reminder of an inaccessible "higher standard," Simpson goes quite far beyond the wistful reflections on the transience of human affairs familiar to any thoughtful traveler toward the end of a voyage never to be repeated. In contrast to the ongoing splendor of the works of art—"the delight of antiquity, the promised delight of futurity"—the sense of ephemeral vulnerability of the viewer is acute: "every spectator who leaves them seems to go away to die." This hyperbolic formulation is followed by an acknowledgment of what it is based on: "a feeling of self-abasement." The beauty and durability of stone makes clear the vulnerable condition of the observer not only because it is closing time and the trip has to end at some point, nor even because this collection will soon be gone. These are simply the accidents of history that make an essential condition poignantly clear. The transience Simpson feels is that of flesh when compared to stone.

The passage pulls itself out of the despair into which Simpson has written himself first with the wonderfully bathetic detail of the attendant gently telling the foreigner lost in reverie before all these beautiful classical nudes that it is closing time. But it is really a multiple set of risings and fallings to gain perspective that allow the text to move on. Simpson has come downstairs (where the statues are on display) and has felt himself lowered further by the experience of gazing on what he admires. Then, in a notably orthodox evocation of the sublime, he proposes an intellectual recovery ("the creature of an hour who gazes at these lifeless monuments has *that* within him without which these monuments had not been, and for which is destined an immortality which will reduce even their duration to a day in time, and a point in eternity"). The human soul is more permanent than stone and includes the creative spark that is able to produce (and recognize) the beauty of the admirable objects all around him. So far this is a loss and recovery that Kant would recognize as sublime. And yet the passage cannot be said to end there. Simpson needs to continue the play of levels. He remembers having seen the whole of Europe in Paris in order to cite what he himself identifies as a hackneyed reflection, "So passeth the glory of the world." Heading out, his attention is called to a crowd of Parisians gazing with their own feelings at a local manifestation of that very phenomenon. "I saw a crowd of amazed Parisians staring up." The amazement he witnesses is a concrete manifestation of a sublime change of condition—the arch of triumph Napoleon commissioned and embellished with the horses looted from Saint Mark's Basilica in Venice in the process of being reconfigured.

The play with levels in this passage that moves between physical conditions of witness—upstairs, downstairs, on a scaffold, on the ground gazing up—and the metaphorical evocation of abased selves and their higher thoughts—the whole of Europe beheld, the passing of the glory of the world witnessed right after seeing the statue that enchants the world—culminates in the point of view of angels. Simpson identifies what he sees as "proving" that Napoleon's hour had passed. But proof is only called for when doubt is possible. The reconfiguration of the arch may be evidence of something more than the defeat on which Simpson settles. He is wrong, for one thing, in identifying the intentional monuments of the emperor ("Napoleon's bas-reliefs") as the objects drawing the attention of the amazed Parisians. Those are still there to this day, meaning whatever they can to the changing city. What is removed is the set of horses that had been wrested from St. Mark's, which had decorated that storied church since they were captured from Constantinople in the thirteenth century and had had pride of place in the triumph celebrating the arrival of the works of art in Paris in 1798. The *quadriga* was claimed for Venice by its Austrian masters and returned to the city in 1815. They then adorned the loggia from which they had been taken until the 1980s, when they were replaced by copies and relocated inside Saint Mark's in order to prevent further damage from pollution.

• • •

Catalogs sometimes talk about provenance. Sometimes they don't. I began this chapter with the story of a collection that moved in a remarkably short span of time from Spanish royal hands to the baggage train of a French usurper to the home of a British commander, where its career has been for the moment stopped. The rapidity with which fundamental shifts in the meanings ascribable to that collection take place should remind us of the contingency of our concepts of art and property, and not only in the revolutionary and Napoleonic periods. Inherited wealth, booty, trophy, gift: I noted above the applicability of any of these terms to identical objects, the speed with which culture can move from one to the other. As Simpson observed to his annoyance, *Le Musée français* blazoned the sources of the works on display at the museum when it was published from 1803 to 1809.[35] The *Musée royal*, issued beginning in 1818, does not do so—except in the case of the Venus de Milo, the acquisition of which is openly presented as a compensation for recent losses. *Destiny* is not the term now, but *chance*—newly valorized as the source of progress in science and in the love of art:

> If the sciences have often owed to chance the most important discoveries by which they have made rapid progress, and the secrets that have been revealed to them, it has no less merited recognition from the fine arts for the treasures by which it has brought them such joy. It is to chance that we owe a host of statues, of medals, and of engraved stones; it brought out from their tombs Herculaneum and Pompeii, those inexhaustible mines of antique monuments that we might call underground museums; and its favors to us have culminated in bringing to light the masterpiece which we are about to consider. The Marquis de Rivière happily acquired it; he hastened to offer it in homage to his majesty, who, by placing it in the Royal Museum, aimed to console it for a part of its losses.[36]

Of course, neither destiny nor chance—*hasard* in the original—brought the Venus de Milo to Paris. When the king receives a tribute that he immediately transforms into a consolation for his people, we see yet another instance of the ability to alter the conditions of a precious object serving as a demonstration (and so a validation) of political power. Like various similar actions typical of the art politics of the era, this one hovers unsteadily between the claims of authority of the legitimate monarch and the vulnerability to popular sentiment bound to be at issue in a period of restoration. The structural similarity between this gesture of benevolence and the one that took place between the king of Spain and Wellington demonstrates that the new relationship between power and symbolic action was not limited in its national reach—that, indeed, it often looked to models (as to rivals) abroad.

The loyalty of the marquis de Rivière to his deposed king had seen him incarcerated by Napoleon for nearly a decade. On his restoration Louis XVIII had made the marquis a duke and ambassador to the Ottoman Porte, the same position Lord Elgin held when he acquired the Parthenon Marbles. If, as Elgin himself tells us, the acquisition of the marbles was in some measure an attempt to outdo Napoleon, we see the lesson returning to France with the new monarch. The sinuous nature of the circuit of patronage only hinted at in the catalog is in part due to the fact that its attempt to perform a kind of self-standing, self-validating power (the monarch defining what a precious object is: property, gift, reward) is dependent on a public performance that is ultimately anything but free or self-validating. In recognition of a marked manifestation of the loyalty he in fact requires to be widespread in order to sustain his position, the king creates an ambassador who then makes a gift to the monarch of an object he is only allowed to remove because he is the king's ambassador. The sovereign ultimately makes the object into an emblem of his benevolence and a compensation for losses visited on his subjects by the very allies who brought him to power. It was neither *hasard* nor destiny that replaced one Venus with another—or rather, it was power trying to wrap itself in a mantle with inevitability on one side and benevolent patronage on the other.

"The report was again current in the gallery," Simpson writes in the same passage in which he poignantly notes the blanks the Prussians are opening up in the museum around him, "that the Apollo was actually coming to England" (218). The final determination of the location of each one of the precious objects was as much a political consideration as anything else.[37] Still, in the incongruous image of a battlefield recovery of stolen canvases, in the king's gift of that treasure to Wellington, as in the controversial permission of the Turkish government that Elgin claimed gave him the right to remove the marbles, and even in the public controversy about buying those marbles, as in the non-event of England acquiring the Apollo Belvedere or the ready replacement of one Venus with another—in all of these instances we see the conditions shaping the modern institution, both practical and emotional. It is not only other museums that will be provoked by the creation and dissolution of an institution such as the Musée Napoléon. Moments of cultural crisis will generate the concepts they need, even quite antithetical concepts. We may think of Simpson's fervid imagination of the original church to which he believed Domenichino's *St. Jerome* was destined to return when we read Jean-Louis Déotte's provocative suggestion that, rather than serving as a location at which innate connections to cultural origins are lost, "it was the museum which invented the concept of natural patrimony."[38]

The Venus de Milo (acquired in 1821) remains at the Louvre in Paris to this day, as emblematic of that collection, not to say of the museal itself, as the *Mona Lisa* (probably acquired by Francis I in 1518) or the Winged Victory of Samothrace (acquired in 1864). I have emphasized in this chapter moments when the question of ownership is not quite settled or not liable to easy moral resolution. Hazlitt's sinuous ruminations on the losses and benefits entailed in the Louvre collection, the complicated question of the disposition of cultural patrimony entailed in Ferdinand's gift of Italian and Spanish Old Masters to the Duke of Wellington—each of these instances is another reminder of the real and still-unresolved crisis we may detect behind George Bankes's bland assurances about the Elgin Marbles and the rhetorical question already quoted: "A notion prevailed that these treasures should be restored to their original owners. But how was this to be done?" I have tried to suggest that the question of restitution, like that of original ownership, remains fully open in the nineteenth century—much as it is today. Bankes's query echoes in the sounding halls of the museum like Simpson's speculative imagination of the response of worshippers to the return of Domenichino's *St. Jerome* to an altar in Rome that never did see it again.

To make a gift is among the clearest claims of ownership. Does Ferdinand have property in the canvases he gives away any more than the Turkish Porte owns the Elgin Marbles or the Venus de Milo? If ownership is determined by who can choose the destiny of works of art, then brute force and the accidents of history that establish where it predominates would be the only standard when it comes to cultural property. While it is not difficult to recognize the incongruity of an English politician making declarations about the just disposition of Greek objects, and while the qualification of the Turkish Porte to decide their fate will seem self-evidently inadequate to anyone currently interested in the topic, the case of Ferdinand only appears to be different. It may seem clear that the king of Spain is uniquely qualified to determine the destiny of a Spanish collection. And yet we might want to hesitate before legitimizing the political structures at play here. Certainly, by the standards of the period, Ferdinand was a legitimate ruler, but to say this is no more than to say that the political standards of the period were even more foreign to modernity than then-current ideas of cultural property. The topic is bound to be confused when we structure our analyses on a simple national axis, which itself is the inheritance of later cultural developments.[39] The largess of the king of Spain, which disarms by its chivalric and apparently disinterested quality, is only superficially distinct from other instances

I have discussed. An exchange as gallant as it is romantic, it seems to breathe the air of a different era. And yet we should pause before putting this story in a distinct register, before endorsing an ethical standard that allows a despotic figure of authority placed on the throne by the force of arms of Britain and its allies to collaborate in the permanent alienation of important art objects from national collections he had had no role in shaping.

That the museum arises in a complicated relation to the nation cannot be surprising. After all, both entities take their modern form around the same time and depend on mutually sustaining and not particularly coherent concepts. The legitimacy of states and of property are no less in question after the Napoleonic era, though the tendency is to foreclose discussion of both when it is not to use one to conclude the conversation about the other. As Miguel Tamen noted some years ago, "there is a link between valuing something for its exemplary properties and not being able to justify the desirability of its preservation without referring to notions such as that of the state."[40] Restoration, legitimate ownership, legitimate sovereignty: these were live and critical questions as the Napoleonic Empire was reassembled into new shapes that nearly always were framed as returns to a status quo, though they inevitably involved shifts in political affiliation the instability of which would determine peace and war in Europe and beyond for centuries to come.

To follow this argument would be to enter into questions of nationhood, property, and political legitimation outside the scope of this chapter, though entirely germane to its arguments. Still, it bears emphasizing that the losses Simpson witnesses at the Louvre and commemorates so poignantly cannot be understood to balance out the never-filled absences at churches and palaces all over Europe without the comforting fiction of the nation (which is the only thing that allows arrival at a new institution to have the quality of a homecoming). More telling than the ethical demand for restitution he voices is the affective evidence of his text. That evidence, like that of so much other writing on the institution at this point of crisis, implies a countervailing possibility of wide applicability: that the museum, precisely because it is not the original home of the work of art, may be the best place to teach the lesson of the aura of the art object. Simpson's experiences, like those of so many in the period, suggest that the barbarism we will keep finding written onto the other side of every document of civilization needs to be understood not as a hidden disfiguring mark, a shocking weakness or blemish, but as a structural necessity.

5

REVELATION AND UNCERTAINTY, OR WHAT YOU SEE IN THE WATER

A single sailor, yet living, dashed in the night against a granite coast,—his body and outstretched hands just seen in the trough of a mountain wave, between it and the overhanging wall of rock, hollow, polished, and pale with dreadful cloud and grasping foam.

John Ruskin, *Modern Painters* V (1860)

STUDY FOR FISH. Coming on at speed, in the Slaver (modern trade?)

Notes by Mr. Ruskin on His Drawings by the Late J. M. W. Turner, R.A.: Exhibited at the Fine Art Society's Galleries (1878)

Apocalypse (It's not the end of the world)

The root meaning of "apocalypse" is revelation, the original Greek indicating uncovering or disclosure. But readers of John of Patmos found something more than a coming to knowledge in the book that brought the word to later ages and languages. The term has come to mean the culmination of history in the destruction of everything we know, a cataclysm the pious are meant to hope for more than fear as the prelude to the arrival of the Messiah, the manifestation of the great inconceivable good that parousia, or presence, will bring to what is left of the world. Still, the cultural appeal of the Apocalypse has tended to reside more in the transient moment of judgment that connects it to our lived experience than in the inconceivable perfection that will follow: sinners punished, the good rewarded, the deity recognizing our worth, humanity recognizing his divinity by witnessing his incontestable (*last*, after all!) recognition of our merits and failings.

It is impossible to miss the lifetimes of uncertainty driving such a flamboyant fantasy of ultimate clarity. In that sense the relationship between revelation and the end of the world indicates more than a confusion of terms. The fantasy of a great reckoning in which evil is identified and routed to the sound of horns, of a public, fully transparent, and authoritative weighing of souls by the archangel Michael once he puts down his sword, marks the inflection point at which divine perfection will meet the long-standing moral catastrophe of human history and clarify all its confusions, as in the central panel of the storied Beaune triptych by Rogier van der Weyden I have reproduced here to stand in for the many related representations of the Last Judgment (fig. 5.1).

I have returned various times in this book to the topic of figures suspended above the earth, so it bears pointing out how the van der Weyden differs from others I have discussed. The painting shows Jesus fully separated from any mortal limits, and in that sense not suspended at all so much as returned to a condition beyond material bounds, hence the elements by which he is located in space. His feet are planted on an orb. His robe falls around the rainbow on which he sits, a beautifully rendered detail indicating not the improbable solidity of that optical phenomenon but the ethereal nature of the exalted Jesus. His gaze, calmly implacable, confirms that he is unlikely to move down or up, as his hands gently indicate the work of judgment taking place. The archangel Michael is also not suspended. He has both feet on the ground of the world as he weighs the souls of the dead, his action bringing the gesture of Jesus to a mundane realm. The other characteristic representation of Michael I should mention here also depicts the archangel mediating between registers to do the work of the divine. The vision artists imagined with relish was not of God's messenger hanging in the air but rather of him hurtling from on high to trample to the ground Satan, himself newly, and permanently, cast out of heaven.[1]

Within history, as an expectation or hope, the Apocalypse carries not just the promise of a revelation of our future (the return to our bodies, eternal punishment or reward) but of a future revelation. God's action in the world will (finally) be undeniably visible—Satan trampled, souls measured. The longing testified to in millennia of visual representations is not for an inconceivable divine peace but for judgment, the settlement of confusions left unresolved up to that point. The comparative nature of Michael's scale, which is designed to counterpose souls, to compare, indicates the *ressentiment* that drives the vision.

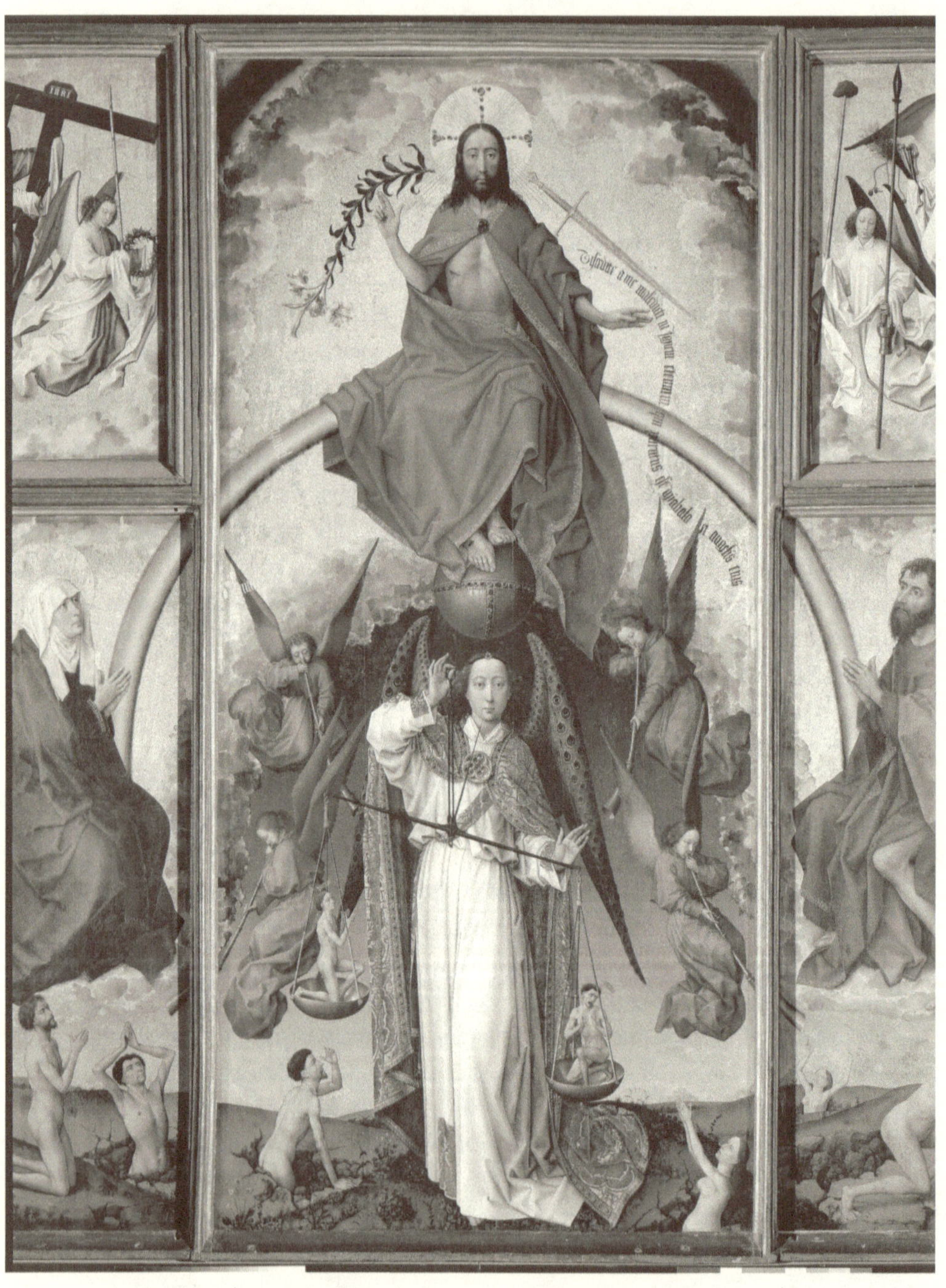

FIGURE 5.1. Rogier van der Weyden, *Altar of the Last Judgement* (1443–52). Oil on panel, partially transferred to canvas, center panel of the polyptych, 110 x 215 cm. Hôtel-Dieu, Beaune. Erich Lessing / Art Resource, NY.

This is no neutral process of evaluation against absolute values: at every point of salvation someone is damned. We cannot know what an infinity of singing the praises of the divine will feel like, but we are experts on what it feels like to see evil unpunished, virtue unrewarded. The relief we can hope for will come from witnessing an incontestable divine assessment, a fulfillment or completion for which all the adjectives allow no repetition, an end to the partial, contingent, and compromised forms not just of knowledge but of existence. Indeed, knowledge and existence will be one in the Apocalypse and its endless aftermath. That's the wish at the heart of the vision: to overcome the gap between manifestation and truth, not just to reach the ultimate interpretation that will end all interpretation but to clarify the confusions of experience that provoke the interpreter's labors. The brassy trumpets blown by angels produce a fanfare announcing the moment of completion that is the promise of the end of time and with it of all that is not known. The angels hold books open not to read them themselves but for us to finally learn everything needful. Revelation is at once a vision and a promise of a final condition of absolute knowledge:

> And the angel which I saw stand upon the sea and upon the earth lifted up his hand to heaven.
>
> And sware by him that liveth for ever and ever, who created heaven, and the things that therein are, and the earth, and the things that therein are, and the sea, and the things which are therein, that there should be time no longer:
>
> But in the days of the voice of the seventh angel, when he shall begin to sound, the mystery of God should be finished. (Rev. 10:5–7)

At the long moment of apocalypse the gap between a deity that knows everything and is eternal and a humanity that is transient and ignorant about the meaning of things will be bridged. That is the angel's promise as he links heaven with the earth and even with the sea on which he miraculously stands. Like the distinctions among elements that mean nothing to angels, time itself will no longer exist to mark the difference between mortal and divine, and the very mystery of God will be finished.

The long-lasting power of the words of John of Patmos derives from an extraordinarily fecund, if contradictory, compound: the interpretation of distressing events on earth (current and historic), the creation of compellingly obscure *new* emblems requiring further elucidation, and the promise of absolute clarity at a future point when knowledge and judgment come together. To link an object in culture to some structure that explains it or gives it meaning—the project we call interpretation in a more mundane realm—implies the closing of a gap in knowledge in order to restore or make visible a prior existing connection that is in some way not self-evident. The process is characteristic of apocalyptic thought in general; every phenomenon can be (really, *needs* to be) associated with the unavoidable, inevitable crisis it anticipates. Each catastrophe is a sign of the times, not another episode in a long sequence of suffering but evidence of a fast-approaching end point at which all events will terminate. These signs, disturbing in themselves, taken together yield the comfort of knowing that what appears to be a distressing trauma may in fact be an indication of profoundly better days ahead. Then again, interpretation evidently flourishes at moments of cultural rupture because that is the only way that novelty can know itself, by recalibrating the meaning of the past. As John of Patmos teaches us, interpretation involves the current lived experience of crisis brought up against the memory of an earlier dispensation. Although apocalypse closes the book and seems so wild a topic compared to the life of Jesus, the adventures of his disciples, and the letters of Paul, its structure shapes the entirety of a text in which the claim of novelty can only be understood as a reminder that the past has not been left behind, that its promise is in the process of being realized.

The New Testament needs to carry the Old as its warrant and support. The Hebrew Bible gains in scope and meaning as it is relegated to the state of being the repository of an extraordinarily significant past. The savior can only be understood when he is recognized to be fulfilling earlier prophecy. As Erich Auerbach demonstrated nearly a century ago, figural reading has to arise in the Christian era, the powerful beginning to a long tradition of finding new meanings in old objects.[2] Interpretation is provoked by crisis because its project is to create links over the gaps the crisis reveals—without thereby repairing the distance. Indeed, interpretation becomes the means of enforcing or establishing a distance that otherwise might not be properly recognized. The prophets mean this new thing to *us*, and so we differ from *you*. Or: *we* are ready to judge this event differently from you, and so we are not a part of the history *you* made. Our interpretation is our difference.

The damage we experience in life most acutely is personal and limited in its scope. We make a wrong step and an ankle is twisted. Or we live long enough and a joint begins to ache not from any trauma but from over- or underuse. Something goes wrong in the way the cells reproduce in the body of a loved one. A profound loss is experienced in a quiet apartment, with the brief aid of expert authorities. The practiced labor of the brisk undertaker's assistants replaces the uncertain aid of doctors. We organize ceremonies to cover over the silence for a brief moment, to make our loss seem more generally applicable before its unique nature returns. And then we commemorate individuals to forget the common nature of the crisis that saddens us. Losses in culture can appear different, but the emotions they provoke are familiar. The relics of a foreign religion stolen and misplaced, the execution of a general in exile on the soil of his captors, the capture or liberation of works of art in order for them to be displayed to a different public at a new location, the theft of works of art from their rightful owners, their restitution to people who had no particular title to them, the methodical and public demolition of broken fragments from the past: all of the topics with which this book has had to do share not only the fact that they call out for a response because of their troubling location at the intersection of beauty and damage. The emotions they generate are displacements of two distinct fears—of insignificance and of irreparable loss—feelings culture is designed to forestall for as long as possible.

When the past is lost, culture will find new beginnings in disaster. That is one way to put the promise of interpretation I have been describing. And it sounds plausible enough, and even comforting. Interpretation is the tool for asserting a new start. There are other ways to arrange the key elements in that sentence, formulations that begin like related paradoxes but cannot sustain the form and feel more concrete than interpretation. Each revolution declares itself ready to start time over—little caring that some are unable or unwilling to recognize the change that revolution is said to mark. And yet the world keeps rediscovering the paradox that the word for new beginnings is also the one we are destined to use for cycles of change, as when Volney writes of "revolutions of empires." We call it a break, and then we start counting, waiting all the time for a new revelation that will indicate the return of a point of crisis that a historical sense insists we see as continuation but that apocalyptic hope wishes to understand as new or perhaps as the penultimate event prior to the final new beginning, that second coming that is meant to stop the count at two. Along with revelation comes the promise of an end that is perpetually deferred and has inevitably been accompanied by an anxious preoccupation with the kinds of perception and understanding we associate with apocalypse, the scanning of the world for signs that meaning is immanent within it. Along with the promise of revelation at some as yet uncertain point in the future comes an example and encouragement for ongoing and constant interpretation. The Hebrew Bible becomes an *Old* Testament with the arrival of the new one, its meanings reshaped to the form of a novel dispensation that needs to be both a complete break and absolute continuity. The present is to be scanned for signs, using many of the same tools and driven by the same hopes and fears as those entailed in new readings of earlier texts. The past becomes a constant resource for possible prognostications about the future we fear or hope for.

All around us lies the wreck of things we have largely lost, or—to put the same matter another way—that only appertain to each one of us in a limited way, which is what can make the study of culture feel like the review of a sad family chronicle, or a walk down a dim portrait gallery by a rejected bastard or by a distant relative slowly realizing she has found her way to an ancestral seat. Using new knowledge and faint half-recognitions, the newcomer finds bearings that a full and entitled sense of belonging will never provide. Can the experience of culture help us to reflect on what we know and fear about the future, absent the hope for that final judgment that reconciles knowledge and experience? It is, after all, not only the promise of divine revelation that has made interpretation an apocalyptic practice.

"I see," we say, meaning "I understand." "Your point of view," we say, meaning that is how *you* see or understand the same thing. And we know there is a greater distance between the two categories than a simple change in person. Now we see as in a mirror darkly; at some later, better point we will see as we do when we are face to face—the improvement being experienced as unmediated insight that takes us beyond the dim reflections of ourselves afforded to our ancestors by the polished metal surfaces they used for mirrors. This book has been concerned with various forms of damage: the breaking of admired things, their theft, even threats to human life such as those a society tacitly accepts or fully endorses when it sends bombers on missions of destruction over foreign cities, when it creates conditions in which displaced people are certain to meet terrible injury, when it pauses its victory parade to torture and execute a rebel general. Retrospect may give these injurious acts the homogenizing treatment we associate with events in the past: this is what Romans did; this is how nations fought then; the situation was complicated, and this is what we had to do, or in any case what we did. But lived experience is different, and its relationship to the future and its judgments is not so clear. Will our actions causing damage be covered over by that kind of retrospective film which looks like understanding and feels like justification? And indeed, how clearly do we see the nature of our actions today?

Faced with a peril bound to change everything at some point in the near future, that is changing so much even as I write, we are not at all unified in our sense of how our culture will react, about seeing or about point of view. It turns out that the question of how to recognize the world is harder than advertised both by common sense and approaches to analysis of cultural objects that keep trying to bring us before the shaping pressures of the material world. Most disturbing of all is the discovery that it is not merely our confusions that mislead us but our apparent lucidities. And the visual is the most consistently shocking source of our failures because its disappointments seem to shake the bedrock on which much of our self-conscious engagement with knowledge rests. My preoccupation throughout this book with the figural and argumentative, not to say conceptual, work done by language related to sight is intended as a reminder of how much is hidden within the apparent transparencies of our lines of vision. Christina Sharpe's powerful understatement brings the reader up short when she addresses this topic in relation to its most clearly manifested failure: "We know that, as far as images of Black people are concerned, in their circulation they often don't, in fact, do the imaging work we expect of them."[3] "When footage of acts of brutality does not result in the correction of abuses by police, by armies, by forces regulating the movements of people at risk at broad or narrow frontiers between nations, as when—in particularly American instances—the murder of children does not eventuate in any change to laws regulating the public availability of weapons designed for mass murder or when convictions for acts of murder clearly captured on visual media are hard-won and rare, we are brought once again before the fact that witnessing injury may well be insufficient stimulus for clear judgment, much less for concerted action. "The imaging work we expect of them" is a mild formulation capturing the unreflective nature of our relationship to images, especially given the recurrent failure ("in fact") in the face of a racism that is more powerful than ocular proof.

The political or simply ethical struggle for truth, *about* truth, was raised forcefully for students of culture when, in response to the elaborate but transparent deceptions carried out in 2003 by the administration of George W. Bush in order to justify America's invasion of Iraq, Bruno Latour asked why critique had "run out of Steam," by which he meant not so much to inquire into anything but to declare his melancholy realization that the critical challenge to ostensibly conventional ideas of truth that had appeared to be such an important and possibly liberatory element in the emergence of theory—or at least that part associated with the term "critique"—had in fact *reduced* the scope of effective responses to dangerous actions by the powerful. Latour's project of imagining anew a positive critical position from which to engage the world is one manifestation of the challenge of addressing the complex network linking perception to recognition and recognition to action.[4]

Certainly, our sophisticated methods of analysis have yielded poor results when it comes to political outcomes. If we compare their record of success in the world to more conventional systems of analysis or values, the moral achievements of critique are vanishingly small. But its failures may best be recognized as symptomatic of the challenging nature of the project critique took on—of linking full knowledge, clear ethical judgment, and effective action in the world. If the angel of history described by Benjamin becomes our presiding deity, it is because of the extraordinarily dynamic combination of perception, feeling, and paralysis he instantiates. In that sense he is yet another fragment from the past made significant by his removal from a whole in which his original role was quite different, in which, after all, a complex messianic return was the hope glimmering beyond the miserable future toward which the angel appears to be bound.[5]

Like individuals born with all the elements in place to determine both future development and ultimate cause of death, it can seem that cultures too are dying their entire life long, damage being the destiny of all human endeavors. But that can only be the end of insight for a circumscribed and ascetic sensibility committed to seeing in their telos all the meaning of phenomena. I have tried to suggest in this book ways in which we might imagine the problems we have in arriving at a consensus about the world around us at moments of crisis as symptomatic of the challenges that present themselves when we attempt to calibrate clarity of perception with moral judgment and with appropriate affect. In the mysteries of the vocabulary culture has developed to reflect on beauty, in the kinds of attention to things implied in the concept, I have identified various relationships to damage and loss and recognition.

As I complete this book, a medical emergency continues to shake the pillars on which contemporary prosperity believes itself to rest, throwing into doubt both the ongoing expansion of wealth on which social systems have premised their value as well as values that antedate those systems but seem to feel more expendable than a generalized sense of affluence and opportunity (which is quite independent of any actual widespread experience of either of those things). As contagion makes us all potentially injurious to each other, its manifestation during the pandemic raises again and again unresolvable questions as to the relative value of various lives, and even the relative value of lives as opposed to ways of life. Confounding as it does mastery and confusion, help and endangerment, and professional measures of risk with personal judgments, the pandemic—understood as a cultural phenomenon—demonstrates the difficulty of seeing damage as it happens, of avoiding throwing it into an ever-deferred future (it may or may not happen this or that way to such and such a person or group) or into a false retrospect (here is the analysis of the event, the list of failures that went into it). But then, understanding the pandemic as a cultural phenomenon was perhaps the hardest part of understanding it at all. In a situation in which science has misleadingly become associated with a simple-minded instrumental clarity, while culture is precisely that realm in which unresolved feelings grounded on vaguely understood but deeply held concepts of identity are valorized, perhaps it was fated to be the case that a crisis in which human values and actions had to match up effectively on a large scale in order for an effective response to be mounted would lead to a disastrous muddle.

I will end this book not on the medical question, however, which, urgent as it is, is likely to feel in retrospect like a sad rehearsal or emblematic prelude to a related crisis of even vaster scope. I will conclude instead with the question of what we see when we look at water. After all, when the pandemic feels fully behind us, we will still have the water to think of, as well as all we have learned about the human capacity for destructive self-deception lived as percipience.

What the Water Tells Us

Two men look out over a bay and reflect on what they see, one with exuberant performative erudition, the other quietly, introspectively, to himself—but not unaffected by his companion:

> God! he said quietly. Isn't the sea what Algy calls it: a great sweet mother? The snotgreen sea. The scrotumtightening sea. *Epi oinopa ponton*. Ah, Dedalus, the Greeks! I must teach you. You must read them in the original. *Thalatta! Thalatta*! She is our great sweet mother. Come and look.
>
> Stephen stood up and went over to the parapet. Leaning on it he looked down on the water and on the mailboat clearing the harbourmouth of Kingstown.
>
> —Our mighty mother! Buck Mulligan said.
>
> He turned abruptly his grey searching eyes from the sea to Stephen's face.

> —The aunt thinks you killed your mother, he said. That's why she won't let me have anything to do with you.
>
> —Someone killed her, Stephen said gloomily.[6]

Buck Mulligan does not see the same ocean as Stephen Dedalus at the beginning of *Ulysses* (1918–20; 1922). His cultured complacency finds an occasion for the ebullient citation of tags from literature classical and modern. The self-regarding expansiveness the sea represents for him is entirely different from the self-lacerating memories that preoccupy Stephen, as are its associations with personal satisfactions. Mother, snot, scrotum: the sea before him is a place of unembarrassed intimacy, pleasure, support. And we remember Buck is carrying a mirror as he rises above the water, "the cracked looking glass" he has stolen from a servant in his aunt's house, a reminder that to see oneself reflected is not to escape servitude or the distortions of injury (Stephen will call this an emblem of Irish art). Buck finds a kindly mother in Swinburne's "Triumph of Time" (1866), neglecting the darker elements of a poem about the end of an affair that shape the vision of the sea as a maternal if incestuous beloved in that work. Stephen sees what there is to see as best he can, a mailboat heading out to sea, a brilliant friend, more verbose and self-regarding than sympathetic to the pain he is exacerbating. Each man discovers what he can in the water, and the distinct associations each brings to bear become evidence and cause of their growing antipathy.

The speaker in Arnold's "Dover Beach" (1867) calls his lover to the window to look at the moonlit ocean, to hear its evocative rhythms. But immediately the meaning of those sensory experiences—sight, sound, the rich sensual manifold entailed in the proximity of the object of erotic attraction—all of these do not prevent but somehow provoke the arrival of a disagreement. In spite of the condition of intimacy with which "Dover Beach" begins—its two lovers, its invitation to stand side by side in the evening at a window by the sea—the experience is ultimately not one that is shareable as an act of witness, because it is not an experience of the world at all but of an extended metaphor. It is (only) the withdrawal of the sea of faith that the speaker hears. The pronominal play of a poem that wants to be about plurality, about what *we* hear or see or think or feel, *together*—otherwise, why is the lover called?—pivots around its near-medial use of the first person. The only time that person talks about himself as an individual is to indicate how alone he is in his perceptions. The *only* in "now I only hear" pulls the speaker away from the beloved just at the moment we feel he would like to claim a shared experience, suggesting either that he alone hears something or that all he hears is something quite different from what Sophocles heard. The final metaphor of this poem that is almost all figure is military: a darkling plain, armies clashing by night. For all its vastness, the metaphor amounts to yet another way of expressing the speaker's individual vulnerability and need. Arnold's flamboyant erudition, his bold shifts from mundane life experiences—hearing the water, the company of a beloved individual—to classical references, cannot disguise the baffled emotion that makes the poem moving.

The plea for fidelity issued by Arnold's speaker is driven by an uncertainty shaped around the evocation of a famously confused military conflict in Thucydides. The allusion has recently been traced to a more immediate event, however, a nighttime battle in the war between British and Sikh forces in 1846.[7] The need for fidelity is all that is certain by the sea, the experience of which initiates a transhistorical reflection on unresolved continuities and breaks: what I hear as opposed to what Sophocles once heard; the ebbs and flows of the sea of faith; the chaotic violence of armies meeting in the dark, whether millennia earlier or a couple of decades before Arnold took pen in hand to write the poem.

To invite a friend or lover to stand beside us and gaze at the water is easily done. But it takes effort to compel assent about what the experience means and a great deal more than sympathy to make others see in that body a Sea of Faith ebbing or a welcoming great sweet mother. Interpretation is a social activity that is experienced as individual. To reflect on what one sees in the world is immediately to introject an interlocutor, and so it is also always to admit the possibility of disagreement. We may be tempted to say that we too hear something of the turbid ebb and flow of human misery in the ocean, but the pressures we are likely to recognize in the sound today are liable to seem anything but metaphoric. The imperative yet never urgent enough question of the rise of global seawater is certainly the most challenging material problem faced by humanity at present, not least because it has proved so difficult not just to do something about it but even to promote a sufficient recognition of the urgency of the crisis—the resistance to urgency often manifesting itself as the refusal of a shared reality. The possibility of common perception and therefore of a common response seems shut to us. In Wilde's quip in "Decay of Lying" (1889) that Wordsworth found sermons under the rocks because he placed them there, we find a memory of Romanticism and a register of the failure of its relationship to nature for later periods. Self comes to the fore just where we might hope the nonself, the natural, should predominate; where we might wish non-self-consciousness should locate itself we find ever more self.[8]

In an essay on the various contradictory meanings of the word "nature," John Stuart Mill reminds us of its use as a name for everything that is *of itself*, without voluntary human intervention—that is, when it is not deployed as a term meaning something much closer to *everything that is not artificial*, including the human (as when we talk about our place in nature); or for *what should be the case* (a usage rarely evoked directly today except in conservative circles but lurking in the background of important ethical tendencies associated with the Left as well).[9] Today, when the situation of human existence in relation to the environment seems so pressing, the relationship of the material to the cultural can seem at once trivial and a matter of life and death. "If only nature *were* unshaped by human intentions!" we might be tempted to exclaim. Or "Would that it were *what should be the case*!" Or even, "Would that the interconnectedness implied in nature being everything could be recognized, could ensure a response approaching the level of responsibility that such a recognition must as a matter of course entail!" Confronted with material facts—astonishing changes in weather patterns, receding glaciers, rising oceans, unquenchable flames devastating forests and darkening the daytime sky of cities far from particular conflagrations—confronted above all with the disconnection between material facts and material actions, a relatively small number of individuals respond with anguish, while another small number respond with hostility. The battle is waged for the response of a majority that seem unable to grasp what is in fact a difficult topic with which to come to grips, one involving at once the need to claim individual agency and responsibility and to recognize a powerful set of losses: of freedom of action, of blithe indifference to the effect of one's actions in the world. The sublime time frames involved in imagining catastrophe paralyze collective action, as what is self-evident in material reality is no more useful or true than the obvious fact of the flatness of the world. The world is round, and it is warming, but Magellan's crew is not returning from their voyage with a thermometer we can all read. Nor is it clear that they would be believed if they did so.

When he needs a figure for the constant change that characterizes our physical existence, which he wants to argue has become an ever-clearer feature of a self-conscious modernity ("the tendency of modern thought"), Walter Pater does two surprising and apparently contradictory things. First, he abandons general formulations and invites his reader to imagine a leap into cool water on a warm day. And then he apparently freezes the moment: "Fix upon it in one of its more exquisite intervals," is his invitation to the reader, "the moment, for instance, of delicious recoil from the flood of water in summer heat." But fixity is only a matter of intervals in a process of constant motion that involves not just what we know but what we *are* ("our physical life," he calls it):

> What is the whole physical life in that moment but a combination of natural elements to which science gives their names? But those elements, phosphorus and lime and delicate fibres, are present not in the human body alone: we detect them in places most remote from it. Our physical life is a perpetual motion of them—the passage of the blood, the waste and repairing of the lenses of the eye, the modification of the tissues of the brain under every ray of light and sound—processes which science reduces to simpler and more elementary forces. Like the elements of which we are composed, the action of these forces extends beyond us: it rusts iron and ripens corn.

The medium into which we have leaped participates in a more than metaphorical way in the nature of our existence (and vice versa). As the unstable, shifting characteristics of the element in which the diver is immersed emerge as the most apt figure for the condition of all things, Pater's imagery shifts uncertainly, trying to capture something of the transient but shaping connections he wants to represent: water, current, web, and then the flame, that flickering, unstable, devouring beauty that paradoxically has so much in common with water in its luminous instability.

> Far out on every side of us those elements are broadcast, driven in many currents; and birth and gesture and death and the springing of violets from the grave are but a few out of ten thousand resultant combinations. That clear, perpetual outline of face and limb is but an image of ours, under which we group them—a design in a web, the actual threads of which pass out beyond it. This at least of flamelike our life has, that it is but the concurrence, renewed from moment to moment, of forces parting sooner or later on their ways.

Pater's elaborate formulations are meant to illuminate something that it is hard to know we are experiencing. To leap into water is to enter the medium that is most like the quality within ourselves that it is most difficult to truly credit—namely, our transience, our brief moment in a world itself characterized by constant change, a mutability that is even more evident in the mental phenomena we call our perceptions. "If we begin with the inward world of thought and feeling," he says, rebeginning his argument in a new paragraph, with a passage in which the evanescent quality of existence is all the clearer, the figures more dangerous, "the whirlpool is still more rapid, the flame more eager and devouring."[10]

Some years ago, the critic Isobel Armstrong published an important study of glass in the nineteenth century, which she addresses as at once medium and object of contemplation. A compound of breath and sand and fire, holding them all in suspension, glass was at once a material object that fascinated the period that saw it produced in ever-larger quantities through new industrial processes and unique as matter precisely because it always opens a view beyond itself.[11] Ruskin reminds us as early as the first volume of *Modern Painters* (1843) that water is the natural phenomenon most similar to glass understood as an object of perception and for that reason most difficult to paint, containing as it does depths and reflective surfaces, lucidities and obscurities. In characteristic fashion, the challenge Ruskin identifies is not simply visual but also involves our knowledge of the formative effects on the world of this medium of sight and object of representations. We don't just look into the water or along its surface, we see its actions shaping everything around us:

> Of all inorganic substances, acting in their own proper nature, and without assistance or combination, water is the most wonderful. If we think of it as the source of all the changefulness and beauty which we have seen in clouds; then as the instrument by which the earth we have contemplated was modelled into symmetry, and its crags chiselled into grace; then as, in the form of snow, it robes the mountains it has made with that transcendent light which we could not have conceived if we had not seen; then as it exists in the foam of the torrent, in the iris which spans it, in the morning mist which rises from it, in the deep crystalline pools which mirror its hanging shore, in the broad lake and glancing river; finally, in that which is to all human minds the best emblem of unwearied unconquerable power, the wild, various, fantastic, tameless unity of the sea; what shall we compare to this mighty, this universal element, for glory and for beauty? or how shall we follow its eternal changefulness of feeling? It is like trying to paint a soul.[12]

The wild, various, fantastic, tameless unity of the sea is like the soul to the human mind in its beauty, changefulness, and glory, which all seems splendid and to be celebrated. And yet the element of water is also evidently even more impossible to assimilate to the mind than it is splendid. It is most like a human soul in the challenge it presents to conceptualization and representation. This passage I have cited from early in Ruskin's career is a prelude for the celebration of Joseph Mallord William Turner's triumphant achievement in capturing this elusive element as much as it is possible to do, in all its modes, including, paradoxically, in the challenge it presents to sight.

More than a decade after the celebration I have just cited, when Ruskin needs an instance to describe the "fallacy caused by an excited state of the feelings, making us, for the time, more or less irrational," on his way to describing a fault in representation "which the mind admits when affected strongly by emotion," he looks to water. And we might remember that it was the "changefulness of feeling" the critic had already identified as characteristic of the sea that made it so difficult to represent and so similar to the human soul. In the treatment of the pathetic fallacy in *Modern Painters* III (1856), we find the two challenges coming together, the instability of the element and the projective power of human emotion:

> Thus, for instance, in Alton Locke,—"They rowed her in across the rolling foam—The cruel, crawling foam." The foam is not cruel, neither does it crawl. The state of mind which attributes to it these characters of a living creature is one in which the reason is unhinged by grief. All violent feelings have the same effect. They produce in us a falseness in all our impressions of external things, which I would generally characterize as the "pathetic fallacy." (Ruskin, 5:205)

It is unfortunate that Ruskin's argument often gets lumped together with a number of other failures or infelicities of interpretation or composition, as though its interest simply came down to a matter of method. Evidently Ruskin has more in mind when he describes a failing that is characteristic of "reason unhinged by grief." How did grief get in here? Grief about what?

The pathetic fallacy would be an absurdly elaborate structure if it had been designed merely to describe the failings of modern writers. The concept makes far more sense as what it is, a key element in Ruskin's diagnosis of the disenchanted character of the modern relationship to the world. The argument in Ruskin loses a great deal of its significance when read in extracts, as it tends to be. Returned to the ambitious account of the changing experience of nature at different historical periods in which it is described, the analytical force of the pathetic fallacy becomes clear.[13] The projection of feelings onto nature, that sign of "a failure in *all* our impressions of external things," is evidence that, absent the fantasy entailed in self-reflection or projection, the world of itself does not reflect things back to us that we are liable to recognize as meaningful. "Reason unhinged by grief" is the *diagnosis* that follows from the symptom of the pathetic fallacy. And the condition is widespread. The diagnostic nature of the fallacy is demonstrated in Ruskin's treatment of William Wordsworth's "The World Is Too Much with Us." "This Sea that bares her bosom to the moon," Wordsworth tells us, in a passage of crucial importance for Ruskin, does not generate the feeling it should, given our modern situation: "For this, for everything, we are out of tune / It moves us not." Out of tune with nature, we are driven to fantasize about seeing ourselves in it, or we confess ourselves nostalgic for times we have never known, when nature's meaning had an undeniable form:

> —Great God! I'd rather be
> A pagan suckled in a creed outworn,
> So might I, standing on this pleasant lea
> Have glimpses that would make me less forlorn;
> Have sight of Proteus rising from the sea
> Or hear old Triton blow his wreathèd horn.[14]

The subject's misery, at first attributed to a lifetime of busy business in "The World Is Too Much with Us"—to getting and spending—is ultimately traceable to the disenchantment of the experience of the world understood not as the framework of existence in which we manage our affairs but as the ground of our being. The world, in the latter sense, is in fact what is not enough with us. (And we may find in this argument an anticipation of Bruno Latour's distinction between "global" and "terrestrial," discussed in Chapter 2.) The speaker is standing on a pleasant lea in order to have a rhyme for sea, because he wants to see more when he looks out over the waters. But it is a frank desire for mystification the poem expresses: to be a pagan suckled in a creed outworn is to be belated, out of time, though that may be the only way to look out at the sea and witness wonders.

Proteus and Triton are challenging old divinities. Triton, once a figure of profound power—a primitive version of Poseidon—had already by the Renaissance been reduced to the role of a harbinger, an announcer of the arrival of others of more importance. A fish below the waist, holding a conch at his lips, he is an image as much for the sound of the sea as for its animal depths. Nevertheless, he has clearly been tamed, becoming merely a decorative bit player, a fountain blowing an endless stream or a herald of Venus in paintings and other graphic representations, blaring an unheard fanfare to announce the coming of uncontrollable beauty or passion. Proteus, son of Poseidon in some traditions, is another anticipator. But, though he has the gift of prophecy, he will only share his knowledge with those who seek him out at his seaside home and have the power to hang on to him in spite of his ferocious animal metamorphoses, as Menelaus does in the the Odyssey, or Aristaeus in Virgil's fourth *Georgic*. So, what does Wordsworth's speaker see if it is not Proteus, the divinity who will prognosticate solely for those who can survive his changes, or Triton, half human, half fish, announcing the advent of some divine glory?[15] He sees nothing that is meaningful: beauty without presence, presence without meaning, a sublime vacuity. Orthodox belief in a creed that is not outworn would lead him to long for another trumpet, for one of those to be blown by the angels at the Last Judgment, for the sound of the final horn. His desires confess a double loss that demonstrates the Wordsworthian roots of "Dover Beach": loss of a faith not outworn and of a fully meaningful experience of the world. Ruskin cites this passage from Wordsworth in the course of his diagnosis of the crisis of a disenchanted modernity in which the most earnest poets and deepest thinkers are "doubtful and indignant," or at best "anxious or weeping" (5:323).

Stephen Dedalus, a hydrophobe, immerses himself as rarely as possible. Nevertheless, he spends a great deal of time thinking about and around water. A man Buck Mulligan saved from drowning recurs to his thoughts throughout the day, emblem of an agency and bravery, not to say recognizable achievement, he fears himself never liable to match. Early in the novel, however, at a key turn in the text, it is perception itself he reflects upon on the beach. If the ineluctable modality of the visible—the non-essential nature of the features of objects we perceive—disturbs him, it is because of his own implication among those objects of perception, the signature of things he is meant to read that are not absolute, primary, fundamental. The Proteus chapter of *Ulysses* is about a wrestling with mutability and signification that involves the subject bodily—as all wrestling will. But it is nevertheless a mental struggle. The long scene that opens the chapter can be off-putting for the first-time reader, owing to its flamboyantly obscure erudition. Yet it can also feel like one of the most pleasant of those in the opening sequence featuring Stephen, owing to its discursive, even conversational, tone. In a way it is the most convivial encounter Stephen has with anyone until he meets Leopold hundreds of pages later, though it is only an encounter with himself.

"Ineluctable modality of the visible": Stephen runs the phrase over the tongue of his mind, as the chapter begins, thinking about Aristotle's reflections on the conditioned nature of perception before giving the flamboyantly abstract phrase a gloss and a location. "Thought through my eyes" is his formulation to describe the modal nature of sight, making the visual a place of knowledge and reflection but not thereby settling matters. To understand perception as thought is to include it in the protean nature of everything else that goes on in the mind. While the body is inevitably implicated in its physical location, that is no answer to the transience of mental states. And so the passage alternates seaside impressions with reflections on philosophy. With all the contingency of someone's handwritten name used as a seal or warrant, the world comes at us identified by its phenomenal nature; like names, it is conditions that we know, not essences. And we remember that the sea was carrying a mailboat when Stephen first looked at it in the novel—so many signatures still floating away from Dublin as Stephen thinks about Aristotle:

> Signatures of all things I am here to read, seaspawn and seawrack, the nearing tide, that rusty boot. Snotgreen, bluesilver, rust: coloured signs. Limits of the diaphane. But he adds: in bodies. Then he was aware of them bodies before of them coloured. How? By knocking his sconce against them, sure.

If the visual is understood to be an experience of transience, of the modal and not of essential conditions, a simple strategy is available when we seek what we call insight: "Shut your eyes and see." And so Stephen does; to know himself as much as possible in relation to the beach as it is, unsigned, unshaped by his mind, he cuts off his lines of sight. But the experiment is flawed in its conception and frightening as an experience:

> Stephen closed his eyes to hear his boots crush crackling wrack and shells. You are walking through it howsomever. I am, a stride at a time. A very short space of time through very short times of space. Five, six: the *nacheinander*. Exactly: and that is the ineluctable modality of the audible. Open your eyes. No. Jesus! . . . Am I walking into eternity along Sandymount strand? Crush, crack, crick, crick.

The self-blinded walker listens to the dry noises of crushed shells and sand and thinks about eternity, poetry, and blind people, about the words we may find for the sounds of damage ("Crush, crack, crick, crick"). But we soon hear a doubled panic set in and shape the conversation Stephen is having with himself, both the fear of the accidents that may befall someone walking sightless and something more terrifying:

> Open your eyes now. I will. One moment. Has all vanished since? If I open and am for ever in the black adiaphane. *Basta*! I will see if I can see.
>
> See now. There all the time without you: and ever shall be, world without end. (31)

"I will see if I can see. / See now." The echoing word that is a homonym for the body of water next to him (and is also present in "seaspawn" and "seawrack") comes back three times, each return with a different meaning. In the first instance, the use of the future tense places the action of knowing or learning or ascertaining under the sign of agency (what I will) that is also an indication of uncertainty (I will see if . . .). In the second, the verb means simply to get a sense of things or perceive through the eyes. Depending on whether we understand it to occur before or after he opens his eyes (which the text leaves indeterminate), the third use oscillates unstably between an imperative (do it—see *now*!) and an expression of comforting reassurance (*see* now, nothing to worry about!) reminding us that we do not lose the world when we do not see it. See now; it's *not* the end of the world. On the contrary, it's a world without end—itself a biblical formulation describing not the human condition in nature but the situation of divinity in eternity understood as a comforting contrast to our mutable existence. The "Jesus!" that is originally an exasperated ejaculation expressing annoyance with himself, perhaps for the cowardice that threatens his experiment in blind experience, returns in the reference to Paul's Epistle to the Ephesians, evoking that traditional source of comfort, the Bible, but also the contrast between human impermanence and an eternal divine, between the partial knowledge of transient things and the absolute knowledge of what is absolutely true because permanent.[16]

A couple of years ago, as I prepared for publication a book on the force of concepts of matter in the nineteenth century and after, one illustration proved hard to find and challenging when I got my hands on it: a print Turner produced for his *Liber Studiorum*, the ambitious collection of engravings of landscapes he brought out between 1807 and 1819. Turner did not ultimately include this piece in the final selection he issued, but Ruskin treasured a proof copy engraved by the artist's own hand, which he wrote about in the following extraordinary terms in *Modern Painters* V (1860), highlighting in particular something he described with the paradoxical term the "work" of death:

> I have not followed out, as I ought to have done, had the task been less painful, my assertion that Turner had to paint not only the labour and the sorrow of men, but their death. There is no form of violent death which he has not painted. Pre-eminent in many things, he is pre-eminent also, bitterly, in this. Dürer and Holbein drew the skeleton in its questioning; but Turner, like Salvator, as under some strange fascination or captivity, drew it at its work. Flood, and fire, and wreck, and battle, and pestilence, and solitary death, more fearful still. The noblest of all the plates of the Liber Studiorum, except the Via Mala, is one engraved with his own hand, of a single sailor, yet living, dashed in the night against a granite coast,—his body and outstretched hands just seen in the trough of a mountain wave, between it and the overhanging wall of rock, hollow, polished, and pale with dreadful cloud and grasping foam. (7:437)

The image is difficult to read in reproduction because it is not easy to make out in the original (see fig. 5.2). Ruskin himself had it reengraved, probably for teaching purposes, at Oxford, and it is more common to find copies of that version, or of another from even later in the century by Sir Frank Short. These unusual returns to such an obscure print indicate both its staying power and the sense that it is challenging to capture all that the work contains. Given that plates of the *Liber Studiorum* are relatively widespread in libraries and museums, and that it is a work in a medium generally associated with reproduction, I was surprised at the elusive nature of this piece. Still, I eventually located the very plate owned by Ruskin, held now at the Museum of Fine Arts in Boston.

I discuss the treatment of the frontispiece of *Liber Studiorum* in *Modern Painters* V at length in the third chapter of this book, where I suggest the importance of the grave in Ruskin's thought on Turner. But the argument about the representation of death is also closely related to the one Ruskin had advanced about the projection of emotion into an otherwise disenchanted natural world in his account of the pathetic fallacy in the third volume of that work. In the engraving of the lost sailor he quite literally finds human pain in the foam—the kind of projection he had deprecated in Kingsley and others. The absence of meaning he had learned about from Wordsworth is given a brutal corrective when such undeniable human suffering is what we find looking out at us from the waves. This is not a re-enchantment of nature, evidently, but a moving vision of loss understood as the mark of true creative achievement. In the astonishing fifth, and final, volume of *Modern Painters* (1860), Ruskin makes

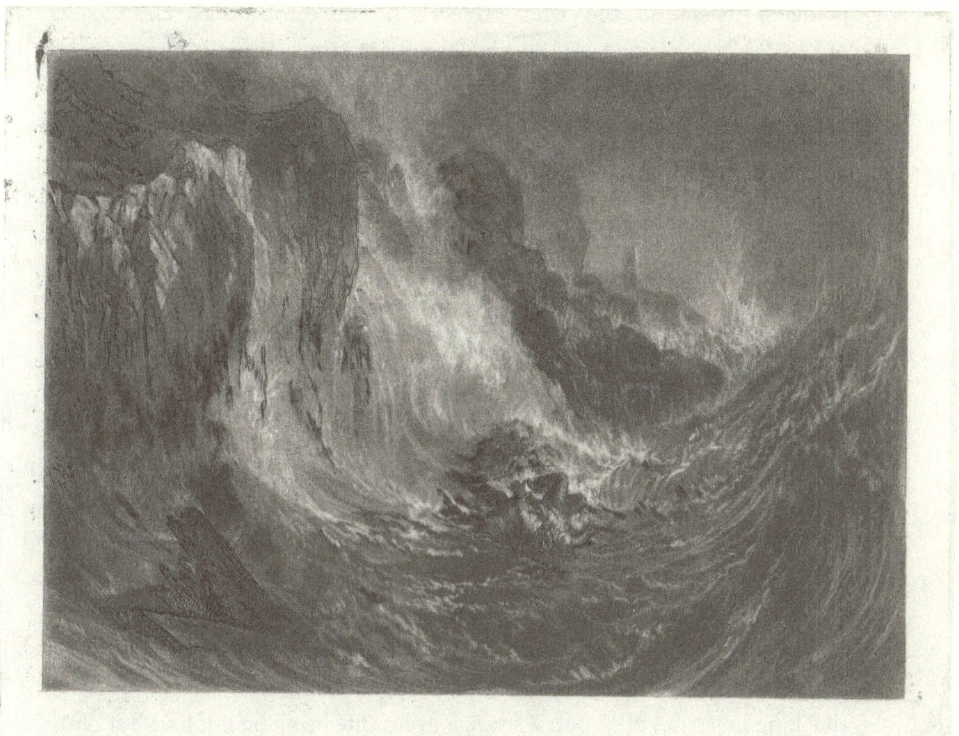

FIGURE 5.2. Joseph Mallord William Turner, *The Lost Sailor* (ca. 1819). Mezzotint and drypoint, engraver's proof, 19.4 x 26.8 cm. Museum of Fine Arts, Boston, Rawlinson 084, bequest of Francis Bullard, M23221. Photo © 2021 Museum of Fine Arts, Boston, MA.

clear what is at stake in this representation when he proposes that the sight of death is at the heart of *every* landscape by Turner, the man he understood to be the greatest modern painter—it is in that melancholy achievement that his modernity and his greatness lie.

While Ruskin's reflection on what is to be discovered in the representation of nature is transhistorical, each manifestation of death he discusses is imagined with great period specificity. The work of every artist is at a fundamental level a response to mortality, but the elements that determine that response will differ, given the cultural relationship to the world that obtains at the time of making. Although, like nature, death itself is a constant, permanent in its inescapability, it is mutable in the ways it is available to culture at different points in history. But the critic's project is not the dispassionate classification of distinctions among eras. Ruskin's argument is meant to culminate in—to explain—what he finds in Turner. What he calls "the English Death" is a particularly modern compound made up of social dislocation and indifference, militarism, economic injustice, and a singularly unmystified relationship to the natural world that is what provokes the modern emergence of the pathetic fallacy, an overcompensating projection of emotions into a nature that is otherwise unmeaning.[17]

Death is, of course, the tendency of all living things until the Apocalypse. The question is how it might be made meaningful before that point. In a rhapsodic account of the topic, Ruskin looks for points of comparison in the achievements of the ancient Greeks and in Dürer's ability to capture the everyday miseries of German life. He even cites the vision of a decayed Italy he finds in those picturesque dark canvases by Salvator Rosa that were so resonant for the Romantics. But these instances do not amount to so many regional and period variations on the same theme. His aim is to insist that there is something particularly modern and uniquely bleak, and (if not *because*) more than merely national, in the compound of military violence and economic oppression that characterizes what he calls "the English Death." The figure he uses for death is a shocking inversion of Venus: a strange Aphrodite bringing not love but death, rising out of the foam and becoming an apocalyptic angel darkening the sea with a significance it has inevitably proved difficult for art to look upon, much less represent:

> And their Death. That old Greek question again;—yet unanswered. The unconquerable spectre still flitting among the forest trees at twilight; rising ribbed out of the seasand;—white, a strange Aphrodite,—out of the sea-foam; stretching its gray, cloven wings among the clouds; turning the light of their sunsets into blood. This has to be looked upon, and in a more terrible shape than ever Salvator or Durer saw it. The wreck of one guilty country does not infer the ruin of all countries, and need not cause general terror respecting the laws of the universe. Neither did the orderly and narrow succession of domestic joy and sorrow in a small German community bring the question in its breadth, or in any unresolvable shape, before the mind of Durer. But the English death—the European death of the nineteenth century—was of another range and power; more terrible a thousand-fold in its merely physical grasp and grief; more terrible, incalculably, in its mystery and shame. (Ruskin, 7:386–87)

While the material elements out of which the English death is compounded are incomparably worse than those of earlier forms of mortality, even that vision of miserable failure is dwarfed by the less tangible qualities Ruskin identifies with "mystery and shame." This death, both material and emblematic, is ubiquitous in Turner's work, Ruskin argues, and it is given in its rawest form in one image, that anomalous plate for Turner's *Liber Studiorum* that Ruskin himself owned and that at first can look to the viewer like a mass of barely differentiated lines.

Turner is famous for his storms, of course, occasions for sublime representations of the workings of nature, including the notorious instance when he was said to have had himself lashed to a mast in order to fully experience the violent action of wind and water (fig. 5.3), an improbable anecdote that takes its force

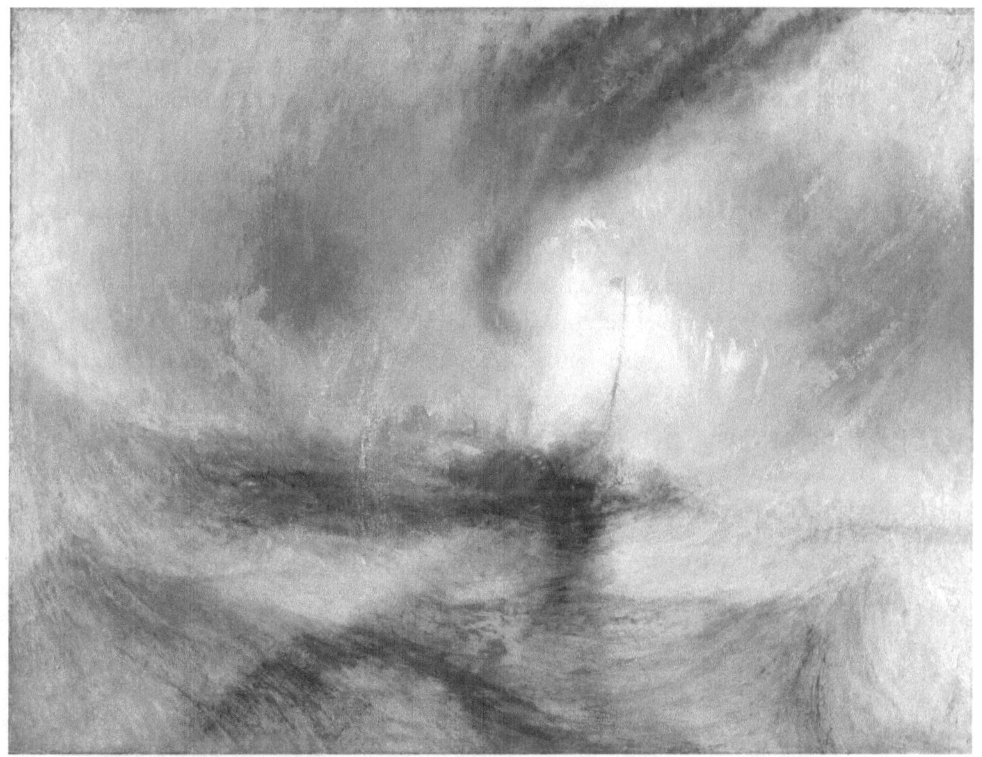

FIGURE 5.3. Joseph Mallord William Turner, *Snow Storm—Steam-Boat off a Harbour's Mouth Making Signals in Shallow Water, and Going by the Lead. The Author Was in This Storm on the Night the Ariel left Harwich* (1842). Oil paint on canvas, 91.5 x 122 cm. Accepted by the nation as part of the Turner Bequest, 1856. Photo: Tate.

from the disjunction between what we see of the water in the normal course of events, what we know about it, and what we want to or are able to safely experience of it. I will return to Ruskin's discussion of this canvas below, but it is worth citing in this context for the contrast it makes with the print. *The Lost Sailor*, also known as *Storm over the Lizard*, is astonishing without in any way being heroic; the umber waves of the print pull the eye into a turbulent space that does not conclusively resolve. The swell on the right is clear, as is the distant lighthouse. But are those waves on the left or rocks battered by foam? It takes several moments to ascertain that they are a fatal combination of both, one that further investigation tells us is typical of the coastline of the Lizard peninsula, a passage on the coast of Cornwall notoriously perilous for ships. Ruskin's "overhanging wall of rock, hollow, polished, and pale with dreadful cloud and grasping foam" captures the interpenetration of elements in the mezzotint. But the title Ruskin uses tells us more and gives us a clue to what is most difficult to see: there is a lost sailor to be found at the center of the turbulent lines once the eye adjusts to the obscurities of the print.

Floating next to a barrel in the middle of the image or perhaps kept afloat by that expedient, lying in any case in an awkwardly foreshortened position, head lower than legs, arms akimbo, all power over his destiny lost, the open-eyed subject experiencing his own English death makes the viewer a witness to something awful about to happen—or worse—in the course of happening. The challenge of the print for the viewer is to recognize the presence of human death. And for Ruskin, the nautical character of this event that is central and yet so easy to miss is part of a challenge at once aesthetic—that is, having to do with the nature of perception—and ethical. "The English death was before his eyes," he writes of the experiences that shaped Turner:

> The life trampled out in the slime of the street, crushed to dust amidst the roaring of the wheel, tossed countlessly away into howling winter wind along five hundred leagues of rock-fanged shore. Or, worst of all, rotted down to forgotten graves through years of ignorant patience, and vain seeking for help from man, for hope in God—infirm, imperfect yearning, as of motherless infants starving at the dawn; oppressed royalties of captive thought, vague ague-fits of bleak, amazed despair. (7:387)

The ocean allows us to rise and fall but not in such a way that perspective is possible, unless we understand the matter metaphorically, as entailing a view of our own helpless involvement in a physical world of which we keep needing to be reminded that we are a vulnerable and barely significant element, seaspawn or perhaps even seawrack, something the ocean swell can call to mind in a comforting or a terrifying way. And we may think here of the nature of the oceanic feeling described in Freud's 1930 *Civilization and Its Discontents*, or of something far less reassuring than the support felt in the womb, the kinds of trauma that project one helpless into the water.[18] In a fascinating study of shipwreck as a figure in philosophy going back to classical antiquity, the philosopher Hans Blumenberg identifies its long-standing power. "Shipwreck, as seen by a survivor," he argues, thinking back to Lucretius and his sources, "is the figure of an initial philosophical experience."[19] In the course of his analysis of a compelling compendium of instances, Blumenberg argues that in spite of the cruel disjunction at its core ("survivor" suggesting not just risk but the death of others), the pleasure that comes from the sight "has nothing to do with a relationship among men, between those who suffer and those who do not; it has rather to do with the relationship between philosophers and reality" (26). Evidently, either the pain of the sight identified by Ruskin has precisely the opposite source or else the critic refuses the distinction.

I have suggested, following Ruskin, that water tantalizes the viewer and challenges the artist with its visual complexity, its combination of translucence and reflection. But, as he also reminds us, it is an element one might associate not only with sight but also with loss of sight. Maritime disaster was never likely to be far away from the thoughts of an island nation dependent on international trade and imperial expansion, a dominant military power the principal strength of which resided in its navy. Indeed, the loss of life at sea is a recurrent theme in nineteenth-century Europe, in painting, prose, and poetry, though the emotional power in their own day of the few instances remembered by current students of art history and literature will tend to be difficult to recognize in an era when oceans are a barrier to fly over rather than the very medium of travel and when goods are transported overseas on massive vessels with small crews not generally native to the territories they serve, a period, also, when significant military struggle has not for a long time been carried out between vast navies as in the past—and notably in the nineteenth century.[20]

In the English context, the words of William Cowper's poignant "Castaway" (1799) resonated throughout the period, though that poem is probably best remembered today as the source of a refrain that keeps rising, in ways at once risible and pathetic, in Mr. Ramsay's consciousness, in Virginia Woolf's *To the Lighthouse* (1927): "We perished each alone." Sensitive as she was to the humor and pathos of Victorian culture and the ways in which its emotionalism was seldom free of a histrionic quality, Woolf has chosen well in making this work echo in Mr. Ramsay's self-obsessed, death-preoccupied mind. The poem memorializes an episode in a true account of a voyage in which a sailor fallen overboard could be provided no succor by his comrades. Attempting to escape an oncoming storm, they hear his cries while he clings to the barrel thrown out to support him as long as his strength lasts. In a shocking turn, however, the close of the text reveals that the entire deeply realized account of suffering at sea is intended to make a comparison to the deeper *emotional* pain felt by the speaker. Commonality is noted, but simply as an exacerbating element in the psychic distress of the self-obsessed speaker whose words echo in Mr. Ramsay's mind: "We perish'd each alone / But I beneath a rougher sea / And whelm'd in deeper gulfs than he."

Cowper's is just one of a large body of texts of remarkable emotional force. The boy in Felicia Hemans's "Casabianca" (1826) stands faithfully on the burning deck until his body is blown onto the main in a violent explosion that makes his loyalty to a dead father that much more poignant and ironic. In a terrible moment in Tennyson's *In Memoriam* (1849), the speaker addresses a mother praying for her sailor son even as his weighted body is being consigned to the depths in another part of the world. It is a theme most beautifully developed, perhaps, in a somewhat anomalous instance, Gerard Manley Hopkins's "Wreck of the Deutschland" (1875–76; published 1916), commemorating the death off the coast of England of five nuns exiled from Germany by the laws constraining their religious freedom.[21] It is hard not to see in the particularly English—that is to say, modern—death represented in the scene that Turner depicts a reminder of the vast risks to which an expanding imperial nation exposed its most vulnerable subjects. The difficulty of making out the sailor is directly related to the print's attempt to capture something of the ultimate (in)significance of this one death, the poignancy depending on its undifferentiated, undifferentiating nature.

A word available to Ruskin, though not to me, is "noble." He says the print of the lost sailor floating in the sea about to destroy him is one of the two *noblest* Turner produced, and it is a word that Ruskin glosses with reference to modesty or humility ("nothing is ever done beautifully," he writes in *Ethics of Dust*, "which is done in rivalship; nor nobly, which is done in pride" (18:319)). It has been difficult to arrive at a satisfactory ethical response to Benjamin's strong proposal that barbarism is on the other side of every document of culture—an idea that shares much with those moments in Ruskin when he proposes we recognize the death at the heart of all significant works of art. The authors may be felt to differ fundamentally in their sense of what it means to take in or perceive a document of civilization because of differences in the kinds of violence that preoccupy them. Still, attention to their commonalities might serve to illuminate the conceptual sophistication of the nineteenth-century critic, the cultural context shaping the claims of the twentieth-century theorist.

We might note as a way of focusing on the concrete violence—even barbarism—suggested in the print that so moves Ruskin that impressment of sailors only ended in Britain with the era of Napoleonic conflict, as long as that observation does not allow us to forget the many and more typical ways in which a society constrains individuals into dangerous or damaging forms of life. There is a still-shocking use of the ocean in *Munera Pulveris* (1862), one of Ruskin's most challenging books on political economy. "Two merchants bid for the two properties," Ruskin writes about a pair of imaginary islands,

> but not in the same terms. One bids for the people, buys them, and sets them to work, under pain of scourge; the other bids for the rock, buys it, and throws the inhabitants into the sea. The former is the American, the latter the English method, of slavery; much is to be said for, and something against, both, which I hope to say in due time and place. (17:256)

In a footnote, Ruskin provides a gloss to this figure designed to appall the ethical imagination of his day, one year into the American Civil War in which the abolitionist sympathies of Britain were clearly engaged. The individuals thrown into the sea, he tells us, are meant to be understood as standing in for the vulnerable Scots and English who were indeed driven out of their homes in massive numbers by landlords eager to turn to the cultivation of sheep, a vast displacement that took place in the later eighteenth and nineteenth centuries, fundamentally reshaping the landscape of the region and the destinies of its people.[22] We hear an echo of this history in a brief but deeply perceptive line in Susan Stewart's *Ruins Lesson*: "Stone cottages or farmhouses abandoned to rubble by famine, clearances, and migration are ruined, yet unmarked; they have something of the pathos of shipwrecks, the most ephemeral and untraceable of ruins" (10). Intended to highlight the unmarked nature of most ruins, the comparison between shipwreck and ruined cottage reminds the reader of the powerful continuities linking those apparently distinct instances in the nineteenth century. Being cast into the sea is a figure for the effect of the indifferent violence of a dehumanizing propertied class. It is also an entirely accurate vision of the outcome of clearances and other crises provoked by landlords that led to the social dislocations and misery attendant on a period of mass migration and the disproportionate presence of Scots overseas, in current and past British dominions and across the military and bureaucratic structures of empire.

Perhaps the most shocking thing about Ruskin's formulation for the modern sensibility is that—as is the case at a number of key junctures in his moral arguments in the middle years of the nineteenth century, the era of greatest British engagement with the evil of American slavery—Ruskin uses slavery as a point of comparison for less clearly recognizable forms of dehumanizing economic oppression. Among the few well-known moments in Ruskin is the remarkable point in "The Nature of Gothic" chapter of *Stones of Venice* II (1853), when he invites his readers to recognize the violence inherent in mass production by seeing themselves as implicated in the destruction brought about by a taste for refined perfection:

> And now, reader, look round this English room of yours, about which you have been proud so often, because the work of it was so good and strong, and the ornaments of it so finished. Examine again all those accurate mouldings, and perfect polishings, and unerring adjustments of the seasoned wood and tempered steel. Many a time you have exulted over them, and thought how great England was, because her slightest work was done so thoroughly. Alas! if read rightly, these perfectnesses are signs of a slavery in our England a thousand times more bitter and more degrading than that of the scourged African, or helot Greek. (10:193)

I have emphasized in this book laborious ways of coming into relationship with beauty and damage, instances in which complicity, responsibility, and the emotions do not line up so as to allow us to easily resolve our judgments in the ethical or aesthetic spheres. Ruskin's work will help me conclude this discussion not only because he is among the most sophisticated theorists on the difficulties entailed in seeing but also because the nuance of his arguments is as often lost sight of as their urgency. The identification of the damage caused by the systems we support through our unreflective relationship to the various luxuries we experience as needs is a step toward the recognition of responsibility for the crushing of selves entailed in the mass production of ornaments in England or glass beads in Venice. Although the modern mind may recoil at the thought of slavery as a point of comparison, it is worth at least pausing to realize that the scandalous juxtaposition was designed to be as shocking in nineteenth-century Britain as it is today.

It will not be news to anyone that moral clarity about an evil being carried out by others elsewhere may blind individuals to ongoing complicity in projects of oppression that it may take only a slight turn of the optic glass to see as closely related to the ones being deprecated—to see them at all. Still, even a subtle literary critic such as Mark Frost suggests that the issue at stake at this moment in "The Nature of Gothic" is the relative value of different categories of individuals. And so he writes of "European lives which, the passage implies, are of greater value."[23] I think this misses the point and even the challenge of Ruskin's formulations. The problem for the modern reader is not that Ruskin thinks the suffering of enslaved Africans matters less than that of Europeans (unless Greece has been removed from Europe) but that he puts slavery on a continuum of evil including ourselves. This approach, like that which proposes the destruction of Scottish lives by their landlords to be related to the enslavement of African people, may or may not appall the modern moral sensibility (as it was designed to do that of the *bien-pensant* nineteenth-century reader). But it merits being looked at squarely, not least because Ruskin is interested in the internalization of forms of subjection, submission, and mastery that are even more urgent questions today than they were in previous centuries. To refuse Ruskin's challenge may seem like a necessary moral position because doing so places certain manifestations of dehumanizing evil outside the range of our everyday and current moral failings. But the refusal can also mislead as to both the nature of our responsibilities in the face of the harms in which we participate and our effectiveness in dealing with these responsibilities.

Orienting oneself properly toward what one is seeing is a challenge of great moral complexity, though one typically given short shrift in polemics that depend on the claim of straightforward clarity of perception. "The greatest thing a human soul ever does in this world is to *see* something and tell what it *saw* in a plain way," Ruskin writes in his chapter on modern landscape in *Modern Painters* III, in the course of laying out the historic crisis at the heart of the pathetic fallacy. He then pushes this formulation toward a claim in which apparent hyperbolic excess in describing two fundamental actions, seeing and talking, is intended to link these notionally simple things together and to associate them with practices that are far from ordinary: "Hundreds of people can talk for one who can think, but thousands can think for one who can see. To see clearly is poetry, prophecy and religion, all in one" (5:333; emphases in the original).

Poetry, prophecy, religion: to see clearly, to speak plainly about what one saw. As readers have discovered over nearly two millennia, to read the book of Revelation is not to be handed the key to a code but to be made privy to an ongoing set of mysteries alongside the promise of a final interpretation. The last days are not characterized by clarity but by extraordinary emblematic excess: dragons with swords coming out of their mouths, books eaten that taste sweet on the way down but then turn bitter, true saviors and false, existing or vanished cities that become symbols of towns that did not exist in nations unimaginable when John sat down to write on Patmos. The emblems of apocalypse demand the revelation that the book promises but cannot fully deliver. If hopes for immediate clarity are disappointed, however, the reader does discover something powerful, a lesson in the identification of signs in the world that has been tantalizing culture into endless variations on interpretation ever since. Some of these signs we might reasonably associate with the difficult task of seeing something and telling what we saw in a plain way, with poetry, prophecy, and, of course, religion.

To see clearly. Critics have long recognized the importance of typology in Ruskin, and indeed it is a central structure in his rational thought and perhaps all the more dominant when his mind is overbalanced. Nobody who did not fear the risk of his own emotions deluding him about the meanings to be found in the world could have articulated with such power the concept of the pathetic fallacy. What happens if we dwell on the difficulty of sight and its potential rewards in Ruskin, if we think of his reflections on the emotions to be found in the water not as a judgment of the moral failures of others but a recognition of a condition in which he too is implicated? The chapter on water in *Modern Painters* I, ends with a passage that has inevitably become notorious in recent years and is worth revisiting here for its instantiation of the difficulties of actually seeing. First the critic celebrates Turner's *Snow Storm* (fig. 5.3), a work he identifies as a challenging register of effort—the painter's and the viewer's—when it comes to being immersed in water as well as taking it in as an object of perception:

> Of course it was not understood; his finest works never are: but there was some apology for the public's not comprehending this, for few people have had the opportunity of seeing the sea at such a time, and when they have, cannot face it.

> To hold by a mast or a rock, and watch it, is a prolonged endurance of drowning which few people have courage to go through. To those who have, it is one of the noblest lessons of nature. (3:571)

Watching, drowning, enduring: a noble lesson in nature? What is the lesson here? Where does its nobility lie? How might we associate this immersion in water with—or distinguish it from—the symptomatic projection of emotion into the waves that is the fallacious response to nature of a disenchanted modernity? Surely a clue about the nobility of the engraving of a man at the brink of death in the obscure lines of *The Lost Sailor* may emerge from reflection on Ruskin's terms. And indeed, it soon becomes clear that the treatment of the difficult nobility of *Snow Storm* is designed as prelude to the discussion of a far fuller but no less difficult representation of death at sea that follows it immediately:

> But, I think, the noblest sea that Turner has ever painted, and, if so, the noblest certainly ever painted by man, is that of the Slave Ship, the chief Academy picture of the Exhibition of 1840. It is a sunset on the Atlantic, after prolonged storm; but the storm is partially lulled, and the torn and streaming rain-clouds are moving in scarlet lines to lose themselves in the hollow of the night. The whole surface of sea included in the picture is divided into two ridges of enormous swell, not high, nor local, but a low broad heaving of the whole ocean, like the lifting of its bosom by deep-drawn breath after the torture of the storm. Between these two ridges the fire of the sunset falls along the through of the sea, dyeing it with an awful but glorious light, the intense and lurid splendour which burns like gold, and bathes like blood. Along this fiery path and valley, the tossing waves by which the swell of the sea is restlessly divided, lift themselves in dark, indefinite, fantastic forms, each casting a faint and ghastly shadow behind it along the illumined foam. They do not rise everywhere, but three or four together in wild groups, fitfully and furiously, as the under strength of the swell compels or permits them; leaving between them treacherous spaces of level and whirling water, now lighted with green and lamp-like fire, now flashing back the gold of the declining sun, now fearfully dyed from above with the undistinguishable images of the burning clouds, which fall upon them in flakes of crimson and scarlet, and give to the reckless waves the added motion of their own fiery flying. Purple and blue, the lurid shadows of the hollow breakers are cast upon the mist of night, which gathers cold and low, advancing like the shadow of death upon the guilty ship as it labours amidst the lightening of the sea, its

> thin masts written upon the sky in lines of blood, girded with condemnation in that fearful hue which signs the sky with horror, and mixes its flaming flood with the sunlight, and, cast far along the desolate heave of the sepulchral waves, incarnadines the multitudinous sea.
>
> I believe, if I were reduced to rest Turner's immortality upon any single work, I should choose this. Its daring conception, ideal in the highest sense of the word, is based on the purest truth, and wrought out with the concentrated knowledge of a life; its colour is absolutely perfect, not one false or morbid hue in any part or line, and so modulated that every square inch of canvas is a perfect composition; its drawing as accurate as fearless; the ship buoyant, bending, and full of motion; its tones as true as they are wonderful; and the whole picture dedicated to the most sublime of subjects and impressions (completing thus the perfect system of all truth, which we have shown to be formed by Turner's works)—the power, majesty, and deathfulness of the open, deep, illimitable sea.

This passage, which is all of Ruskin that some people know, has become a touchstone for discussions of the engagement with and neglect of the evil of slavery in nineteenth-century culture. There are two places critics typically go as they declare that either Ruskin or Turner is failing to engage with slavery or else that he is doing so brilliantly (see fig. 5.4). On balance, when weighing up Ruskin's failure, there is the claim that he says almost nothing about the fact that the ship being represented is devoted to that most immoral and shameful project, the shipping of captive human beings as property in order to subject them to a lifetime—indeed a multigenerational period with no set term—of further violence and oppression. And more, that he does not note that those in control on board the ship have manifested the ultimate logic of the dehumanizing brutality they serve by making the calculation of profit and loss that indicates to them they are better off throwing sick and dead human beings overboard rather than giving them the care to which we tell ourselves we believe every individual is entitled when at risk or after death. All Ruskin gives us is a bare statement without the expressions of dismay we have come to expect when these topics are addressed: "She is a slaver, throwing her slaves overboard. The near sea is encumbered with corpses." On the other side of the scale is what Ruskin does say about what he sees in the image. Here are a few of the terms one might cite:

> The intense and lurid splendor which burns like gold and bathes like blood.
> Faint and ghastly shadow
> Advancing like the shadow of death upon the guilty ship

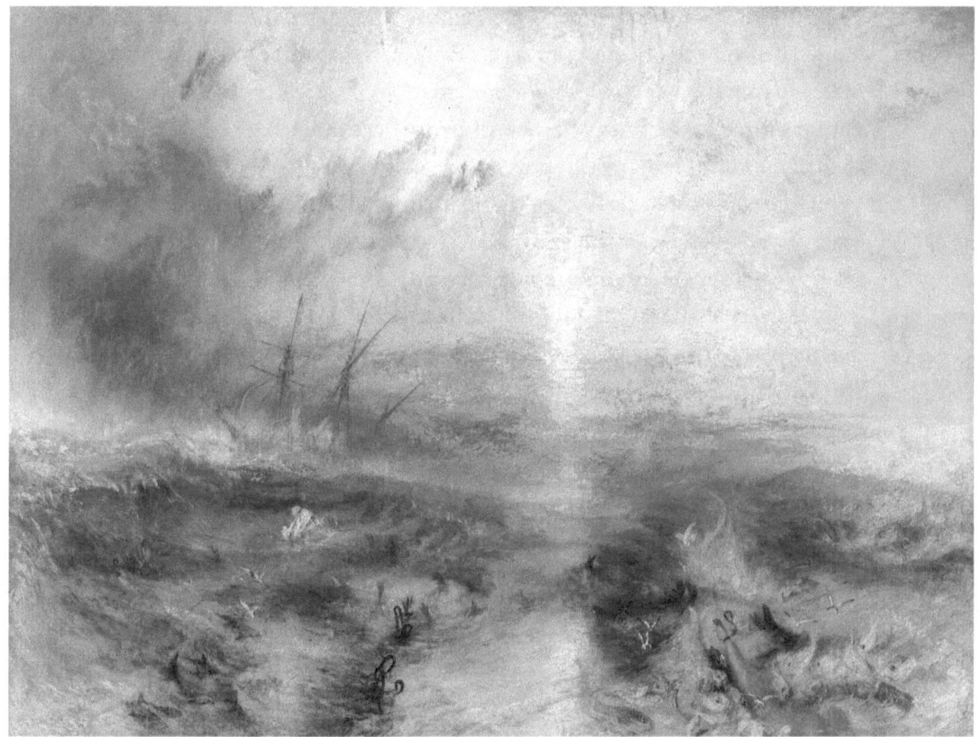

FIGURE 5.4. John Mallord William Turner, *Slave Ship* (*Slavers Throwing Overboard the Dead and Dying, Typhoon Coming On*) (1840). Oil on canvas, 90.8 × 122.6 cm. Boston, Museum of Fine Arts, Henry Lillie Pierce Fund. Photograph © 2021, Museum of Fine Arts, Boston, MA.

> Its thin masts written upon the sky in lines of blood girded with condemnation
> That fearful hue which signs the sky with horror, and mixes its flaming blood with the sunlight
> The desolate heave of the sepulchral waves.
> The power, majesty, and deathfulness of the open, deep, illimitable sea

What a sorry pass I find myself moved to as a critic! Like a lawyer for the defense before a skeptical court, first I cite the long passage, as though it were a piece of punctiliously untainted evidence. Then I pull out just a selection of the language in the passage that tells *me* that at every turn its author is no less engaged with the moral catastrophe represented by the action of the slavers than any of his judgmental readers might think themselves to be. But after that

I really don't know what more to say to those who pretend that Ruskin is ignoring what is in a sea he describes as "deathful," who claim to be unable to see the condemnation of a ship the representation of which is described as "written upon the sky in lines of blood girded with condemnation." "Girded with *condemnation*!" I find myself moved to write yet again, as though the extra ink in my repetition, italicization, and impatient exclamation mark will budge the scale of our archangel Michaels. But, of course, I am hardly the first to see what is everywhere apparent in Ruskin's text. And unsurprisingly, though to surprisingly little avail, many attentive critics have pointed out with compelling force the impossibility of statements about the painting and about Ruskin's response that nevertheless keep being made.[24] And, of course, Ruskin anticipated the problem. What did he say about a related painting? "There was some apology for the public's not comprehending." After all, "few people have had the opportunity of seeing the sea at such a time, and when they have, cannot face it."

If Paul Gilroy did not initiate the contemporary tradition of not facing Ruskin's text, he certainly gave it an important impetus when he briefly touched on the topic in his groundbreaking *Black Atlantic*, deprecating what he calls "Ruskin's inability to discuss the picture except in terms of what it revealed about the aesthetics of painting water," citing as evidence the fact that "he relegated the information that the vessel was a slave ship to a footnote in the first volume of *Modern Painters*."[25] Possibly the keyword in Gilroy's brief account is "information," as that is precisely *not* what is missing from a text in which Ruskin says as clearly as possible what the title of the painting would also inform anyone: "The noblest sea that Turner has ever painted, and, if so, the noblest certainly ever painted by man, is that *of the Slave Ship*." I put the words in italics as an indication of my despair that they will be read by those who, to paraphrase Gilroy, are unable to discuss the picture except in terms of what it reveals Ruskin missed in it. So, if the "information" Gilroy claims to miss is there, what is this thing he is calling information that can be felt as absent when it is quite palpably present?[26]

Ian Baucom reads substantially more than one paragraph of Ruskin before weighing in on what the critic is missing. But his account relies on limiting the reach of an argument the complexity of which he evidently partially recognizes but cannot quite credit:

> Enjoined to devote ourselves alternately to the surface and the reflected "above," our eyes are forbidden permission to peer beneath the water, or told that there

> is no beneath, that what is visible below the surface is merely an inverse image of that which floats above. Turner's peculiar genius, Ruskin argues, derives from his brilliant exploitation of this optical ballet of surface and reflection, and from his refusal to allow us to delve beneath the water. "We are not," Ruskin insists, "allowed to tumble into it and gasp for breath as we go down, we are kept upon the surface" (3:359). "We," apparently, are not the jettisoned slaves, who have no choice but to tumble into the water, to gasp for breath as they go down beneath a surface on which a Victorian public, freed from the obligation to wonder what lies beneath these waters, can see itself reflected.[27]

Like the perpetual indignation of Caliban in Wilde's preface to *Dorian Gray*, it is unclear if all this critical affect comes from seeing or *not* seeing one's own face looking back from the mirror of Turner's painting or Ruskin's analysis. But is seeing all of right and wrong we have in the world? And is it as easy as Wilde's Caliban thinks it should be? We do other things aside from looking. For example, we spend a great deal of time getting and spending, which may contribute to our inability to see things in the water.

At times contemporary criticism astounds one with its impoverished relationship to sight, seeming to believe that all that is missing is an unobstructed view (more *information*, perhaps) of what is the case in order for goodness to prevail. And yet, what if we *cannot* see? What if when we do see, we still do not judge rightly? What if when we see and know, we still act wrongly? What would it mean if the Victorian public had indeed seen itself reflected in the waters of the slave ship, a response Ruskin certainly would have desired but did not, evidently, think of as being bound to happen as a matter of course? And let us say it clearly so it is heard: "we" are not the enslaved people dead and dying in the image—and no viewer has ever been that impossible thing. The real questions is why we might think that identifying with the drowned is more of a moral position than identifying with the sailors on the ship.

As Mark Frost says in a cogent response to the line of argument followed by Baucom and others, "Nor does Ruskin ever 'forbid' readers to look beneath the surface of water. He merely points out that it is impossible to do so from a distance." Frost thoughtfully insists on the limits of an analysis that separates Ruskin's aesthetic thought from his morality. But perhaps the problem is not that his critics miss that connection but that they wish it were otherwise.[28] Frost discusses Sarah Fulford's characteristic claim that though the slaves are "reduced to merely a footnote," they haunt the language of his response, an analysis that in the first instance requires ignoring what Ruskin is doing in order to discover that he has done it in spite of himself. "Had Europeans been depicted drowning," Fulford writes, "one wonders whether Ruskin would have paid so much attention to the glorious hues of Turner's sunset."[29] This would be a serious charge if we did not have Ruskin's account of the noble plate of the drowned sailor to reflect on, if there weren't a large number of astonishingly beautiful Turner seascapes without slavers or dying people for Ruskin to have singled out for praise. But it may turn out that the presence of Europeans in the water is more marked than Fulford would like to recognize.

The structure of false accusation and easy defense ultimately hides what is truly and irrecoverably troubling about the painting and the critic's account of it, which is the challenging position in which the viewer is placed in relation to injury. While many nineteenth-century critics found the style of the painting incoherent, or what they understood as a floating chain inverisimilitudinous, the challenge the image presents for the contemporary viewer is ultimately traceable to the fact that it shows us the face of damage unrelieved by the kinds of things in which culture has lately suggested we find some relief—things we sometimes call information but which are not ultimately that at all. The painting illustrates no agency, either on the part of the victims or the perpetrators. Worse, perhaps, it places them both in circumstances in which their fates are not clearly distinguishable. We know individuals on board the ship are responsible and that individuals in the water are suffering terribly in the moment the painting represents. But the ship is not an agent, and neither is the storm or the water or the animals in the water following their natural instincts.

When it was displayed at the Royal Academy, the painting was accompanied by a passage of poetry from Turner's *Fallacies of Hope* providing a kind of moral gloss:

> Aloft all hands, strike the topmasts and belay;
> Yon angry setting sun and fierce-edged clouds
> Declare the Typhon's coming.
> Before it sweeps your decks, throw overboard
> The dead and dying—ne'er heed their chains
> Hope, Hope, fallacious hope!
> Where is thy market now?

The location of the speaker is unstable in a text that moves quickly from the vain attempt of the sailors to save themselves from the destructive winds coming on—the actions relayed in an imperative form, as if the speaker were the captain of the ship—to the order to jettison the dead and dying in an undifferentiated action combining sacrilegious indifference and murder, to abandoning the ship entirely in a second-person address to those on board ("Before it sweeps *your* deck"). The final ironization of aspirations (or fallacious hopes) at the close seems to include in its judgment at once the hope for survival and for profit from human suffering, and so it needs to be entirely the expression of someone outside the events depicted. Evidently this view of the subject of the painting, which Paul Gilroy himself has described as illuminating the painter's "elemental despair for which the morality of the traffic in slaves offered a striking and appropriate symbol," suggests something quite a distance from indifference.[30]

Is it his ironies that are unbearable and make so many critics think that Turner is missing what he is in fact showing? The subjects being hurt are given no agency, which appalls our sense of what we want to see represented. The ship moves off in one direction, back and left, its sails furled so as to minimize the damage from the wind; there is nothing else the crew will be able to do to save themselves from danger. And we have no idea of the ultimate fate of the vessel or the men on board it. The dead and dying follow another course, though they are floating in the same ocean. Hands rise from the water hopelessly, as no help will come. A leg is tossed by the waves, suggesting the loss of motive power of a corpse. The painting as a whole insists on the recognition of a set of denials: the slavers have denied the humanity of those they have treated as property and to whom they have refused aid or comfort. Casting these people overboard is the ultimate manifestation of a logic that has been true since before the enslaved people were brought on board: a human connection that should entail recognition, solidarity, and care has been ruptured. That is clear enough. The other lost connection is harder to assimilate as a lesson: the power of nature and the vicissitudes of fortune make the moral compromises the slavers live with not just ethically catastrophic but a practical failure. The sea is a reminder of the core fact of the shared humanity that has been denied, of the vulnerability that could lead to a recognition of commonality, even to an act of caretaking.

Phlebas the Phoenician, a fortnight dead,
Forgot the cry of gulls, and the deep sea swell
And the profit and loss.
A current under sea

Picked his bones in whispers. As he rose and fell
He passed the stages of his age and youth
Entering the whirlpool.
                    Gentile or Jew
O you who turn the wheel and look to windward,
Consider Phlebas, who was once handsome and tall as you.[31]

That is the entirety of the "Death by Water" section of Eliot's *The Waste Land*: profit forgotten, difference forgotten (Gentile or Jew or Phoenician), undifferentiated death becoming an emblem of an inevitable shared fate. (And we may remember that the Phoenician sailor enters the poem first in an act of highly ironized fortune-telling by the congested Madame Sosostris.) As the sailors on board the guilty ship look to save themselves but not their cargo, nature ironizes their ambitions and their sense of distinction from those they have cast away.

The themes of Turner's painting are utterly dark and difficult. Christina Sharpe is moved by it to an extensive reflection on the nature of the animal consumption and decomposition that follows death at sea, reminding her readers of the inevitable and ongoing circulation of human material, a grimly imagined and moralized version of the insight we saw in Pater's account of the place of human material in nature.[32] Today, even more than in the day it was painted, *The Slave Ship* leaves the viewer suspended in an impossible space, a situation evidently intolerable for a line of criticism demanding that most unlikely thing, adequate representation and appropriate ethical commitment, when adequacy can only be established by the guarantee of full sympathetic engagement (of maker, of viewer), and ethical commitment is limited to moments of adequate identity with suffering subjects. Far closer to the dying than to the ship but looking from a place of safety and so sharing more with the men trying to make an escape, temporarily spared the destiny of those before us, we cannot save the dying, and even our judgment is bound to be too late. "Few people have had the opportunity of seeing the sea at such a time, and when they have, cannot face it," Ruskin wrote in a passage I cited above explaining why Turner's seascapes can be so hard to understand but that makes little sense if it is just about how rare it is to expose oneself to the dangers of a storm at sea (or to have the "opportunity to do so"). "To hold by a mast or a rock, and watch it, is a prolonged endurance of drowning which few people have courage to go through." Needless to say, this is an experience of seeing, facing, watching, and enduring that fewer have had today than in the nineteenth century. Even fewer would endorse the idea that such an experience would be liable to prove "one of the noblest lessons of nature" (3:571).

The tendency to see too many of our own feelings reflected in nature is characteristic of modernity as Ruskin understood it, as is the centrality of death in every significant work of art. Negotiating between the widespread and symptomatic fallacy of a pathos that projects its feelings onto a disenchanted world and a drive to identify in admired representations of nature signs of the modern death that is compounded of cruel indifference, brutal violence, and something more, a surplus in excess of death that is beautiful precisely because it does not deny our fatal condition, there is no question that Ruskin's project matches up uneasily with a modern sensibility that thinks it wants to see with great precision, that claims to want information, but that does not want to see what Ruskin cannot avoid recognizing. And so two options typically open up. We can pretend Ruskin missed what was right in front of him—and indeed what he spoke about—or we can judiciously reflect on the historical moment in which his work, or Turner's for that matter, might be understood to make sense. Following the latter approach we review the most likely sources for the ship, and we remind ourselves of the conference on abolition that took place as Turner painted or of the memoirs of slavers and antislavers he would have known.

But Turner's painting is unsettling for too many reasons. Chief among them, as I have noted, is the conflict between the clarity of the crimes it memorializes—enslavement, murder—and the lack of a fixed point of view and agents. Beyond these challenges, as all the critics remind us, there is the obscurity of the artist's own position in relation to the events represented—which has been postulated as ranging from complicity to indifference to committed resistance. The historical gap in which the painting exists, it bears saying, has always (even in its own day) made its moral tenor uncertain. It was painted well after Britain had abolished slavery on its soil and during a period of great antislavery activism during which Britain was engaged (with mixed success) in interdicting the trade on the high seas, while wealthy interests still profited from slavery that had remained legal in the Caribbean into the 1830s. Turner's work has been associated with an abolitionist Congress in 1840, but also with the famous episode of the *Zong*, in which enslaved people were cast overboard in order to be able to claim their deaths as a loss for the purposes of insurance, a notorious case that was tried in England in 1781 to a morally calamitous verdict.[33] Even when slavery was abolished in the Caribbean in 1834, it was an ongoing activity in that great trading partner and autonomous British creation, the United States. So, the moral standpoint for our own day—almost as obsessed with locating the historical moment of a cultural event as with ascertaining the proper degree of blame—is liable to be unstable. We can tell ourselves that the lack of clarity is a fault or an attempt to hide something. But painting a thing and talking about it strike me as far from the most efficient ways to try to hide it. The painting is not, and never was, a seascape into which a slave ship has intruded and brought in its train a set of cruel associations. It is not an attempt to represent nature that has been interrupted by the presence of horrible murder that the painter has illustrated inadequately because its victims do not fall in with his plan to capture beauty or sublimity or the surface of water. To think of the image this way may be to suffer from interference from later modes of representation, as though the painter were a photographer, as though documentary realism were the only project when pain is before us or when moral failure is to be represented.

Auden suggested a long time ago that the indifference of the world to our pain—and to the pain we cause—is the most striking characteristic of the Old Masters. Reading criticism of Turner's painting and of Ruskin's response, the powerful insight of the poet become clearer, notably the idea that *moderns* may be particularly prone to forgetting what the Old Masters never did (and my reading requires an emphasis on the first word of the following passage, but evidently all the moral power of the work resides in such an emphasis):

> They never forgot
> That even the dreadful martyrdom must run its course
> Anyhow in a corner, some untidy spot
> Where the dogs go on with their doggy life and the torturer's horse
> Scratches its innocent behind on a tree.[34]

While Auden proposes that it is characteristic of modernity to keep forgetting that it is a fundamental part of human suffering that the world is deeply indifferent to it, Ruskin urges a different reckoning. Still, the demand that we look for the injury in the work of art may be understood as arising from a related recognition that a relationship to pain is part of what a noble work of art will relay to the viewer—even when no cure is offered.

The catalog of his collection of Turner's drawings that Ruskin was working on in the late 1870s as one of the debilitating mental crises that characterized his later years came on him makes poignant reading. In it we find an extraordinary note about a watercolor study for the painting he had by that point sold because it was too painful to live with, suggesting not simply his allegorical understanding of the work but his urgent response to what he saw in the water: "STUDY FOR FISH. Coming on at speed, in the Slaver (modern trade?)."[35] The parenthesis proposes an allegorical reading of a fragment with profound implications for the painting as a whole. If the fish in the water coming to feast on the living and the dead, all open eyes and even more open implacable mouths, are understood to stand for modern trade, who are the slaves, what is the ship? What is the relationship between the slave trade that—I have been suggesting—can only be understood as a self-evident evil in Turner and an implacable, devouring modern trade that provides the ultimate moment of brutal consumption?

Is it possible that the frequent claim of moral failure in relation to the painting is an indication of resistance to an ongoing moral crisis that we do not want to talk about, in which long-dead agents are not the most interested parties? While slavery has been abolished as a legal practice, so that ships no longer *openly* roam the oceans with a cargo of humanity to be sold or murdered or claimed as lost cargo for insurance purposes, the injuries of a devouring global trade fill the waters all around us. I have not found the sketch Ruskin describes, but then the frenzied, ravening, implacable consumption one sees in the painting itself is distressing enough to illustrate what Ruskin is calling "modern trade." The dead and dying are set upon at all angles with the ferocious intention and lack of clear volition we associate with animal instinct, actions compounding the evil of death with a loss of identity and even clear agency for agent and victim. I have reproduced another study of fish Ruskin owned, which he also identifies in the catalog immediately below the one I have been discussing and in a clearly analogous form as a sketch for the *Slaver*. This image he reads as a figure for "modern philosophy" parallel to the image of brutal, implacable "modern trade"—and offering an inadequate response to the evil before it: "Looking up to the sky, in the Slaver (Modern Philosophy)" (13:469). Mouths agape, unseeing eyes raised above them: it is hard to say if these creatures have come to speak or to consume whatever falls into their maws (fig. 5.5).

I found a copy of *The Lost Sailor* at a major collection that had it erroneously listed—as many do—as a print from the original plate by Turner. Ruskin himself had commissioned the work, probably in the 1870s when he was putting together a collection of reproductions for students of art at Oxford (fig. 5.6). I have to admit I was pleased when I first came across this print, as I knew it would reproduce so much more clearly than the challenging original, which I hoped at that point in my ignorance was itself a poor or late printing or a copy.

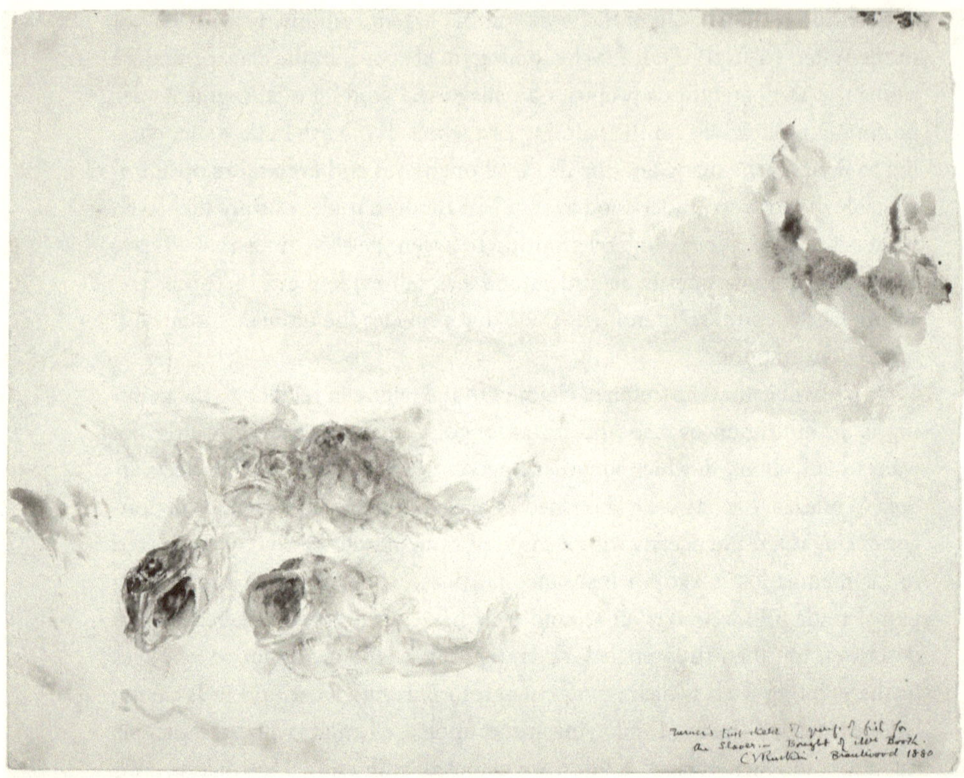

FIGURE 5.5. First sketch of group of fish for Turner's *Slaver*, purchased by John Ruskin in 1880. Robert H. Taylor Collection of English and American Literature, Manuscripts Division, Department of Special Collections, Princeton University Library, Princeton, NJ, RTC01.

But it was immediately apparent when I sat before the work that for all of its nicely rendered feeling of depth, its bright foam and dark stones, the problem at the heart of the copy resided precisely in its straightforward clarity: the staring eyes of the dying man losing the solemnity of death in the zigzag lines of hair. This is not what Turner created, this clear, defined, pathetic grotesque. This is not the noble plate. And it is an ongoing problem in discussions of Turner that some of his most moving effects are difficult to see in reproduction: the force of the light is deadened on the page of the book, the power of an ocean swell shrunk by the limits of the printed volume. As an oil painting or a complex mezzotint is reduced to just another image in a world filled with so many, the ostensible subject inevitably comes to the fore, the work's existence as an object meaning so little.

I have been highlighting the elements that have made *The Slave Ship* and Ruskin's reading of it so hard to see in recent years. But it would be wrong to avoid the most troubling reason of all. It is hard to get away from the simple fact that Ruskin has contempt for modern concepts of freedom—and that he sees them as continuous with our modern failures of perception. He thinks we are not free, that our desires enslave us to our detriment and cause us unreflectively, and sometimes even as we vaunt our emancipatory sentiments, to enslave others. He sees our confused desires and our complicity as moral failings.

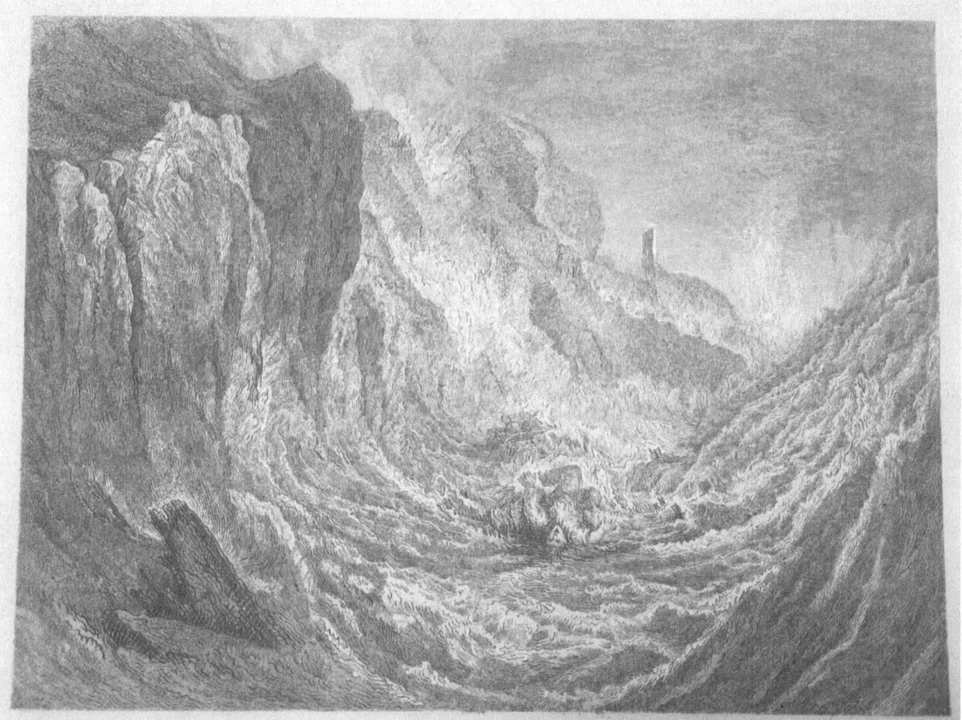

FIGURE 5.6. J. Fisher (England), after Joseph Mallord William Turner, *The Lost Sailor*, from *Liber Studiorum*. Etching and mezzotint, 25.2 x 30.5 cm. Art Gallery of New South Wales, gift of Mrs. Arthur Acland Allen through the Empire Art Loan Collection Society, 1939, 2000.181. Photo: AGNSW.

Is he wrong? More troubling, perhaps, he includes among our mystified desires distant political goals he sees as tending to promote the neglect of our complicity in ongoing acts of forced, dehumanizing labor. And here an important historical dimension can enter our study of Ruskin and the representation of what the water shows us if we allow it to. Is the end of slavery the beginning of freedom? Is what we call freedom a common experience?[36]

For decades a moral convention has pulled particular instances of damage out of the general run of human events, identified them as evils so distinct that to approximate them to others would be to deny their pernicious nature. This approach, which is designed to honor and even preserve the unspeakable character of a particular episode of trauma, sometimes does so at the cost of pulling the event out of history, a permanent exception that nevertheless points a powerful moral lesson. But there is room to ask if this moral convention that identifies evil with exception does not lessen its moral value. *If not now, when?* can become a ritualized memory of urgency that translates into its opposite: if then, never before or after. *Never again* risks becoming a tendentious claim of distinction that may well inhibit the moral sympathies it aims to galvanize.

In an uncommonly interesting study I mentioned briefly above, *Shipwreck with Spectator*, Hans Blumenberg has tracked back to its uses in early Greek philosophy the meanings of the metaphor of a spectator safe on land looking out to sea at the injuries attendant on a shipwreck. Blumenberg's work is not simply a study in continuities, however, and he identifies a fundamental and quite moving turn in the meaning of the metaphor in the nineteenth century. His instances from this period show the transformation of the figure from one intended to evoke the relationship between the philosopher and a mutable nature into one illustrating a complex sensibility involving at once reflection on the contemporary moment and the realization of failed moral responsibility. Blumenberg first cites that grim philosopher, Arthur Schopenhauer, who "fully decodes the identicalness of the human subject in both positions, the position of those who are going down and that of the spectator" (59), before turning to a line of argument that makes a surprising swerve from historical evidence to something more, to the ethical challenge to be found in the identification of the drowned and the viewer who sees them from apparent safety:

> Considered quantitatively the nineteenth century was surely *the* epoch of shipwrecks. Down to the sinking of the *Titanic*, nature's force manifested itself more

> convincingly than ever before; in the nineteenth century, England alone lost five thousand men a year through ships going down—off the British coast there were 700 shipwrecks in the first six months of 1880, and in the first six months of 1881, 919—in whose memory, J.M.W. Turner set up a last fierce monument of romantic longing for death. In spite of this reality, the shipwreck metaphorics was completely occupied by the newly emerging historical consciousness and its insoluble dilemma of theoretical distances versus living engagement. (67)

"Theoretical distances versus living engagement." Blumenberg does not specify what Turner painting he has in mind, but it is probably *The Shipwreck* from 1805. What the philosopher captures with real clarity, however—not to say pathos—is an insoluble condition that makes the representation of injury at sea recognizable as more than a document of history, as in itself instantiating the gap between perception and engagement, between theorizing and living. A few pages later Blumenberg addresses himself to a turn of phrase that he finds repeatedly in the lectures of the historian Jacob Burckhardt when the latter attempts to account for the fear of looming uncertainty in contemporary culture. It is a formulation that makes Schopenhauer's insight about the identicalness of situation of "those who are going down and the spectator" more fully historical. And Burckhardt's words might be read as a gloss on the pathetic fallacy as much as on the lines carved onto the plate of the drowned sailor that are so hard for the eye to make out: "Times of dread and deepest woe may be coming," the historian declares, sounding a note combining anxiety and uncertainty. "We would like to know the waves on which we sail across the ocean; but we ourselves are these waves."[37]

To look at nature and find meaning we may not approve looking back at us; to look at a work of art and see not just pain but a painful indictment: I have emphasized what I understand to be a tradition of extraordinary misreading of Turner's painting and Ruskin's account of it not because I think I can compel assent when the clear evidence of the canvas or printed page is disallowed by the rules of our ethical-aesthetic courts, but because I see the crisis in interpretation provoked by painting and text as characteristic of the challenge of seeing our condition reflected in the water. The pathetic fallacy that shows us only what we already know or believe we feel; the sea that tells us nothing at all; the vision of death or murder absent the sight of agency: in the seaspawn and seawrack we are liable find a memory of meaning that feels substantive and fatal alongside a representation unable to support the meaning we want to give it, leaving in its wake a troubling sense of complicity, uncertainty, even fear.

• • •

What *you* see in the water, I wrote, in the subtitle to this chapter, as though I knew you, as though I were qualified to identify your responses, as though I were putting myself into every category of perception or subjecthood available. This tendentious interpellation, like that entailed in the "we" and "us" I use in the paragraphs before this one, is in fact typical of my instances, as much of Wordsworth's declaration that the world is too much with "us," an observation that is evidently driven by that individual disappointment eventuating in a cry that can only be of the speaker, as of Arnold's lonely companioned speaker in "Dover Beach" ("I only"), or of the shifts from "I" to "he" to "you" and back in Stephen Dedalus's meditations on the beach, or even of Walter Pater's generalizing claims about an experience that can seem so individual, the refreshing dive into a body of water on a hot day, used as an instance of "our physical life" (as though we shared *that* most personal thing, one could complain—as though we *didn't*, someone else might answer). "You who turn the wheel" are invited to "consider" the fate of Phlebas the Phoenician, his bones picked in whispers by the sea.

It is not just the relative clarity of bones we might find in the water, however. And the play of pronouns will not always identify commonality. Sometimes it comes as a challenge. I mentioned the treatment of the breakdown of the human form in Christina Sharpe's *In the Wake* earlier in this chapter. As she works to imagine the effects of being thrown overboard on bodies that had undergone the abuse and starvation characteristic of the slave ship, Sharpe's reflections on decomposition as a form of permanence resist reduction to the evacuation of difference motivating Eliot in the passage from *The Waste Land* I have cited. The loss of particularity, of individuation, of separation is also at the heart of the political and ethical meaning of dangerous water in the work of two recent poets who have drawn on *The Slaver* in the course of their reflections on race in history and therefore today. In *Turner* (1995), David Dabydeen captures the combination of moral crisis and uncertainty in the painting and its reception with one elegant and troubling conceit: his speaker, one of the doomed selves forever floating in the water in the painting, suspended in the catastrophe the artist created, gives Turner's name to both the pedophile captain of the ship and to a child conceived from his violent abuse and cast overboard stillborn. The serious play with the name makes it a permanently alienated second person, as well as a substantive that amounts to no more than a circular verb capturing the contingent suspended, unresolved, inconclusive motion of a body in the water: a turner/Turner:

I gather it to my body, this grain,
This morsel slipped from the belly of moon,
And name it Turner and will instruct it
In the knowledge of landscapes learnt as the ship
Plunged towards another world we never reached.[38]

Neither Turner ever arrives at an end point, nor does either turner ever return, caught up as they are in a cyclic motion that painfully recapitulates the injury of being born out of the deracinating intimate violence of slavery. But this impossible, unrealizable self he meets in the water is an object of frustrated fascination to the speaker, who keeps working to remember (indeed, to fantasize) an origin its sea-born alter ego could never know. What the speaker always hears in return, however, is not recognition of that unshareable lost beginning but insult. And indeed, the project of instruction the speaker undertakes, driven by his invented memories of origins, is bound to fail. The incongruous promise to learn about landscapes (I . . . will instruct it / In the knowledge of landscapes") is an evocation of the genre associated with the work of the painter who is the original source of the name. But the category becomes grotesquely useless when wielded by a sea-borne figure attempting to speak of it to an inchoate sea-born entity for whom no relationship to either land or memory is possible ("landscapes learnt as the ship / Plunged towards another world we never reached"). Inevitably, Turner is unteachable. Instead of recognition of the lesson of a common past in which he instructs this figure he so welcomes, the speaker hears from the creation of displacement and abuse that is another vision of himself another name, one linking both speakers in the optic of the brutal white agents who have determined their fate. Having no context but the maelstrom into which it was born, it (and the objectifying pronoun is a deliberate confession of the indeterminacy of this being's nature and the dehumanization that is its cause) finds a name for the speaker and for itself and refuses all instruction in the fantasies of memory proposed by its longing counterpart. Not even a fantasy of return is available for *this* turner. It demonstrates instead the one lesson it learned about itself from birth, culminating in the dark final section of the long poem, of which I will just cite the opening. The speaker has tried to take on the projects of Turner the artist, to make landscapes, to wield the colors of the sea. But Turner, the creation of slavery, has only one word for itself or the speaker, a color become an insult meant to divide it from the speaker who is also itself:

> "Nigger," it cries, loosening from the hook
> Of my desire, drifting away from
> My body of lies. I wanted to teach it
> A redemptive song, fashion new descriptions
> Of things, new colours fountaining out of form.
> I wanted to begin anew in the sea
> But the child would not bear the future
> Nor its inventions, and my face was rooted
> In the ground of memory, a ground stampeded
> By herds of foreign men who swallow all its fruit. (25.1–8)

In these selves stripped of a place of origin by the act of removal, and of an arrival by being cast overboard, Dabydeen projects a heartbreaking failed romance of impossible memory evidencing at every point the fecundating power of violence.

As a memorial to the cruelty and violence of the Middle Passage, Turner's painting has played an important role in recent African American writing. We find it, perhaps most surprisingly, at the end of Claudia Rankine's *Citizen*, that volume of poems devoted to race as it is lived in America, which opens with a disquieting sequence of memories of racial injuries made all the more immediate and difficult by being relayed in an implacable second person designed to trouble the conventional structures of witness or narration. In an uncomfortable and irresolvable exploding at once of group and individual identity, of culpability as well as evasion, everything that happens in this opening section is happening to *you*. Turner's painting, briefly alluded to in an essay on Serena Williams in the volume, appears entirely unglossed at its end, along with a detail showing the fish attacking the body in the foreground.[39] Rankine does not versify the work in any way because, in a text preoccupied at every turn by the refusal to see and haunted by the memory of what was revealed by the rising floodwaters of Katrina about the failure of recognition of damaged Black lives in America, she would like the sight of this painting from the past at least to speak for itself, to bear witness to continuities she wants to understand as impossible to deny. It is a bold use of a work Ian Baucom, not without reason, has described with evocative paradox as "a representative image of what we do not see" (*Specters*, 275). But perhaps that is why it tantalizes, why it keeps a surprising contemporary and American relevance. The crisis of Katrina, which is the place where the painting finds its closest evocation in Rankine's volume, is presented by the poet as at once immediately urgent and historic, a compound of real-time failure to rescue and evidence of long-standing and ongoing systemic racism, all captured with the relentless amnesiac immediacy and mystifying sentimentality characteristic of the American news media when it is brought before any crisis.

The play between news, information, knowledge, and ethical failure is captured in a video collaboration with John Lucas, the script of which Rankine includes in *Citizen* and which is composed of quotations related to the storm and its aftermath compiled from CNN reporting. The difficult work of the poem here, as throughout, is to memorialize a specific acute moment of suffering while indicating that the sense it is distinct—or new(s)—is precisely the problem:

> The fiction of the facts assumes innocence, ignorance,
> lack of intention, misdirection; the necessary conditions
> of a certain time and place.[40]

"The fiction of the facts" is the assumption of a lack of responsibility that is in itself a denial of complicity, of the necessary conditions that were already there and are being hidden by misdirection. The moral failure the poet challenges has at its heart the historical limitations of responses that appear to offer a clear-eyed view of events but do so at the cost of committing to an idea of their *limited* nature:

> He said, I don't know what the water wanted. It wanted to
> show you no one would come.
> He said, I don't know what the water wanted. As if then
> And now were not the same moment. (85–86)

"As if then / And now were not the same moment." Dabydeen thanks Jack Lindsay, the biographer of Turner and one of the few authors to take Turner's poetry seriously, in his acknowledgments, reminding us of the particularly textual nature of his use of the painting, highlighting by contrast Rankine's use of the work as *visual* material.[41] She emphasizes this motivation in her discussion of the topic during an interview in which she indicates that it was the painting itself she wanted to bring before her readers—a kind of ocular evidence of the undeniable—and of the relationship between then and now:

> I thought, "Gosh, this problem has been around since the market—since black bodies were part of the market. When they were objects. When they were considered property." And that equation between whiteness and the black body as property of whiteness is the equation we can't get out of. . . . I wanted to end [*Citizen*] with Turner because people always say, "Well, I didn't know. It wasn't my intention. I wish I had known more about this." But Turner knew better in the 1800s. He knew better. And this is 2015. So, there it was. The end.[42]

"I . . . they . . . they . . . we . . . I . . . I . . . my . . . I . . . I . . . He." This informal moment, with its brief snippets of internalized conversation and ventriloquized defensive dialogue, is in itself a reminder of the importance of the pronominal play in *Citizen*, its function as a way to mark the intersection of impossible ignorance and complicity at which a crisis is manifested and denied.[43] To know better in this formulation is not simply to be better informed (to have more or more-accurate information about resources not mobilized for rescue, say, or about the presence or lack of intention). It means to recognize what one already knows—for example, that the situation of the people in trouble during a flood did not begin with the most recent rainfall. Claudia Rankine's colloquial usage and her straightforward juxtaposition of historical periods amounts to a sophisticated reminder of both the power and limits of the apparently self-evident.

We look at the sea and the struggle over interpretation begins. Rankine proposes we look to the past and locate not a constant mystification of what we should see but a kind of clarity that includes the challenging irresolutions inherent in an unclaimed responsibility linking us to prior instances of damage and to ongoing processes in which we still have a role to play. Similarly, "The end," as she uses it here, means not an apocalyptic revelation in which judgment is outsourced to a divinity with the perfect ability to measure souls and thereby complete history. Rather, it is meant to suggest—as Rankine's use of the second person does in her poetry—the need to finish with obfuscation about the nature of inextricable complicity. To end this way is to begin.

So there it was. The end.

ACKNOWLEDGMENTS

This is the second book I send to press as a global pandemic rages, this one reaching completion on the anniversary of the day on which I watched from the roof of my home as a plume of smoke rose from the place where two towers I had never liked had stood, making them suddenly mean things they never could have prior to that moment. While it is certain that the losses and fears of the years between 9/11 and the current medical crisis shaped this project in ways I can recognize and probably in ways that are still opaque to me, one thing that has become ever clearer during that long period is the gratitude I feel for those who have sustained and inspired my work in a world in which so much is unpredictable aside from risk and loss.

It would have been impossible for me to conceive, much less write, this book without the year I spent at the American Academy in Rome as a Rome Prize and ACLS/Burkhardt Fellow in 2004. The Relics Discussion Group that convened itself while I was there was an important intellectual resource, and what I learned from our conversations continues to orient me in my work. From among those who participated I will mention in particular Walter Cupperi, Mary Doyno, Maria Elena Gonzales, Elizabeth Marlowe, Richard Neer, Andrea Volpe, and Justin Walsh.

Closer to home, I have received a great deal of encouragement at key moments from Deans and Chairs at Rutgers University, starting, to my great good fortune, with Barry Qualls and the late Cheryl Wall, extraordinary models of graceful mentoring and collegiality. Most recently, Rebecca Walkowitz as dean, and Meredith McGill as chair, provided timely support at a key juncture, as well as cheerful encouragement.

A number of scholars at Rutgers and elsewhere have inspired this project and its author over the years. I have reason to be grateful to James Eli Adams, Isobel Armstrong, John Belton, Lynn Festa, Kate Flint, Lauren Goodlad,

Billy Galperin, Colin Jager, Jonathan Kramnick, John Kucich, David Kurnick, George Levine, Leah Price, Elaine Scarry, Michelle Stephens, Helen Vendler, Lynn Wardley, and Carolyn Williams. My collaboration with fellow directors at the Rutgers British Studies Center, Seth Koven, and Carla Yanni, has been a delight and a lesson in the styles of supportive interdisciplinary thought.

I would like to record here my gratitude to three scholars who provided more encouragement than they could have realized at key moments in the prehistory and long emergence of this project simply by their gracious responses to an interloper from abroad: Dominique Poulot at Université Paris 1, Panthéon-Sorbonne, whose kind welcome and receptiveness gave a last push to my thoughts about topics he has studied with a subtlety and nuance to which I can only aspire; Corrado Bologna, at the time at La Sapienza in Rome, more recently at Scuola Normale Superiore di Pisa, whose urbane reflections on art and literature were a model and a stimulus for taking my work in unexpected directions; and Nicholas Shrimpton, at Oxford, the scholar who, with patience and a wonderfully open spirit, guided my first steps with John Ruskin.

As I came to the end of this project, I was fortunate to acquire new interlocutors who led me to new resources and ideas in a number of fast-developing fields. I would like to thank, Fiona Greenland, Morag Kersel, Erich Hattala Matthes, Trinidad Rico, and, and especially Liz Marlow, who convened us. To these names I would add with gratitude that of Sadia Abbas, who in a brief period has proved a fruitful and helpful interlocutor on the topics addressed in these pages.

Marshall Brown and Garrett Stewart commented on material that helped shape this project, including some that ended up on the cutting room floor in revision, but that nevertheless helped me to conceive of the work in its current form. I am extraordinarily grateful for their distinct models of collegial aid, as I am to Billy Galperin at Rutgers, who read an entire early version of the volume and provided his usual incisive guidance. The work benefited immensely from the perspicacious and generously detailed comments of two anonymous readers for Stanford University Press. Their extraordinary insight into what this book could be led me to a clearer sense of my project, and a full recasting of its structure.

I am grateful to thoughtful interlocutors who helped me work through this material at The Birkbeck Centre for Nineteenth-Century Studies; the University of Birmingham; Columbia University, the CUNY Graduate Center; Indiana University; Université Paris 1, Panthéon-Sorbonne, Université Paris 8,

Vincennes-Saint-Denis; Maison des Sciences de l'Homme, Paris Nord; Yale University; as well as at the North American Victorian Studies Association Annual Conference in Phoenix Arizona in 2008. An earlier, and much shorter version of Chapter Four appeared in the *Proceedings of the Modern Language Association* as "Owning Art after Napoleon: Trophy, Symbol, and the Question of Restitution at the Birth of the Museum" (Spring 2010).

I should also say that while kind friends and colleagues did their best, I am solely responsible for the positions I maintain on these pages, and for any errors even their help was unable to prevent me from committing.

I have had reason to be especially grateful to librarians and curators for help acquiring images during this complicated period of partial-openings and odd hours. My thanks to the staff at the Art and Architecture Collection at the New York Public Library, the Art Gallery of New South Wales, The Firestone Library at Princeton University, the Department of Special Collections at Stanford University Libraries, and the Watson Library at the Metropolitan Museum. I would like to express here my gratitude to John Russell for his extraordinary generosity in allowing me to select an image from among his stunning photographs of sites of looting in Iraq.

At Rutgers this book had the benefit of Caolan Madden's imaginative, sensitive, and careful work as a research assistant and original copy editor. Jake Romanow's punctilious subsequent attentions helped tame a later version of the manuscript. New administrative duties came my way as I was undertaking revisions, and I'd like to register here my gratitude to the extraordinary faculty and staff at the Rutgers Writing Program, for their inspiring dedication during a difficult period. I owe a more personal debt to my two chief collaborators, Lynda Dexheimer and Ali Sperling, for their insistence that I get back to this book, and for the work they took on in order to help me do so.

Faith Wilson Stein's long-standing commitment to this project and its author led me to produce a kind of book I had not anticipated, but that I am very glad to see in print. At Stanford I also deeply appreciated the engaged and imaginative work of Erica Wetter and Caroline McKusick, as well as of Gigi Mark, a kind and supportive production editor, and Christine Gever, the alert and thoughtful copy editor. I am glad to have had Mary Mortensen's nuanced and patient work on the index.

Writing during the crises that have characterized recent years is only possible, for me because of the ongoing support of friends and family, whether we are able to meet in person or not. It gives me great pleasure to acknowledge here Tim Dowling, Molly Finnerty, Maria Elena Gonzales, Jane Harvey, Oliver Herring, Kamron Keshtgar, Jonathan Kramnick, Peter Krashes, Julian Loose, Meredith McGill, Rita Pomade, Rachel Porter, Maureen Siegel, Reka Siegel, and Kate Telscher. My brother, Stefan Siegel, continues to be what he has been from the outset, a good-humored source of affection and good sense.

Nancy Yousef, best reader first and last, improved everything that is good in this book, and tried her best with the rest. Our daughter, Silvia, continues to make my life more radiant and amusing than I could have thought possible before I met her. I thank her here for those moments when she left me to my work, and for those when she interrupted me.

Brooklyn, September 11, 2021

NOTES

PREFACE

1. Job 38–42. KJV, *The Holy Bible* (New York: Meridian, 1974). The figure of Job is identified as a foundational element in the rise of theodicy in Susan Neiman's important study, *Evil in Modern Thought: An Alternative History of Philosophy* (Princeton, NJ: Princeton University Press, 2002). See, e.g., 18, 100.

2. Elaine Scarry's discussion of what she calls "the inexpressibility of physical pain" is still the most developed discussion of the topic. See *The Body in Pain: The Making and Unmaking of the World* (Oxford: Oxford University Press, 1985), 3–19.

3. Rose Macaulay, *Pleasure of Ruins* (London: Thames & Hudson, 1953).

4. Jo Tollebeek and Eline van Assche, *Ravaged: Art and Culture in Times of Conflict* (Brussels: Mercatorfonds, 2014); Lucia Allais, *Designs of Destruction: The Making of Monuments in the Twentieth Century* (Chicago: University of Chicago Press, 2017); Gerard Passannante, *Catastrophizing: Materialism and the Making of Disaster* (Chicago: University of Chicago Press, 2019); Brian Dillon, *Ruin Lust: Artists' Fascination with Ruins from Turner to the Present Day* (London: Tate, 2014); Susan Stewart, *The Ruins Lesson: Meaning and Material in Western Culture* (Chicago: University of Chicago Press, 2020).

5. Dario Gamboni, *The Destruction of Art: Iconoclasm and Vandalism since the French Revolution* (London: Reaktion Books, 2018).

6. Sigmund Freud, *The Interpretation of Dreams* [1900], vols. 4 and 5 of *The Standard Edition of the Complete Psychological Works of Sigmund Freud*, trans. and ed. James Strachey in collaboration with Anna Freud (London: Hogarth Press, 1953–66).

7. See the Introduction for further discussion of these topics.

8. The subtitle of Susan Stewart's *The Ruins Lesson: Meaning and Material in Western Culture* only suggests the intricate relationships the book addresses, but all the substantives are closely connected: ruins, meaning, the material. At the heart of Passannante's *Catastrophizing* is the claim that the imagination of injury is a characteristic manifestation of the emergence of a powerful materialism in intellectual culture. See also the place of broken remains from the past in my own discussion of material topics in *Material Inspirations: The Interests of the Art Object in the Nineteenth Century and After* (Oxford: Oxford University Press, 2020), 145–245. The movement in Bruno Latour's

work between emphasizing a profoundly material (though not materialist) revision of what we call the social and reflecting on historic and current accounts of damage ("the anthropology of iconoclasm") is particularly striking. See "What Is Iconoclash? Or Is There a World beyond the Image Wars?," in *Iconoclash: Beyond the Image Wars in Science, Religion, and Art*, ed. Latour and Peter Weibel (Cambridge, MA: MIT Press, 2002), 16–40. See also Latour, *Reassembling the Social: An Introduction to Actor-Network-Theory* (Oxford: Oxford University Press, 2005), 110n141.

9. Eve Kosofksy Sedgwick, "Paranoid Reading and Reparative Reading, or, You're So Paranoid, You Probably Think This Essay Is About You," in *Touching Feeling: Affect, Pedagogy, Performativity* (Durham, NC: Duke University Press, 2003), 123–51. Cf. the specter of injury in this formulation of Latour's: "The urge for debunking has become the best way to protect the analyst from even hearing the scream of those they misinterpret" (*Reassembling*, 100n131).

10. Harold E. Raugh, Jr., *The Victorians at War, 1815–1914: An Encyclopedia of British Military History* (Santa Barbara, CA: ABC-CLIO, 2004), xiii.

INTRODUCTION: RUIN AND RECOGNITION AT THE ARCH OF TITUS

1. There is no better indication of the extraordinary sophistication of recent discussion of restitutions than the ostensible indifference about ultimate outcomes assumed by some of its most passionate proponents. See, e.g., Dan Hicks's call for "a commitment to take no interest in the use of an object after a return is made." *The Brutish Museums: The Benin Bronzes, Colonial Violence and Cultural Restitution* (London: Pluto Press, 2020), 238; subsequent references will appear in parentheses in the text. Hicks draws on a consensus that has emerged in the field of anthropology in relation to human remains and sacred objects that might need to be buried or be allowed to decay once they are returned. It bears saying that the most extreme version of the emergent argument about absolute restitution is liable to contradict the tendencies of an important line of recent work on the social lives (or the "biographies") of objects. It will be hard to reconcile a sense that any existence away from the original source is not so much a life as an ongoing moral error in need of correction (even a kind of death) with the dynamic, sociologically inflected interest in human networks that shape the complex and varied reception of objects in the world. For what is certainly the most important recent document on restitution, see Felwine Sarr and Bénédicte Savoy, *The Restitution of African Cultural Heritage: Towards a New Relational Ethics*, trans. Drew S. Buck, November 2018, http://restitutionreport2018.com/, 28–29; subsequent references will appear in parentheses in the text. For a useful set of earlier resources and legal statements contextualizing the discussion of restitution, see Lyndell V. Prott, *Witnesses to History: A Compendium of Documents and Writings on the Return of Cultural Objects* (Paris: UNESCO, 2009). Foundational texts on the social life of objects include Arjun Appadurai, "Introduction: Commodities and the Politics of Value," in *The Social Life of Things: Commodities in Cultural Perspective*, ed. Appadurai (Cambridge: Cambridge University Press, 1986),

3–63; Igor Kopytoff, "The Cultural Biography of Things: Commoditization as a Process," in Appadurai, *Social Life of Things*, 64–91; and Chris Gosden and Yvonne Marshall, "The Cultural Biography of Objects," *World Archaeology* 31 (1999): 2, 169–78.

2. On triumphs, see Mary Beard, *The Roman Triumph* (Cambridge, MA: Harvard University Press, 2007); and Ida Östenberg, *Staging the World: Spoils, Captives, and Representations in the Roman Triumphal Procession* (Oxford: Oxford University Press, 2009). On the relationship between the triumph and the arch, see two essays in *Koine*: Mediterranean Studies in Honor of R. Ross Holloway, ed. Derek B. Counts and Anthony S. Tuck (Oxford, UK: BAR, 2009): Jodi Magness, "Some Observations on the Flavian Victory Monuments of Rome," 35–40; and Naomi J. Norman, "Imperial Triumph and Apotheosis: The Arch of Titus in Rome," 41–53.

3. Brooke Foss Westcott (B. F. Dunelm), introduction to William Knight, *The Arch of Titus and the Spoils of the Temple* (London: Religious Tract Society, 1896), 9–12, at 9, 11. Knight was the long-serving canon of St. Michael's Church in Bristol. Originally published in 1867, his account of the destruction of the arch as a fulfillment of biblical prophecy was brought out in this substantially cheaper popular edition in 1896, with the introduction of Westcott, an important nineteenth-century theologian and biblical scholar, particularly noted for his collaboration in an influential edition of the New Testament.

4. The standard source on the arch is Michale Pfanner, *Der Titusbogen* (Mainz: Verlag Philipp von Zabern, 1983). On the Napoleonic restorations, see Ronald T. Ridley, *The Eagle and the Spade: The Archaeology of Rome during the Napoleonic Era, 1809–1814* (Cambridge: Cambridge University Press, 1992). Ridley points out the weakened condition in which the structure had been left by the French (96). See also David Watkin, *The Roman Forum* (Cambridge, MA: Harvard University Press, 2009), 178–92; and Jukka Jokilehto, *A History of Architectural Conservation* (London: Routledge, 2011), 69–86, esp. 82–85. On the political context for the renovations, see Christopher Johns, *Antonio Canova and the Politics of Patronage in Revolutionary and Napoleonic Europe* (Berkeley: University of California Press, 1998), esp. 78–81; and Stephen L. Dyson, *Archaeology, Ideology, and Urbanism in Rome from the Grand Tour to Berlusconi* (Cambridge: Cambridge University Press, 2019), 33–56.

5. Fergus Millar rightly insists that "what we persistently call the arches of Emperors or members of their families were in fact, in all known cases, arches *to* them, dedicated by the Senate and the People of Rome." Fergus Millar, "Last Year in Jerusalem: Monuments of the Jewish War in Rome," in Jonathan Edmondson, Steve Mason, and James Rives, *Flavius Josephus and Flavian Rome* (Oxford: Oxford University Press, 2005), 102–28, at 120. How we understand agency when acts of homage to power are at issue is always a matter of political disposition, however, meaning that the common usage may nevertheless be quite accurate, both in its suggestion of possession and in its ambiguity. Millar's chapter provides a helpful account of the political context for the construction of the arch, including a forceful argument that it participated in a much larger program of commemoration of a war on which the new imperial family staked its prestige and so its claim to power.

6. Tyler Lansford, *The Latin Inscriptions of Rome* (Baltimore: Johns Hopkins University Press, 2009), 65.

7. Earlier interventions and inscriptions commemorating the repurposing of pagan material did not typically celebrate the process of renovation, focusing instead on the exorcising of pagan elements and consecration for divine purposes. See various instances cited by Susan Stewart, *The Ruins Lesson* (Chicago: University of Chicago Press, 2020), 54–56.

8. On the sources of the arch in Baghdad, see Kanan Makiya's extraordinary *The Monument: Art and Vulgarity in Saddam Hussein's Iraq* (London: I. B. Tauris, 2001). Makiya points out that the length of the forearms and fists of Hussein reproduced for the monument match the height of the Arc de Triomphe (3).

9. See Steven Fine's various studies of the menorah and its history, including "'When I Went to Rome . . . There I Saw the Menorah': The Jerusalem Temple Implements in Rabbinic Memory, History, and Myth," in his *Art, History and the Historiography of Judaism in Roman Antiquity* (Leiden: Brill, 2014); "Who Is Carrying the Temple Menorah? A Jewish Counter-narrative of the Arch of Titus Spolia Panel, *IMAGES* 9 (2016), 19–48; and *The Menorah: From the Bible to Modern Israel* (Cambridge, MA: Harvard University Press, 2016). See also Leon Yarden, *The Spoils of Jerusalem on the Arch of Titus : A Reinvestigation* (Göteborg: P Åströms, 1991).

10. The extraordinary range of Dario Gamboni's *The Destruction of Art*, which includes sustained treatment of modern art movements in which destruction plays a part as well as discussion of the sociological and psychological drives toward vandalism, makes the work singularly useful in moving the topic beyond its conventional limits. See Dario Gamboni, *The Destruction of Art: Iconoclasm and Vandalism since the French Revolution* (London: Reaktion Books, 1997; rev. ed. 2018).

11. Walter Benjamin, "On the Concept of History," in *Selected Writings*, vol. 4: *1938–1940*, ed. Howard Eiland and Michael W. Jennings, trans. Edmund Jephcott et al. (Cambridge, MA: Harvard University Press, 2003), 389–400, at 392; subsequent references will appear in parentheses in the text.

12. Knight, *Arch of Titus*, 50. "Nowhere," the bishop writes toward the end of his introduction to the volume, "is it more easy to recognize how the Divine and human . . . work together than in the last scenes of Jewish national life which Canon Knight has portrayed" (Westcott, in Knight, *Arch of Titus*, 12).

13. On this complex figure who linked Jewish, Greek, and Roman culture, see the collection of essays in Edmondson, Mason, and Rives, *Flavius Josephus and Flavian Rome*. On spectacle in his work, see Honoria Howell Chapman, "Spectacle in Josephus' Jewish War," in Edmondson, Mason, and Rives, *Flavius Josephus and Flavian Rome*, 289–313. For an attempt to read Josephus's account of the war and the triumph somewhat against the grain of the celebration, see Christopher A. Frilingos, "More Than Meets the Eye: Incongruity and Observation in Josephus's Account of the Triumph of Vespasian and Titus," *History of Religions* 57, no. 1 (2017): 50–67.

14. Flavius Josephus, *War of the Jews: Works of Flavius Josephus*, trans. William Whiston (London: William Allason and J. Maynard, 1818), 4:250; subsequent references

will appear in parentheses in the text. Whiston's 1737 translation, widely reprinted throughout the nineteenth century, was the most common source in the period.

15. Millar, *Last Year in Jerusalem*, 101.

16. On prisoners at triumphs, see Beard, *The Roman Triumph*, 107–42; and Östenberg, *Staging the World*, 128–63. Beard expresses some skepticism about the customary nature of the practice of executing important captives as a culmination of the triumph (129–31). Östenberg is more willing to credit the typical character of the practice suggested by Josephus (see 151, 160–63). There is, in any case, no reason to doubt Simon's fate.

17. Alois Riegl, "The Modern Cult of Monuments: Its Character and Its Origin" [1903], trans. Kurt W. Forster and Diane Ghirardo, *Oppositions: A Journal for Ideas and Criticism in Architecture* 25 (1982): 21–50, at 29.

18. Sigmund Freud, *Civilization and Its Discontents* [1930], trans. James Strachey (New York: Norton, 1962), 16–18.

19. On political struggles over antiquities in India, see Tapati Guha-Thakurta, *Monuments, Objects, Histories: Institutions of Art in Colonial and Postcolonial India* (New York: Columbia University Press, 2004), especially the nuanced and thought-provoking chapter titled "Archaeology and the Monument: On Two Contentious Sites of Faith and History" (268–303).

20. For an account of the imperial politics involved in Titus's return, see Brian W. Jones, "Titus in the East, A.D. 70–71," *Rheinisches Museum für Philologie* 128, no. 3/4 (1985): 346–52.

21. On EUR, see Dyson, *Archaeology, Ideology, and Urbanism*, 189–94. Some halls of the museum opened in 1952, the rest in 1955. For a useful contextualization of an institution he describes as the one "which best embodied archaeological continuity from the fascist era to the 'quiet years' of postwar Rome," see ibid., 211.

22. On the *Forma Urbis*, or Severan Marble Plan, see Stephen L. Dyson, *Rome: A Living Portrait of an Ancient City* (Baltimore: Johns Hopkins University Press, 2010), 206. On the display of the *Forma Urbis* at the Vatican, see ibid., 13. On the casts of Trajan's column, see also Anna Pasqualini, "L'Antiquaria di gesso: Passato e futuro del Museo della civiltà romana all'EUR," *Mediterraneo antico* 9, no. 2 (2006): 1–16. The most detailed account on the history of the reproductions, which were originally commissioned by Napoleon III and produced between 1861 and 1862, is Clotilde D'Amato, "La Colonna Traiana: Da simbolo ideologico a modello materiale; Manifattura e diffusione dei calchi," in *Tra Damasco e Roma: L'architettura di Apollodoro nella cultura classica*, ed. Fiorella Festa Farina, Giuliana Calcani, Constantino Meucci, Maria Letizia Conforto, and Amr N. Al Azm (Rome: "L'Erma" di Bretschneider, 2001), 227–45.

23. Morley Safer's 1965 reporting from Cam Ne for CBS is often cited as an important turning point in American responses to the war. https://www.pri.org/stories/2016-05-20/morley-safers-coverage-vietnam-war-changed-everything.

24. The relationship between deeply sophisticated and politically engaged theories and their later applications would be interesting to trace in detail, but that is a topic outside the scope of this project. Among the important sources for the critical tradition,

we might cite Max Horkheimer and Theodor Adorno, whose *Dialectic of Enlightenment* (1944/1947), ed. Gunzelin Schmid Noerr, trans. Edmund Jephcott (Palo Alto, CA: Stanford University Press, 2002), developed the richest critique of modern aspirations to knowledge of the period, and Michel Foucault, whose early work in particular—including *The Order of Things: An Archaeology of the Human Sciences* (1966), trans. A. M. Sheridan Smith (London: Tavistock, 1970), and *Discipline and Punish: The Birth of the Prison* (1975), trans. Alan Sheridan (New York: Penguin, 1977)—laid the groundwork for the recurrent association of knowledge and power in later critics. The 1960s and early 1970s also saw the rise of a number of influential challenges to vision and representation, drawing on the theories of Jacques Lacan, especially feminist insights into the inequity of the relationship of the sexes to the visual sphere. Laura Mulvey's seminal "Visual Pleasure and Narrative Cinema" (1975) is among the most powerful of the founding arguments in this arena. See Mulvey, *Visual and Other Pleasures* (Houndmills, Basingstoke, UK: Palgrave Macmillan, 1989), 14–26. In art history itself, Griselda Pollock pioneered a robust challenge to art-historical conventions ratifying a fundamentally masculine story about art linked to a characteristically male way of seeing. See, e.g., "Modernity and the Spaces of Femininity," in *Vision and Difference: Feminism, Femininity, and the Histories of Art* (1988), which should be read alongside Pollock's bracing introduction to a later edition of the volume (London: Routledge, 2003), xvii–xxxviii, 70–127, and also her more recent *Differencing the Canon: Feminist Desire and the Writing of Art's Histories* (London: Routledge, 1999).

25. The list of influential critical approaches to institutions of culture is a long one. Among representative instances one might cite are Theodor Adorno, "Valery Proust Museum," in Adorno, *Prisms*, trans. Samuel and Shierry Weber (Cambridge, MA: MIT Press, 1967), 175–85; Ivan Karp and Steven D. Lavine, eds., *Exhibiting Cultures: The Poetics and Politics of Museum Display* (Washington, DC: Smithsonian Institution, 1991); Pierre Bourdieu, *Distinction: A Social Critique of the Judgment of Taste* (1979), trans. Richard Nice (Cambridge, MA: Harvard University Press, 1984); Pierre Bourdieu and Alain Darbel, *The Love of Art: European Art Museums and Their Public* (1969), trans. Caroline Beattie and Nick Merriman (Palo Alto, CA: Stanford University Press, 1990); and Amy K. Levin, ed., *Gender, Sexuality, and Museums* (New York: Routledge, 2010). Recent polemical responses to the collection and display of specific collections associated with brutal acts of imperial violence may be read as representing novel departures based on new insights or knowledge or newly principled subjects, but it is difficult to disassociate their most forceful claims from the traditions to which they seem so closely allied. See, e.g., Ariella Aïsha Azoulay, *Potential History: Unlearning Imperialism* (London: Verso, 2019), esp. 1–161; and Dan Hicks, *Brutish Museums*. For Azoulay, in particular, the question of cultural property ties into a broader tradition of postwar critique of Enlightenment thought, of which her book is a particularly florid manifestation. Though her broad historical sweep often takes in earlier periods, her conceptual touchstones are consistently drawn from the Enlightenment, and the revolutions she deprecates are the foundational ones from that period. See, e.g., her account of "unlearning" concepts including "citizen," "art," sovereignty, and human rights, along with

the categories "new" and "neutral" (11), or her description of "the historical fetishization of the French and American revolutions" (357), or her attempt to bring Kant into her analysis ("Undoing imperial violence means undoing time, space, and the body politic as given forms of experience," 152–53), or her concern that her arguments might be mistaken for those of Burke (38).

26. The two founding documents in this area are impressive and deeply informed works of singular rhetorical force: Eve Kosofksy Sedgwick, "Paranoid Reading and Reparative Reading, or, You're So Paranoid, You Probably Think This Essay Is About You," in *Touching Feeling: Affect, Pedagogy, Performativity* (Durham, NC: Duke University Press, 2003), 123–51; and Bruno Latour, "Why Has Critique Run Out of Steam? From Matters of Fact to Matters of Concern," *Critical Inquiry* 30 (2004): 225–48. For a later polemic on the issues, see Rita Felski, *The Limits of Critique* (Chicago: University of Chicago Press, 2015). For a bracing recent challenge addressing the affective drives of the critique of critique and presenting a trenchant challenge to unspoken assumptions written into its characteristic styles, see David Kurnick, "A Few Lies: Queer Theory and Our Method Melodramas," *English Literary History* 87, no. 2 (2020): 349–74.

27. The apparently self-evident nature of violence is a recurrent pressure on theories of reading for depth. The lies that surrounded the Gulf War motivate Latour's pioneering work, and injuries from Abu Ghraib to Katrina are cited in the introduction to an important special issue of the journal *Representations* on "surface reading." As the editors note, "The assumption that domination can only do its work when veiled, which may once have sounded almost paranoid, now has a nostalgic, even utopian ring to it." Stephen Best and Sharon Marcus, "Surface Reading: An Introduction," *Representations* 108, no. 1 (2009): 1–38, at 9. Or as Sedgwick herself asks in a passage cited in the same issue: "Why bother exposing the ruses of power in a country where, at any given moment, 40 percent of young black men are enmeshed in the penal system?" Sedgwick, "Paranoid Reading," 140; cited in Emily Apter and Elaine Freedgood, "Afterword," in Best and Marcus, "Surface Reading: An Introduction," 139–45, at 145.

28. Simon Gikandi's *Slavery and the Culture of Taste* (Princeton, NJ: Princeton University Press, 2011) is a rare example of a work in which the intersection of violence and aesthetics is explored in ways that illuminate both categories.

29. Two forceful recent instances of this approach are Hicks, *Brutish Museums*; and Azoulay, *Potential History*, esp. 1–161.

30. See a passage later in the book linking the museum with military innovations typically associated with the well-established moral catastrophe of the First World War, though most of them were originally exploited in the colonial sphere: "The ethnological museum must take its place alongside the fortified trench, barbed wire, the Maxim machine gun, and the tank, as part of the coming techno-brutality of the twentieth century" (193).

31. Thomas Hobbes develops the topic of the state of war in *De Cive* (1642) and *Leviathan* (1651). On war as the description of the lived experience of racial inequality, see Haile Selassie's 1963 speech to the United Nations in which he declares that "until the philosophy which holds one race superior and another inferior is finally and

permanently discredited and abandoned, until there are no longer any first-class and second-class citizens of any nation, until the colour of a man's skin is of no more significance than the colour of his eyes, until the basic human rights are equally guaranteed to all, without regard to race—until that day, the dream of lasting peace and world citizenship and the rule of international morality will remain but a fleeting illusion, to be pursued but never attained." "Address by His Imperial Majesty Haile Selassie I, Emperor of Ethiopia," United Nations General Assembly, New York, October 4, 1963, United Nations General Assembly, 18th session, Official Records, 1–4, at 3. When he adapts the speech for his song "War," Bob Marley abridges the emperor's periphrasis on the absence of peace into a galvanizing, totalizing refrain: "Everywhere is war." "War," *Rastaman Vibration*, Bob Marley & The Wailers, Island Records, 1976.

32. Bruno Latour's "Why Has Critique Run Out of Steam" begins with a war-weary tone, "Wars. So many wars," suggesting fatigue with the proliferation of the phenomenon in the world. Ambitious recent attempts to address the cultural force of war include Mary Favret, *War at a Distance: Romanticism and the Making of Modern Wartime* (Princeton, NJ: Princeton University Press, 2009); Jan Mieszkowski, *Watching War* (Stanford, CA: Stanford University Press, 2012); Paul Saint-Amour, *Tense Future: Modernism, Total War, Encyclopedic Form* (Oxford: Oxford University Press, 2015); Nathan K. Hensley, *Forms of Empire: The Poetics of Victorian Sovereignty* (Oxford: Oxford University Press, 2016); and Nasser Mufti, *Civilizing War: Imperial Politics and the Poetics of National Rupture* (Evanston, IL: Northwestern University Press, 2017). See also an important essay by David L. Clark, "Unsocial Kant: The Philosopher and the Un-regarded War Dead," *Wordsworth Circle* 41, no. (2010): 60–68. Scholarship to cite in the visual arts includes Lucia Allais, *Designs of Destruction: The Making of Monuments in the Twentieth Century* (Chicago: University of Chicago Press, 2018), which places the development of institutions of preservation in the context of twentieth-century military conflict; and the essays collected in Jo Tollebeek and Eline van Assche, *Ravaged: Art and Culture in Times of Conflict* (Brussels: Mercatorfonds, 2014). Influential earlier resources for thought in this area include Karl Schmitt, *The Concept of the Political* (1932), trans. George Schwab (Chicago: University of Chicago Press, 2007), 25–37, 78–79; Michel Foucault, *Society Must Be Defended: Lectures at the Collège de France, 1975–1976*, trans. David Macey (New York: Picador, 2003), 43–64; and Elaine Scarry, "The Structure of War," in *The Body in Pain: The Making and Unmaking of the World* (New York: Oxford University Press, 1985), 60–157.

CHAPTER 1: RISING ABOVE THE RUINS

1. See Siegel, *Material Inspirations: The Interests of the Art Object in the Nineteenth Century and After* (Oxford: Oxford University Press, 2020), 51–63. For the account of the transfiguration and its aftermath that Raphael brings together in the painting, see Matt. 17:1–9.

2. Friedrich Nietzsche, *The Birth of Tragedy and Other Writings*, ed. Raymond Geuss and Ronald Speirs, trans. Ronald Speirs (Cambridge: Cambridge University Press, 1999), 26.

3. "sublime, adj. and n.," *OED Online*, June 2021, https://www-oed-com.proxy.libraries.rutgers.edu/view/Entry/192766?rskey=3yBwCn&result=1.

4. See Immanuel Kant, *Critique of the Power of Judgment* [1790], trans. Paul Guyer and Eric Matthews (Cambridge: Cambridge University Press, 2002), 128–59. For a nuanced recent account of the history of the concept, see Robert Doran, *The Theory of the Sublime from Longinus to Kant* (Cambridge: Cambridge University Press, 2015). I take Doran's emphasis on what he calls "the moral-subjective orientation and sociocultural implications" of sublimity to be in harmony with my own approach, although Doran's focus on transcendence in some ways works against the moral claims I am making (57).

5. Gerard Passannante, *Catastrophizing: Materialism and the Making of Disaster* (Chicago: University of Chicago Press, 2019), 22. See also the chapter titled "Disaster before the Sublime; or Kant's Catastrophes," 192–235. Passannante's fascinating topic is what he calls "imaginative disasters," that is, visions of injury the mind creates as it reflects on the material nature of existence. In his effort to argue for the significance of these fictive episodes in the history of philosophy, Passannante contrasts their relative neglect to the widespread interest in "real disasters" and what he calls "the empirical study of disaster and the history of its interpretation." When it comes to ruins, his contrast between real and imaginative is probably too stark.

6. Susan Stewart, *The Ruins Lesson: Meaning and Material in Western Culture* (Chicago: Chicago University Press, 2020), 1.

7. The tendency to limit reflection in the face of damage has sometimes been understood as a politically progressive response to injury, one premised on the acknowledgment that when it comes to a foundational trauma, the seriousness of the condition is marked by its resistance to analysis. See Ruth Leys's account of the ways in which the traumatic event has been "dissociated from normal mental processes of cognition" and therefore "cannot be known or represented" in *Trauma: A Genealogy* (Chicago: University of Chicago Press, 2000), 266. Leys's book challenges the premises behind such an approach, which she associates with Cathy Caruth's work, esp. *Trauma: Explorations in Memory* (Baltimore: Johns Hopkins University Press, 1995); see Leys, *Trauma*, 266–97. As the editors of a recent collection attempting to move beyond the limits set by founding texts on the topic put it, "The phenomenon of trauma as an aporetic event . . . has the dual effect of unsettling reductive readings of trauma but also entrenching trauma studies in repetitions of the moment when thought reaches its limit." Eric Boynton and Peter Capretto, "The Limits of Theory in Trauma and Transcendence," in *Trauma and Transcendence: Suffering and the Limits of Theory*, ed. Boynton and Capretto (New York: Fordham University Press, 2018), 1–14, at 2.

8. Doran addresses the challenging nature of the translation of *hypsos*, which indicates "'height,' 'elevation,' or 'loftiness,'" terms in many ways less metaphorically available than "the sublime." He cites the instance of the ocean, which may be sublime but is never elevated (39–40), a topic that will return in the final chapter of this book.

9. On "modernatist thought," see Rancière, "The Distribution of the Sensible: Politics and the Aesthetics," in *The Politics of Aesthetics: The Distribution of the Sensible* [2000], trans. Gabriel Rockhill (London: Continuum, 2004), 12–45, esp. 26–28;

subsequent references will appear in parentheses in the text. Friedrich Schiller is probably the key point of reference on the topics that concern Rancière in this text. See *The Aesthetic Education of Man* [1794], trans. and with intro. by E. M. Wilkinson and L. A. Willoughby (Oxford: Oxford University Press, 1982). Rancière's later work touches on Schiller's sources, notably on Johann Joachim Winckelmann, a topic Rancière turns to when he engages more concretely with the history of art in texts such as *Aisthesis: Scenes from the Aesthetic Regime of Art*, trans. Zakir Paul (London: Verso, 2011).

10. On the beautiful, see Kant, *Critique of the Power of Judgment*, 89–124.

11. Jean-François Lyotard, *The Differend: Phrases in Dispute* [1983], trans. Georges Van Den Abbeele (Minneapolis: University of Minnesota Press, 1988), 179.

12. Georg Wilhelm Friedrich Hegel, *Philosophy of Right* [1821], trans. T. M. Knox (Oxford: Oxford University Press, 1967), 10.

13. Lyotard, *The Differend*, 179–80. The same argument and names are recapitulated elsewhere in Lyotard's oeuvre, e.g., "A Missive on Universal History," in *The Postmodern Explained: Correspondence 1982–1985*, trans. Don Barry, Bernadette Maher, Julian Prefanis, Virginia Spate, and Morgan Thomas (Minneapolis: University of Minnesota Press, 1992), 23–38, at 29.

14. With Lyotard in mind, the historian Anson Rabinbach writes of "the banality of catastrophe," a situation in which "Auschwitz has become intellectual shorthand" for a generalized condemnation of "the ethical, technological and political structures of the modern world." Rabinbach, *In the Shadow of Catastrophe: German Intellectuals between Apocalypse and Enlightenment* (Berkeley: University of California Press, 1997), 12, 14. In her discussion of a related tendency in Giorgio Agamben, Amanda Anderson describes "a modernity in which a Holocaust hue covers all of political life." *Bleak Liberalism* (Chicago: University of Chicago Press, 2016), 3–4.

15. Rancière, *Politics of Aesthetics*, 9–10. For an ambitious and nuanced account of Rancière's response to Lyotard's sublime, addressing the political project inherent in the former's response to the aesthetic theories of Kant and Schiller, see Tina Chantner, "The Artful Politics of Trauma: Rancière's Critique of Lyotard," in Boynton and Capretto, *Trauma and Transcendence*, 121–41.

16. Jean-François Lyotard, "After the Sublime, the State of Aesthetics," in *The Inhuman: Reflections on Time*, trans. Geoffrey Bennington and Rachel Bowlby (Cambridge, UK: Polity, 1991), 142; italics in the original. The sublime was a career-long interest of Lyotard's to which he frequently returned. For more technical and historical accounts of the subject, see also "The Sublime and the Avant-Garde" in ibid., 89–107; and Lyotard, *Lessons on the Analytic of the Sublime* [1991], trans. Elizabeth Rottenberg (Palo Alto, CA: Stanford University Press, 1994). Robert Doran points out that Lyotard and his followers press Kant's argument into the topic of limits of representation, which is entirely outside the scope of the philosopher's original discussion of "the experience of unboundedness" (Doran, *Theory of the Sublime*, 270). On the distinctions drawn between thing and object in recent theoretical work, an issue that Lyotard and Rancière are referencing in the passages quoted, see Siegel, *Material Inspirations*, esp. 1–46.

17. Lyotard, "The Sublime and the Avant Garde," 99. The argument is anticipated in *The Postmodern Condition: A Report on Knowledge* [1979], trans. Geoff Bennington and Brian Massumi (Manchester, UK: Manchester University Press, 1984), 77–80. It is possible to find more nuance in the treatment of time in the third *Critique* than Lyotard does. See Paul Guyer's description of Kant's sublime as both "a single yet complex feeling" and "a sequence of feelings." Guyer, *Kant and the Experience of Freedom: Essays on Aesthetic and Morality* (Cambridge: Cambridge University Press, 1996), 204. Guyer is cited by Passannante, who glosses the topic reasonably enough: "Kant wants it both ways" (Passannante, *Catastrophizing*, 232). For a bracing contemporary challenge to Lyotard's treatment of the sublime non-event as a response to the prospect of nuclear war, see Klaus R. Scherpe, "Dramatization and De-dramatization of 'The End': The Apocalyptic Consciousness of Modernity and Post-modernity," trans. Brent O. Peterson, *Cultural Critique*, no. 5 (1986–87): 95–129, esp. 128–29.

18. Siegel, *Material Inspirations*, 138–41.

19. On the intersection of the experience of damage with reflection on matter in earlier periods, see especially Passannte's *Catastrophizing* and Stewart's *Ruins Lesson*. Passannante's description of what he calls catastrophizing as "the imaginative and often involuntary creation of speculative disasters as an expression of and response to materialist philosophies and forms of explanation" (1) suggests the epistemological issues shaping the relationship between beauty and damage. But the ethical and even emotional questions soon make themselves known in his account of knowledge. See, e.g., a formulation such as the following: "The making of catastrophe is both a vehicle by which materialism aims to represent the world and the most telling symptom of the malady it sometimes becomes" (2)—which would be an excellent gloss for Benjamin's angel of history as I understand it.

20. Walter Benjamin, "On the Concept of History," in *Selected Writings*, vol. 4: 1938–1940, ed. Howard Eiland and Michael W. Jennings, trans. Edmund Jephcott et al. (Cambridge, MA: Harvard University Press, 2003), 392; emphases in the original.

21. Rancière, "Distribution of the Sensible, 29. "Twentieth and twenty-first century understandings of trauma have long dwelt in the province of the sublime," notes Ian Baucom in the course of a thoughtful account of the topic. More uncharitably, one might identify the length of the period he marks out as evidence of the conventional nature of the relationship. Baucom, *Specters of the Atlantic: Finance Capital, Slavery, and the Philosophy of History* (Durham, NC: Duke University Press, 2005), 254; see also 131–32. On the ethical and conceptual limits of imagining the Holocaust as fated terminus, see Michael André Bernstein, *Foregone Conclusions: Against Apocalyptic History* (Berkeley: University of California Press, 1995). Among the most cited evocations of the Holocaust as the preeminent site of the unthinkable and therefore inexpressible in the intellectual tradition I have been addressing is a stunning passage from Maurice Blanchot, which binds up the topic in a network of inhibitions and questions eventuating in a silence paradoxically provoked by a cry so vast as to be uncountable:

> The holocaust, the absolute event of history—which is a date of history—that utter-burn where all history took fire, where the movement of Meaning was swallowed up, where the gift, which knows nothing of forgiving or of consent, shattered without giving place to anything that can be affirmed, that can be denied—gift of every passivity, gift of what cannot be given. How can it be preserved, even by thought? How can thought be made the keeper of the holocaust where all was lost, including guardian thought?
>
> In the mortal intensity, the fleeing silence of the countless cry.

Maurice Blanchot, *The Writing of the Disaster* [1980], trans. Ann Smock (Lincoln: University of Nebraska Press, 1988), 47.

22. See "From Thomas Jefferson to Volney, 17 March 1801," Founders Online, National Archives, https://founders.archives.gov/documents/Jefferson/01-33-02-0289.

23. Constantin François Chassebœuf, comte de Volney, *A New Translation of Volney's Ruins, or Meditations on the Revolution of Empires* (Paris: Leyrault, 1802), 1:2–3; subsequent references, all from this volume, will appear in parentheses in the text.

24. Volney spent the years 1782 to 1785 in the Middle East and published *Voyage en Égypt et Syrie* in 1787. The account of Palmyra in that volume is also adapted from Robert Wood and James Dawkins, *The Ruins of Palmyra, Otherwise Tedmor, in the Desart* (London: Robert Wood, 1753), as are some of the illustrations he provides for the city and the Temple of Bel. See Volney, *Voyage en Syrie et en Égypt pendant les anneés 1783, 1784, et 1785* (Paris: Volland, 1787), 2:256–65.

25. Siegel, *Desire and Excess: The Nineteenth-Century Culture of Art* (Princeton, NJ: Princeton University Press, 2000), 30–36. On Wood and Dawkins and Volney, see Stewart, *Ruins Lesson*, 202–4, 213–15.

26. Wood and Dawkins, *Ruins of Palmyra*, 21. There are doubts about the identity of the author of the treatise on the sublime in modern criticism (see Doran, *Theory of the Sublime*, 25–31), but the only question entertained by Wood and Dawkins is whether Longinus was *originally* from Palmyra, the connection between place and philosopher-statesman being amplified in a note of antiquarian fussiness: "It is not certain that Longinus was a Palmyrene, though very probably he was of some part of Syria. But which argues the most flourishing state of letters in a country, to have given birth to a great genius, or to have given him honour and support?" (21n).

27. For a sense of the conventional nature of the traveler's complaint, see Laurence Goldstein's description of "the principal features of the ruin sentiment in the eighteenth century," the assertion that "Providence controls the course of human events, a belief both comforting and horrifying." Laurence Goldstein, *Ruins and Empire: The Evolution of a Theme in Augustan and Romantic Literature* (Pittsburgh: University of Pittsburgh Press, 1977), 5.

28. Amanda Anderson, *The Powers of Distance: Cosmopolitanism and the Cultivation of Detachment* (Princeton, NJ: Princeton University Press, 2001), 6. Hans Blumenberg identifies the figure of an observer rising to find an ampler, more rational view as a variation on that of the spectator watching a shipwreck from safety, a metaphor that he finds

characteristic of the modern sensibility: "A novel variety of the shipwreck metaphor, one found only in the modern epoch, is first produced by the Enlightenment's cosmic exoticism. . . . Its fundamental idea was that reason might be better represented on the moon or in another alien world than it is on earth and by men. The imagination was then bound to be continually stimulated to picture how the earth would be seen from the point of view of such a higher rationality." Hans Blumenberg, *Shipwreck with Spectator* [1979], trans. Steven Rendall (Cambridge, MA: MIT Press, 1997), 32. I will return to the topic of shipwreck, and to Blumenberg, in the final chapter of this book. On the place of Middle Eastern antiquities in Enlightenment thought, see Aaron Tugendhaft, *The Idols of Isis* (Chicago: University of Chicago Press, 2020), 35. It bears saying that the ruins of Palmyra are different from those on which Tugendhaft focuses because of their relative youth and their closer implication with European history than the Assyrian material at issue when the focus is Iraq.

29. "Among those events likely to change the political system of Europe that seem to have multiplied in recent years," Volney had written in his 1788 book on the subject, "there is without doubt none that promises consequences as far reaching as the war that has recently broken out between the Turks and the Russians." Volney, *Considerations sur la guerre actuelle des Turcs* (London, 1788), 1; my translation.

30. Mary Favret, *War at a Distance: Romanticism and the Making of Modern Wartime* (Princeton, NJ: Princeton University Press, 2010), 193; subsequent references will appear in parentheses in the text.

31. See Favret's culminating chapter, "Viewing War at a Distance," 187–229.

32. Felicia Hemans, "Casabianca," in *Felicia Hemans: Selected Poems, Prose, and Letters*, ed. Gary Kelly (Peterborough, ON: Broadview Press, 2002), 300–301; Alfred Tennyson, "The Charge of the Light Brigade," in *The Poems of Tennyson*, 2nd ed., 3 vols., ed. Christopher Ricks (Harlow, Essex, UK: Longman, 1987).

33. For Briseis and Andromache, see *The Iliad*, trans. Robert Fagles (New York: Penguin Books, 1990), bks. 1 and 22. For the love and death of Dido, see *The Aeneid*, trans. David Ferry (Chicago: University of Chicago Press, 2017), bk. 4.

34. In a recent popular history, Alan Forrest writes of visitors reporting with little comment the screams of the dying and peasants dragging off the dead with fishhooks. *Waterloo* (Oxford: Oxford University Press, 2015), 120–23.

35. Susan Sontag, *Regarding the Pain of Others* (New York: Picador, 2003), 44–45; subsequent references will appear in parentheses in the text. On the history of publication of Goya's prints and their early reception, see Alan E. Smith, "La recepción de la primera edición de Los desastres de la Guerra de Goya (marzo, 1863) en el Madrid del joven Galdós," *Bulletin of Spanish Studies* 86, no. 4 (2009): 459–74. For an important recent study of the intersection of photography and war that resists the certainty that it is through visual evidence—whether of the human gaze or the camera—that a clear sense of the experience of military conflict will be established, see "Looking at the Dead," in Jan Mieszkowski, *Watching War* (Stanford, CA: Stanford University Press, 2012), 96–143. See also Rachel Teukolsky's thoughtful account of the challenging pressure of the real in representing war in the nineteenth century and today, "Realism's War Pictures: Reality

Effects in the Illustrated Newspaper," in Teukolsky, *Picture World: Image, Aesthetics and Victorian New Media* (Oxford: Oxford University Press, 2020), 84–142.

CHAPTER 2: HEIGHT AND DAMAGE / VIRTUAL REALITY

1. Percy Bysshe Shelley, "Ozymandias," in *Shelley's Poetry and Prose: Authoritative Texts, Criticism*, ed. Donald H. Reiman and Neil Fraistat, 2nd ed. (New York: Norton, 2002), 109–10. Out of the large body of work on poetry and ruins, which typically revolves around Renaissance or Romantic topics, we might highlight Roland Mortier, *La poétique des ruines en France: Ses origins, ses variations, de la Renaissance à Victor Hugo* (Geneva: Library Droz, 1974); Laurence Goldstein, *Ruins and Empire: The Evolution of a Theme in Augustan and Romantic Literature* (Pittsburgh: University of Pittsburgh Press, 1977); Leonard Barkan, *Unearthing the Past: Archaeology and Aesthetics in the Making of Renaissance Culture* (New Haven, CT: Yale University Press, 2001); Andrew Hui, *The Poetics of Ruins in Renaissance Literature* (New York: Fordham University Press, 2017); and Sophie Thomas, *Romanticism and Visuality: Fragments, History, Spectacle* (New York: Routledge, 2008). Susan Stewart's magisterial, *The Ruins Lesson: Meaning and Material in Western Culture* (Chicago: University of Chicago Press, 2019), is certainly the boldest and most far-ranging account of the topic.

2. John Keats, "On Seeing the Elgin Marbles," in *Keats's Poetry and Prose: Authoritative Texts, Criticism*, ed. Jeffrey N. Cox (New York: Norton, 2009), 73.

3. Blanchard Jerrold and Gustave Doré, *London: A Pilgrimage* (London: Grant & Co., 1872).

4. Thomas Babington Macaulay, review of *The Ecclesiastical and Political History of the Popes of Rome, during the Sixteenth and Seventeenth Centuries*, by Leopold Ranke, trans. Sarah Austin [London, 1840], first published in the *Edinburgh Review* 72 (1840); in *Critical and Historical Essays Contributed to the Edinburgh Review*, 5th ed., 3 vols. (London: Longman, Brown, Green, and Longmans, 1848), 3:207–54, at 209. On the backgrounds to this image, see William Colenso, "A Few Remarks on the Hackneyed Quotation of 'Macaulay's New Zealander'" [1882], in *Three Literary Papers* (Napier, NZ, 1883), 36–41.

5. John Ruskin, *"A Joy for Ever" and The Two Paths, with Letters from the Oxford Museum and Various Addresses 1856–1860*, in *The Works of John Ruskin*, ed. E. T. Cook and Alexander Wedderburn, Library Edition, 39 vols. (London: George Allen, 1903–12), 16:64–65.

6. See Anthony Vidler, "The Paradoxes of Vandalism: Henri Grégoire and the Thermidorian Discourse on Historical Monuments," in *The Abbé Grégoire and His World*, ed. Jeremy D. Popkin and Richard H. Popkin (Dordrecht: Kluwer Academic Publishers, 2000), 129–56, at 130. On the context for Grégoire's work and historiographical debates on the topic, see Bronisław Baczko, "The Vandal People," in *Ending the Terror: The French Revolution after Robespierre* (Cambridge: Cambridge University Press, 1994), 185–223. For Grégoire's own reports to the national convention, see Henri Grégoire, *Rapport sur les destructions opérées par le vandalisme et les moyens de le réprimer*

(August 1794); *Second rapport sur le vandalisme* (November 1794); and *Troisième rapport sur le vandalisme* (December 1794). The reports are reproduced in Henri Grégoire, *Oeuvres* (Nedelm, Liechtenstein: KTO Press, 1977), 2:257–78, 321–32, 335–57. See also Miguel Tamen, *Friends of Interpretable Objects* (Cambridge, MA: Harvard University Press, 2001), 51–57. For a nuanced and sophisticated biography that is notably illuminating on the later reception of this complex figure, see Alyssa Goldstein Sepinwall, *The Abbé Grégoire and the French Revolution: The Making of Modern Universalism* (Berkeley: University of California Press, 2005). On the history of the Vandals, and on the tradition that culminated in their association with the destruction of antiquities, see Andrew Merrills and Richard Miles, *The Vandals* (Chichester, West Sussex: John Wiley, 2009), esp. 9–16. Work on iconoclasm and vandalism in the French Revolution has proliferated in recent years. See Chapter 3 for more on this topic and a fuller—though still very partial—bibliography.

7. Tamen, *Friends of Interpretable Objects*, 55; subsequent references will appear in parentheses in the text. On ignorance as "a key concept in the stigmatization of iconoclasm," see Dario Gamboni, *The Destruction of Art: Iconoclasm and Vandalism since the French Revolution* (London: Reaktion Books, 2018), 19. Indeed, a great deal of the interest of the recent resurgence of work in this area resides in the discovery of deeply informed motivations for carrying out acts of damage. See, e.g., the collection edited by Stacy Boldrick, Leslie Brubaker, and Richard Clay, *Striking Images, Iconoclasms Past and Present* (Farnham, UK: Ashgate, 2013); and Bruno Latour and Peter Weibel, eds., *Iconoclash: Beyond the Image Wars in Science, Religion, and Art* (Cambridge, MA: MIT Press, 2002). Ambitious earlier attempts to reflect on the intellectual backgrounds of iconoclasm include Alain Bensançon, *The Forbidden Image: An Intellectual History of Iconoclasm* [1994], trans. Jane Marie Todd (Chicago: University of Chicago Press, 2000); and the works of David Freedberg, many of whose shorter pieces on the topic were recently collected as *Iconoclasm* (Chicago: University of Chicago Press, 2021).

8. On the rise of the museum in relation to the violence of the Revolution, see Louis Réau, *Histoire du vandalisme: Les monuments détruits de l'art français* (Paris: Hachette, 1959), a work especially interesting for its combination of tendentious judgments with a long perspective on a theme the author traces back as far as the Huguenots. Also see Stephen Bann, "Poetics of the Museum: Lenoir and Du Sommerard," in *The Clothing of Clio: A Study in the Representation of History in Nineteenth-Century France* (Cambridge: Cambridge University Press, 1994), 77–92; and Francis Haskell, "The Musée des monuments français," in *History and Its Images: Art and the Interpretation of the Past* (New Haven, CT: Yale University Press, 1993), 236–52. More recent work includes Alexandra Stara, *The Museum of French Monuments, 1795–1816: Killing Art to Make History?* (Milton Park, Abingdon, UK: Routledge, 2013).

9. Aaron Tugendhaft, *The Idols of Isis from Assyria to the Internet* (Chicago: University of Chicago Press, 2020), 73. Attempts to think about the cultural forces shaping contemporary iconoclasm include Tugendhaft's brief monograph, as well as the essays in *Idol Anxiety*, the collection he edited with Josh Ellenbogen (Chicago: University of Chicago Press, 2011). Important articles locating the actions of ISIS in a broader

cultural context include Finbarr Barry Flood, "Idol-Breaking as Image-Making in the 'Islamic State,'" *Religion and Society: Advances in Research* 7 (2016): 116–38, which builds on his extraordinarily compelling "Between Cult and Culture: Bamiyan, Islamic Iconoclasm, and the Museum" (*Art Bulletin* 84, no. 4 (2002): 641–59) in order to lay out the historically specific version of Islam shaping the iconoclasm of ISIS and place it in relation to the iconoclasm of secular modernity enshrined in the museum itself. See also Pierre Centlivres, *Les Bouddhas d'Afghanistan* (Lausanne: Éditions Favre, 2001), for a sophisticated attempt to locate the decision to destroy the statues in relation to the immediate political aspirations of the Taliban. For an account insisting on the modern nature of acts of violence often identified as atavistic, see Sadia Abbas, "Nikes in Nineveh: Daesh, the Ruin and the Global Logic of Eradication," in *Edinburgh Companion to the Postcolonial Middle East*, ed. Anna Ball and Karim Mattar (Edinburgh: Edinburgh University Press, 2019), 293–308. Ömür Harmanşah makes a particularly strong case for seeing the production of ISIS videos not as documentation of the actions of committed iconoclasts but as the end product—a set of propaganda images diffused largely through social media: "ISIS, Heritage, and the Spectacles of Destruction in the Global Media," *Near Eastern Archaeology* 78, no. 3 (2015): 170–77. Kavita Singh develops a sobering and thought-provoking analysis of the destruction of the Buddhas at Bamiyan as part of a Taliban campaign against the Hazara ethnic minority in *Museums, Heritage, Culture: Into the Conflict Zone* (Amsterdam: Reinwardt Academy, Amsterdam University of the Arts, 2014), 29–54. Looting and destruction of objects are not identical practices, of course, though they sometimes overlap. For a useful collection of essays on legal, historical, and policy topics related specifically to Iraq, see Lawrence Rothfield, *Antiquities under Siege: Cultural Heritage Protection after the Iraq War* (Lanham, MD: AltaMira Press, 2008).

10. See Freedberg, *Iconoclasm*: "Once again the question of why people destroy images comes to the fore. Is it because they matter so little, or because they matter too much?" (xxvi). But this excellent question about the proper amount of mattering can cut in more than one direction. What we ask about will become more gripping and difficult, it seems to me, when it is not only the passions of the iconoclast that are probed.

11. See Chap. 1. See also the discussion of intentional and unintentional monuments in Chap. 3 of this book. On "vandalism" and "iconoclasm" as terms, see Gamboni, *Destruction of Art*, 22–26.

12. See the works cited in note 9 above, especially the essays by Flood, as well as Dario Gamboni's "World Heritage: Shield or Target?," *Conservation: The Getty Conservation Institute Newsletter* 16, no. 2 (2001): 5–11.

13. For a particularly thoughtful account of Ruskin's place in the universalization of concepts of cultural heritage that had typically emerged as national concerns, see Françoise Choay, *L'allegorie du patrimoine* (Paris: Éditions du Seuil, 1992), 109.

14. On the worship practices of the Ruskins, and specifically the influence of Scottish Evangelical elements, see Tim Hilton, *John Ruskin* (New Haven, CT: Yale University Press, 2002), 19–22.

15. Gamboni, *Destruction of Art*, 13. Gamboni goes on to argue for what he calls the heuristic value of violence for those interested in thinking of autonomy as a historical and historiographical construct. "Since the history of art history is so closely associated with that of the growing autonomy of art," he declares convincingly, "the historiography of iconoclasm cannot but possess a normative, even programmatic dimension" (20). As he notes later in the course of his discussion, the implicit argument in antivandalism discourse in the eighteenth century came down to autonomy: "art does not serve any master, therefore it must not be destroyed" (149).

16. When Mary Favret writes, in the course of a brief account of the complex challenges of defining war, of "anointing our own perplexity with . . . war's sublime effects," I take her to be evocatively capturing the ways in which the sublime may be a symptom disguised as an explanation. She is doing more than mooting another option when she notes that "a less sublime, more historically circumscribed approach to the question of war's meaning can be told." Favret, *War at a Distance: Romanticism and the Making of Modern Wartime* (Princeton, NJ: Princeton University Press, 2010), 174.

17. *The Displaced*, directed by Imraan Ismail and Ben C. Solomon, creative direction by Chris Milk and Jake Silverstein (Hollywood, CA: Vrse.works, 2015), https://www.nytimes.com/video/magazine/100000005005806/the-displaced.html.

18. *Take Flight*, directed by Daniel Askill, written by Lorin Askill, Daniel Fletcher, and Gregory Stern (New York: The New York Times Magazine and Radical Media, 2015), https://www.nytimes.com/video/magazine/100000004084936/take-flight.html.

19. Marcus Wohlsen, "Google Cardboard's *New York Times* Experiment Just Hooked a Generation on VR," *Wired*, November 9, 2015, https://www.wired.com/2015/11/google-cardboards-new-york-times-experiment-just-hooked-a-generation-on-vr/.

20. The situation has only continued to worsen, to the point that the United Nations refers to the period 2010–20 as "a decade of displacement." *Global Trends: Forced Displacement in 2019* (Copenhagen: United Nations High Commissioner for Refugees, 2020), 4. Report available at http://www.unhcr.org/refugee-statistics.

21. Cf. Tugenhaft on video games (*Idols of ISIS*, 82–89), especially his resistance to what he describes as the obscuring of "the human capacity for political judgement and responsibility" (89).

22. See Stewart Brand, "Why Haven't We Seen the Whole Earth Yet?," in *The Sixties: The Decade Remembered Now, by the People Who Lived It Then*, ed. Lynda Obst (New York: Random House / Rolling Stone Press, 1977), 168. See also Andrew Kirk, *Counterculture Green: The "Whole Earth Catalog" and American Environmentalism* (Lawrence: University Press of Kansas, 2007).

23. This version of the inception story is from an interview with Brand (July 17, 2001), in Fred Turner, *From Counterculture to Cyberculture: Stewart Brand, the Whole Earth Network, and the Rise of Digital Utopianism* (Chicago: University of Chicago Press, 2006), 69.

24. Stewart Brand, "History: Some of What Happened around Here for the Last Three Years," in *The Last Whole Earth Catalog: Access to Tools* (Menlo Park, CA: Portola Institute, 1971), 439–41, at 439.

25. Bruno Latour, *Down to Earth: Politics in the New Climatic Regime*, trans. Catherine Porter (Cambridge, UK: Polity Press, 2019), 19; emphasis in the original. Subsequent references will appear in parentheses in the text.

26. See Deodato Tapete and Francesca Cigna, "Detection of Archaeological Looting from Space: Methods, Achievements and Challenges," *Remote Sensing* 11, no. 20 (2019): 2389, https://doi.org/10.3390/rs11202389.

27. https://www.globalxplorer.org/. See also https://www.nationalgeographic.com/history/article/archaeologists-parcak-globalxplorer-looting-ted-prize.

28. The concept of looting always involves conflict between extremely local and far larger concepts of social organization. For a thought-provoking and sophisticated study of the topic in a European context, see Fiona Greenland, *Ruling Culture: Art Police, Tomb Robbers, and the Rise of Cultural Power in Italy* (Chicago: University of Chicago Press, 2021). See also the work of Morag Kersel on communities involved in making claims for antiquities, including "Transcending Borders: Objects on the Move," *Archaeologies* 3, no. 2 (2007): 81–98; and "When Communities Collide: Competing Claims for Archaeological Objects in the Market Place," *Archaeologies* 7, no. 3 (2011): 518–37. For a sense of the varied motivations and actors involved in the specific case of Iraq, see the essays in Rothfield, *Antiquities under Siege*, 1–73.

29. Robert Wood and James Dawkins, *The Ruins of Palmyra, Otherwise Tedmor, in the Desart* (London: Robert Wood, 1753), 13; subsequent references will appear in parentheses in the text.

30. See Richard Stoneman, *Palmyra and Its Empire: Zenobia's Revolt against Rome* (Ann Arbor: University of Michigan Press, 1992), 4.

31. On the Arch of Titus and the Temple of Peace, see the Introduction to this book.

32. On the history of the menorah and other relics from the temple, see especially the works of Steven Fine cited in the Introduction. Fine mentions yet another tradition that traces the removal of the relics from the temple to the sack of the city in 455 by Vandals led by Gaiseric (Fine, *The Menorah: From the Bible to Modern Israel* [Cambridge, MA: Harvard University Press, 2016], 46). On this later sack, see also Peter Heather, *The Fall of the Roman Empire: A New History of Rome and the Barbarians* (Oxford: Oxford University Press, 2006), 379; and Guy Halsall, *Barbarian Migrations and the Roman West* (Cambridge: Cambridge University Press, 2007), 254–56.

33. Jacobus de Voraigne, *The Golden Legend*, trans. William Granger Ryan (Princeton, NJ: Princeton University Press, 1993), 1:38–39.

34. One historian refers to "one of the most civilized sacks of a city ever witnessed." Heather, *Fall of the Roman Empire*, 227; see also Halsall, *Barbarian Migrations and the Roman West*, 216–17.

35. Immanuel Kant, *Critique of the Power of Judgment* [1790], trans. Paul Guyer and Eric Matthews (Cambridge: Cambridge University Press, 2002), 129.

36. For a nuanced account of the critique of the distanced view, see Amanda Anderson, *The Powers of Distance: Cosmopolitanism and the Cultivation of Detachment* (Princeton, NJ: Princeton University Press, 2001), 3–33. The most interesting recent polemic on this topic is certainly Bruno Latour's account of the desire "to know in the very

same way everything that happens on earth as if one had to see it from afar" (*Down to Earth*, 69).

37. In an important study, Jan Mieszkowski traces the impossibility of arriving at a fixed vantage point when it comes to the observation of war to military developments in the Napoleonic era. Mieszkowski, *Watching War* (Stanford, CA: Stanford University Press, 2012), 1–29. "The more self-aware the audience to war is about the significance of its own status as a viewing force," Mieszkowski writes about the cultural effect of this development, "the more unsure it becomes about the meaning of what it is watching and its relationship to it captures something we see in the constantly shifting views" (29). A slightly earlier date for the phenomenon is suggested by what we see illustrated in Volney.

38. "Palmyra was at all times a natural emporium for the merchandize [*sic*] coming from India by the Persian Gulph," notes Volney, "which, from thence by way of the Euphrates or the Desert was conveyed into Phoenicia, and Asia minor, to diffuse its varied luxuries among numerous nations with whom they were always in great request. Volney, *Travels through Syria and Egypt* (London: G. G. J. and J. Robinson, 1788), 2:289. Cf. Wood and Dawkins, *Ruins of Palmyra*, 19–20. See also Volney, *Ruins*, 7. For an account of the centrality of the city to major networks of trade, see Diederik Burgersdijk, "Palmyra on the Silk Road: Terrestrial and Maritime Trading Routes from China to the Mediterranean," *Talanta. Proceedings of the Dutch Archaeological and Historical Society*, 51 (2019): 246–57. It is an important issue in Stoneman, *Palmyra and Its Empire*, 31–49. See also Paul Veyne, *Palmyra: An Irreplaceable Treasure*, trans. Teresa Lavender Fagan (Chicago: University of Chicago Press, 2017), 3–6, 18–27. The revisionist history of Peter Frankopan, *The Silk Roads: A New History of the World* (New York: Vintage, 2017), highlights connections that were clearer to eighteenth-century writers than they have been in later eras.

39. On Bamiyan as an important node on the Silk Road and so a "crossroads of the world," at which "influences from India, China, Greece and Persia mingled in the arts," see Singh, *Museums, Heritage, Culture*, 33. See also Frankopan, *The Silk Roads*, 60. See also the essays in Masanori Nagaoka, ed., *The Future of the Bamiyan Buddha Statues: Heritage Reconstruction in Theory and Practice* (Paris: UNESCO Publishing, 2020). Sadia Abbas's argument that important historical networks that undermine national and continental divisions "have yet to find an adequate engagement in postcolonial studies" is relevant here. But it is not only in postcolonial studies that deep and long-standing connections have been neglected. See Abbas, "Neither Greek nor Indian: Space, Nation and History in *River of Fire* and *The Mermaid Madonna*," in *The Postcolonial Contemporary: Political Imaginaries for the Global Present*, ed. Jini Kim Watson and Gary Wilder (New York: Fordham University Press, 2018), 164–85, at 172.

CHAPTER 3: TERROR AND JUDGMENT / DATING THE RUINS

1. "Changed by our special pressures, subdued by our skepticism, the paradigms of apocalypse continue to lie under our ways of making sense of the world," wrote Frank

Kermode in pioneering 1965 lectures, published in 1966 as *The Sense of an Ending*, which still offer helpful insights on the ongoing influence of apocalyptic themes and indeed anticipate some sophisticated recent formulations. See also Kermode's epilogue to the work he produced in 2000, which places the development of that work in the context of the ongoing fear of nuclear conflagration. Kermode, *The Sense of an Ending: Studies in the Theory of Fiction* (Oxford: Oxford University Press, 2000), 28, 181–97. On the secularization of disaster that characterizes modernity after the Enlightenment, see Marie-Hélène Huet, *The Culture of Disaster* (Chicago: University of Chicago Press, 2012).

2. John Ruskin, *Modern Painters* V, in *The Works of John Ruskin*, ed. E. T. Cook and Alexander Wedderburn, Library Edition, 39 vols. (London: George Allen, 1903–12), 7:435. The five volumes of *Modern Painters* (1843–60) comprise volumes 3–7 of the Library Edition. Subsequent references will appear in parentheses in the text by Library Edition volume and page number.

3. Though it focuses on an earlier period, Susan Stewart's treatment of the linking of ruins and landscapes in fanciful frontispieces to collections of prints is worth citing here. (And certainly both Turner and Ruskin are keenly aware of historical precedents.) "Out of the North," Stewart writes about engravers in the Netherlands in the sixteenth century in language that touches on principal concerns of Ruskin, "come two dominant strands of ruins imagery—the landscape and the allegory." Stewart's point is not simply that "ruins imagery gave temporal poignancy to these modes in both painting and printmaking" (Stewart, *The Ruins Lesson* [Chicago: University of Chicago Press, 2020], 151), but that the material nature of printmaking gives it an inherent relationship to ruins and ruination—as the plate is scratched and bitten into to make the image in the first instance, and then as the lines on the plate decay over the run of prints (158–63). Stewart's argument will also be relevant when I return to Turner's prints in my last chapter. On Ruskin's own sensitivity to the material nature of the medium, see Siegel "The Ruined Cathedral, Black Arts, and the Grave in Engraving: Ruskin and the Fatal Excess of Art," in *Material Inspirations*, 249–74. On later developments in the fine arts print and damage, see Dario Gamboni, *The Destruction of Art: Iconoclasm and Vandalism since the French Revolution* (London: Reaktion Books, 2018), 150.

4. On the figure on the beach in Ruskin, see Siegel, "Strange Aphrodite," in *Material Inspirations*, 122–41.

5. Ezek. 26:7–12, KJV, *The Holy Bible* (New York: Meridian, 1974); subsequent references will appear in parentheses by chapter and verse in the text.

6. See Herwig Wolfram's fascinating *History of the Goths*, trans. Thomas J. Dunlap (Berkeley: University of California Press, 1988).

7. Historians have been keenly aware of the challenging nature of this period of transition, of course. Works to cite include the revisionist projects of Eamon Duffy, including *The Stripping of the Altars: Traditional Religion in England, c. 1400–1580* (New Haven, CT: Yale University Press, 1992; 2nd ed., 2005); and before him, Christopher Haigh, *The English Reformation Revised* (Cambridge: Cambridge University Press, 1987). On the iconoclasm that accompanied religious developments, see Margaret Aston's

groundbreaking studies, especially *Broken Idols of the English Reformation* (Cambridge: Cambridge University Press, 2016). A context for later historiographical debates is to be found in the important recent collection edited by Alexandra Walsham, Brian Cummings, Bronwyn Wallace, and Ceri Law, *Memory and the English Reformation* (Cambridge: Cambridge University Press, 2020). In the introduction to this work the editors note the ways "the protracted religious revolution of the sixteenth and seventeenth centuries involved a concerted attempt to reshape social memory" and in particular "to disguise its own novelty, to obscure the dramatic rupture it had wrought" (3). On the centrality of the Reformation in the development of European ideas of the meaning of objects from the past, see Walter Benjamin, *Origin of the German Trauerspiel* [1928], trans. Howard Eiland (Cambridge, MA: Harvard University Press, 2019). See also Siegel, *Material Inspirations*, 228–45.

8. On Ruskin's use of "grave," see Siegel, *Material Inspirations*, 264–74. On "The Two Boyhoods," see 122–35.

9. For a challenge to the association of Benjamin's work with disasters it did not anticipate but with which it is frequently linked, see Susannah Young-ah Gottlieb, *Regions of Sorrow: Anxiety and Messianism in Hannah Arendt and W. H. Auden* (Palo Alto, CA: Stanford University Press, 2003), 248–49.

10. Sigmund Freud, *Beyond the Pleasure Principle*, trans. James Strachey (New York: Norton, 1961).

11. As Benjamin tells us, the actual name of the work is *Angelus Novus* ("On the Concept of History," 392). Paul K. Saint-Amour proposes the idea of "dissident temporalities": "We need a loose rubric," he writes, "for work that applies skeptical pressure to reflexive invocations of the future. Call it *critical futurities*: scholarship that takes as its object past and present conscriptions of the 'future,' the rhetoric, poetics, and ideology of such conscriptions, and their ethical, political, and historiographic import." Saint-Amour, *Tense Future: Modernism, Total War, Encyclopedic Form* (Oxford: Oxford University Press, 2015), 23, 24, emphasis in the original; subsequent references will appear in parentheses in the text. Paraphrasing David Scott, *Conscripts of Modernity: The Tragedy of Colonial Enlightenment* (Durham, NC: Duke University Press, 2004), Saint-Amour adds a diagnostic element to his analysis, suggesting not only that "thwarted expectation can become encysted in our histories to the detriment of self-understanding and commitment in the present," but that while "past narratives about the future are crucial historical artifacts . . . these artifacts need not be permitted to dictate the conditions of their reception and interpretation" (32).

12. Wendy Brown, "Resisting Left Melancholy," *boundary 2* 26, no. 3 (1999): 19–27, at 26, https://muse.jhu.edu/. Brown is, of course, describing a condition that substantially postdates Benjamin. For a more dynamic vision of the critic's project that insists on its distance from melancholic stasis, see Klaus R. Scherpe, "Dramatization and De-dramatization of 'The End': The Apocalyptic Consciousness of Modernity and Post-modernity," trans. Brent O. Peterson, *Cultural Critique*, no. 5 (1986–87): 95–129, an essay intended to resist Benjamin's apocalyptic sensibility being subsumed in 1980s

postmodern thought. "In Benjamin's work," writes Scherpe, "the negation of the naive belief in progress leads neither to his relinquishing historical reason, nor to an aesthetic program of contemplative or militant indifference" (106).

13. Heather Love, *Feeling Backward: Loss and the Politics of Queer History* (Cambridge, MA: Harvard University Press, 2007), 148–49; subsequent references will appear in parentheses in the text. To Love, Brown's call for an investigation of feelings sounds "at times more like a request that such feelings should not exist" (149).

14. For further discussion of these passages, see Chaps. 1 and 2.

15. At the core of Amanda Anderson's recent attempt to recover the significance of liberal writers is her identification of their achievement with a "governing bleakness of outlook" that has more typically been recognized (and valued) in writers associated with the intellectual Left. This outlook she identifies as having been shaped as much for members of the Frankfurt School and for liberals such as Lionel Trilling by "a post-catastrophic response to the war, to fascism, and to disappointment with the Soviet experiment." Amanda Anderson, *Bleak Liberalism* (Chicago: University of Chicago Press, 2016), 99. The critique of liberalism that has been so important to ostensibly radical theoretical orientations, Anderson proposes, changes in its nature if one sees both developments as responses to the same catastrophes (99–114). Anderson's compelling argument, it bears saying, is also a striking object lesson in how much misery has been valorized in postwar intellectual culture.

16. Colin Frost, "What Would Jack Bauer Do," *Globe and Mail*, June 16, 2007, https://www.theglobeandmail.com/news/national/what-would-jack-bauer-do/article687726/. The justice's words are symptomatic of a desire to make real the urgencies of the fictional show that is a widespread phenomenon among conservatives in the period. Indeed, "'24': An hour of realism" was a headline in the *Washington Times* on April 27, 2005. "If there's a bomb about to hit a major U.S. city and you have a person with information," one of the creators of the show, Joel Surnow, is quoted as saying in the piece, his hypothetical expressed with the immediacy of a simple conditional tense before concluding in a hyperbole that interpellates the second person as agent of violence and judge of its ethical force, "if you don't torture that person, that would be one of the most immoral acts you could imagine." https://www.washingtontimes.com/news/2005/apr/27/20050427-085529-9412r/. It would be impossible to overstate the political work *24* was seen to do in its day, when a conservative think tank as distinguished as the Heritage Foundation hosted a panel discussion in 2006 with an astonishing question openly mooted in its title: "'24' and America's Image in Fighting Terrorism: Fact, Fiction, or Does It Matter?" To indicate not simply the cultural cachet of the show but the importance of its open embrace of the combination of urgency and artifice, we might note that among the people in attendance to discuss whether distinguishing fact or fiction mattered in the fight on terrorism were the then-current secretary of homeland security and coauthor of the PATRIOT Act, Michael Chertoff, who made remarks, and Associate Justice Clarence Thomas. Rush Limbaugh moderated a conversation that included actors and writers from the show, as well as scholars. https://www.c-span.org/video/?193133-1/public-image-us-terrorism-policy.

17. Scarry, *Thinking in an Emergency* (New York: Norton, 2011), xiv. Scarry gives a sense of the seamless nature of the shift between the abdication of responsibility held to be necessary as the result of becoming a nuclear state and the justification based on the ostensible fear of terrorism (5–6). See especially "The Claim of Emergency," a section of the chapter "The Seduction to Stop Thinking" that lays out the paradox of a critical need to act that is divorced from the process of thought (7–10).

18. See the bibliographical notes on vandalism, iconoclasm and Grégoire in Chapter 2 of this volume. There is some small debate as to priority in the use of the term "vandalism," but no source dates it to a time before the Revolution, and they all concur on the centrality of Grégoire's reports in popularizing its use. The literature on vandalism in the French Revolution is large and constantly growing. Réau is still a useful, if tendentious, source: Louis Réau, *Histoire du vandalisme: Les monuments détruits de l'art français* (Paris: Hachette, 1959). More recently, see the essays in Philippe Bordes and Régis Michel, eds., *Aux armes et aux artes! Les artes de la Révolution* (Paris: A. Biro, 1988); as well as Emmet Kennedy, *A Cultural History of the French Revolution* (New Haven, CT: Yale University Press, 1989), esp. 197–234. Édouard Pommier's *L'art de la liberté* (Paris: Gallimard, 1991) is an important resource, esp. 93–166. See also the wide-ranging papers collected in Simone Bernard-Griffits, Marie-Clude Chemin, and Jean Ehrard, eds., *Révolution française et "vandalism révolutionnaire"* (Paris: Universitas, 1992). On the political and intellectual implications of the abbé's work, see especially Dominique Poulot's "Revolutionary 'Vandalism' and the Birth of the Modern Museum: The Effects of the Representation of Modern Cultural Terror," in *Art in Museums*, ed. Susan Pearce (London: Athlone, 1995), 192–214. On the revolutionary calendar, see Kennedy, *Cultural History*, 345–52.

19. M. H. Carnot, *Mémoires de Grégoire, ancien évêque de Blois*, 2 vols. (Paris, 1837), 345; cited in Anthony Vidler, "The Paradoxes of Vandalism: Henri Grégoire and the Thermidorian Discourse on Historical Monuments," in *The Abbé Grégoire and His World*, ed. Jeremy D. Popkin and Richard H. Popkin (Dordrecht: Kluwer Academic Publishers, 2000), 129–56, at 138. Richard Clay rejects the term "vandalism" as reductive and pejorative in a study emphasizing the popular agents of revolutionary violence rather than the intellectuals characterizing their actions. See Clay, *Iconoclasm in Revolutionary Paris: The Transformation of Signs* (Oxford, UK: Voltaire Foundation, 2012).

20. Abbé Henri Grégoire, *Rapport sur les inscriptions des monumens publics* (Paris: National Convention, 1794).

21. On the intersection of new concepts of the past and future in the revolutionary period, see especially Reinhart Koselleck, *Futures Past: On the Semantics of Historical Time*, trans. Keith Tribe (New York: Columbia University Press, 2004). For more recent reflections on the topic of critical futurity, see two works produced in tandem by Michael André Bernstein and Gary Saul Morson: Bernstein, *Foregone Conclusions: Against Apocalyptic History* (Berkeley: University of California Press, 1995); and Morson, *Narrative and Freedom: The Shadows of Time* (New Haven, CT: Yale University Press, 1994).

22. "La France est vraiment un nouveau monde. Sa nouvelle organisation sociale présente un phénomène unique dans l'étendue des âges; et peut-être n'a-t-on pas encore

observé qu'outre le matériel des connoissances humaines, par l'effet de la révolution elle possède exclusivement une foule d'élémens, de combinaisons nouvelles, prises dans la nature, et d'inépuisables moyens pour mettre à profit sa résurrection politique." Grégoire, *Rapport sur les destructions opérées par le Vandalisme et les moyens de le réprimer* (Paris: Convention nationale, 1794), 22–35. All the translations from Grégoire are mine unless otherwise indicated.

23. "Sous le despotism, le people étoit compté pour rien; actuellement il est ce qu'il doit être, c'est-à-dire tout. Les monumens publics doivent donc lui rappeler son courage, ses triomphes, ses droits, sa dignité; ils doivent parler un langage intelligible pour tous, et qui soit le véhicule du patriotisme et de la vertu, dont le citoyen doit se pénétrer par tous les sens." Grégoire, *Rapport sur les inscriptions*, 4–5.

24. Quoted in Joseph L. Sax, "Heritage Preservation as a Public Duty: The Abbé Grégoire and the Origins of an Idea," *Michigan Law Review* 88 (1989): 1142–69, at 1153. For more of these stark declarations and treatment of the debate around the values they represented, see Pommier's chapter "De l'inconoclasme au patrimoine," in *L'art de la liberté*, 93–166.

25. "Sans doute il faut que tout parle aux yeux le langage républicain." Grégoire, *Rapport sur les destructions opérées par le Vandalisme*, 11.

26. "Les monumens du moyen âge formeront des suites intéressantes, sinon pour la beauté du travail, au moins pour l'histoire et la chronologie." Grégoire's argument for continuity anticipates the value of specialized fields of study yet to emerge, notably art history: "There are also monuments, which, lacking the seal of genius, are precious for the history of art" (Il est d'ailleurs des monumens, qui, sans avoir le cachet du géni, sont précieux pour l'histoire d'art"). Grégoire, *Rapport sur les destructions opérées par le Vandalisme, 20, 25.*

27. Gamboni, *Destruction of Art*, 39; see also 40–46.

28. On the project of the Encyclopedia, see Saint-Amour, *Tense Future*, 190–98.

29. Alois Riegl, "The Modern Cult of Monuments: Its Character and Its Origin" [*Moderne Denkmalkultus: Sein Wesen und seine Entstehung*], trans. Kurt W. Forster and Diane Ghirardo, *Oppositions: A Journal for Ideas and Criticism in Architecture* 25 (1982): 21–50, at 26; subsequent references will appear in parentheses in the text.

30. See, e.g., his first essay on vandalism, "Modern Rome has no more great men. But her obelisks, her statues, attract the attention of the learned world. Some Englishman spent two thousand guineas to see the monuments that adorn the banks of the Tiber. Certainly, if our victorious armies penetrate Italy, the taking of the Apollo Belvedere and the Hercules Farnese would be the most brilliant conquest. It is Greece that decorated Rome; but should the masterpieces of the Greek republics decorate a nation of slaves? The French Republic ought to be their final home." (Rome moderne n'a plus de grands hommes; mais ses obélisques, ses statues, appellent les regards de l'univers savant. Tel Anglais dépensoit deux mille guinées pour aller voir les monumens qui ornent les bords du Tibre. Certes, si nos armées victorieuses pénètrent en Italie, l'enlèvement de l'Apollon du Belvédère et de l'Hercule Farnèse seroit la plus brillante conquête. C'est la Grèce qui a décoré Rome; mais les chef-d'œuvres des républiques grecques doivent-ils

décorer le pays des esclaves? La République française devroit être leur dernier domicile.) Grégoire, *Rapport sur les destructions opérées par le Vandalisme*, 27.

31. Sax, "Heritage Preservation as a Public Duty," 1142. See also Astrid Swenson, *The Rise of Heritage: Preserving the Past in France, Germany and England, 1789–1914* (Cambridge: Cambridge University Press, 2013), 25–35.

32. For the expansion of the scope of care that accompanied the development of the concept of heritage, see Françoise Choay, *L'allegorie du patrimoine* (Paris: Éditions du Seuil, 1992); and David Lowenthal, *Possessed by the Past: The Heritage Crusade and the Spoils of History* (New York: Free Press, 1996). For an important account focusing on the institutionalization of the process in the twentieth century, see Lucia Allais, *Designs of Destruction: The Making of Monuments in the Twentieth Century* (Chicago: University of Chicago Press, 2018).

33. From the long list of works touching on the intersection of damage and restoration, we might cite Réau, Gamboni, and Choay. Choay is particularly subtle on the distinctions and similarities in the French and English relationships to the topic in the nineteenth century.

34. On the intellectual backgrounds to Riegl's argument, see Michael Gubser, *Time's Visible Surface: Alois Riegl and the Discourse on History and Temporality in Fin-de-Siècle Vienna* (Detroit: Wayne State University Press, 2006); and Margaret Olin, "The Cult of Monuments as a State Religion in Late 19th Century Austria," *Wiener Jahrbuch für Kunstgeschichte* 28 (1985): 177–98. See also Karen Bassi, *Traces of the Past: Classics between Archeology and History* (Ann Arbor: University of Michigan Press, 2016), 108–12.

35. William Shakespeare, *Shakespeare's Sonnets,* ed. Katherine Duncan-Jones (London: Arden Shakespeare, 2010), 147, lines 13–14.

36. *Entwicklungskette*, or "chain of development," the term Riegl uses, has a long history in German thought. To write, as Benjamin does, of *eine Kette von Begebenheiten*, or "a chain of incidents," is to rupture the relationship between event and telos. Benjamin, "Über den Begriff der Geschichte," in *Gesammelte Schriften*, ed. Rolf Tiedman and H. Schweppenhäuser (Frankfurt am Main: Suhrkamp, 1980), 1:691–704, at 697. Riegl, *Der moderne Denkmalkultus* (Vienna: Braumüller, 1903), 2. Evidently Riegl's vision owes a debt to the powerful tradition of thinking about development associated with sources on which Benjamin also draws and which he modifies, notably Schiller and Hegel. On Benjamin's nineteenth-century sources, see Michael Löwy, *Fire Alarm: Reading Walter Benjamin's "On the Concept of History"* [2001], trans. Chris Turner (London: Verso, 2005), 64. On Benjamin's response to Riegl's work, see Giles Peaker, "Works That Have Lasted . . . Walter Benjamin Reading Alois Riegl," in *Framing Formalism: Riegle's Work*, ed. Richard Woodfield (London: Routledge, 2001), 291–310.

37. Immanuel Kant, *Critique of the Power of Judgment* [1790], trans. Paul Guyer and Eric Matthews (Cambridge: Cambridge University Press, 2002), 148.

38. The precursors are typically responses to the Thirty Years' War, such as the prints of Jacques Callot published as *The Miseries of War* (1633) and—in literature—Hans Jakob Christoffel von Grimmelhausen's *Simplicius Simplicissimus* (1668). But for a revealing sense of the difficulty of finding the moral grounding of the Callot for the

modern viewer, see Diane Wolfthal, "Jacques Callot's *Miseries of War*," *Art Bulletin* 59, no. 2 (1977): 222–33. See also Hilliard T. Goldfarb, "Callot and the Miseries of War: The Artist, His Intentions, and His Context," in Goldfarb and Reva Wolf, *Fatal Consequences: Callot, Goya, and the Horrors of War* (Hanover, NH: Hood Museum of Art, 1990), 13–26. On Goya, see also Chap. 1 of this volume.

39. G. W. F. Hegel, *Aesthetics: Lectures on Fine Art*, trans. T. M. Knox (Oxford: Oxford University Press, 1975), 2:1059. The lectures were delivered in the first decades of the nineteenth century and first compiled in 1835. The whole passage running from 1058 to 1062 is of interest.

40. Mary Favret, *War at a Distance: Romanticism and the Making of Modern Wartime* (Princeton, NJ: Princeton University Press, 2010), 177; subsequent references will appear in parentheses in the text.

41. Jan Mieszkowski notes about this period that "the new notion of the citizenry as a conglomeration of individuals mobilized to wage war was paralleled by the equally novel idea that the populace was now united in its status as an audience viewing the conflict." Mieszkowski, *Watching War* (Stanford, CA: Stanford University Press, 2012), 3.

42. Gamboni, *Destruction of Art*, 49; see also 56. On the ways in which concepts of vandalism put into question ideas of social progress, see 61.

43. See Saint-Amour, "On the Partiality of Total War," in *Tense Future*, 47–89, esp. 55–60. See also "Visions of Total War," in Mieszkowski, *Watching War*, 144–72.

CHAPTER 4: OWNING ART AFTER NAPOLEON

1. C. M. Kaufmann documents the exchange between Wellington and Ferdinand and the subsequent history of the Wellington collection in *Catalogue of Paintings in the Wellington Museum* (London: Her Majesty's Stationery Office, 1982). Elizabeth Longford discusses the trophies won at this decisive battle in *Wellington: The Years of the Sword* (New York: Harper and Row, 1969), 316, 318, 334.

2. Walter Benjamin, "On the Concept of History," in *Selected Writings*, vol. 4: *1938–1940*, ed. Howard Eiland and Michael W. Jennings, trans. Edmund Jephcott and others (Cambridge, MA: Harvard University Press, 2003), 389–400, at 392; subsequent references will appear in parentheses in the text. For more extended discussions of the essay, see the Preface to this book and Chaps. 2 and 3.

3. On the antimuseal tradition, see Siegel, *Desire and Excess: The Nineteenth Century Culture of Art* (Princeton, NJ: Princeton University Press, 2000), 3–10.

4. Matthew Arnold, "Sweetness and Light," in Arnold, *Culture and Anarchy and Other Writings*, ed. Stefan Collini (Cambridge: Cambridge University Press, 1993), 58–80.

5. Work on cultural property, which has been taking place in museum studies, art history, archeology, and anthropology, as well as in other fields, has reached new levels of political commitment and intellectual sophistication in recent years. Jordanna Bailkin provides a conceptually generative historical study in *The Culture of Property: The Crisis of Liberalism in Modern Britain* (Chicago: University of Chicago Press, 2004).

For the rich international legal response, see Barbara Hoffman, ed., *Art and Cultural Heritage: Law, Policy, and Practice* (Cambridge: Cambridge University Press, 2006); and Ana Filipa Vrdoljak, *International Law, Museums and the Return of Cultural Objects* (Cambridge: Cambridge University Press, 2006). Wilhelm Treue and Margaret Melanie Miles view the question in a broad historical context; see Treue, *Art Plunder: The Fate of Works of Art in War and Unrest*, trans. Basil Creighton (New York: John Day, 1961); and Margaret Melanie Miles, *Art as Plunder: The Ancient Origins of Debate about Cultural Property* (New York: Cambridge University Press, 2008). Hoffman is interesting on the question of restitution, but see also James Cuno, *Who Owns Antiquity? Museums and the Battle over Our Ancient Heritage* (Princeton, NJ: Princeton University Press, 2008); and Cuno, ed., *Whose Culture? The Promise of Museums and the Debate over Antiquities* (Princeton, NJ: Princeton University Press, 2009); Jeanette Greenfield, *The Return of Cultural Treasures* (Cambridge: Cambridge University Press, 1996); John Henry Merryman, *Imperialism, Art, and Restitution* (Cambridge: Cambridge University Press, 2006); and the challenging papers collected in *Who Owns Objects? The Ethics and Politics of Collecting Cultural Artefacts*, ed. Eleanor Robson, Luke Treadwell, and Chris Gosden (Oxford, UK: Oxbow, 2006). It bears saying that the issues involved in different areas, though they will frequently inform each other, are often driven by quite distinct field and institutional histories—not to mention political considerations. For a discussion of recent polemics related to restitution, see the Introduction to this volume.

6. Historians of the Louvre have done important work laying out the practical and conceptual effects of this period in the history of the museum. See especially Dominique Poulot, *Musée, nation, patrimoine, 1789–1815* (Paris: Gallimard, 1997); and Poulot, ed., *Patrimoine et modernité* (Paris: L'Harmattan, 1998). In *Une histoire des musées de France, XVIIIe–XXe* (Paris: La Decouverte, 2005), Poulot gives an evocative double title to the section on the Musée Napoléon: "La construction de la légitimité muséale: La naturalization des oeuvres" (The construction of museal legitimacy: The naturalization of works of art), the colon holding in balance the artifice of institutional legitimacy on one side and the bold suggestion that the national affiliations of works of art may be subject to the same kinds of alterations as human citizenship itself on the other. See also Jean-Louis Déotte, "Rome, the Archetypal Museum, and the Louvre, the Negation of Division," in *Art in Museums*, ed. Susan Pearce (London: Athlone, 1995), 215–32; and Hans Belting, "The Farewell to *Apollo*," in Belting, *The Invisible Masterpiece* [1998], trans. Helen Atkins (London: Reaktion Books, 2001), 27–49. My discussion focuses on the museum in the early years of the nineteenth century; nevertheless, Andrew McClellan, *Inventing the Louvre: Art, Politics, and the Origins of the Modern Museum in Eighteenth-Century Paris* (Cambridge: Cambridge University Press, 1994), is a vital resource.

7. André Malraux, *Psychologie de l'art*, vol. 1: *La musée imaginaire* (Geneva: A. Skira, 1947), 14–15.

8. On the Arch of Titus, see the Introduction to this volume and Chap. 2. On the theft of relics, see Patrick J. Geary, *Furta Sacra: Thefts of Relics in the Central Middle Ages*, rev. ed. (Princeton, NJ: Princeton University Press, 1990); on the remains of Saint Mark, in particular, see 87–102.

9. The *Oxford English Dictionary* dates the first use of the term in English to 1837, but even in French it was a fairly recent formulation, first proposed in the work of a French noble emigrant writing in the period of Napoleonic supremacy. "Lorsque l'on est issu d'une famille illustre, l'on doit apprendre à ses enfants que si le public est disposé à honorer en eux le mérite de leurs parents, il s'attend à en trouver les traces chez leurs descendants; le respect que l'on accorde généralement à la naissance est loin d'être gratuit. Noblesse oblige." Pierre-Marc-Gaston de Lévis, *Maximes et réflexions sur différents sujets de morale et de politique* [1808] (Paris: P. Didot, 1810), 23–24.

10. On the vast reach of these European conflicts, see Alexander Mikaberidze, *The Napoleonic Wars: A Global History* (Oxford: Oxford University Press, 2020.

11. Important compendia included the volumes produced by the great antiquarian Bernard de Montfaucon, *L'antiquité expliquée et représentée en figures* (1719–24), and by the founder of art history, Johann Joachim Winckelmann, *Monumenti Antichi Inediti* (1767), as well as the *Specimens of Antient Sculpture* published by the Society of Dilettanti in 1809, together with works by many less prestigious followers. On this topic, see Siegel, *Material Inspirations* (Oxford: Oxford University Press, 2020).

12. Unable to remove the fresco itself from the walls of the Vatican, the French had acquired the cartoon for the work from Milan. See Martin Rosenberg, "Raphael's *Transfiguration* and Napoleon's Cultural Politics," *Eighteenth-Century Studies* 19, no. 2 (1985–86): 180–205, at 190. For the broader context of reception of Raphael, see also Rosenberg's *Raphael and France: The Artist as Paradigm and Symbol* (College Park: Pennsylvania State University Press, 1995); and Jean-Pierre Cuzin et al., *Raphaël et l'art français* (Paris: Réunion des musées nationaux, 1984).

13. On the history of the reception of these statues, see Francis Haskell and Nicholas Penny, *Taste and the Antique: The Lure of Classical Sculpture, 1500–1900* (New Haven, CT: Yale University Press, 1981). See also Siegel, *Desire and Excess* and *Material Inspirations.*

14. "Dans le cours de vos victoires vous avez conquis les principaux chefs-d'oeuvre des beaux-arts, et vous en avez enrichi la France. La collection des gravures qui peut les faire connaître à l'Europe entire est un hommage qui vous est dû. Nous vous l'offrons avec reconnaissance et respect." Dedication, *Le Musée français, ou recueil de gravures d'après les plus beaux tableaux, statues et bas-reliefs qui composent la collection nationale*, vol. 1 (Paris, 1803). All translations from these volumes are mine. The publication history of this collection of prints is complicated, and with good reason. The project was begun in the ancien régime, but continued through the revolutionary and Napoleonic periods and then the restoration. So, both political circumstances and the nature of the national collection were changing around it. The plates were issued in fascicles over time, meaning that bound volumes differ somewhat in their arrangement—and that circumstances could sometimes outpace the plans of its authors. By far the fullest treatment of this endeavor is still George D. McKee, "The Musée Français and the Musée Royal: A History of the Publication of an Album of Fine Engravings with a Catalogue of Plates and a Discussion of Similar Ventures" (MA thesis, University of Chicago, 1981). McKee treats the *Musée français* and the *Musée royal* as one album. I tend to separate the two titles, but there were many continuities in their production.

15. "Ce monument fait pour passer à la postérité la plus reculée, sera le témoignage éternel de la munificence de Bonaparte, qui a fait don de la Vénus de Médicis au Musée français, et doit servir à constater pour jamais la reconnaissance des beaux arts envers leur illustre bienfaiteur." *Le Musée français, ou recueil de gravures d'après les plus beaux tableaux, statues et bas-reliefs qui composent la collection nationale*, vol. 4 (1809). See Edward P. Alexander's "Dominique Vivant Denon and the Louvre of Napoleon: The Art Museum as Symbol of National Glory," in *Museum Masters: Their Museums and Their Influence* (Walnut Creek, CA: Altamira Press, 1995), 79–112; on the medal, see 94. See also Belting, *Invisible Masterpiece*, 29–30.

16. For a related observation about the visual representation of the looting, see the discussion of Benjamin Zix's drawings of Vivien Denon in Alice Mae Littman Goff, "To the Vandals They Are Stone: A Profane Pre-history of the German Temple of Art, 1794–1830" (PhD diss., University of California, Berkeley, 2015), 22–23.

17. "La Grèce les céda; Rome les a perdus; / Leur sort changea deux fois, il ne changera plus"; my translation. Quoted in Charles Saunier, *Les conquêtes artistiques de la Révolution et de l'Empire: Reprises et abandons des Alliés en 1815* (Paris: Renouard, 1902), 37. Saunier is the best early source for the history of Napoleonic looting; on the arrival and procession, see 36–38. Dorothy Mackay Quynn, "The Art Confiscations of the Napoleonic Wars" *American Historical Review* 50, no. 3 (1945): 437–60, is still a useful source. See also Wayne Hanley, *The Genesis of Napoleonic Propaganda, 1796–1799* (New York: Columbia University Press, 2005), esp. chap. 4, "Art as Bonaparte's Tool of Propaganda"; and Wayne Sandholtz, *Prohibiting Plunder: How Norms Change* (New York: Oxford University Press, 2007), esp. chap. 3, "Napoleonic Plunder and the Emergence of Norms." The most detailed and thought-provoking recent study of the cultural effects of the lootings and restitutions is probably Goff's dissertation, which has a wider conceptual and historical scope than its Prussian focus might suggest.

18. On the Louvre under Napoleon, see the works already cited on the museum, as well as more specialized studies, including Cecil Gould, *Trophy of Conquest: The Musée Napoléon and the Creation of the Louvre* (London: Faber & Faber, 1965); and Francis Henry Taylor, *The Taste of Angels: A History of Art Collecting from Rameses to Napoleon* (Boston: Little, Brown, 1948), 542–89. See also Philippe Malgouyres, *Le Musée Napoléon* (Paris: Louvre, 1999); and Thierry Lentz, Isabelle Leroy-Jay Lemaistre, Anne Dion-Tenenbaum, and Sylvain Laveissière, *Napoléon et le Louvre* (Paris: Louvre, 2004). Philippe Bordes provides an informed critical perspective on recent revaluations of the imperial Louvre; see "Le Musée Napoléon," in *L'empire des muses: Napoléon, les arts et les lettres*, ed. Jean-Claude Bonnet (Paris: Belin, 2004).

19. Thomas Lawrence, *The Life and Correspondence of Sir Thomas Lawrence*, ed. D. E. Williams (London: Colburn and Bentley, 1831), 1:338.

20. Michael Faraday, *The Life and Letters of Faraday*, ed. Bence Jones (London: Spottiswoode, 1870), 1:92. See Goff, "To the Vandals They Are Stone," 44–51, for a thoughtful account of a related ambivalence among German writers.

21. For a detailed contemporary account of the restitution, see Helen Maria Williams, *A Narrative of the Events Which Have Taken Place in France from the Landing of*

Napoleon Bonaparte on the First of March, 1815, till the Restoration of Louis XVIII (London, 1815), 220–47; subsequent references will appear in parentheses in the text. See also Taylor, *Taste of Angels*, 571–89; and Haskell and Penny, *Taste and the Antique*, 114–16. On Wellington's role and his sense of the political considerations involved, see his dispatch to Castlereagh of September 23, 1815, in *Hansard Parliamentary Debates*, 1st ser. (1803–20), February 1, 1816, cols. 301–5; subsequent references will appear in parentheses in the text. Elizabeth Eastlake gives a good review of the politics of the process from the English point of view in "Galleries of the Louvre," *Quarterly Review* 117 (1865), 287–323.

22. On Canova's role in relation to the Chiaramonte gallery and its decoration, see Ulrich Hiesinger, "Canova and the Frescoes of the Galleria Chiaramonti," *Burlington Magazine* 120, no. 907 (October 1978): 654–63, 665. On the history of the restitutions, and especially Canova's role, see Haskell and Penny, *Taste and the Antique*, 108–16; Christopher M. S. Johns, *Antonio Canova and the Politics of Patronage in Revolutionary and Napoleonic Europe* (Berkeley: University of California Press, 1998), esp. 123–94; and Katharine Eustace, "Questa Scabrosa Missione: Canova in Paris and London in 1815," in Eustace, *Canova: Ideal Heads* (Oxford, UK: Ashmolean, 1997), 9–38. See also Thomas Crow, *Restoration: The Fall of Napoleon in the Course of European Art, 1812–1820* (Princeton, NJ: Princeton University Press, 2018), 93–125. Nineteenth-century sources indicate that while Lawrence's portrait of George IV was originally given pride of place in the painting collection, either in an antechamber or at the conclusion of the sequence of Old Masters, it was often felt to be out of place and at times was removed to other locations.

23. *Hansard Parliamentary Debates*, June 7, 1816; see cols. 1027–40. See also William Hamilton, *Memorandum on the Subject of the Earl of Elgin's Pursuits in Greece* (Edinburgh: Balfour, Kirkwood & Co., 1810). For Canova's letter see the *Report from the Select Committee of the House of Commons on the Earl of Elgin's Collection of Sculptured Marbles* (London: John Murray, 1816), xxiii.

24. January 6, 1802; cited in Holger Hoock, "The British State and the Anglo-French Wars over Antiquities, 1798–1858," *Historical Journal* 50 (2007): 49–72, at 61. On the topic of national rivalries over culture, see also Hoock's *Empires of the Imagination: Politics, War, and the Arts in the British World, 1750–1850* (London: Profile, 2010).

25. See Francis Haskell, *Rediscoveries in Art: Some Aspects of Taste, Fashion and Collecting in England and France* (Oxford: Phaidon, 1976); and Elizabeth Gilmore Holt, *The Triumph of Art for the Public* (Garden City, NY: Anchor Books, 1979).

26. William Hazlitt, *Complete Works*, ed. P. P. Howe (London: J. M. Dent, 1930–34), 8:14; subsequent references to Hazlitt will be drawn from this edition and appear in parentheses in the text.

27. For an anticipation of this sentiment often cited as the beginning of a modern heritage sensibility, see Antoine-Chrysostome Quatremère de Quincy's 1796 *Letters to Miranda*, in *Letters to Miranda and Canova on the Abduction of Antiquities from Rome and Athens*, trans. Chris Miller and David Gilks (Los Angeles: Getty Research Institute, 2012). See also Dominique Poulot's important introductory essay for this volume, "The Cosmopolitanism of Masterpieces," 1–91.

28. Felicia Hemans, *The Restoration of the Works of Art to Italy* (Oxford: R. Pearson, 1816), lines 1–4.

29. James Simpson, *Paris after Waterloo: Notes Taken at the Time and Hitherto Unpublished* (London: William Blackwood and Sons, 1853), 118; subsequent references will appear in parentheses in the text.

30. The artist James Stothard gives a good sense of the speed of the process of removal in a letter from this period: "Most of all, I was delighted with the assemblage of paintings to be viewed and compared with each other; the altar-pieces of Rubens, with his school, covered the most space, and made a splendid show," he notes. But that show had a set term: "On the Monday of the second week I had been at Paris, they began to take down all the altar-pieces by Rubens, and whatever belonged to Flanders, Holland, and Germany. This afforded me an opportunity to inspect Rubens on the ground. On the Thursday of this second week, we made a day to visit Versailles and St. Cloud. On my return not a picture of Rubens remained on the walls of the Louvre." Anna Eliza Bray, *Life of Thomas Stothard* (London: John Murray, 1851), 73.

31. Cf. Dominique Poulot on Quatremère de Quincy's "demand for a 'destination'" in "The Cosmopolitanism of Masterpieces," 1. See also 27–34, which addresses Quatremère de Quincy's *Considerations morale sur la destination des ouvrages de l'art* ("Moral considerations concerning the destination of works of art"), a text from 1815 and thus closely contemporary with Simpson's reflection. On the topic in the period, see also Édouard Pommier, "La Révolution et le destin des oeuvres d'art," in Quatremère de Quincy, *Lettres à Miranda*, ed. Pommier (Paris: Macula, 1989), 56–57; and Dario Gamboni, *The Destruction of Art: Iconoclasm and Vandalism since the French Revolution* (London: Reaktion Books, 2018), 46.

32. In "To the Places Where They Were to Be Found Previously: The Restoration of Prussian Art Collections, 1814–1815," chap. 3 of "To the Vandals They Are Stone: A Profane Pre-history of the German Temple of Art, 1794–1830" (PhD diss., University of California, Berkeley, 2015), Alice Mae Littman Goff describes in admirable detail the aspirations and only partial successes of German attempts at restitution, along with the distinct ideas of return that emerged in that context (67–101). For a study of the Italian case that documents the emergence of Italian art institutions in response to Napoleonic-era developments, as well as the small number of paintings that were returned to the churches from which they were taken, see Michelle L. Clarabut, "Overcoming the Past: An Examination of the Repatriation of Italian Painting in Post-Napoleonic Italy" (PhD diss., Royal Holloway and Bedford New College, University of London, 2017). Clarabut calculates that approximately 40 percent of the paintings taken were returned and indicates the patchy success rate of various areas, with Rome getting back less than a quarter of the thirty-five works removed, while the Vatican got back both of its canvases. She also helpfully emphasizes the removal of works to collections outside of Paris, their location making restitution more difficult. (236–47).

33. "Repatriation in Foreign-Ruled States" is the neutral but thought-provoking title of an important chapter by Clarabut identifying the practical and political challenges

facing areas that included such important art centers as Venice and Milan, among others (107–50).

34. James Thomson, "Summer," in *The Seasons*, ed. James Sambrook (Oxford: Oxford University Press, 1981), 1347. "Could great men thunder / As Jove himself does," begins the famous speech from Shakespeare's *Measure for Measure*, with which Simpson evidently references Napoleonic overreaching, "Jove would ne'er be quiet, / For every pelting, petty officer / Would use his heaven for thunder." It is that characteristic of human vainglory, the mistaking of "a little brief authority" for a status of greater permanence and mightier significance warranting the creation of monuments, that makes the kinder angels weep while splenetic mortals laugh as the markers of transient glory outlast those who commission them. William Shakespeare, *Measure for Measure*, ed. A. R. Braunmuller and Robert N. Watson (London: Arden Shakespeare, 2020), 2.2.136–49.

35. See Poulot, "Cosmopolitanism of Masterpieces," on emergent concepts of individual property in relation to those of *cultural* property, in particular "the triumph of exclusive ownership, personal or national" (29) following the French Revolution.

36. "Si les sciences ont dû souvent au hasard les découvertes les plus importantes par les progrès rapides qu'elles leur ont fait faire et les secrets qu'elles leur ont dévoilés, il n'a pas moins mérité la reconnoissances des beaux arts, par les trésors dont il leur a livré la jouissance. C'est au hasard que l'on est redevable d'une foule de belles statues, de médailles, et de pierres gravés antiques; il a fait sortir de leurs tombeaux Herculanum et Pompéi, ces mines inépuisables de monuments antiques, et qu'on pourroit appeler des musées souterrains; et il nous a comblés de ses faveurs en rendant à la lumière le chef-d'ouvre dont nous allons nous occuper. M. le marquis de Rivière avoit eu le bonheur de l'acquérir; il s'est empressé d'en faire hommage à Sa Majesté, qui, en le plaçant dans son Musée royal, a voulu le consoler d'une partie de ses pertes"; my translation. Henri Laurent, *Le Musée royal* (Paris: P. Didot, 1818), n.p. McKee points out that the Venus de Milo is the only art object illustrated in the series that was not in French hands in 1815. McKee, "Musee," 81. Indeed, its anomalous position is highlighted by the fact that while the sculpture was only discovered in 1820, the plate illustrating it is to be found in a volume dated two years earlier.

37. Simpson first mentions the possibility he always deprecates (and yet more than a little supports) during an extensive discussion of the statue earlier in the text. "Had the report turned out true (which I never believed) that it was to be presented to the British nation, in full compensation for their concern in the deliverance of the world, it must have been inaugurated in a temple built for the purpose" (152). Full compensation and a splendid new temple: it is not even a subtext of this passage that if everyone got what they deserved, the Apollo would have ended up in London in a purpose-built museum.

38. Déotte, "Rome, the Archetypal Museum, and the Louvre," 223.

39. For a sophisticated account of the peculiar nature of a national identity subtended by a relationship to objects clearly not created by that nation, see Fiona Rose-Greenland, "The Parthenon Marbles as Icons of Nationalism in Nineteenth-Century Britain," *Nations and Nationalism* 19, no. 4 (2013): 654–73. See also Kavita Singh's reflections on the challenging topic of repatriation when the status of a nation is contested,

"Repatriation without *Patria*: Repatriation for Tibet," *Journal of Material Culture* 15, no. 2 (2010): 131–55.

40. Miguel Tamen, *Friends of Interpretable Objects* (Cambridge, MA: Harvard University Press, 2001), 73. On this link, see also Chapter 2 of this volume.

CHAPTER 5: REVELATION AND UNCERTAINTY, OR WHAT YOU SEE IN THE WATER

1. See Rev. 12:7–9, KJV, *The Holy Bible* (New York: Meridian, 1974); subsequent references to the Bible will appear in parentheses in the text.

2. Auerbach speaks of "the strangely new meaning of *figura* in the Christian world." Erich Auerbach, "Figura" [1938], *Scenes from the Drama of European Literature* (Minneapolis: University of Minnesota Press, 1984), 11–76, at 28. While I am emphasizing the Christian moment of apocalyptic thought, it bears saying that both the significance ascribed to violent destruction and the prophetic voice with which that significance is identified have roots in the Old Testament. On this topic, see Susan Stewart's discussion of what she calls "planned obsolescence in the Hebrew scripture": Stewart, *The Ruins Lesson* (Chicago: University of Chicago Press, 2020), 44–47; subsequent references will appear in parentheses in the text.

3. Christina Sharpe, *In the Wake: On Blackness and Being* (Durham, NC: Duke University Press, 2016), 116. Sharpe's account of the work of recent Black artists and critics emphasizes the links connecting their representation of the limits of visual experience (as a source of empathy, as a form of evidence, or as a call to action) with the injuries associated with the ongoing failures their projects illuminate. When she describes what she calls "Black annotation and Black redaction" as "another effort to try to look, to try to really see" (117), we may understand the repetition of "try," like the vaguely emphatic but compelling "really," to be indications of the difficulty of the project (to look, to really see) she is describing.

4. See the discussion of Latour in Chapter 2.

5. Messianic elements, of course, run through Benjamin's essay, but as an illustration of their importance I will just cite the final words of the text, which, as currently presented in the standard edition, ends with a paragraph A and a paragraph B, both of which close on the topic. Paragraph A's reflection on prognostication ends with the proposition that for the Jews the future was not homogeneous, empty time because "every second was the small gateway in time through which the Messiah might enter." Paragraph B, on the historical disjunctions that interest the historical-materialist critic, concludes with the establishment of "a conception of the present as now-time shot through with splinters of messianic time." Walter Benjamin, "On the Concept of History," in *Selected Writings*, vol. 4: *1938–1940*, ed. Howard Eiland and Michael W. Jennings, trans. Edmund Jephcott and others (Cambridge, MA: Harvard University Press, 2003), 389–400, at 397. On the historical context for this element in Benjamin, see Anson Rabinbach, "Between Enlightenment and Apocalypse: Benjamin, Bloch and Modern German Jewish Messianism," *New German Critique*, no. 34 (1985): 78–124. See also Susannah

Young-ah Gottlieb, *Regions of Sorrow: Anxiety and Messianism in Hannah Arendt and W. H. Auden* (Palo Alto, CA: Stanford University Press, 2003).

6. James Joyce, *Ulysses*, ed. Hans Walter Gabler (New York: Vintage, 1986), 4–5; subsequent references will appear in parentheses in the text.

7. Walter H. Kokernot, "'Where Ignorant Armies Clash by Night' and the Sikh Rebellion: A Contemporary Source for Matthew Arnold's Night-Battle Imagery," *Victorian Poetry* 43, no. 1 (2005): 99–108, www.jstor.org/stable/40002810.

8. Oscar Wilde, "The Decay of Lying," in *Complete Works of Oscar Wilde*, vol. 4, ed. Josephine M. Guy (Oxford: Oxford University Press, 2007), 72–103, at 83.

9. John Stuart Mill, "Nature," in *Three Essays on Religion*, ed. Lou Matz (Peterborough, ON: Broadview Press, 2009), 65–104.

10. Walter Pater, *The Renaissance: Studies in Art and Poetry*, ed. Donald L. Hill (Berkeley: University of California Press, 1980), 186–87.

11. Isobel Armstrong, *Victorian Glassworlds* (Oxford: Oxford University Press, 2008).

12. John Ruskin, *Modern Painters* I, in *The Works of John Ruskin*, ed. E. T. Cook and Alexander Wedderburn, Library Edition, 39 vols. (London: George Allen, 1903–12), 3:494. The five volumes of *Modern Painters* comprise volumes 3–7 of the Library Edition. Subsequent references will appear in parentheses in the text by Library Edition volume and page number.

13. The discussion of the "pathetic fallacy" is central to the argument about landscape in history running from just before "On Classical Landscape" to "Medieval Landscape" to "Modern Landscape." See *Modern Painters* III (5:197–387). On the context for the emergence of the pathetic fallacy, see also Jonah Siegel, *Material Inspirations: The Interests of the Art Object in the Nineteenth Century and After* (Oxford: Oxford University Press, 2020), 185–88.

14. William Wordsworth, "The World Is Too Much with Us," in *21st-Century Oxford Authors: William Wordsworth*, ed. Stephen Gill (Oxford: Oxford University Press, 2010), 237.

15. On prophetic Proteus and his shocking transformations, which include turning into fire and water itself, see Virgil, *The Georgics of Virgil*, trans. David Ferry (New York: Farrar, Straus & Giroux, 2005), 171–83. See also Homer, *The Odyssey*, trans. Robert Fagles (London: Penguin Books, 1996), 136–37. On Triton, see Hesiod, where he is a far more significant deity than later visual representations would suggest: "great, wide-ruling Triton, . . . he owns the depths of the seas . . . an awful god." Hesiod, *Theogony*, in Hesiod, *The Homeric Hymns and Homerica*, trans. Hugh G. Evelyn-White, Loeb Classical Library (Cambridge, MA: Harvard University Press, 1967), 149, line 930.

16. The entire passage in Paul is based on the limits of phenomenal knowledge of the world (comprehending length, breadth, depth, and height) contrasted with faith in absolute and permanent categories as grounding phenomena: "That Christ may dwell in your hearts by faith; that ye, being rooted and grounded in love, May be able to comprehend with all saints what is the breadth, and length, and depth, and height; And to know the love of Christ, which passeth knowledge, that ye might be filled with all the fulness

of God. Now unto him that is able to do exceeding abundantly above all that we ask or think, according to the power that worketh in us, Unto him be glory in the church by Christ Jesus throughout all ages, world without end. Amen" (Eph. 3:17–21).

17. On "the English Death," see also Siegel, *Material Inspirations*, 122–41.

18. Sigmund Freud, *Civilization and Its Discontents* [1930], trans. James Strachey (New York: Norton, 1962), 11–15.

19. Hans Blumenberg, *Shipwreck with Spectator: Paradigm of a Metaphor for Existence* [1979], trans. Steven Rendall (Cambridge, MA: MIT Press, 1997), 12; subsequent references will appear in parentheses in the text. On the centrality of danger at sea in the history of the word "peril"—and on the ways in which the term has at its root the risk presented by both financial speculation and nature itself, see Marie-Hélène Huet, *The Culture of Disaster* (Chicago: University of Chicago Press, 2012), 3.

20. Théodore Géricault's 1819 sensation, *The Raft of the Medusa*, is probably the most famous instance of the visual representation of shipwreck, but it was a frequent theme. On the English context, see T. S. R. Boase, "Shipwrecks in English Romantic Painting," *Journal of the Warburg and Courtauld Institutes* 22, no. 3/4 (1959): 332–46. See also Barry Venning, "A *Macabre* Connoisseurship: Turner, Byron and the Apprehension of Shipwreck Subjects in Early Nineteenth-Century England," *Art History* 8, no. 3 (1985), 303–19; and Christine Riding, "Shipwreck in French and British Visual Art, 1700–1842: Vernet, Northcote, Géricault, and Turner," in *Shipwreck in Art and Literature*, ed. Carl Thompson (New York: Routledge, 2013), 112–32.

21. William Cowper, "The Castaway," in *The Poems of William Cowper*, ed. John D. Baird and Charles Ryskamp (Oxford: Oxford University Press, 1995), 3:214–16; Virginia Woolf, *To the Lighthouse* (New York: Harcourt, Brace, Jovanovich, 1981); Felicia Hemans, "Casabianca," in *Felicia Hemans: Selected Poems, Prose, and Letters*, ed. Gary Kelly (Peterborough, ON: Broadview Press, 2002), 300–301; Alfred, Lord Tennyson, *In Memoriam*, ed. Erik Gray, 3rd Norton Critical Edition (New York: W. W. Norton, 2020); Gerard Manley Hopkins, "Wreck of the Deutschland," in *The Major Works*, ed. Catherine Phillips (New York: Oxford University Press, 2002), 110–19. To this small representative list of verse one should probably add Edgar Allan Poe's sublime evocation of death and desperate survival in his 1841 story "Descent into the Maelstrom," in *Complete Tales and Poems*, ed. Hervey Allen (New York: Modern Library, 1965), 127–40.

22. "A pregnant paragraph," reads Ruskin's own gloss on the passage, "meant against English and Scotch landlords who drive their people off the land." Ruskin, *Munera Pulveris* [1862], in *The Works of John Ruskin*, 17:256n. On this topic, see two books by T. M. Devine, *To the Ends of the Earth: Scotland's Global Diaspora, 1750–2010* (London: Allen Lane, 2011), and *The Scottish Clearances: A History of the Dispossessed, 1600–1900* (London: Allen Lane, 2018). For an ambitious argument that places the fate of the Scots and other dispossessed groups within the British Isles in relation to the development of modern racialized thought, see Cedric Robinson, *Black Marxism: The Makings of the Black Radical Tradition* (Chapel Hill: University of North Carolina Press, 2000), 24–43, 67–68.

23. Mark Frost, "'The Guilty Ship': Ruskin, Turner and Dabydeen," *Journal of Commonwealth Literature* 45 (2010), 371–88, at 381, 373–74.

24. For subtle and clear accounts of the painting and Ruskin's response, see Leo Costello, "Turner's *The Slave Ship* (1840): Towards a Dialectical History Painting," in *Discourses of Slavery and Abolition: Britain and Its Colonies, 1760–1838*, ed. Brycchan Carey, Markman Ellis, and Sara Salih (New York: Palgrave Macmillan, 2004), 209–22; and especially the magisterial work of Marcus Wood, which has been an important resource for my own remarks on the painting: *Blind Memory: Visual Representations of Slavery in England and America* (Manchester, UK: Manchester University Press, 2000), 41–76.

25. Paul Gilroy, *The Black Atlantic: Modernity and Modern Consciousness* (London: Verso, 1993), 14. For a more nuanced though less frequently cited account of the painting, see also Gilroy's 1990 talk "Arts of Darkness: Black Art and the Problem of Belonging to England," reprinted in his *Small Acts: Thoughts on the Politics of Black Cultures* (London: Serpent's Tail, 1993), 74–85.

26. Abigail Ward follows Gilroy's line of reading in *Black Atlantic*. "John Ruskin's description of the painting," she writes, acknowledging the conventional nature of the account she is about to endorse, "has become infamous . . . because it only mentions the drowning slaves in passing." As she indicates, this failure is seen as somehow more widespread than even Ruskin's astonishing blindness to what was in front of him, becoming a tradition of neglect: "His comments have become characteristic of a tradition of reading Turner's painting which fails to see the jettisoned slaves." It turns out that Ward, like Gilroy, has in mind another neglect altogether, one that arguably does more to ignore what is in front of the face of anyone who looks at the Turner or the Ruskin: "Turner's attempts to deny black people an active role in nineteenth-century Britain." In an extraordinary act of critical projection, it turns out that Ward herself sees in the water not what is there but what isn't. In Ruskin's failure to see what she describes with chilling coolness as "the jettisoned slaves," she sees more than even a failure of perception or representation: she sees the denial of the agency of Black people in Britain. Abigail Ward, "'Words Are All I Have Left of My Eyes': Blinded by the Past in J. M. W. Turner's *Slavers Throwing Overboard the Dead and Dying* and David Dabydeen's 'Turner,'" *Journal of Commonwealth Literature* 42 (2007): 47–58, at 48.

27. Ian Baucom, "Charting the 'Black Atlantic,'" *Postmodern Culture* 8, no. 1 (1997): 12–13. See also Baucom's ambitious chapter "To Tumble into It, and Gasp for Breath as We Go Down: The Idea of Suffering and the Case of Liberal Cosmopolitanism," in his *Specters of the Atlantic: Finance Capital, Slavery, and the Philosophy of History* (Durham, NC: Duke University Press, 2005), 267–96, a subtle reading of the political stakes inherent in the ethical and affective projects involved in Turner's painting and its making that anticipates some of my own claims, though it orients them in an entirely different direction.

28. Frost, "'The Guilty Ship,'" 373–74.

29. Sarah Fulford, "David Dabydeen and Turner's Sublime Aesthetic," *Anthurium: A Caribbean Studies Journal* 3, no. 1 (2005): 1–21. This argument is addressed in Frost, "'The Guilty Ship,'" 374–75.

30. Gilroy, "Arts of Darkness," 81–82.

31. T. S. Eliot, "Death by Water," in *The Waste Land* (New York: Vintage, 2021), 68.

32. . See Sharpe, *In the Wake*, 40–41.

33. See M. NourbeSe Philip's long poem *Zong!* (Middletown, CT: Wesleyan University Press, 2008), based on the event and the case. See also Sharpe, *In the Wake*, 34–39—though the event and the cultural responses it has provoked are evoked throughout the book.

34. W. H. Auden, "Musée des Beaux Arts," in *Selected Poems: Expanded Edition*, ed. Edward Mendelson (New York: Vintage International, 2007), 87. In his magisterial account of Turner's canvas in relation to slavery, Marcus Wood cites the painting by Brueghel that Auden references in the course of his discussion of the tragically comic poignancy of legs projecting above the water.

35. Ruskin, *Notes by Mr. Ruskin on his Drawings by the late J. M. W Turner, R. A. Exhibited at the Fine Arts Society's Galleries* [1878], in *The Works of John Ruskin*, 13:393–485, at 469; cited in Wood, *Blind Memory*, 58. This pamphlet underwent various changes in its many editions; for details see 13: liv–lv, 393–402.

36. For an extraordinarily compelling reading of the continuities into which we might place Turner's painting, see Sharpe, who not only emphasizes various elements going back to the Middle Passage as phenomena shaping and distorting Black life in what she calls "the wake," but links them to other failures of care and attention, notably the European response to the refugee crisis in the waters of the Mediterranean. Her treatment of the Turner (*In the Wake*, 36) is part of a compelling discussion around the term "ship." On freedom, see Sharpe's characterization of living "in the wake of the unfinished project of emancipation" (5).

37. Jacob Burckhardt, *Einleitung in die Geschichte des Revolutionszeitalters* [1867] (Introduction to the history of the revolutionary age), qtd. in Blumenberg, *Shipwreck with Spectator*, 69. Blumenberg is fascinated by the return of this figure in various versions of the lectures Burckhardt delivered on the French Revolution in the late 1860s as the historian attempts to illustrate the difficulty of subjects living in the aftermath of the Revolution achieving an objective standpoint from which to reflect on its meaning. See ibid., 69–73.

38. David Dabydeen, *Turner* (Leeds, UK: Jonathan Cape, 2010), sec. 16, 1–5. See Sharpe, *In the Wake*, on the ship as womb, an idea she in part develops from Édouard Glissant's *Poetics of Relation* [1990], trans. Betsy Wing (Ann Arbor: University of Michigan Press, 1997), which she cites at the opening of the section titled "The Belly of the Ship," 73–81.

39. "From the start many made it clear Serena would have done better struggling to survive in the two dimensionality of a Millet painting, rather than on their tennis court—better to put all that strength to work in their fantasy of her working the land, rather than be caught up in the turbulence of our ancient dramas, like a ship fighting a storm in a Turner seascape." Claudia Rankine, *Citizen: An American Lyric* (Minneapolis: Graywolf, 2014), 26.

40. Claudia Rankine, *Citizen*, 83.

41. See Jack Lindsay, *Turner: His Life and Work* (St. Albans, UK: Panther Books, 1973), esp. 7, 72–87. See also Jack Lindsay, ed., *The Sunset Ship: The Poems of J. M. W. Turner* (Lowestoft, Suffolk, UK: Scorpion Press, 1966).

42. https://radioopensource.org/claudia-rankine/#.

43. Rankine's serious play with personal pronouns returns in the title of a more recent work, *Just Us*. Something that does not quite sound like justice is what we hear in a word describing a limiting condition (just) alongside another indicating recognition of a shared one (us). Or is what we hear a word describing a limit recognized (*only* us) that can sound like something close to (but not quite) the hope for a better community (us joined in justice)? Like the simple word "Citizen" in the title of her earlier volume, the language here works to unsettle an assumption of commonality by demanding its recognition even as the text registers its limits. See also Rankine's treatment of "we" in the course of her discussion of *e pluribus unum*: "But who is this 'we'? / Is it even possible to form a 'we'? / Is this even the question?" *Just Us: An American Conversation* (Minneapolis: Graywolf Press, 2020), 332–33.

INDEX

The authorized representative in the EU for product safety and compliance is:
Mare Nostrum Group
B.V Doelen 72
4831 GR Breda
The Netherlands

www.ingramcontent.com/pod-product-compliance
Lightning Source LLC
LaVergne TN
LVHW041112080826
845145LV00007B/1781

* 9 7 8 1 5 0 3 6 3 2 1 5 8 *